HORIZONTAL RIGHTS

A powerful, privately-owned television channel refuses to air an advertisement advocating equal rights for the LGBT community. A prestigious club bars women from standing for executive positions. A homeowner refuses to rent their house to a person on grounds of their race. Each of these real-life cases involves the exercise of private power, which deprives individuals of their rights. Can these individuals invoke the Constitution in response?

Horizontal Rights: An Institutional Approach brings a fresh perspective to these age-old yet fraught issues. This book argues that constitutional scholarship and doctrine, across jurisdictions, has proceeded from an inarticulate premise called 'default verticality.' This is based on a set of underlying philosophical assumptions which presumes that constitutional rights are presumptively applicable against the State, and need special justification to be applied against private parties.

Departing from default verticality and its assumptions, this book argues that constitutional rights should apply horizontally between private parties where the existence of an economic, social or cultural institution creates a difference in power between the parties, and allows one to violate the rights of the other. The institutional approach aims to be both theoretically convincing, as well as providing a workable model for constitutional adjudication. It applies both to classic issues such as restrictive covenants, as well as cutting-edge contemporary legal problems around the regulation of platform work and the distribution of property upon divorce. This promises to be an exciting new contribution to the global conversation around constitutional rights and private power.

Horizontal Rights

An Institutional Approach

Gautam Bhatia

•HART•

OXFORD • LONDON • NEW YORK • NEW DELHI • SYDNEY

HART PUBLISHING

Bloomsbury Publishing Plc

Kemp House, Chawley Park, Cumnor Hill, Oxford, OX2 9PH, UK

1385 Broadway, New York, NY 10018, USA

29 Earlsfort Terrace, Dublin 2, Ireland

First published in Great Britain 2023

A catalogue record for this book is available from the British Library.

A catalogue record for this book is available from the Library of Congress.

ISBN: HB: 978-1-50996-761-2
ePDF: 978-1-50996-763-6
ePub: 978-1-50996-762-9

Typeset by Compuscript Ltd, Shannon

To Sandy
and the Research Group

Acknowledgements

THIS BOOK BEGAN life as a DPhil thesis at the University of Oxford, between 2018 and 2021. I am deeply grateful to my supervisor, Professor Sandy Fredman, and the Oxford Human Rights Research Group (RG), where its arguments took form, shape and flesh. Sandy was with the project from its beginning – as a thousand-word outpouring of vague thoughts misleadingly labelled as a 'proposal' – to its end, as the book that you now hold in your hands. At RG, Tom Lowenthal, Jason Brickhill, Nomfundo Ramalekana, Sanya Samtani, Tristan Cummings, Rishika Sahgal, Gauri Pillai, Farrah Raza, Monica Arango, Meghan Campbell, Njodi Ndeunyema, Anjali Rawat, Sarah Horsch Carsley and Lydia Mugambe were all extraordinarily generous with their time, going over multiple drafts and iterations of every argument. They were encouraging when they needed to be and tough when it was merited, but always entirely constructive.

Professors Ann Davies and Alan Bogg examined the thesis with rigour, kindness and generosity. They provided immensely helpful feedback about how to improve its arguments. Their comments formed the basis upon which I converted the thesis into a book manuscript. I am deeply grateful to them.

Meghan Finn read the thesis and provided invaluable comments on my engagement with South African law. Walter Khobe did the same for Kenyan law. I am grateful to both of them for their time, freely given.

'He would walk into my mind as if it were a town, and he a torchlight procession of one, lighting up the streets', said Norman MacCaig about Hugh MacDiarmid. I can think of no better description for Madhubala P's intellectual contribution at the final steps of this project, in helping me move somewhat closer to the clarity of thought and language that we all hope to attain.

Through the five years of this project, my parents have been engaged interlocutors from the beginning to the end. Their confidence in me – which is far greater than my confidence in myself – ensured that the PhD-and-book process never got too lonely or too frightening.

The copy of the book that you hold in your hands exists because of the work of many individuals at Hart Publishing: editorial director Sinead Moloney, who was my first contact at Hart; Sasha Jawed, who has handled the process until the end; Chris Myers, who copy-edited the manuscript; Grace Ridge, the cover designer; Tom Adams, the production manager; and many others, whose work is invisible, but not unacknowledged. I am grateful to all of them.

Perhaps the truest form of academic tribute is the footnotes section. I am grateful to all those whose work and writing have shaped and influenced my own thoughts for the better, whom I have argued with and against, and whose imprints are visible throughout this book.

Table of Contents

Acknowledgements .... *vii*
Table of Cases .... *xi*
Table of Authorities .... *xvii*

PART I
THEORY

1. **The Default Vertical Approach** 3
   - I. Introduction 3
   - II. The *Civil Rights Cases* 6
   - III. Sovereignty 10
   - IV. Freedom 15
   - V. Individual Responsibility 18
   - VI. Alternative Bases for Default Verticality 23
   - VII. The Contingency of the Public/Private Divide: The Case of India 25
   - VIII. Conclusion 29

2. **State Action** 31
   - I. Introduction 31
   - II. The Public Character of Private Actors 34
   - III. Critique 42
   - IV. Insights 44

3. **Indirect and Direct Horizontality** 46
   - I. Introduction 46
   - II. Indirect and Direct Horizontality: A Typology 48
   - III. Indirect Horizontality: Forms and Limits 51
   - IV. Direct Horizontality: What It Solves (and What It Doesn't) 63
   - V. Conclusion 69

4. **Two Models of Bounded Horizontality** 71
   - I. Introduction 71
   - II. Two Contemporary Accounts of Bounded Direct Horizontality 73
   - III. Strengths and Weaknesses: An Analysis 79
   - IV. Conclusion: Towards the Institutional Model 84

5. The Institutional Approach ... 86
I. Introduction ... 86
II. The Institutional Approach: Philosophical Foundations ... 92
III. The Judicial Antecedents of the Institutional Approach ... 97
IV. The Institutional Approach in India ... 105
V. The Institutional Approach and the Assumptions of Default Verticality ... 122
VI. The Institutional Approach and Private Law Regimes ... 130

PART II
APPLICATION

6. Application I: Platform Work ... 137
I. Introduction ... 137
II. Why Platform Work? ... 141
III. Constitutionalising Labour and Employment Rights ... 144
IV. The Institutional Model as Applied to the Labour Market ... 149
V. The Institutional Model as Applied to Platform Work ... 152
VI. Applying Rights According to the Institutional Model ... 158
VII. Conclusion ... 170

7. Application II: Domestic Relationships and Unpaid Labour ... 173
I. Introduction ... 173
II. Contextualising the Issue ... 181
III. The Applicability of the Institutional Approach ... 185
IV. Application and Remedies ... 189
V. Conclusion ... 198

8. The Prospects of the Institutional Approach ... 200
I. Introduction ... 200
II. The Institutional Approach: A Summary ... 201
III. Contemporary Prospects ... 209
IV. Conclusion ... 226

Bibliography ... 227
Index ... 239

Table of Cases

South African Cases

AAA Investments (Proprietary) Ltd v Micro Finance Regulatory Council 2006 (11) BCLR 1255 (CC) 35, 39
AB v Pridwin Preparatory School 2020 (9) BCLR 1029 212
Allpay Consolidated Investment Holdings (Pty) Ltd v Chief Executive Officer of the South African Social Security Agency (No 2) 2014 (6) BCLR 641 (CC) 40, 42
Bhe v Magistrate, Khayelitsha 2005 (1) SA 580 (CC) 180
Calibre Clinical Consultants (Pty) Ltd v National Bargaining Council for the Road and Freight Industry [2010] 4 All SA 561 .... 35, 43–44
Certification of the Constitution of the Republic of South Africa, 1996 (10) BCLR 1253 (CC) 209
Daniels v Scribante 2017 (8) BCLR 949 (CC) 211–13
Du Plessis v De Klerk, 1996 (5) BCLR 658 .... 3–4, 18, 55, 62, 64, 101–02, 131, 209, 212, 214
Governing Body of the Juma Musjid Primary School v Essay NO 2011 (8) BCLR 761 (CC) 210
Jackson v Metropolitan Edison Co 419 US 345 (1974) 4, 17, 35–38, 40–41, 43, 82
Khumalo v Holomisa 2002 (8) BCLR 771 (CC) 41–42, 48, 210, 212
Murray v Minister of Defence 2009 (3) SA 130 (CA) 145, 161
South African National Defence Union v Minister of Defence 2007 (8) BCLR 863 (CC) 145

Canadian Cases

David Heller v Uber Technologies 2019 ONCA 1 (Court of Appeal for Ontario) 104
Fraser v Ontario (Attorney General) (2008) 92 OR (3d) 481 (Supreme Court of Ontario) 165
Health Services & Support v British Columbia [2007] 2 SCR 391 .... 145, 150, 165
Kenya Bus Service Ltd v Attorney General [2005] KLR 788 .... 3, 214
McKinney v University of Guelph [1990] 3 SCR 229 .... 3, 15–16, 44
Re Drummond Wren (1945) OR 778 (Ont HC) 59
RWDSU v Dolphin Delivery Ltd [1986] 2 SCR 573 49

Kenyan Cases

Agnes Nanjala William v Jacob Petrus Nicholas Vandergoes, MSA CA Civil Appeal No 127 of 2011 (UR) (Court of Appeal of Kenya) 196–97
CMN v AWM, Environment and Land Case 208 of 2012 (High Court of Kenya)....196
Duncan Muriuki Kaguuru v Baobab Beach Resort and Spa Ltd, Petition No 223 of 2012 216
Federation of Women Lawyers v Attorney-General, Petition No 164B of 2016, High Court of Kenya 196–97
Isaac Ngugi v The Nairobi Hospital, Petition No 407 of 2012 216
Jemimah Wambui Ikere v Standard Group Ltd, Petition No 466 of 2012....216
Kenya Bus Service Ltd v Attorney General [2005] KLR 788 .... 3, 214
Law Society of Kenya v Betty Sungura Nyabuto, Petition 21 of 2010....215
Mwangi Stephen Mureithi v Hon'ble Danile Toroitch Arap Moi, Petition No 625 of 2009, 17 (High Court of Kenya) 215
Peter Mburu Echaria v Priscilla Njeri Echaria, Civil Appeal No 75 of 2001 (Court of Appeal of Kenya)....196
Rose Wangui Mambo v Limuru Country Club, Constitutional Petition No 160 of 2013 216
Stephen Saitoti Kapaiku v Cocacola Sabco Nairobi Bottlers Ltd, Petition No 338 of 2012 216
Uhuru Muigai Kenyatta v Nairobi Star Publications Ltd, Petition No 187 of 2012 215

US Cases

Barsky v Board of Regents of University of State of New York 347 US 442 (1954) 4
Blum v Yaretsky 457 US 991 (1981) 11, 36–37, 41, 43
Burton v Wilmington Parking Authority 365 US 715(1961) 35–36
Coppage v Kansas 236 US 1 (1915) 20
Cotter v Lyft 13-cv-04065-VC (11 March 2015) (District Court for the Northern District of California)....142
Douglas O'Connor v Uber Technologies No C-13-3826 EMC, 11 March 2015 (Northern District of California) 142
Dynamex v The Superior Court of Los Angeles County Ct App 2/7 B249546 (Supreme Court of California) 142
Evans v Newton 382 US 296 (1965)....38
Ex Parte Virginia 100 US 333 (1879) 9
Flagg Bros Inc v Brooks 436 US 149 (1978) 11–13, 37

Fletcher v Peck 10 US (6 Cranch) 87 (1810) 19
Griggs v Duke Power Co 401 US 424 (1971) 100
Hosanna-Tabor Evangelical Lutheran Church and School v Equal Employment Opportunity Commission 565 US 171 (2012) 112
Hudgens v NLRB 424 US 507 (1976) 38, 40
Jackson v Metropolitan Edison Co 419 US 345 (1974) 4, 17, 35–38, 40–41, 43, 82
Jones v Alfred H Mayer Co 392 US 409 (1968) 100
Lawson v Grubhub Case No 15-cv-05128-JSC (8 February 2018) (District Court of the Northern District of California) 142
Local 590 v Logan Valley 391 US 308 (1968) 38
Lochner v New York 198 US 45 (1905) 7, 20
Lugar v Edmondson Oil Co 457 US 922 (1982) 16
Marsh v Alabama 326 US 501 (1946) 38–41
Monroe v Pape 365 US 167, 255 (1961) 15
Moose Lodge No 107 v Irvis 407 US 163 (1972) 11, 36
NLRB v Jones & Laughlin Steel Corp 301 US 1 (1937) 145
Nevada Department of Human Resources v Hibbs 538 US 721 (2003) 184
New York Times v Sullivan 376 US 254 (1964) 48–49
Public Utilities Commission v Pollack 343 US 451 (1952) 35
Razak v Uber CA No 16-573 (11 April 2018) (District Court for the Eastern District of Pennsylvania) 142
Reitman v Mulkey 387 US 369 (1967) 43, 99
Rendell-Baker v Kohn 457 US 830 (1981) 37, 40, 43
San Francisco Arts and Athletics v USOC 483 US 522 (1986) 37
Shelley v Kraemer 334 US 1 (1948) 16, 56–57, 74–75, 80, 99, 127
Slaughter-House Cases 83 US 36 (1873) 10
Texas Department of Housing and Community Affairs v Inclusive Communities Project 576 US 519 (2015) 100, 132
Trustees of Dartmouth College v Woodward 17 US (4 Wheat) 518 (1819) 19
United States v Cruikshank 92 US 542 (1875) 9, 17, 39
Vega v Postmates 2018 NY Slip Op 4610 (21 June 2018) (Appellate Division of the Supreme Court of New York) 142
Virginia v Rives 100 US 313 (1880) 9, 20

Indian Cases

Indian Medical Association v Union of India (2011) 7 SCC 179 .... 106–15, 133
Indian Young Lawyers' Association v The State of Kerala, Writ Petition (Civ) No 373 of 2006 (Supreme Court of India) 110, 112
Olga Tellis v Bombay Municipal Corporation, AIR 1986 SC 180 188

Pradeep Kumar Biswas v Indian Institute of Chemical Biology (2002) 4 SCC 111 35
S Vasudevan v SD Mital, AIR 1962 Bom 53 105

German Cases

25 BVerfGE 256 (1969) ('Blinkfuer') 104
Burgschaft Case, BVerfGE 89, 214, NJW 1994 36 53
BVerfGE 7, 198 (1958) 52
BVerfGE 81, 242, 7 January 1990 (*Handelsvertreter*) 103–04

ECJ Cases

Association de médiation sociale v Union locale des syndicats CGT and Others ECLI:EU:C:2014:2 ....66, 89, 156
Case 26/62 *Van Gend en Loos v Nederlandse Administratie der Belastingen* [1963] ECR 1 65
Case 36/74 *Walrave and Koch v Association Union Cycliste International* [1974] ECR 01405 65
Case 43/75 *Defrenne v SABENA (No 2)* [1976] ECR 455 65
Case C-144/04 *Walter Mangold v Rudiger Helm* [2005] ECR I-09981 66
Case C-281/98 *Angonese v Cassa di Risparmio di Bolzano SpA* [2000] ECR I-04139 65
Case C-282/10 *Maribel Dominguez v Centre informatique du Centre Ouest Atlantique* ECLI:EU:C:2011:559 66
Case C-320/16 *Uber v Bensalem*, Case (10 April 2018) 142
Case C-411/98 *Angelo Ferlini v Centre Hospitalier de Luxembourg* [2000] ECR I-08081 65
Case C-624/19 *K and Ors V Tesco Stores* 2nd Chamber, 3 June 2021 66
Case C-91/92 *Paola Faccini Dori v Recreb Srl* [1994] ECR I-3325 66
Defrenne v SABENA (No 2) [1976] ECR 455 65
Sindicatul 'Pastorul Cel Bun' v Romania [2014] 58 EHRR 10 166

Irish Cases

Attorney General [SPUC] v Open Door Counselling Ltd [1988] IR 593 68
Byrne v Ireland [1972] 1 IR 241 67
Educational Company of Ireland Ltd v Fitzpatrick (No 2) [1961] IR 345 67
Hanrahan v Merck Sharp and Dohme [1988] ILRM 629 (SC) 68

Hayes v INTO [1987] ILRM 651 67
Hosford v John Murphy & Sons Ltd [1988] ILRM 300 (HC) 68
Meskell v CIE [1973] IR 121 .... 64, 67
Murtagh Properties v Cleary [1972] IR 330 67
SPUC v Grogan [1989] IR 760 68
W v Ireland (No 2) [1997] 2 IR 141 (HC) 68

UK Cases

Hall v Bull [2013] UKSC 73 225
Independent Workers' Union of Great Britain v The Secretary of state for Works and Pensions [2020] EWHC 3050 (Admin) 138, 169
Lee v Ashers Baking Company Ltd [2018] UKSC 49 225
Re S (A Child) [2005] 1 AC 593 219
The Independent Workers Union of Great Britain v The Central Arbitration Committee [2021] EWCA Civ 952 ....158, 166
Uber BV v Aslam [2018] EWCA Civ 2748 .... 104, 138, 167–68
Uber BV v Aslam [2021] UKSC 5 168

New Zealand Cases

Allan v Allan (1990) 7 FRNZ 102 (HC) 194
B v B [2016] NZHC 1201 192
Clayton v Clayton [Vaughan Road Property Trust] [2016] NZSC 29 193
Dalton v Dalton [1979] 1 NZLR 113 (CA) 192
Martin v Martin [1979] 1 NZLR 97 (CA) 192
P v P [1980] 2 NZLR 278 (CA) 192
Reid v Reid [1979] 1 NZLR 572 (CA) 193–94
Williams v Williams [1979] 1 NZLR 122 (CA) 192

Other Authorities

C-176/12 *Association de médiation sociale v Union locale des syndicats CGT and Others* ECLI:EU:C:2014:2 .... 66, 89, 156
De Geillustreerde Pers NV v The Netherlands App no 5178/71, Commission (Plenary) Report (31) (ECHR) 222
Inake v Deliveroo 6622665 CV EXPL 18–2673 (July 23 2018) (Court of First Instance, Amsterdam) 142
Maurice Tomlinson v TVJ and Ors [2020] JMCA Civ 52 217

Michael Kaseris v Rasier Pacific, VOF [2017] FWC 6610 (Australian Fair Work Commission) 142
Pallage v Rasier [2018] FWC 2579 (Australian Fair Work Commission)........ 142
Sindicatul 'Pastorul Cel Bun' v Romania [2014] 58 EHRR 10 166
Swedish Engine Drivers' Union v Sweden [1976] ECHR 2 165
T-494/92, Corte Constituticional de Colombia........ 188, 195–96

Table of Authorities

Constitutions and Legislation

Basic Conditions of Employment Act 1997 145
Civil Rights Act 1964, Pub L 88–352) (Title VII) 100
Civil Rights Act 1964, Title II – Public Accommodation, 42 USC 2000 107
Civil Rights Act 1875, 18 Stat 335–37, s 2, http://legisworks.org/sal/18/stats/STATUTE-18-Pg335a.pdf 7
Constitution of India 1949 .... 25, 49, 118
Constitution of Kenya 2010 .... 29, 49, 63, 196, 214
Constitution of the Republic of South Africa 1996 .... 29, 39, 41, 49, 65, 145, 209
Constitution of the United States of America 1787 .... 7, 9, 19
Employment Equity Act 1998 145
Employment Rights Act 1996 167
Labour Relations Act 1995 145
Property (Relationships) Act 1976 192–93
Protection of Women from Domestic Violence Act 2005 195

Miscellaneous

Parliament of India, *Constituent Assembly Debates, vol III*, 1 May 1947, www.constitutionofindia.net/constitution_assembly_debates/volume/3/1947-05-01 26
Parliament of India, *Constituent Assembly Debates*, *vol VIII*, 29 November 1948, https://indiankanoon.org/doc/1464664/ 26
Parliament of India, *Constituent Assembly Debates, vol XI*, 25 November 1949, https://indiankanoon.org/doc/792941/ 119
Parliament of India, *Constituent Assembly Debates: vol VII*, 29 November 1948, https://indiankanoon.org/doc/1464664/ 107–08

International and Supranational Instruments

Charter of Fundamental Rights of the European Union 2000 (2000/C 364/01) 146

Directive 2009/38/EC of the European Parliament and of the Council of 6 May 2009 165
European Social Charter (Revised), Strasbourg, 3.V.1995 164
ILO Declaration on Fundamental Principles and Rights at Work (1998), www.ilo.org/declaration/thedeclaration/textdeclaration/lang–en/index.htm 146

Part I

Theory

1

The Default Vertical Approach

I. INTRODUCTION

IN THIS OPENING chapter, I set out the foundational assumptions that underlie a common and widespread intuition in contemporary constitutionalism: the intuition that constitutional bills of rights are primarily addressed to the state, and aim to constrain its power. The purpose of this chapter is to provide the necessary context, in relation to which the arguments of the succeeding chapters can be assessed. In chapters two and three, I examine how certain jurisdictions have attempted to extend the reach of bills of rights to non-state parties and whether – and to what extent – the methods they have used remain wedded to the foundational assumptions set out in this chapter. I find that existing approaches remain tied to one or more assumptions, and that the alternative – 'direct horizontality' – is unworkable unless constrained in certain ways. In chapter four, I consider two contemporary scholarly models of horizontality, and argue that while they provide us with certain important insights, there remain gaps. Finally, in chapter five, I advance an alternative model of horizontality ('the institutional model'), and argue that this model is attractive in large part because it successfully jettisons these foundational assumptions, which are no longer of normative relevance in today's world. Part II of this book – chapters six, seven and eight – explores the application of the institutional model to certain existing, real-world situations.

* * * * *

'*Most commonly* we think of the Constitution as the law that defines and limits the reach of the State' (emphasis added).[1] This sentence – including the qualifier at the beginning – is likely to command reflexive agreement from most students of contemporary constitutionalism.[2] The qualifier suggests that while

[1] RS Kay, 'The State Action Doctrine, the Public–Private Distinction, and the Independence of Constitutional Law' (1993) 10 *Constitutional Commentary* 329, 338.

[2] For a range of judicial opinions that express this intuition, drawn from different jurisdictions, see, eg *Du Plessis v De Klerk* 1996 (5) BCLR 658, [154] (Madala J, concurring/dissenting) (Constitutional Court of South Africa); *McKinney v University of Guelph* [1990] 3 SCR 229, 262 (Supreme Court of Canada); *Kenya Bus Service Ltd v Attorney General* [2005] KLR 788 (High Court of Kenya).

constitutions are no longer thought of *exclusively* in terms of state power, the state remains firmly at the centre of constitutional imagination.[3] A constitution may well perform ancillary tasks, but its 'most critical and distinctive function [remains] … to provide law for the lawmaker'.[4] This 'essential dichotomy … between deprivation [of rights] by the State … [and deprivation by] private conduct',[5] the former presumptively the subject of constitutional concern and the latter presumptively not, 'is the basis for the distinction between public and private activities'[6] – ie the public/private divide – in the sense that shall be discussed in this book. This divide, it is often argued, is 'constitutive for constitutionalism'.[7]

The public/private divide is visible most starkly in bills of rights, which – despite occasional departures[8] – are overwhelmingly directed at the state. As Dieter Grimm points out, in a historical analysis of the origins of bills of rights, 'fundamental rights excluded those areas from the state's authority to rule … in which the private and not the public interest was primary. They thus marked the boundary between the state and society.'[9]

This is no longer exclusively true, as the second and third chapters shall discuss. However, the 'vertical' character of bills of rights (applicable against the state), along with the public/private divide that is constituted by, and constitutive of, this character, remains the default mode of thinking across jurisdictions.[10]

In this opening chapter, I identify three conceptual assumptions that I believe are integral to this approach to constitutionalism (for the purposes of this book, I shall call it the 'default vertical approach', or 'default verticality'). These assumptions shall be studied in the context of the constitutional jurisprudence of the USA and the scholarly debates around it. There are two reasons for (largely) limiting the enquiry in this opening chapter to the USA. First, the default vertical approach – as legal doctrine – had its origins in US constitutional

[3] D Gibson, 'The Charter of Rights and Private Litigation' (1982–83) 12 *Manitoba Law Journal* 213, 215 (discussing the Canadian context).

[4] S Gardbaum, 'The Horizontal Effect of Constitutional Rights' (2003) 102 *Michigan Law Review* 387, 394.

[5] *Jackson v Metropolitan Edison Co* 419 US 345 (1974) 349.

[6] E Chemerinsky, 'Rethinking State Action' (1985) 80 *Northwestern University Law Review* 503, 504.

[7] D Grimm, *Constitutionalism: Past, Present, and Future* (Oxford University Press, 2016) 29.

[8] See the essays in D Oliver and J Fedtke (eds), *Human Rights and the Private Sphere: A Comparative Study* (Routledge, 2007), discussing the (limited) ways in which some jurisdictions depart from the default model.

[9] Grimm, *Constitutionalism* (n 7) 52. See also *Barsky v Board of Regents of University of State of New York* 347 US 442 (1954) (Douglas J, dissenting), noting that the US bill of rights is about what Government 'may not take away'. ibid 473.

[10] See, eg *Du Plessis v De Klerk* (n 2) [45] ('Entrenched Bills of Rights are ordinarily intended to … protect against legislative and executive action') and the authorities in n 2.

jurisprudence.[11] It has been subsequently exported across the globe,[12] but remains closely associated with the USA through the 'state action doctrine' (ie a doctrine that, in a certain set of narrow circumstances, treats the actions of private parties as those of the state; this will be discussed in more detail in chapter two). And secondly, by the time that the other jurisdictions studied in this book came to grapple with issues surrounding the vertical and horizontal character of rights, the state action doctrine was already long established and well developed. For these reasons, in isolating the conceptual foundations of the default vertical approach, the focus will be on the USA.

I shall begin with an account of the *Civil Rights Cases* of 1883, a set of cases widely accepted as representing one of the first substantive judicial articulations of the default vertical approach (section II). I shall go on to discuss the conceptual underpinnings of the default vertical approach, which I believe can be reduced to three core concepts, articulated in specific and concrete terms: sovereignty (section III), freedom (section IV) and individual responsibility (section V). I do not claim that these concepts were consciously incorporated by the framers of the US Constitution into the text of the document, or specifically in the minds of judges while interpreting it.[13] What I do claim, however, is that these concepts represent a plausible and persuasive justification for the default vertical approach. As scholars have noted, on its own terms, the default vertical approach is counterintuitive and remains unconvincing without a further, underlying normative foundation.[14] Intuitively, why *should* constitutional rights be limited to constraining the state, when non-state parties also seem to frequently be in positions to affect precisely those interests that the rights are designed to protect? It is these assumptions, I will argue, that constitute that normative foundation.

Two caveats are in order. First, it may be pointed out that the three interlocking assumptions do not form the only plausible bases of default verticality. It could be argued, for example, that a constitution's concern is with the allocation of public power between public institutions; or that political liberalism's

[11] Dowdle and Wilkinson label it the 'structural-liberal' approach to constitutionalism, and trace its roots to the founding of the US Constitution: MW Dowdle and MA Wilkinson, 'Introduction' in MW Dowdle and MA Wilkinson (eds), *Constitutionalism beyond Liberalism* (Cambridge University Press, 2017) 1, 1.

[12] ibid.

[13] For a detailed discussion about the concepts of federalism, natural rights, consent and structural constraints upon government, all of which played a role in drafting the Constitution and the bill of rights, see TB McAffee, 'Restoring the Lost World of Classical Legal Thought: The Presumption in Favor of Liberty over Law and the Court over the Constitution' (2006–07) 75 *University of Cincinnati Law Review* 1499.

[14] See, eg F Michelman, 'Constitutions and the Public/Private Divide' in M Rosenfeld and A Sajo (eds), *The Oxford Handbook of Comparative Constitutional Law* (Oxford University Press, 2012) 299; G Peller and M Tushnet, 'State Action and a New Birth of Freedom' (2004) 92 *Georgia Law Journal* 779, 790.

vision of state neutrality is founded on the premise that there is a special valence to state-sanctioned denigration of certain forms of life. To this, I will flag two responses: (i) that some of the alternative bases – on closer scrutiny – are similar to one or more of the three assumptions that I discuss; and (ii) that while some of them do justify a heightened concern with state action, they do not justify why – at least presumptively – constitutional rights ought *not* to apply to private relations. The strongest source of that justification, I will argue, is located in the three assumptions of sovereignty, abstract freedom and individual responsibility (section VI).

Secondly, it is not my case that the three assumptions outlined above continue to be followed, even in the USA.[15] It is clear that jurisdictions across the world are increasingly moving away from them, in different ways and to different degrees: whether by constitutionalising horizontal rights, or – which is more frequent – legislatively intervening in the 'private sphere' (through, for example, civil rights laws). The purpose of the following enquiry is to isolate these assumptions so that they can serve as measures for jurisdictions and models that, to various extents, have begun to question or interrogate the default vertical approach.

Lastly, it is now well accepted that the default vertical approach arose out of a specific set of historical circumstances and that, for all its intellectual dominance, as well as dominance in terms of global constitutional design, it is not the only way to think about constitutionalism.[16] I will conclude this chapter, therefore, by taking a brief look at India, a jurisdiction where, for historical reasons, the state did not always monopolise the thinking about constitutions and rights. The text of the Indian Constitution, with its unusually concrete horizontal rights provisions, reflects the contingent character of the default vertical approach, and the possibility of imagining a different model altogether (section VII). This model will be taken up in detail in chapter five.

II. THE *CIVIL RIGHTS CASES*

The *Civil Rights Cases* involved a constitutional challenge to the Civil Rights Act of 1875. The Civil Rights Act was a reconstruction-era federal law that was primarily aimed at securing the civil rights of newly emancipated Black US citizens. It did so by prohibiting race discrimination in access to 'accommodations,

[15] See, eg L Seidman and M Tushnet, *Remnants of Belief: Contemporary Constitutional Issues* (Oxford University Press, 1996); Peller and Tushnet, 'State Action and a New Birth of Freedom' (n 14) 792.

[16] Grimm, *Constitutionalism* (n 7); Dowdle and Wilkinson, *Constitutionalism beyond Liberalism* (n 11); MJ Horwitz, 'The History of the Public/Private Distinction' (1982) 130 *University of Pennsylvania Law Review* 1423, 1426.

advantages, facilities and privileges of inns, public conveyances on land or water, theatres, and other places of public amusement'.[17] Further, it penalised individuals who acted in contravention of this prohibition.[18]

The Civil Rights Act of 1875 was enacted to implement the promise of the Thirteenth and Fourteenth Amendments to the US Constitution, framed in the aftermath of the US Civil War and the dismantling of slavery. The Thirteenth Amendment proscribed slavery and involuntary servitude, while the Fourteenth Amendment stated – in the relevant part – that '[No] State [shall] deprive any person of life, liberty, or property, without due process of law; nor deny to any person within its jurisdiction the equal protection of laws'.[19] In defence of the law, it was argued that the Civil Rights Act was enacted under the authority of both these Amendments. The challengers contended, however, that the Thirteenth Amendment was simply inapplicable to straightforward racial discrimination that did not amount to slavery. As for the Fourteenth Amendment, they contended that it was directed only against the state. It did not authorise the federal Congress to regulate *private* conduct – ie to 'adjust … the social rights of men and races in the community'.[20]

It is important to clarify here that a primary issue in the *Civil Rights Cases* was about the reach of *federal* power, arising out of the specific relationship between the national government and the state governments in the USA. The challengers did not raise – and the Supreme Court did not consider – the question of whether government *in general* possessed the power to enact a statute such as the Civil Rights Act and legislatively intervene in the 'private sphere' (although successful challenges of that nature become commonplace a few decades later, in the *Lochner* era[21]). The issue, rather, was whether the national Congress doing so was consistent with the federal division of powers.

In order to answer the federal question, however, the Supreme Court had to *first* answer the (separate) question of whether the Fourteenth Amendment covered private conduct or not. This is because, according to Section 5 of that Amendment, the federal Congress had been granted the power to 'enforce, by appropriate legislation, the provisions of this article'.[22] Consequently, if the guarantee of equal protection of laws applied to private conduct, there could be no doubt that the federal Congress was empowered to pass the Civil Rights Act.

Therefore, in my analysis of the *Civil Rights Cases*, I will confine myself to the Court's consideration of this preliminary question, crucial to the constitution of the public/private divide. For the reasons that I have provided above, I believe

[17] Civil Rights Act 1875, 18 Stat 335–37, s 2, http://legisworks.org/sal/18/stats/STATUTE-18-Pg335a.pdf.

[18] ibid.

[19] Constitution of the United States of America 1787, Fourteenth Amendment, s 1.

[20] *The Civil Rights Cases* 109 US 3 (1883) 22.

[21] See, eg *Lochner v New York* 198 US 45 (1905).

[22] Constitution of the United States of America 1787, Fourteenth Amendment, s 5.

that this part of the Court's reasoning is cleanly separable from its consideration of the federal question (which I propose to bracket for the purposes of the present argument).

The Supreme Court agreed with the challengers, and struck down the Act by an 8–1 majority. The majority chose to interpret the Thirteenth Amendment narrowly, observing that there existed 'distinct notions of what … [slavery] was and what were its necessary incidents'.[23] These included compulsory restraints on movement, prohibitions upon contracting, holding property, testifying in court and so on. In other words, according to the Supreme Court, slavery was a condition of legal subordination, marked by a set of formal and legal prohibitions and disabilities. The Thirteenth Amendment, which applied against private parties, therefore only empowered the federal Congress to 'declare and vindicate those fundamental rights which appertain to the essence of citizenship'.[24] In the opinion of the Court, however, the Civil Rights Act went much beyond that, (impermissibly) seeking to adjust 'social rights'.[25]

Consequently, even though the Thirteenth Amendment did depart from the default vertical approach by applying inter se between private parties, the Supreme Court chose to interpret it narrowly, thus depriving it of much of the force that it might have had. This interpretive approach makes sense as long as we think of the default vertical approach as 'default', and horizontality as an exception that must be strictly construed.

Justice Harlan dissented. I shall take up his dissent in greater detail in chapter five. Here, it is sufficient to flag an important element of his reasoning. 'Slavery', he observed, 'was the moving or principal cause of the adoption of [the Thirteenth] amendment, and … that *institution* rested wholly upon the inferiority, as a race, of those held in bondage' (emphasis added).[26] Consequently, by protecting the legal rights of the newly emancipated Black people from discriminatory conduct – rights that were ordinarily available and exercised by all other 'freemen' – the Civil Rights Act was only removing the 'burdens which lay at the very foundation of the *institution of slavery* as it once existed' (emphasis added).[27]

Justice Harlan took what we may call an 'institutional view' of constitutional rights. While the majority was correct in identifying certain specific prohibitions and disabilities that characterised slavery, Justice Harlan did not limit himself to that. He recognised that what gave these specific formal features their force was that they were part of the *institution* of slavery, which, in turn, was based on certain foundational practices. These practices could be reflected in more ways

[23] *The Civil Rights Cases* (n 20) 28.
[24] ibid.
[25] ibid.
[26] ibid 38 (Harlan J, dissenting).
[27] ibid 40 (Harlan J, dissenting).

than just through the list of legal prohibitions and disabilities that the majority judgment recognised. Consequently, the reach of the Thirteenth Amendment would extend to all the concrete manifestations of the institution of slavery – including, naturally, the denial of civil rights.

This institutional model of horizontality is what I shall develop further in chapter five, but I depart from it now. What of the Fourteenth Amendment? Here, the majority held that

> it is *State action* of a particular character that is prohibited. Individual invasion of individual rights is not the subject matter of the amendment ... until some State law has been passed, or some State action through its officers or agents has been taken, adverse to the rights of citizens sought to be protected by the Fourteenth Amendment, no legislation of the United States under said amendment, nor any proceeding under such legislation, can be called into activity. (emphasis added)[28]

Building upon, and taking forward, existing contemporary precedent,[29] the *Civil Rights Cases* marked the beginnings of the well-known 'state action doctrine', which continues to this day. It was accompanied, as well, by the origin of the public/private divide in constitutionalism, which took the form of a separation between 'state action' and 'individual invasion' of rights. The majority located this analysis in the text of the Fourteenth Amendment, noting that because the Fourteenth Amendment 'prohibits *the State* from denying to any person the equal protection of laws'(emphasis added),[30] a 'law ... without any reference to adverse State legislation'[31] would not fall within its protective scope.

As Frank Michelman points out, however, this is not a conclusion that is necessarily dictated by the text of the Fourteenth Amendment. Reading the relevant words of the Fourteenth Amendment – 'No state shall ... deprive any person or life, liberty, or property without due process of law'[32] – Michelman notes that:

> It is child's play to explain how the state, as the sovereign source of the common law, is responsible for every failure of the common law to provide relief against one or another exercise of power by one member of society against another.[33]

And if the state is responsible for that failure, it must be held to account for it. This, of course, forms the basis of what we today recognise as the familiar concept of positive rights and positive duties, and one that has strong support

[28] ibid 12–13.

[29] *United States v Cruikshank*, 92 US 542 (1875); *Virginia v Rives* 100 US 313 (1880); *Ex Parte Virginia* 100 US 333 (1879). These cases all considered the interpretation of the Fourteenth Amendment, and were cited in *The Civil Rights Cases* (n 20).

[30] *The Civil Rights Cases* (n 20) 18.

[31] *The Civil Rights Cases* (n 20) 18–19.

[32] Constitution of the United States of America 1787, Fourteenth Amendment, s 1.

[33] F Michelman, 'W(h)ither the Constitution?' (2000) 21 *Cardozo Law Review* 1063, 1076. See also HW Horowitz, 'The Misleading Search for "State Action" under the Fourteenth Amendment' (1957) 30 *Southern California Law Review* 208. This argument shall be discussed in greater detail in ch 2.

in international and comparative law, as well as in scholarly literature.[34] Indeed, Justice Bradley – who authored the majority opinion in the *Civil Rights Cases* – had himself hinted at such an understanding of the Fourteenth Amendment in a prior judgment, before resiling from it in favour of the state action doctrine.[35] Michelman therefore argues that the basis of the state action doctrine is not conceptual, but 'a normative political theory that our judges attribute to the Constitution'.[36] In the next three sections, I will attempt to excavate the fundamentals of that 'normative political theory'.

III. SOVEREIGNTY

In this section, I shall argue that the default vertical approach's central concern with constraining the state's powers depends upon identifying and isolating a set of distinctive attributes (of the state), which are normatively salient from the perspective of whom a bill of rights should be addressed to. I will further argue that it is the conception of sovereignty and sovereign power – uniquely located within the state, and distinct from other forms of power – that appears to be the most plausible candidate for the job.

The manner in which this emerges is set out by Frank Michelman (among others). Michelman outlines a four-step process that concludes with the establishment of the default vertical approach:

> A demand for effective imposition, on powers that form and roam in society, of peace- and order-keeping by means of the issuance of positive laws backed by sufficient force (a legally ordered society) which implies, second, for each self-standing territory or population, the concentration in a single institutional nexus (the state) of these positive-legislating, order-keeping powers and functions; and so implies also, third, a vesting in that same institutional nexus of the sole, final disposition over deployments of coercive powers (state monopoly of lawful force); and then, finally and recursively, fourth, a demand for *subjection of these state concentrated powers* – which themselves now appear as an imposing instance of powers forming and roaming – to positive legal controls: in other words, constitutional government, government under law. (emphasis added)[37]

In other words, the default vertical approach depends upon a clean separation between 'state' and 'society', where, in the words of Dieter Grimm, 'society was stripped of all ruling authority … the authority to rule was completely deprivatized, but needed to be legally constrained *precisely on account of its*

[34] See, eg S Fredman, *Human Rights Transformed: Positive Rights and Positive Duties* (Oxford University Press, 2008).

[35] *Slaughter-House Cases* 83 US 36 (1873).

[36] Michelman, 'W(h)ither the Constitution?' (n 33).

[37] Michelman, 'Constitutions and the Public/Private Divide' (n 14) 305–06.

concentration in the state' (emphasis added).[38] It is this concentration of power in a 'single institutional nexus (the state)' that we commonly understand as the modern concept of 'sovereignty'.

The doctrinal role played by sovereignty in the construction of the default vertical approach can be illuminated by how it has been articulated in some of the judgments that refer to it, even though it is not spelt out in its entirety. Consider, for example, *Flagg Bros Inc v Brooks*[39] – an often-studied judgment, and one of the foundational 'state action' cases in the USA. In *Flagg Bros*, the respondent-individuals were evicted from their homes, and their goods were warehoused by the petitioner-storage company. On the respondents' failure to settle their accounts, the petitioner proposed to sell the goods. This action – which was sanctioned by the law of the State of New York – was challenged on the basis that it violated the due process clause of the Fourteenth Amendment. The respondents, in short, had been deprived of their property without adequate process. Rejecting the challenge, Chief Justice Rehnquist – writing for the majority – held that there was no 'state action', as the New York law, 'recognizing the traditional place of private arrangements in ordering relationships in the commercial world, can hardly be said to have delegated to Flagg Brothers an *exclusive* prerogative of the *sovereign*' (emphasis added).[40]

Chief Justice Rehnquist differed from the finding of the Court of Appeals, which had held that through its law, the State of New York had 'delegated to the warehouseman a portion of its *sovereign monopoly* power over binding conflict resolution' (emphasis added).[41] He also differed from Justice Stevens, who, in his dissenting opinion, observed that 'the ... power to order binding, nonconsensual resolution of a conflict between debtor and creditor'[42] was, indeed, a function 'historically', 'traditionally', or 'uniquely' 'associated with *sovereignty*' (emphasis added).[43]

What united all three opinions, however, was a consensus that the Fourteenth Amendment was limited to acts that were characteristic of sovereignty. The Court of Appeals and Chief Justice Rehnquist insisted that only acts that were the exclusive prerogative of sovereignty were covered, while Justice Stevens adopted a more generous formulation, covering actions traditionally or historically associated with sovereignty.[44] The unified judicial vision, nonetheless, was

[38] Grimm, *Constitutionalism* (n 7) 16.

[39] *Flagg Bros Inc v Brooks* 436 US 149 (1978).

[40] ibid 160. See also *Blum v Yaretsky* 457 US 991 (1981) 1012.

[41] *Flagg Bros* (n 39) 149. For other judgments of the Supreme Court placing emphasis on whether there existed a state-conferred 'monopoly', see, eg *Moose Lodge No 107 v Irvis* 407 US 163 (1972), 177.

[42] ibid 171, 176.

[43] ibid 171.

[44] For an analysis of the difference between the majority and the dissent on this point, see P Brest, 'State Action and Liberal Theory: A Casenote on *Flagg Brothers v Brooks*' (1982) 130 *University of Pennsylvania Law Review* 1296.

that there was something about the concept of sovereignty, and a set of core acts that were uniquely associated with sovereignty, which attracted constitutional concern. These acts could not be performed by non-state actors, unless the state authorised them to do so through an act of delegation of sovereignty. In those – and only in those – cases would the state action doctrine apply, and the non-state actor be made subject to the relevant provisions of the bill of rights.[45]

This understanding of sovereignty explains the structure of the *Flagg Bros* judgment(s). Chief Justice Rehnquist held that the challenge to the New York statute was, effectively, a challenge to the State of New York's *acquiescence* (through the statute) to the private recourse Flagg Brothers took to recover its debts. But because what Flagg Brothers was doing was a private act, which did not involve any delegation of sovereignty on the part of the State of New York, the challenge under the Fourteenth Amendment had to fail. On the other hand, Justice Stevens's dissent rested upon the finding that a challenge could be brought under the Fourteenth Amendment precisely because, *through its acquiescence*, the New York statute in effect delegated a function of sovereignty to a private party to perform.

What is so distinctive about sovereignty – and the powers uniquely attached to it – that justifies this view? As shown in the paragraph above, Michelman suggests that it lies in the classical understanding of sovereignty, which views the state 'as the monopolist of *lawful* force, the *sole power* from the reach of whose command there is virtually no exit' (emphasis added).[46] I will now unpack that summary. It is important to understand that a significant part of the work in this articulation is being done by the word 'lawful'. It is trite to note that, as an empirical matter, the state does not possess a 'monopoly' over the use of force. This was recognised by Chief Justice Rehnquist in *Flagg Bros* itself, when he noted that, hypothetically, a stronger party could physically deprive a weaker party of its property and sell it, and that this would not constitute a violation of the Fourteenth Amendment.[47] In other words, therefore, as Chief Justice Rehnquist discussed extensively in the first part of his judgment, if the State of New York itself (through one of its officials) had deprived the respondents of their property, it would have been an exercise of sovereignty that would have been hit by the Fourteenth Amendment. However, the same act, when it was performed by Flagg Brothers (a private party), was exempt from Fourteenth Amendment scrutiny – unless, of course, it could be traced back to the state in some relevant way, such as sovereign delegation. On this point, as we have seen, the majority held that it could not, while Justice Stevens held that it could. Thus, the issue is not that the state exercises a monopoly over force (it does not);

[45] As Martin Loughlin points out, in the development of concepts, 'the state and sovereignty are inextricably linked'. M Loughlin, *The Foundations of Public Law* (Oxford University Press, 2010) 184.

[46] Michelman, 'Constitutions and the Public/Private Divide' (n 14) 301.

[47] *Flagg Bros* (n 39) 157.

rather, as Michelman suggests above, it is that the state, in its capacity qua the sovereign, exercises a monopoly over the legal authority to stipulate when and how force could be used.

Indeed, this very distinction formed the heart of the reasoning in the *Civil Rights Cases*, which, as we have seen above, inaugurated the state action doctrine. The majority judgment in the *Civil Rights Cases* drew a crucial conceptual distinction between an 'impairment' of a (constitutional) right and an 'invasion' of that right:

> [C]ivil rights, such as are guaranteed by the Constitution against State aggression, *cannot* be impaired by the wrongful acts of individuals, unsupported by State authority in the shape of laws, customs, or judicial or executive proceedings. The wrongful act of an individual, unsupported by any such authority, is simply a private wrong, or a crime of that individual; an invasion of the rights of the injured party, it is true, whether they affect his person, his property, or his reputation; but if not sanctioned in some way by the State, or not done under State authority, *his rights remain in full force*, and may presumably be vindicated by resort to the laws of the State for redress. (emphasis added)[48]

Consequently, as specified in the context of *Flagg Bros*, the same action (as a factual matter) would either be an impairment of a constitutional right or a 'mere' invasion (with the right remaining intact), depending upon the actor. This should make it clear, therefore, that the US Constitution is concerned not with the actual power exercised by the state (a power that is exercised by non-state parties to different degrees as well), but by its normative character (which is exclusively an attribute of the state, flowing from sovereignty).

This normative character – as I discussed above – refers to the state's monopoly over the lawful (or 'legitimate'[49]) use of force. The idea is refined further by Kay, who (like Michelman) argues that 'the unique power of the State' lies in its acts of law-making – that is, the 'authority to prescribe rules of conduct binding on individuals'.[50] It is this exercise of power that Kay sees as 'qualitatively different from any other in society',[51] and therefore the subject of constitutional concern.

We are now in a position to link this up with the articulation of sovereignty in *Flagg Bros*. The state action doctrine is based upon a conception of sovereignty that vests in it a specific and defined set of attributes, and a set of acts

[48] *The Civil Rights Cases* (n 20) 17.

[49] J Thomas, 'Our Rights, but Whose Duties? Re-conceptualizing Rights in the Era of Globalization' in T Kahana and A Scolnicov (eds), *Boundaries of State, Boundaries of Rights: Human Rights, Private Actors, and Positive Obligations* (Cambridge University Press, 2016) 1, 22.

[50] Kay, 'The State Action Doctrine, the Public-Private Distinction, and the Independence of Constitutional Law' (n 1) 343. See also Loughlin, *The Foundations of Public Law* (n 45) 196; Thomas, 'Our Rights, but Whose Duties?' (n 49) 22; PB Miller, 'Principles of Public Fiduciary Administration' in Kahana and Scolnicov, *Boundaries of State, Boundaries of Rights* (n 49) 251, 256.

[51] Kay, 'The State Action Doctrine, the Public-Private Distinction, and the Independence of Constitutional Law' (n 1) 352.

that are unique to and characteristic of it. The difference between sovereign and non-sovereign powers or acts (flowing from those powers) is what accords normative salience to limiting constitutional bills of rights to addressing only the state.

As an aside, this argument is congruent with (although it does not depend upon) accounts that trace the development of the concept of sovereignty in intellectual history. According to these accounts, for a variety of historical reasons, sovereignty came to be clothed with the attributes of indivisibility and supremacy, linked with legislative authority and concentrated within the state, in the political thought before and leading up to the revolutionary period and the drafting of the first modern constitutions.[52] Jean Thomas notes, therefore, that the 'philosophical understanding' of rights was (and in some respects, still is[53]) 'tied to the social contract tradition [of Hobbes, Locke, and Rousseau] in … [which] the moral universe is defined by the relationship between a single ruler and the ruled'.[54] Of course, this did not necessarily end with the US revolution: the lingering shadow of sovereignty in political theory was perhaps best summed up by Foucault's famous injunction to 'cut off the King's head'.[55]

Characterising sovereignty as a unitary – rather than a dispersed – concept, and as the sole attribute of the state, is essential, as we saw at the beginning of this section, to Michelman's four-step analysis of the default vertical approach. Without committing to the correctness of the above account as a matter of history, or as a matter of the historical development of political thought, the key idea remains the same: it is the concept of sovereignty that seems to drive the normative wedge between the exercise of state power (salient with respect to constraints established by bills of rights) and the exercise of non-state power (subject to state-made 'ordinary law', but not constrained by bills of rights).

However, there remains a final part of the analysis that is missing. Michelman's four-step account brings us to the justification for limiting the (centralised, concentrated) power of the state through a bill of rights, but it does not tell us why *only* state power ought to be so constrained. In other words, while the concept of sovereign power is a necessary condition for the default vertical approach, it cannot be a sufficient condition as well. It cannot, by itself, answer critics who point to how exercises of *other* kinds of power can also affect vital interests that would go unprotected without the shield of a bill of rights.

[52] See, eg Loughlin, *The Foundations of Public Law* (n 45) ch 7. See also Grimm, *Constitutionalism* (n 7) 4; N MacCormick, *Questioning Sovereignty: Law, State, and Nation in the European Commonwealth* (Oxford University Press, 1999) ch 8.

[53] J Griffin, *On Human Rights* (Oxford University Press, 2008) 13.

[54] Thomas, 'Our Rights, but Whose Duties?' (n 49) 11. For an account of the origins of this concept of sovereignty and its association with legislative power in the political thought of Jean Bodin, who preceded Hobbes, Locke and Rousseau, see Q Skinner, *The Foundations of Modern Political Thought, vol 2: The Age of Reformation* (Cambridge University Press, 1978) 289–90.

[55] M Foucault, 'Truth and Power' in *Power/Knowledge* (C Gordon ed, Pantheon, 1980).

An answer, of sorts, was provided in the *Civil Rights Cases*, where the majority noted that individuals affected by private power could always seek their remedies under statute or common law.[56] As Erwin Chemerinsky points out, this argument has a respectable vintage. At the time of the framing of the US Constitution (according to Chemerinsky), existing common law was deemed sufficient to protect rights from private invasion. The purpose of the bill of rights was simply to extend those common law rights to the domain of state action, and fill in the legal vacuum. This would, effectively, make the domain of rights gapless.[57]

However, as the majority's own reference to statute (in addition to common law) shows, a few decades after the framing of the US Constitution, it had already become clear that the bill of rights and the common law did not, by themselves, make the domain of rights gapless. Consequently, a few decades further on, the argument of the *Civil Rights Cases* was developed further by Frankfurter J in a dissenting opinion, when he conceded that private actors and institutions *could* offend the rights of others, but that 'government can either regulate these or create distinct bodies for the protection of human rights and the advancement of human dignity'.[58]

Thus, the argument, put in the broadest way, holds that while the state – being the sovereign lawmaker – needs to be constrained through a bill of rights because it is by definition above (ordinary) law, private parties fall under the purview of the state. Consequently, remedies against their acts must be sought by taking recourse to the state's (ordinary) law-making power. This completes Michelman's argument by providing the flip side to the fourth step, and combining the argument for why the state should be constrained by a bill of rights with the argument for why non-state parties should not – ie the default vertical approach.

IV. FREEDOM

However, whatever the merits of the fifth step as a textual exegesis of the US Constitution, as a conceptual claim, it falls short. This is because it has no answer to why a constitution *should* leave crucial rights to the mercies of non-constitutional law. To put the point another way: the fact that sovereign power stands uniquely above and beyond the reach of ordinary law provides us with good reasons to constrain the exercise of that power through, for example, a constitutional bill of rights. However, the fact that the exercise of non-sovereign

[56] *The Civil Rights Cases* (n 20).

[57] E Chemerinsky, 'Rethinking State Action' (1985) 80 *Northwestern University Law Review* 503.

[58] *Monroe v Pape* 365 US 167, 255 (1961) (Frankfurter J, dissenting). For an expression of exactly the same argument by the Supreme Court of Canada, see *McKinney v University of Guelph* (n 2) 262.

power *could* be constrained through ordinary law does not provide us with a reason not to protect rights against non-sovereign actors, especially given that protective laws may often not exist.

What is required, therefore, is an additional affirmative reason in support of the default vertical approach. This reason was articulated by the US Supreme Court in stark terms in *Lugar v Edmondson Oil Co*, where it noted that the state action doctrine 'preserves *an area of individual freedom* by limiting the reach of federal law' (emphasis added).[59] This justification, based on individual freedom or personal autonomy, has been accepted by both scholars[60] and courts[61] as one of the normative bases (whether right or wrong) of the default vertical approach: that is, limiting or constraining the power of the state *ipso facto* promotes the values of freedom and autonomy,[62] or a 'concept of a private sphere … [that] preserves a space for individual flourishing that the state might otherwise destroy'.[63] As Gardbaum frames the argument: 'limiting the scope of constitutional rights to the public sphere enhances the autonomy of citizens, preserving a heterogeneous private sphere free from the uniform and compulsory regime constructed by constitutional norms'.[64]

According to this argument, therefore, freedom (or autonomy) is the second axis along which the public/private divide turns. The domain of the private sphere – which is defined by the quality of freedom – is constructed by the set of rights that constrain the state from acting in that domain. The concern of the state, in other words, is limited to establishing 'public order' within which the autonomous society could remain 'free'.[65]

Of course, this articulation of freedom has been extensively criticised as being internally incoherent, apart from long being eroded by extensive civil rights legislation, across jurisdictions, that imposes obligations on private parties[66]

[59] *Lugar v Edmondson Oil Co* 457 US 922 (1982), 936. While the specific reference in the quote is only to 'federal law' (because the case arose in that context), the context makes it clear that the nature of the Court's observation was not limited to federalism concerns.

[60] For an analysis of the historical co-dependency between the concepts of limiting arbitrary power and promoting (liberal) individual freedom, see K Whittington, 'Constitutionalism' in R Scott and S Kosslyn (eds), *Emerging Trends in the Social and Behavioral Sciences* (John Wiley, 2015), https://doi.org/10.1002/9781118900772.etrds0051. See also L Henkin, '*Shelley v Kraemer:* Notes for a Revised Opinion' (1962) 110 *University of Pennsylvania Law Review* 473, fn 11.

[61] *McKinney v University of Guelph* (n 2) 262.

[62] This is what Dowdle and Wilkinson define as the foundational assumption of the 'structural-liberal approach' to constitutionalism. See Dowdle and Wilkinson, 'Introduction' (n 11). See also H Hershkoff, 'Privatising Public Rights: Common Law and State Action in the United States' in Kahana and Scolnicov, *Boundaries of State, Boundaries of Rights* (n 49) 129, 138; H Hershkoff, 'The Private Life of Public Rights: State Constitutions and the Common Law' (2013) 88 *New York University Law Review* 1, 4.

[63] L Seidman, 'The State Action Paradox' (1993) 10 *Constitutional Commentary* 379, 401.

[64] Gardbaum, 'Horizontal Rights' (n 4) 394–95.

[65] Loughlin, *The Foundations of Public Law* (n 45); see also Grimm, *Constitutionalism* (n 7) ch 1.

[66] See, eg Seidman, 'The State Action Paradox' (n 63). For a defence of the argument, see TP Lewis, 'Book Review: Larry Alexander & Paul Horton, *Whom Does the Constitution Command?*' (1991) 8 *Constitutional Commentary* 486, 500–01.

(albeit accomplished through the parliamentary or congressional route). Nonetheless, its role as one of the supporting pillars of the default vertical approach to constitutionalism makes it worthwhile to examine it further. It is clear that the conception of freedom at stake here is a de-materialised one – ie it is an abstract conception that pays no heed to the socio-economic conditions of the actors, which determine if the freedom they enjoy is meaningful in any sense.[67] This is accomplished – to draw upon an old and venerable tradition of thinking about the concept, going back at least to Hobbes[68] – by limiting freedom to that gained from the exercise of coercive state power, and not considering freedom to act in a certain way.

Cass Sunstein deepens the analysis by pointing out that this conception of freedom takes the existing distribution of resources as natural, and mandates individuals to exercise their freedom within the boundaries of that distribution[69] (or, in Grimm's words, within 'an existing condition of liberty'[70]). Once again, this point is made – with candour – within US constitutional doctrine. In the *Civil Rights Cases*, both the majority and the dissenting minority agreed that it was not open to the government to 'adjust social rights'[71] (the dissenters simply argued that that was not what the Civil Rights Act was doing). The argument was framed even more clearly a few years before the *Civil Rights Cases*, in another Reconstruction-era judgment called *United States v Cruikshank*, where the Supreme Court noted that the Fourteenth Amendment protected 'the individual from the arbitrary exercise of the powers of government, unrestrained by the *established principles* of private rights and distributive justice' (emphasis added).[72] But perhaps most tellingly, almost a century after the *Civil Rights Cases*, the Supreme Court found an absence of 'state action' with respect to a regulated corporation delivering electricity to a city-wide area on the basis (inter alia) that it was a 'natural monopoly'.[73] The juxtaposition of the words 'natural' and 'monopoly' – which resulted in the entity being held to be unconstrained by the bill of rights – suggests a normative theory according to which the outcomes

[67] Dowdle and Wilkinson, 'Introduction' (n 11).

[68] T Hobbes, *Leviathan* (First published 1651, Penguin Books, 1968) Part II, ch 21; see also PS Atiyah, *The Rise and Fall of the Freedom of Contract* (Oxford University Press, 1985) 43. For a critique of Atiyah that aligns with the arguments in this book, see B Mensch, 'Freedom of Contract as Ideology' (1981) 33 *Stanford Law Review* 753.

[69] C Sunstein, *The Partial Constitution* (Harvard University Press, 1998) Introduction. For an account of how a key concern behind the framing of the US Constitution was protecting the existing distribution of, and entitlement to, property, see J Nedelsky, *Private Property and the Limits of American Constitutionalism* (University of Chicago Press, 1990).

[70] Grimm, *Constitutionalism* (n 7) 86. See also Peller and Tushnet, 'A New Birth of Freedom' (n 14) 791. For a defence of the argument that distributional issues should be left entirely outside the remit of the Constitution and subject to the political process, see L BeVier and J Harrison, 'The State Action Principle and Its Critics' (2010) 96 *Virginia Law Review* 1767.

[71] *The Civil Rights Cases* (n 20) 22.

[72] *United States v Cruikshank* 92 US 542 (1876) [19].

[73] *Jackson v Metropolitan Edison Co* 419 US 346 (1974), n3.

of unregulated markets are deemed 'natural' (and therefore non-salient) and constitutive of the normative baseline. From this baseline, state action is then treated as a departure, and consequently subjected to the bill of rights.

As in the case of sovereignty, this argument is supported by (although it does not depend upon) studies in the historical development of political thought. On one set of accounts, for example, the American Revolution (culminating in the drafting of the US Constitution[74]) was fuelled by a rising bourgeoisie arrayed against the old feudal order and an absolutist state.[75] In this context, one of the ideological drivers of the period (and not just in the USA) was the belief that freedom could be best achieved by constraining the power of the sovereign to interfere with the 'autonomy of social sub-systems … allow[ing] them to develop according to their own criteria of rationality free from political direction. Equal individual freedom for all served as the medium for this autonomy.'[76] In other words, the deprivatisation of rulership (as discussed in the previous section on sovereignty) was accompanied by a corresponding privatisation of society.[77] It is therefore unsurprising that the conception of abstract freedom that is constitutive of the public/private divide leaves – as discussed above – the existing social and (particularly) economic order intact (or, as Atiyah puts it, 'equal freedom before the law and *in the marketplace*' (emphasis added)[78]).

V. INDIVIDUAL RESPONSIBILITY

In the previous section, we saw that the default vertical approach articulates a conception of freedom that treats individuals as abstract wills, shorn of the material background within which freedom can be exercised and made meaningful. This abstraction of individual difference, in turn, rests upon an assumption that, in the private domain, parties engage with each other as legal equals. As Van der Walt points out, this is visible from the terminology itself: the word 'vertical' – used to describe the relationship between individual and state – suggests that the two parties to the relationship stand at different, almost opposing, levels;

[74] And, for that matter, the French as well.

[75] For judicial endorsement of this view – in support of the default vertical approach – see, eg *Du Plessis v De Klerk* (n 2) [101] (Ackermann J, concurring).

[76] Grimm, *Constitutionalism* (n 7) 50; on the specific subject of the economy, see Atiyah, *The Rise and Fall of the Freedom of Contract* (n 68) 118: 'political and economic liberties [in the 17th century] … were not so easily disentangled'. See also K Polanyi, *The Great Transformation: The Political and Economic Origins of Our Time*, 2nd edn (Beacon Press, 2001).

[77] Michelman, 'Constitutions and the Public/Private Divide' (n 14).

[78] Atiyah, *The Rise and Fall of the Freedom of Contract* (n 68) 77. For a book-length exploration of linkages between the 19th-century rise of capitalism and the concept of legal freedom, see E Pashukanis, *The General Theory of Law and Marxism* (Routledge, 2001); M Dimick, 'Pashukanis' Commodity-Form Theory of Law' in P O'Connell and U Ozsu (eds), *The Research Handbook on Law and Marxism* (Edward Elgar, 2021) 115.

whereas the word 'horizontal' indicates flattening – that the parties are operating within the same plane:

> The separation of law from socio-economic history on which late 19th century jurisprudence came to insist programmatically – when jurisprudence came to ignore socio-economic baseline questions dogmatically … made it plausible to look upon public law relations as vertical power relations (between superiors and inferiors) and upon private law relations as horizontal relations (between equals).[79]

As the above quote indicates, much like the conception of freedom, this conception of equality and responsibility depends upon separating law from the material (socio-economic) bases that form the environment within which individuals act.[80] And once this background is taken out of the equation – or, to put it more precisely, rendered non-normative – it can be argued that because individuals within the private sphere are operating within the same plane, the correct characterisation of their relationship is not that of a rights holder and a duty bearer. Rather, it is of two contracting parties who are responsible for setting the terms of their relationship, characterised by the legal concept of the contract. These parties, therefore, cannot claim the protection of the rights framework.

This third axis of the default vertical approach is also indicated in the *Civil Rights Cases*, where the majority judgment drew a direct comparison between the legislative interference wrought by the Civil Rights Act and potential legislative interference with the power to contract.[81] As Ira Nerken points out in her analysis of the judgment, the majority viewed civil rights violations in the 'private sphere' as 'discrete, isolated, individual transactions, the outcome of which was determined by the individual circumstances'.[82] The majority's suggestion to the victims of discrimination – that they take up their grievance with the local state authorities[83] – further indicates that it considered the set of individual transactions that the Civil Rights Act sought to take cognisance of and proscribe as 'a bargain between equal citizens in a neutral state'.[84] Nerken makes the additional important point – one that I shall return to in chapters four and five – that a corollary of this set of assumptions involving freely contracting citizens who

[79] J van der Walt, *The Horizontal Effect Revolution and the Question of Sovereignty* (De Gruyter, 2014) 6.

[80] Van der Walt calls this the 'programmatic erasure of baseline questions from the attention of legal doctrine'. ibid 40.

[81] See, eg The Constitution of the United States of America 1787, Art I, s 10, Clause I (the 'Contract Clause'). See also *Fletcher v Peck* 10 US (6 Cranch) 87 (1810); *Trustees of Dartmouth College v Woodward* 17 US (4 Wheat) 518 (1819).

[82] I Nerken, 'A New Deal for Fourteenth Amendment Rights: Challenging the Doctrinal Bases of the Civil Rights Cases and State Action Theory' (1977) 12 *Harvard Civil Rights-Civil Liberties Law Review* 297, 321.

[83] *The Civil Rights Cases* (n 20).

[84] Nerken, 'A New Deal for Fourteenth Amendment Rights' (n 82) 322.

must be held responsible for the bargain they make is 'an atomization of social problems'.[85] In other words, instead of treating private discrimination as an instance of institutional racism, the majority viewed it as a set of isolated events, detached from its institutional background.

While the link between the default vertical approach and the concept of individual responsibility was only implicit in the *Civil Rights Cases*, it was spelt out with much greater clarity in *Virginia v Rives*,[86] one of the three state action cases that preceded the *Civil Rights Cases*. Elaborating upon the interpretation of the Fourteenth Amendment, the concurring opinion in *Rives* noted that:

> The denial of rights or the inability to enforce them, to which the section refers is, in my opinion, such as arises from legislative action of the State, as, for example, an act excluding colored persons from being witnesses, making contracts, acquiring property, and the like. With respect to obstacles to the enjoyment of rights arising from other causes, persons of the colored race *must take their chances* of removing or providing against them *with the rest of the community*. (emphasis added)[87]

Just as the *Civil Rights Cases* majority drew a distinction between 'impairment' (caused by the state, subject to the bill of rights) and 'invasion' (caused by private parties, unconstrained by the bill of rights), with the right itself remaining ostensibly intact in case of an 'invasion', *Rives* also sought refuge in terminology. When the state acted, it was a 'denial' of rights, and the bill of rights was immediately attracted. On the other hand, the acts of non-state parties constituted mere 'obstacles', which were of no constitutional concern.

But the terminology again is revealing. A denial of rights immediately suggests moral culpability and the need for a remedy. An 'obstacle', on the other hand, suggests a natural impediment that, as *Rives* notes, individuals take responsibility for negotiating past or around. This 'naturalness', and therefore normative insignificance, of certain kinds of inequalities was made particularly clear in *Coppage v Kansas*,[88] a judgment delivered during the peak of the *Lochner* era (which represented the high-water mark of the supremacy of the freedom of contract in US jurisprudence). Striking down a law that restrained an employer from inserting a clause in the employment contract prohibiting the employee from joining a labour union, the Supreme Court noted that:

> [I]t is from the nature of things impossible to uphold *freedom of contract* and the right of private property without at the same time recognising as legitimate *those inequalities of fortune* that are the necessary result of the exercise of those rights. (emphasis added)[89]

[85] ibid 335.
[86] *Virginia v Rives* 100 US 313 (1880).
[87] ibid 333.
[88] *Coppage v Kansas* 236 US 1 (1915).
[89] ibid 17.

The link between the concept of individual responsibility ('freedom of contract') and the treatment of the background socio-economic context as non-normative ('inequalities of fortune') was thus made clear. As Van der Walt points out, the dichotomy was between the propositions that 'any tolerance of hierarchies in public life must be subjected to express and conscious justification … [while] private hierarchies must generally be tolerated as natural outcomes of virtuous diligence and natural talent'.[90]

Furthermore, this way of thinking was not limited to the doctrinal jurisprudence of the USA. In his study of the evolution of private law in the Western legal world, Gonçalo de Almeida Ribeiro makes the following observation about the prevailing legal philosophy on the European continent, at around the same time that cases such as *Rives* were being decided:

> Within a rightful legal order, persons *waive their rights at their discretion*, enter contracts that oblige them before other persons, and *are liable to right their wrongdoings* – in the eyes of the law they are abstract wills, *universally free and equal.* Savigny and his followers held this theory to be immanent in a major division of the legal order they called 'patrimonial law', comprising the law of obligations and property law – that is, human relations over commodified goods. The nineteenth century jurists contrasted this patrimonial law, essentially universal, with both public law, a normative order that expresses the particularities of a people, and family law, a realm of private relations between unequal and mutually dependent persons (husband/wife, father/child, and master/servant). (emphasis added)[91]

As with sovereignty and freedom, this third axis of the default vertical approach is congruent with a dominant intellectual current of the time, as well as the evolving material social relations. The mechanism of the contract was viewed as freeing individuals from (feudal) hierarchies that were symbolised by predetermined status.[92] Henry Maine's influential book, *Ancient Law*, written in 1861 – just a few years before *Rives* and the *Civil Rights Cases* were decided – became particularly famous for arguing that the development of society resulted in a shift from 'status' to 'contract': private law was characterised by its obliviousness towards individual status, and by treating parties as equal, autonomous agents.[93] And this was achieved through the central, structuring legal device of the *contract.*

[90] Van der Walt, *The Horizontal Effect Revolution* (n 79) 6; see also ch 1, dealing in particular with the arguments of Maine, Austin and Kennedy.

[91] G de Almeida Ribeiro, *The Decline of Private Law: A Philosophical History of Liberal Legalism* (Hart Publishing, 2019) 7.

[92] For an account of status-based restrictions in pre-Industrial Revolution England, see, eg Polanyi, *The Great Transformation* (n 76) 92.

[93] H Maine, *Ancient Law* (first published 1861, Cambridge University Press, 2013).

Maine was far from the only person to make this point: in his critique of political economy, Karl Marx – to whom I shall return later in this book – noted that 'the exchange of exchange values is the productive, real basis of all *equality* and *freedom*'.[94] In his analysis of this passage, Marcel Van Der Linden notes that:

> If person A and person B want to do business because A offers a commodity for which B is prepared to pay money, then A and B must recognise each other as contracting parties with equal negotiating rights, as owners of private property, each with their own independent will. Freedom and equality of negotiating status are therefore structural elements in the exchange process between commodity owners.[95]

Writing in the same tradition, a few decades after Marx, Evgeny Pashukanis argued that the 'general structure of bourgeois law, including its system of rights and its pretence of formal equality, represents a formalisation of the social relations of capitalist society'.[96] Interestingly, interpreters of Pashukanis have argued – in language strikingly similar to that deployed by Nerken (see above) – that, in essence, his commodity-form theory of law argues that the capitalist exchange economy and a legal regime that treats individuals as '"atomized" legal personalities'[97] are co-constitutive. We can therefore see the link between the idea of (atomised) individual responsibility, the legal device of the contract and the emerging capitalist economy in the backdrop of which both the above concepts evolved.

Indeed – and to deepen the argument further – this development was reflected *within* the evolution of contract law itself. In response to an emerging market economy, the nineteenth century saw the triumph of the 'will' theory of contract, which consciously rejected material differences between contracting parties and assumed equality in all normative respects.[98] As Horwitz puts the point:

> Substantive justice, according to the earlier view [of contract law], existed in order to prevent men from using the legal system in order to exploit each other. But where things have no 'intrinsic value', there can be no substantive measure of exploitation and the parties are, by definition, equal. Modern contract law was thus born

[94] K Marx, *Grundrisse. Foundations of the Critique of Political Economy (Rough Draft)* (M Nicolaus trans, Penguin, 1973) 245. See also K Marx, *The German Ideology* (Progress Publishers, 1968); K Marx, *Capital: vol 1* (Penguin, 1990) 280; the analysis in D McLoughlin and T Hurzeler, 'Marx on the Factory Act: Law, Exploitation and Class Struggle' in O'Connell and U Ozsu, *The Research Handbook on Law and Marxism* (n 78) 21, 31.

[95] M Van der Linden, *Workers of the World: Essays Toward a Global Labor History* (Brill, 2011) 60. See also K Saito, *Capital, Nature, and the Unfinished Critique of Political Economy: Karl Marx's Ecosocialism* (Monthly Review Press, 2017); Pashukanis, *The General Theory of Law and Marxism* (n 78).

[96] A White, 'Marxism, Labour and Employment Law and the Limits of Legal Reform in Class Society' in O'Connell and U Ozsu, *The Research Handbook of Law and Marxism* (n 78) 299, 304.

[97] Dimick, 'Pashukanis' Commodity-Form Theory of Law' (n 78) 115, 121.

[98] MJ Horwitz, 'The Historical Foundations of Modern Contract Law' (1974) 87 *Harvard Law Review* 917.

> staunchly proclaiming that all men are equal because all measures of inequality are illusory.[99]

Consequently, and moving beyond the realm of contract, in a broader sense, the dominant intellectual view was that:

> the principle of equal freedom, which prevented the rule of some members of society over others and permitted obligations between citizens solely *on a voluntary basis*, provided protection against private exploitation or domination. In this way, everyone had the opportunity to pursue their own advantage, and no one could be compelled to engage in transactions to their own detriment. Thus, voluntary agreement – whatever form it might take – engendered no injustice. (emphasis added)[100]

Thus, as Gonçalo de Almeida Ribeiro notes, there was a 'structural homology between the will theory and the picture of the exchange economy, particularly with respect to the abstract conception of the person common to both'.[101] Consequently, to the extent that the private sphere was composed of autonomous individuals contracting on a voluntary basis, everyone could be held responsible for the outcomes of these freely bargained-for contracts. The domain of the private sphere could thus remain insulated from the application of rights.[102]

VI. ALTERNATIVE BASES FOR DEFAULT VERTICALITY

It is important to acknowledge that the three assumptions outlined above do not exhaust the range of accounts that have been offered as potential justifications for default verticality. It may be argued, for example, that a constitution's focus upon the state flows not from assumptions about sovereignty, freedom and responsibility, but, more simply, from the presumption that a constitution's role is to allocate public power between different institutions and not beyond (a point buttressed by the fact that in the international and supranational domain, the addressee of laws and norms is the state).

[99] ibid 918–19. See also Horwitz, 'The History of the Public/Private Distinction' (n 16) 1425; Atiyah, *The Rise and Fall of the Freedom of Contract* (n 68) 61–62; for a broader view, see K Polanyi, 'The Fascist Virus' in *Economy and Society: Selected Writings* (Polity Press, 2018) 108, 117, and other essays in the same volume.

[100] Grimm, *Constitutionalism* (n 7) 188. See also CB Macpherson, *The Political Theory of Possessive Individualism* (Clarendon Press, 1962) 3; Atiyah, *The Rise and Fall of the Freedom of Contract* (n 68) 70. For a contrary view, see J Gordley, *The Philosophical Origins of the Modern Contract Doctrine* (Oxford University Press, 1993).

[101] G de Almeida Ribeiro, *The Decline of Private Law: A Philosophical History of Liberal Legalism* (Hart Publishing, 2019) 175. See also D Kennedy, 'The Role of Law in Economic Thought: Essays on the Fetishism of Commodities' (1985) 34 *American University Law Review* 939, 953.

[102] For an account of the overlapping, yet different, way in which this affected the institution of the family, see F Olsen, 'The Myth of State Intervention in the Family' (1985) *Journal of Law Reform* 835. See also De Almeida Ribeiro, *The Decline of Private Law* (n 101) discussing Savigny's jurisprudence.

While this is true on its own terms, I suggest that at the root of this presumption is, again, the idea of indivisible sovereignty, located within the state. That constitutions are assumed to address themselves only to one form of power is itself drawn from prior assumptions about which forms of power are normatively salient, back to the conception of the public/private divide with which I began this chapter. That divide, I suggested, was most plausibly explained by a certain conception of sovereignty, which, when taken in conjunction with conceptions of abstract freedom and individual responsibility, provided a justification for prioritising public power over non-public power (as far as constitutional bills of rights are concerned).

It may also be argued that the tradition of political liberalism provides an alternative justification for default verticality: liberal neutrality is founded upon the premise that there is a qualitative distinction between state action and non-state action when it comes to issues such as the public stigma associated with state disfavour – or favour – towards certain basic goods and forms of life. The purpose of bills of rights, therefore, is to ensure state neutrality between different visions of the good.

Three responses can be made to this. The first is that, to an extent, the argument from liberal neutrality is already contained within the second of default verticality's assumptions: abstract freedom. As discussed above, abstract freedom contains a set of arguments that posit state action as a unique and uniquely salient threat to human flourishing. However, while this is a necessary condition for default verticality, it is not a sufficient one.

This is because, and secondly, while the argument from liberal neutrality arguably explains why *some* rights ought to be presumptively addressed to the state (for example, the right to non-discriminatory treatment), it does not explain why this is true for rights *in general*. In chapter five, for example, I will consider the horizontal application of the right against forced labour. This right is not connected to ideas of liberal neutrality and anti-perfectionism. Consequently, the argument from state neutrality is only a partial explanation for default verticality.

Thirdly, it is also partial in another sense. Liberal neutrality justifies a heightened focus – or concern – with state action when it comes to the application of constitutional rights. It does not, however, explain the flip side: why constitutional rights should *not* presumptively apply to private relations (especially if other reasons, independent of liberal neutrality, exist). In this context, it is important to recall that the three interlocking assumptions outlined above do not exist in silos, but reinforce each other, and together constitute the foundation of default verticality: that is, they justify not only a heightened concern for state action, but also – through abstract freedom and individual responsibility – the presumption against extending constitutional rights to private relations (and consequently require special justification when this is done).

In sum, therefore, it is true that there exists a range of arguments that may be advanced to support default verticality. However, what I have tried to show in this section is that while these arguments explain certain aspects of default verticality – or come at the problem from one angle – it is the three interlocking assumptions of sovereignty, abstract freedom and individual responsibility that possess significant explanatory force when it comes to assessing default verticality as a whole.

VII. THE CONTINGENCY OF THE PUBLIC/PRIVATE DIVIDE: THE CASE OF INDIA

It is almost trite to argue that there is nothing 'natural' about the default vertical approach, and that it arose out of a specific and contingent set of historical circumstances.[103] Such is the dominance that it has exercised over contemporary constitutional imagination, however, that it is often difficult to imagine what an alternative may look like. As I shall argue in chapters two and three, even jurisdictions that consciously attempt to depart from the default vertical approach continue to operate within the framework of at least one – if not more – of the founding assumptions outlined above.

The contingent character of those assumptions is revealed, however, when we consider certain provisions of the Indian Constitution. I shall examine the case of the Indian Constitution in greater detail in chapter five, and restrict myself to an outline here. At first glance, the Indian Constitution's bill of rights suggests that it fits comfortably within the contours of the default vertical approach. The bill of rights begins with a definition of the 'state',[104] and contains a series of familiar-sounding proscriptions upon state power.[105] This is unsurprising. As a survey of the Constituent Assembly Debates reveals, the framers of the Indian Constitution were (not atypically) heavily influenced by prominent constitutional models in existence at the time: primarily, the US model, but also the constitutions of Ireland and Japan (among others), which did not, in any significant way, depart from the default vertical approach.

However, the story does not end there. The bill of rights also has four provisions that apply inter se between private parties. Article 15(2)(a) of the Constitution stipulates that

> no citizen shall, on grounds only of religion, race, caste, sex, place of birth or any of them, be subject to any disability, liability, restriction or condition with regard to access to shops, public restaurants, hotels and places of public entertainment.[106]

[103] Dowdle and Wilkinson, 'Introduction' (n 11).
[104] Constitution of India 1949, Art 12.
[105] See, eg ibid Arts 14 (equal protection of laws), 15 (non-discrimination) and 21 (life and personal liberty).
[106] ibid Art 15(2).

Article 17 states that '"Untouchability" is abolished and its practice in any form is forbidden'.[107] Article 23(1) provides that 'traffic in human beings and *begar* and other similar forms of forced labour are prohibited'.[108] And Article 24 prohibits child labour in hazardous industries.[109]

There is a family resemblance between these provisions of the Indian Constitution and the Thirteenth Amendment of the US Constitution (which shall be discussed in chapter five). Beyond that, however, what is immediately noticeable about these provisions is their specificity. Unlike departures from the vertical model (considered in chapters two and three) that are framed in the language of *principle* – such as the 'public function test' or 'indirect horizontality' – leaving courts to provide concrete content to the stated principle on a case-by-case basis, the provisions of the Indian Constitution refer to a very categorical set of *acts*, and make no reference whatsoever to the state. This suggests that at the time of the framing of the Indian Constitution, there existed a set of known injustices that were inflicted by non-state parties and that were salient enough to be directly proscribed under the Constitution, instead of leaving it up to Parliament. Constitutional history supports this point. The debates around these clauses were accompanied by vivid illustrations of what the framers had in mind: barbers' salons under Article 15(2),[110] stigmatic social practices under Article 17[111] and inter-generational debt-bondage under Article 23[112] (among other things). One of the purpose(s) of the Indian Constitution, therefore, was evidently to address these specific 'legacies of injustice'.[113]

What were these injustices that prompted a departure from the premises of the default vertical model? A clue to the provenance of the horizontal rights provisions in the Indian Constitution is available in legal history. Commentators have pointed out how a distinctive feature of pre-colonial governance in India was the idea of 'layered sovereignty': a significant part of what we consider 'law-making' today was the domain of 'self-regulating communities', which were independent with respect to their 'internal organization'.[114] Crucially, from its

[107] ibid Art 17.
[108] ibid Art 23(1).
[109] ibid Art 24.
[110] Parliament of India, *Constituent Assembly Debates, vol VIII*, 29 November 1948, https://indiankanoon.org/doc/1464664/.
[111] ibid.
[112] Parliament of India, *Constituent Assembly Debates, vol III*, 1 May 1947, www.constitutionofindia.net/constitution_assembly_debates/volume/3/1947-05-01.
[113] R Teitel, 'Transitional Jurisprudence: The Role of Law in Political Transformation' (1997) 106 *Yale Law Journal* 2009, 2014.
[114] See eg N Dirks, *Castes of Mind: Colonialism and the Making of Modern India* (Princeton University Press, 2001); S Kaviraj, *Trajectories of the Indian State: Politics and Ideas* (Permanent Black, 2010); R Singha, *A Despotism of Law* (Oxford University Press, 1998); describing the thought of Rabindranath Tagore ('the laws of the state had limited jurisdiction and were subordinated to the rules of right conduct prescribed by community practices'), see also P Chatterjee, 'Nationalism, Internationalism, and Cosmopolitanism: Some Observations from Modern Indian History' (2016) 36 *Comparative Studies of South Asia, Africa and the Middle East* 320, 331.

very beginning, colonial rule was characterised by a (tactical) policy of leaving this structure largely intact. As early as 1792, it was stated British policy that there would be no interference with the 'personal laws' of the communities.[115] The very use of the phrase 'personal law' is telling, demonstrating that what we understand today as 'law-making power' (including, in the Indian case, the rules governing marriage, divorce, tenancy and inheritance) was habitually exercised by non-state parties (albeit, admittedly, with the sufferance of the colonial 'sovereign'). Consequently, the unitary conception of sovereignty that lies at the heart of the default vertical approach arguably did not possess the kind of normative salience during the evolution of rights-thinking in colonial India.

It is therefore unsurprising that as the language of rights developed and evolved in colonial India, it took two distinct forms: the familiar language of civil and political rights against despotic foreign rule, but also a vocabulary of rights available to individuals against *community-based* action, which had no state involvement of any kind. This vocabulary included the rights of women in the context of patriarchal family structures. For example, the nineteenth century saw three great movements involving the rights of widows to remarry, raising the age of consent and ending the practice of *sati* (the burning of a widow on her husband's funeral pyre). In all these movements, women as rights-bearing subjects were framed more in opposition to the community than to the state.[116]

In the period following shortly after, there were movements, as well, for recognition of rights against community-sanctioned ostracism and exclusion, primarily organised along the lines of caste. From the latter part of the nineteenth century, the colonial government had begun to receive petitions and complaints from individuals about social and spatial segregation, which was enforced by caste diktats.[117] In the twentieth century, these complaints evolved into the language of civil rights and public law, but directed *against* the operation of such social interdicts. For example, in one of his first legal submissions to the government, BR Ambedkar – who would later become the main draftsperson of the Indian Constitution – insisted on an 'anti-boycott law', which would penalise the practice of social and economic boycotts inflicted by dominant castes upon subordinate castes.[118] In the succeeding years, various government committees recognised the reality of a socially sanctioned, but highly effective, network of prohibitions and exclusions, ranging from the occupation a person could undertake to the public utilities that she could access. For this reason, some of the

[115] S Kaviraj, *The Imaginary Institution of India* (Permanent Black, 2010) 12.

[116] T Sarkar, 'A Prehistory of Rights: The Age of Consent Debate in Colonial Bengal' (2000) 26 *Feminist Studies* 601, 606; see also T Sarkar, 'Something Like Rights? Faith, Law and Widow Immolation Debates in Colonial Bengal' (2012) 49 *Indian Economic and Social History Review* 295.

[117] E Zelliott, *Ambedkar's World* (Navayana, 2012) 14.

[118] BR Ambedkar, *What Congress and Gandhi Have Done to the Untouchables* (Samyak Prakashan, 1945), http://www.satnami.com/WHAT%20CONGRESS%20AND%20GANDHI%20HAVE%20DONE%20TO%20THE%20UNTOUCHABLES.pdf.

early legislative proposals to deal with the issue not only proposed outlawing discriminatory laws, but also 'customs or *usages*'[119] (emphasis added) (ie long-standing traditional patterns of behaviour) that had discriminatory effect. It was these insights that eventually found their way into the Indian Constitution through Article 15(2), which prohibits denial of access or service in the 'private' economic domain.

The nature of the powers exercised by groups also reveals why, in addition to sovereignty, assumptions about freedom and individual responsibility also did not (necessarily) limit the imagination of the constitutional framers. It would, after all, be difficult to argue that in the context of layered sovereignty, where groups exercised systematic coercive power through a range of social and economic sanctions, 'freedom' was what remained after constraining only state power. In a society where economic boycott was regularly used as a method of enforcing social discipline, it would be equally difficult to argue that freely contracting individuals faced each other as abstract equals in a horizontal plane. It is therefore my contention – which I shall develop in greater detail in chapter five – that a history in which groups, communities and institutions exercised power in their respective domains, distinct and separate from the state, meant that the default vertical approach did not enjoy the kind of monopoly over the minds of the framers of the Indian Constitution that it did elsewhere. Consequently, as observed above, while most of the provisions of India's fundamental rights chapter do indeed apply to the state, the Constitution also contains a set of provisions that appear to flow from an entirely distinct constitutional imagination, one that is not constrained by the assumptions underlying the default vertical approach and accords no special role for the state.

This is also because by 1947, more than 150 years after the framing of the US bill of rights, there had been ample time to study the default vertical approach and draw upon it, but also learn from its errors. Tellingly, in an initial Note to the Constituent Assembly on the subject of fundamental rights, BR Ambedkar singled out the default vertical approach, and criticised the assumption of 'constitutional lawyers' that 'the enactment of fundamental rights is enough to safeguard their liberty and that nothing more is called for … that where the State refrains from intervention in private affairs – economic and the social – the residue is liberty'.[120]

Noting further that

> the useful remedy adopted by democratic countries … to *limit* the power of Government to impose arbitrary restraints in political domain and to *invoke* the ordinary power of the legislature to restrain the more powerful individual from imposing arbitrary restraints on the less powerful' (emphasis added)[121]

[119] Zelliott, *Ambedkar's World* (n 117).

[120] BR Ambedkar, 'Memorandum and Draft Articles on the Rights of States and Minorities, 24 March 1947' in B Shiva Rao (ed), *The Framing of India's Constitution*, vol II (NM Tripathi, 1966) 84, 100.

[121] ibid.

had proven 'inadequate', Ambedkar outlined an alternative vision that would take into account differential, institutional power relations within society. It is this vision – largely passed over in silence in comparative constitutional literature – that (as I shall argue in chapter five) helps us to construct a convincing model of horizontal rights. This is a model that does not suffer from the shortcomings of the existing (chapters two and three) models that continue to place the state at the centre of the analysis.

VIII. CONCLUSION

More than two centuries after the framing of the US Constitution's bill of rights, in a world that has changed beyond recognition, the default vertical approach continues to exercise a powerful sway over constitutional imagination. For example, Section 8 of the Constitution of South Africa (adopted in 1996) provides that the bill of rights shall bind 'all organs of state',[122] and shall bind natural or juristic persons 'if, and to the extent that, it is applicable, taking into account the nature of the right and the nature of any duty imposed by the right'.[123] Thus, while it is taken for granted that a bill of rights, by its very nature, applies to the state, there is only a qualified recognition that in some (undefined) cases, it *might* apply in some sense to non-state parties.

In this introductory chapter, I have attempted to account for the (continuing) normative plausibility of the default vertical approach. I have argued that the three interlocking conceptions of sovereignty, freedom and individual responsibility combine to isolate the state as a *uniquely significant* centre of power, which must therefore be constrained by a bill of rights. Sovereignty vests in the state a monopoly over legitimate coercion (expressed primarily through the authority of law-making), and therefore qualitatively differentiates between state and non-state power. The existence of this power presents a unique threat to abstract freedom, narrowly defined as the absence of coercion. And the uniqueness of the threat flows from the fact that while natural and juristic persons interact with each other from a position of formal legal equality – and are thus individually responsible for shaping their relationships with each other – the state (through its exercise of sovereign power) stands above this plane of interaction.

The three conceptions, therefore, are mutually reinforcing,[124] and together place the state at the centre of constitutional imagination, as the primary subject

[122] Constitution of the Republic of South Africa 1996, s 8(1).

[123] Constitution of the Republic of South Africa, 1996, s 8(2); but see also Constitution of Kenya 2010, which makes no such distinction. For a discussion of horizontality doctrine in both jurisdictions, see ch 8 of this book.

[124] See, eg Atiyah, *The Rise and Fall of the Freedom of Contract* (n 68) 71 (drawing the link between sovereignty and contract); Lewis, 'Book Review' (n 66) 501 (drawing the link between freedom and contract); see also S Mau, *Mute Compulsion: A Marxist Theory of the Economic Power of Capital* (Verso, 2023), for a more conceptual argument about the link between freedom and contract.

of a bill of rights. In the next two chapters, I shall argue that prevailing judicial models that depart from the default vertical approach nonetheless continue to subscribe to one or more of its foundational assumptions. For this reason, the solutions they offer to the problems of the default vertical approach remain partial and unsatisfactory. This, then, sets the stage for chapter five, where I shall discuss the 'institutional approach'. I will argue that by repudiating each of the three foundational assumptions, the institutional approach can potentially make up for these shortcomings, and provide a model of constitutional rights that has liberated itself from the shackles of the state.

2

State Action

I. INTRODUCTION

IN CHAPTER ONE, I set out the three conceptual assumptions that underlie the default vertical approach to understanding constitutional bills of rights: sovereignty, freedom and individual responsibility. Notwithstanding the default vertical approach, constitutional and appellate courts in multiple jurisdictions apply bills of rights to actions of non-state parties in certain circumstances. In this second chapter, I examine one of the archetypical models that exemplifies a 'departure' from verticality. I argue that even in doing so, courts remain wedded to one or more of the conceptual assumptions underlying the default vertical approach. Popularly known as the 'state action doctrine', this approach 'attributes' the acts of a non-state body to the state, by virtue of a formal or real connection that exists between the two. I argue that this approach – which takes different forms in different jurisdictions – continues to treat the concept of unitary, centralised sovereignty as uniquely salient when it comes to the application of bills of rights. It is therefore unsatisfactory. At the same time, one aspect of this approach – which focuses upon the private party's capacity or ability to impact rights – contains the kernel of a more satisfactory account, which will be developed in chapter five.

* * * * *

The default vertical approach holds that bills of rights are primarily designed to apply to the state, and that consequently, the application of constitutional rights to non-state parties stands in need of special justification. In chapter one, I focused on the 'vertical' component of this approach, interrogating the conceptual assumptions that make the relationship between the individual and the state central to the application of bills of rights. In this chapter and the next, I shall examine its 'default' character by demonstrating how even departures from verticality remain bound to one or more of its founding assumptions.

Departures from the default vertical approach have received sustained focus and critique in the existing literature. According to scholarly accounts, they can be broadly classified as follows:[1] first, approaches that ask what a private party *is* or *does* (considered in this chapter); and secondly, approaches that seek to indirectly reach the acts of a private party by going *through* the state ('indirect horizontality', considered in the next chapter).

In examining these approaches, my analysis in this chapter and the next shall be comparative. I shall not, however, undertake a jurisdiction-by-jurisdiction approach, as some scholars have done.[2] Instead, I shall focus on the archetypal approaches outlined above, and examine how they have been treated by certain prominent constitutional and appellate courts. In doing so, my selection of jurisdictions attempts to follow a principle of broad geographical, historical and size-based representativeness within the English-speaking constitutional world. Thus, this chapter considers the USA (which, as discussed in chapter one, has been a dominant influence when it comes to the default vertical approach), India (a Global South constitutional democracy with more than a billion people, whose constitution was framed during the first wave of British decolonisation) and South Africa (another post-colonial nation, whose constitution was framed towards the end of the twentieth century).[3] The next chapter also considers Germany (which is not an English-speaking jurisdiction, but whose concept of indirect horizontality has influenced constitutional jurisprudence worldwide), Ireland (whose constitutional tort doctrine is arguably a form of direct horizontality) and – briefly – the Court of Justice of the European Union. I recognise that the cases I discuss may not be representative of the *only* way in which a particular jurisdiction treats the question at issue. Inconsistencies and outliers are features of every legal system where the doctrine of precedent has some role to play. The purpose of analysing these cases is to demonstrate how the archetypal approaches (discussed above) are given concrete content through the process of judicial reasoning, often in more than one jurisdiction.

I also acknowledge that there exist jurisdictions such as Greece,[4] Spain[5] and Colombia[6] where constitutional doctrine has considered the horizontal

[1] W Rivera-Perez, 'What's the Constitution Got to Do with It? Expanding the Scope Of Constitutional Rights into the Private Sphere' (2012) 1 *Creighton International and Comparative Law Journal* 189; J Thomas, *Public Rights, Private Relations* (Oxford University Press, 2015) ch 1; S Gardbaum, 'The "Horizontal Effect" of Constitutional Rights' (2003) 102 *Michigan Law Review* 387.

[2] For an example of this approach, see J Mathews, *Expanding Rights' Reach: Constitutions, Private Law, and Judicial Power* (Oxford University Press, 2018), comparing the USA, Canada and Germany.

[3] It is important to note that the Canadian 'governmental functions' approach follows the same logic as the state action approaches in the USA and South Africa, but is narrower in its operation. Consequently, for the purposes of this book, Canadian jurisprudence will not add significantly to the scope of the argument.

[4] C Akrivopoulou, 'Greece: Taking Private Law Seriously in the Application of Constitutional Rights' in D Oliver and J Fedtke (eds), *Human Rights and the Private Sphere: A Comparative Study* (Routledge, 2007) 157.

[5] A Rodriguez Liboreiro, 'Spain: A Jurisdiction Recognising the Direct Horizontal Application of Human Rights' in Oliver and Fedtke, *Human Rights and the Private Sphere* (n 4) 378.

[6] Rivera-Perez, 'What's the Constitution Got to Do with It?' (n 1) 203–07.

application of rights, but whose approaches may not sit easily with the archetypes discussed in this chapter and the next. In that sense, I make no claim to comprehensiveness. However, within the constraints of theme, space and language in the context of this book, I hope to advance a somewhat representative account of the English-speaking democratic-constitutional world.

With these preliminary remarks, we now come to the subject matter of this chapter: the 'public character of private actors' (section II). This first set of approaches focus on how closely connected a private party is to the state in its composition (section IIA), its functioning (section IIB), its ability to impact fundamental rights (section IIC), or some combination of the three. If the connection is proximate enough, the acts of the private party are deemed 'attributable' to the state, and it is subjected to the bill of rights (in that jurisdiction). In order to avoid confusion, it is important to note that these approaches are conceptually distinct from approaches that place positive obligations upon the state to protect individual rights. The result of a finding of 'attribution', rather, is that it is the private body that is subjected to the bill of rights, by virtue of its resemblance to the state.

There is no dearth of scholarly criticism of these approaches. For example, the US 'state action' doctrine – an exemplar of the first category – has been famously called 'a conceptual disaster area'.[7] Criticisms of this kind focus on how the line-drawing exercise to determine what constitutes enough proximity to the 'state' is unsatisfactory (and that, as a corollary, the line should be drawn elsewhere[8]), or even indicate that it is inherently arbitrary and incapable of principled delineation.[9] It is not my purpose in this chapter to reiterate these criticisms. My focus lies elsewhere. I shall demonstrate how, even as they purport to 'depart' from verticality by applying bills of rights against private parties, these approaches continue to be bound by the conceptual assumptions of the default vertical approach. In other words, by equating a private party to the state (the first category), these 'departures' still place the state at the heart of their analysis.

For example, within the conceptual framework of 'attribution', this category of approaches invariably ends up focusing on questions such as whether

[7] CL Black Jr, 'The Supreme Court, 1966 Term – Foreword: "State Action", Equal Protection, and California's Proposition 14' (1967) 81 *Harvard Law Review* 71, 95.

[8] See, eg D Barak-Erez, 'Civil Rights in the Privatized State: A Comparative View' (1999) 28 *Anglo-American Law Review* 503, 517; AA Berle Jr, 'Constitutional Limitations on Corporate Activity – Protection of Personal Rights from Invasion through Economic Power' (1952) 100 *University of Pennsylvania Law Review* 933, 952; S Sedley, 'No Ordinary Law' (2008) 30(11) *London Review of Books*, www.lrb.co.uk/the-paper/v30/n11/stephen-sedley/no-ordinary-law.

[9] See, eg Thomas, *Public Rights, Private Relations* (n 1) 17. See also Mathews, *Expanding Rights' Reach* (n 2) ch 4. F Michelman, 'Constitutions and the Public/Private Divide' in M Rosenfeld and A Sajo (eds), *The Oxford Handbook of Comparative Constitutional Law* (Oxford University Press, 2012) 300; P Brest, 'State Action and Liberal Theory, A Casenote on *Flagg Brothers v Brooks*' (1982) 130 *University of Pennsylvania Law Review* 1296.

the state has 'delegated' its functions to a private party or whether a private party possesses a 'monopoly' over a domain in a manner similar to the state. The ideas of both delegation and monopoly hark back to the unitary, centralised and monopolistic conception of sovereignty that constitutes the first assumption of the default vertical approach (section III). These approaches, therefore, are deficient in vital ways. However, they also have elements that can provide us with valuable insights in building a more convincing model. For example, a focus upon a private party's *impact* upon (or ability to impact) the rights protected by a constitution can serve as a vital building block (section IV), a proposition that I shall develop further in chapter five.

II. THE PUBLIC CHARACTER OF PRIVATE ACTORS

The default vertical approach – as I argued in chapter one – is premised upon the assumption that sovereign power, concentrated within the state, possesses unique normative salience in relation to threats to individual interests, and therefore in relation to invoking and applying constitutional rights. Whatever the intuitive plausibility of this assumption at the time of its origin, the rise of the modern administrative state in the twentieth century, its undertaking of far-reaching welfare functions and the subsequent outsourcing and privatisation of those very functions have cast significant stress upon the clean(er) separation between state and non-state power.[10] These developments have given rise to the first category of departures from the default vertical approach – the subject matter of this chapter – which Jean Thomas usefully labels 'the inadequate constraint' hypothesis: 'states are performing "intrinsically" public or state-like functions by delegation – through contract or outright privatization – to corporations, leaving quintessentially state functions improperly constrained and supervised'.[11]

The inadequate constraint hypothesis remedies this lacuna by asking whether a sufficient degree of 'functional equivalence'[12] exists between the private party and the state. If the answer is 'yes', then the private party is subjected to the bill of rights *as if* it were the state. Equivalence is determined through a range of overlapping tests. In the interests of conceptual clarity, these can be broadly classified into: tests asking what a body *is* (ie its composition and character), what it *does* (ie its activities and tasks), and the kinds of impact it can have on

[10] A Supiot, 'The Public–Private Relation in the Context of today's refeudalisation' (2013) 11 *International Journal of Constitutional Law* 129.

[11] J Thomas, *Public Rights, Private Relations* (n 1) 10.

[12] H Hershkoff, 'The Private Life of Public Rights: State Constitutions and the Common Law' (2013) 88 *New York University Law Review* 1, 12.

individual interests and rights. In practice, of course, courts employ a combination of some or all of these tests in order to determine functional equivalence.[13]

A. What a Private Party 'Is'

Private bodies are subject to bills of rights if they are, to all appearances, indistinguishable from the state. After a few decades of vacillation, the Indian Supreme Court finally held that it would decide this question by applying a straightforward test of control: does the state exercise 'functional, financial, and administrative control'[14] over the private party? It is difficult to imagine what remains after taking away finances, functions and administration. Indian jurisprudence, therefore, presents the archetype of the situation where the legal form is the only relevant difference between the state and the private party. In a similar, although less stark, fashion, the extent of ministerial control over a formally 'private' body engaged in regulating the practice of microlending was one of the important factors that led the South African Constitutional Court to subject it to the Bill of Rights, as an 'organ of state' under the South African Constitution.[15]

Not every jurisdiction, however, insists on such near-effacement of the identity of the private party before subjecting it to a bill of rights. The state's 'involvement with' or 'participation in' a private activity can often suggest a sufficiently close 'relation'[16] or 'nexus'[17] between the two as to warrant the application of the bill of rights. This relationship is determined by a number of factors. For example, in *Public Utilities Commission v Pollack*, the extensive regulatory supervision undertaken by the Public Utilities Commission (a state agency) over the activities of Pollack (the owner of the streetcar-and-bus system in Washington DC) was deemed a close enough nexus by the US Supreme Court to subject the latter to the provisions of the Bill of Rights.[18] In *Burton v Wilmington Parking Authority*, the Respondent – an agency of the State of Delaware – leased an integral part of its parking-building space to a restaurant, while also providing it with necessary electricity and gas. A combination of these

[13] For one of the clearest examples of this, see the judgment of the South African Supreme Court of Appeal in *Calibre Clinical Consultants (Pty) Ltd v National Bargaining Council for the Road and Freight Industry* [2010] 4 All SA 561 (Supreme Court of Appeal), which applied some combination of almost all the tests discussed below.

[14] *Pradeep Kumar Biswas v Indian Institute of Chemical Biology* (2002) 4 SCC 111. The Supreme Court was interpreting Art 12 of the Indian Constitution, which imposes the bill of rights upon state organs and 'other authorities'.

[15] *AAA Investments (Proprietary) Ltd v Micro Finance Regulatory Council* 2006 (11) BCLR 1255 (CC) [44].

[16] *Public Utilities Commission v Pollack* 343 US 451 (1952), 462.

[17] *Jackson v Metropolitan Edison Co* 419 US 345 (1974), 351.

[18] *Public Utilities Commission v Pollack* (n 16).

factors was sufficient for the Supreme Court to hold that racial discrimination in denial of services undertaken by the private respondent (the restaurant) brought it within the scope of the bill of rights, as the state had taken 'responsibility'[19] for the actions of the restaurant.

Demonstrating, however, that these enquiries were all a matter of degree, in *Moose Lodge v Irvis*, the US Supreme Court refused to hold a bar liable for racial discrimination even though its licence was provided under a state regulatory scheme because 'the symbiotic relationship between lessor and lessee that was present in Burton'[20] was not present here. Consequently, the mere fact of state regulation was not sufficient, as the private party must be operating within 'a framework of extensive state supervision and control'.[21] The result of the difference, of course, was that while the respondent in *Burton* was held liable for racial discrimination under the Constitution, Moose Lodge escaped liability.

While judges in the majority and the dissent in the USA have disagreed with each other over whether, in particular cases, the facts justify a finding of 'state action' or not, they have been united over the principles governing the enquiry. Abstracting from the specifics of when 'involvement' or 'participation' is deemed 'sufficiently close', judges have repeatedly held that the underlying principle is whether the private body's acts are 'attributable to the State'[22] or may be treated 'as that of the State'.[23] It is in this sense that the state remains central to the enquiry: if the key is whether the state is 'responsible' for the private party's action or whether the private party's action is 'attributable' to the state, then the normatively significant actor remains the state. The success of the claim then depends on how effectively the private party can be assimilated to the classical understanding of 'state' under the default vertical approach.

B. What a Private Party 'Does'

There are occasions, however, when a private party does not retain a tangible 'nexus' with the state (or a state agency) either in formal or in real terms. In such situations, the focus shifts the nature of the *functions* that it performs, and whether there is a sufficiently close relationship in terms of those. For example, in terms of Canadian jurisprudence, which puts the point most clearly and narrowly, is the private party performing 'governmental functions'?[24]

[19] *Burton v Wilmington Parking Authority* 365 US 715 (1961), 722.

[20] *Moose Lodge v Irvis* 407 US 163 (1972), 175.

[21] *Jackson v Metropolitan Edison Co* (n 17) 362 (Douglas J, dissenting).

[22] ibid 359.

[23] *Blum v Yaretsky* 457 US 991 (1982), 1004.

[24] For reasons explained previously, I do not explore Canadian jurisprudence in this chapter. For an account, see Mathews, *Expanding Rights' Reach* (n 2).

As I will argue subsequently, this category of approaches remains bound to one of the underlying assumptions of default verticality: that of centralised and unitary sovereignty. This is made clear if we pay close attention to how courts decide whether a private party's conduct bears a sufficiently close relationship with the state. The following discussion, therefore, is organised around three themes that play a role in these cases: an emphasis on the 'traditional' functions of the state (i), and the markers that are used to decide that issue: delegation (ii) and monopoly (iii).

(i) The 'Traditional' Functions of the State

Naturally, functional equivalence requires a prior account of what constitutes a 'state function', with which equivalence is being drawn. In the previous chapter, I briefly discussed the US Supreme Court's decision in *Flagg Bros*, which asked whether the private party performs a function that has 'traditionally [been] the exclusive prerogative of the State'.[25] This expression has been a staple feature in US Supreme Court judgments both before and after *Flagg Bros*.[26] The use of the word 'traditionally' indicates that the focal point of the enquiry is historical. And, indeed, the disagreements between the majority and the dissenting opinions in state action cases have often revolved around the kinds of functions that the state has been historically expected to perform. As I shall highlight subsequently, this approach ignores Andrew Clapham's straightforward insight that 'the classic duties of the State may vary over time'.[27] Instead, it locks in (descriptive) assumptions about what the state *once did* into (normative) judgements about what it *now should do*.

Additionally, there is no clarity on precisely how far back into the past the historical enquiry needs to go. In *Flagg Bros* itself, for example, Justice Marshall (in dissent) accused the majority of attempting to resolve the issue in a 'historical vacuum', and noted that 'by ignoring this history, the Court approaches the question before us as if it can be decided without reference to the role that the state has *always played* in lien execution by forced sale' (emphasis added).[28] And in *Rendell-Baker v Kohn*, which concerned the status of a private school that entered into an arrangement with the state to meet the educational needs of 'maladjusted' students, the fact that '*until recently* the State had not undertaken to provide education for students who could not be served by traditional public schools' (emphasis added)[29] was an important factor in the majority's refusal to subject it to the bill of rights.

[25] *Flagg Bros v Brooks*, 436 US 149 (1978).

[26] *Jackson v Metropolitan Edison Co* (n 17); *Rendell-Baker v Kohn* 457 US 830 (1981) 842; *Blum v Yaretsky* (n 23); *San Francisco Arts and Athletics v USOC* 483 US 522 (1986).

[27] A Clapham, *Human Rights in the Private Sphere* (Oxford University Press, 1996) 259.

[28] *Flagg Bros v Brooks* (n 25) 168 (Marshall J, dissenting).

[29] *Rendell-Baker v Kohn* (n 26) 842.

(ii) Markers of State Functions I: Delegation

The backward-looking nature of the enquiry, which ties it to the state (and, in particular, to the 'traditional' conception of what the state should look like) is exemplified by two of the most prominent indicia applied by the courts: *delegation* and *monopoly*. The prominent concerns of the courts revolve less around the rights bearer and her relationship with the private party, and more around whether the state is attempting to 'evade' its constitutional responsibilities by delegating functions to private parties. For example, in *Evans v Newton*, which involved a challenge to a town administering a large private park along racially segregated lines, in its capacity as the trustee of a bequest, the US Supreme Court noted that the issue was whether 'private individuals or groups are *endowed by the State* with powers or functions governmental in nature' (emphasis added).[30] The point was made more expressly in *Local 590 v Logan Valley* when the Court considered the issue of peaceful picketing in the loading porch of a privately owned shopping centre: 'the State may not delegate the power, through the use of its trespass laws, wholly to exclude those members of the public wishing to exercise their First Amendment rights on the premises'.[31]

The hold of the delegation argument is visible perhaps most starkly in judicial disputes over the interpretation of the US Supreme Court's famous judgment in *Marsh v Alabama*. In *Marsh*, the Court held that the First Amendment to the US Constitution (guaranteeing the freedom of expression and religion) applied to a 'company town' (ie a town that, in every respect, functioned as a town, but was privately owned). A member of the Jehovah's Witnesses, therefore, could exercise their constitutional right to distribute leaflets in the streets of the town.[32] The Court in *Marsh* based its holding on a number of arguments, such as the diminishment of property interests when an individual 'opened up' their property for use of the public, the existence of a 'public function' and the importance of keeping traditional channels of communication – such as sidewalks and roads – open.[33] Subsequently, however, attempts by the Court to expand the scope of the state action doctrine by invoking some of these broader arguments – for example, in *Logan Valley*, as discussed above – were unable to command a permanent majority, and the Court ultimately interpreted *Marsh* as being a case about delegation[34] – an argument that only Justice Frankfurter

[30] *Evans v Newton* 382 US 296 (1965) 299.

[31] *Local 590 v Logan Valley* 391 US 308 (1968), 319. *Logan Valley* was subsequently overturned, but not on this point.

[32] *Marsh v Alabama* 326 US 501 (1946).

[33] ibid 506.

[34] *Hudgens v NLRB* 424 US 507 (1976), 519: '[*Marsh*] involved the assumption by a private enterprise of all of the attributes of a state-created municipality and the exercise by that enterprise of semiofficial municipal functions as a delegate of the State.' See also *Jackson v Metropolitan Edison Co* (n 17) 372 (Marshall J, dissenting).

had made in his concurring judgment: 'a company-owned town is a town. In its community aspects it does not differ from other towns. These community aspects are decisive in adjusting the relations now before us.'[35]

Understanding the departure from the default vertical approach in the language of delegation has influenced constitutional thought beyond the borders of the USA. Under the South African Constitution, for example, the Bill of Rights binds all 'organs of state'.[36] An organ of state is defined, in turn, as an entity performing a public function in terms of national legislation.[37] Admittedly, the higher courts in South Africa have not (yet) had the occasion to develop a body of long-standing jurisprudence (as in the USA).[38] However, in one of the first cases, *AAA Investments* – concerning the conduct of a nominally 'private' body that regulated micro-lending, discussed above – in which it did have an opportunity to explore the definition of 'organ of state' (and thereby the underlying foundations of extending the bill of rights to bodies performing public functions), the South African Constitutional Court expressly chose to follow US and Canadian jurisprudence. After engaging in a lengthy survey of the law in those jurisdictions, it observed that 'our Constitution ensures, *as in Canada and the United States*, that government cannot be released from its human rights and rule of law obligations simply because it employs *the strategy of delegating its functions* to another entity' (emphasis added).[39] On the facts of the case, what weighed with the Court (apart from ministerial control, discussed above, and another factor, discussed below), was that the minister who was required by statute to oversee the micro-lending industry had '*passed on* [that] regulatory duty' (emphasis added).[40]

(iii) Marker of State Functions II: Monopoly

The third factor that weighed with the South African Constitutional Court in *AAA Investments* comes through most clearly in the concurring opinion of O'Regan J. Endorsing the judgment of the High Court (which was overturned on appeal by the SCA), O'Regan J observed that 'no lender may lawfully operate without registering with the Council … in that sense, the rules are coercive and

[35] *Marsh v Alabama* (n 32) 510–11.

[36] Constitution of South Africa 1996, s 8(1).

[37] ibid s 239.

[38] For a genealogy and analysis, which also discusses, inter alia, some of the issues raised in this chapter pertaining to the nature of the state, see M Finn, 'Organs of State: An Anatomy' (2015) 31 *South African Journal on Human Rights* 631.

[39] *AAA Investments (Proprietary) Ltd v Micro Finance Regulatory Council* 2006 (11) BCLR 1255 (CC) [40].

[40] ibid [43]. While I shall explore South African jurisprudence in greater detail later in ch 3, the purpose of this example is merely to demonstrate how delegation as an archetypal concept has obtained cross-jurisdictional currency as a justification for departing from the default vertical approach.

general in their effect'.[41] In other words, the Council's monopoly over regulating micro-lending – backed up by coercion – brought it into the 'public' side of the public/private divide.[42] Similarly, in *Allpay Consolidated Investment Holdings v Chief Executive Officer (No 2)*, the Constitutional Court noted that Cash Paymaster Services – a private limited company in charge of distributing social security payments – was an organ of state because, having signed an exclusive contract with the state social security agency, it had become the 'gatekeeper' of the right to social security – and thereby was 'the operational arm of the … administration'.[43]

Similarly, while US judges have been careful to specify that monopoly is not a dispositive factor in determining the existence of state action, it has always been a relevant factor. In *Marsh*, for example, the company town's exclusive control – through its property rights – of the 'channels of communication'[44] weighed with the Court in invoking the First Amendment. And in their dissenting opinions in *Jackson* and *Hudgen*, Justices Douglas and Marshall found that the electricity company's monopoly over municipal power supply[45] and the shopping centre's monopoly over the channels of *effective* communication when it came to company policies[46] amounted to 'displacing' the state and taking over its functions.

The vocabulary of displacement brings us back to the concept with which this section began: like the cases that focus on the character of the private party, cases focusing on functions also come back to the question of attributability. In his dissent in *Jackson*, Marshall J noted that in performing vital public functions, private parties acted as 'surrogates'[47] of the state; in *Kohn*, he went even further, holding (also in dissent, although not on this point) that private conduct 'impregnated with … governmental character … can be regarded as governmental action'.[48] Whether delegation, monopoly or the character of the private body, it is this inability to depart from the paradigm of the state – even while departing from default verticality – that, I shall argue, continues to bind these approaches to the assumption of sovereignty that underlies default verticality.

[41] ibid [122].

[42] 'I cannot therefore agree with the conclusion of the Supreme Court of Appeal that, properly construed, the Rules are private in character.' ibid.

[43] *Allpay Consolidated Investment Holdings (Pty) Ltd v Chief Executive Officer of the South African Social Security Agency (No 2)* 2014 (6) BCLR 641 (CC) [55].

[44] *Marsh v Alabama* (n 32) 507.

[45] *Jackson v Metropolitan Edison Co* (n 17) 361.

[46] *Hudgens v NLRB* (n 34) 540. Although not directly addressed, there seems to be a tension between the relevance of monopoly in these cases and the concept of a 'natural monopoly', evolving out of an unregulated market, which was discussed in a previous generation of US cases. See ch 1.

[47] *Jackson v Metropolitan Edison Co* (n 17) 372.

[48] *Rendell-Baker v Kohn* (n 26) 847.

C. The Private Body's Capability to Affect Rights

In chapter one, I set out Frank Michelman's important insight, that the 'concentration [of legitimate coercive power] in a single institutional nexus (the state)'[49] was responsible for presenting it as a unique threat to core individual interests. This was one of the major reasons for subjecting the state to constitutional control through a bill of rights, while leaving it free to deal with 'private' invasions of rights through legislation.[50] Pared down to its essentials, this bare logic suggests an alternative method of departing from the default vertical approach, one that can bypass the Ptolemaic epicycles of control, delegation, monopoly and attributability.[51]

The tentative beginnings of this method are found in *Marsh v Alabama* before it was watered down to the delegation argument by future judgments. What the majority in *Marsh actually* said was that 'whether a corporation or a municipality owns or possesses the town *the public in either case has an identical interest* in the functioning of the community in such manner that the channels of communication remain free' (emphasis added).[52] In other words, it was the company town's ability to impact a vital constitutional interest – by virtue of its ownership of the town – that justified subjecting it to the bill of rights. A few decades later, more tentative steps were taken in the judgment of the South African Constitutional Court in *Khumalo v Holomisa*, within the framework of a more facilitative Constitution. Section 8(2) of the South African Constitution provides that the bill of rights binds a natural or juristic person in certain circumstances, 'taking into account the nature of the right and the nature of any duty imposed by the right'.[53] In *Khumalo*, the question before the Court was whether the law of defamation was consistent with the free speech guarantee of the Constitution. To answer that question, however, the Court decided to first examine whether the right to free speech was horizontally applicable.[54] Answering in the affirmative, the Court noted that:

> given the intensity of the constitutional right in question, coupled with *the potential invasion of that right which could be occasioned by persons other than the state or*

[49] Michelman, 'Constitutions and the Public/Private Divide' (n 9) 305–06; see also RS Kay, 'The State Action Doctrine, the Public–Private Distinction, and the Independence of Constitutional Law' (1993) 10 *Constitutional Commentary* 329.

[50] Rivera-Perez, 'What's the Constitution Got to Do with It?' (n 1).

[51] In his dissenting opinion in *Blum v Yaretsky*, Justice Brennan referred to the 'complex and opaque regulatory frameworks' that the courts needed to pierce through to get *to* the state. *Blum v Yaretsky* (n 23) 1012 (Brennan J, dissenting).

[52] *Marsh v Alabama* (n 32) 507. See also Douglas J's dissent in *Jackson*: 'When power is denied a householder, the home, under modern conditions, is likely to become unlivable.' *Jackson v Metropolitan Edison Co* (n 17) 360 (Douglas J, dissenting).

[53] Constitution of the Republic of South Africa 1996, s 8(2).

[54] Note that the Court would not have needed to do so, had it found – as other jurisdictions have – that common law, emanating from the state, must *ipso facto* comply with the Constitution. I will study this approach in the next section.

> *organs of state*, it is clear that the right to freedom of expression is of direct horizontal application in this case. (emphasis added)[55]

While the Constitutional Court in *Khumalo* did not explain this any further, in legal scholarship, the argument is articulated in its most straightforward form by Daphne Barak-Erez. Barak-Erez argues that instead of focusing upon the private party accused of violating rights, our starting point should be the rights bearer. We therefore begin from the premise that in our society, every individual is entitled to certain basic goods (including rights and freedoms). Any entity – private or public – that is in a position to impact that entitlement is subjected to the same standards as imposed upon the government.[56] This approach, Barak-Erez argues, allows us to address 'the challenges posed by the realities of the new state'[57] – in particular, the large-scale privatisation of welfare functions. Indeed, the South African Constitutional Court gestured towards this in *Allpay* (discussed above) when it noted that Cash Paymaster Ltd, through its contract with the state social security agency, exercised control over individuals' ability to exercise their constitutional right to social security.[58]

In more formal terms, and in line with the typology discussed above, Jean Thomas labels this the 'vulnerable valuable interests diagnosis':

> A third important way of describing the situation is that crucial interests are going unprotected. This way of thinking says that people's interest in freedom from summary execution and torture, for instance, is radically under-protected when Shell, for example, can participate in the violation of those interests and have claims brought against it in the United States under the *Alien Tort Claims Act* thrown out partly on the basis that its actions are insufficiently connected to a government to be eligible for accountability.[59]

III. CRITIQUE

As the very label 'functional equivalence' suggests, this set of approaches depends upon finding points of overlap – in character, functions or impact – between the private party and the state. The more one can 'equate' the private party with (what we think of as) the state, the greater chance of having it subjected to the bill of rights. This is reflected, for example, in the US state action cases, where the majority and dissenting opinions regularly disagree on the application of the test but agree on the principle that, ultimately, in some way, if a private party is to be bound by the Bill of Rights, its actions must be 'attributable' to the state.

[55] *Khumalo v Holomisa* 2002 (8) BCLR 771 (CC) [33]. See also the discussion of Irish constitutional cases in Rivera-Perez, 'What's the Constitution Got to Do with It?' (n 1).

[56] Barak-Erez, 'Civil Rights in the Privatized State' (n 8) 519.

[57] ibid 517.

[58] *Allpay Consolidated Investment Holdings* (n 43) [54].

[59] Thomas, *Public Rights, Private Relations* (n 1) 10–11.

It intuitively follows that functional equivalence leaves untouched the assumptions underlying the default vertical approach. As Barak-Erez acknowledges, the result is that 'the distinction between public and private can be preserved while acknowledging that the line between the two should now be drawn differently'.[60] This is particularly obvious with the approach outlined in section IIA, where the whole enquiry is about how much 'control' the state has over a private party, or how 'entangled' it is. It is also pervasive (albeit to a subtler degree) in section IIB, where the emphasis shifts to functions. For example, the focus on 'delegation' rests upon an ideological conception of what the state is and what it should be doing. In his concurring opinion in *Reitman v Mulkey* (a case involving an amendment to the Californian Constitution that would have allowed racially restrictive covenants), for example, Justice Douglas asked about the role of the state in its 'historical and classical sense'.[61] Justice Brennan's opinion in *Blum v Yaretsky* was premised upon the responsibilities of the state in 'in an era of active governmental intervention to tackle social ills'.[62]

The problem, however, is not simply that the delegation argument appears to turn upon whether a majority on the bench believes that the state should be the nightwatchman of classical liberal theory or the welfare state of the mid-twentieth century,[63] or take some other historical form altogether. The problem is also that, whatever vision of the state one operates with, it remains centred as a unique, normatively significant threat to rights. In other words, the 'functions' in question are not considered on their own terms, but whether they can, in some way, be associated with the state. It is *that* association which determines the question of whether the performance of those functions needs to respect rights. This is evident from how judges in both the USA and South Africa have rejected looking at functions purely from the perspective of their potential to impact the 'public interest', and insisted on a further, tangible connection with the state.[64] In *Jackson*, for example, the US Supreme Court caricatured the argument by dismissively observing that 'doctors, optometrists, lawyers, Metropolitan, and Nebbia's upstate New York grocery selling a quart of milk'[65] were all enterprises 'affected with a public interest',[66] but 'without more',[67] did not fall within the contours of state action. In *Calibre Clinical Consulting*, the South African Supreme Court of Appeal noted that there was no support, either in South African case law or in cases from abroad (in this case, the USA, Canada and the

[60] Barak-Erez, 'Civil Rights in the Privatized State' (n 8) 506–07.
[61] *Reitman v Mulkey* 387 US 369 (1967), 386 (Douglas J, concurring).
[62] *Blum v Yaretsky* (n 23) 1012 (Brennan J, dissenting).
[63] Thomas, *Public Rights, Private Relations* (n 1) 17. For a discussion of the same issue in the South African context, see JD van der Wyver, 'The Private Sphere in Constitutional Litigation' (1994) 57 *Tydskrif vir Hedendaagse Romeins-Hollands Reg* 378, 391.
[64] And in Canada, a jurisdiction that I have flagged, but not discussed, in this chapter.
[65] *Jackson v Metropolitan Edison Co* (n 17) 354. See also *Rendell-Baker v Kohn* (n 26) 842.
[66] ibid.
[67] ibid.

UK), for the proposition that if 'the public has an interest in the manner in which [a private body's] powers are exercised or its functions are performed',[68] it is therefore subjected to the Bill of Rights. The SCA then went on to define 'public function' – the specific term used in the Constitution – in terms of the state, by observing that public functions were those pertaining to the people as a whole, 'which is pre-eminently the terrain of government'.[69]

The assumptions underlying the default vertical approach are even clearer when we consider the element of 'monopoly' as one of the components of functional equivalence. The idea of the 'monopoly' (whether it is monopoly over the supply of a particular service or monopoly over coercive power in specific sectors, both of which are considered above), by its very nature, harks back to the conception of sovereignty located at a single, indivisible point, and therefore a unique threat to core individual interests.

What the monopoly argument misses, however, is that a *particular* private party need not occupy the position of a monopolist for it to effectively threaten rights. It could, rather, be one among many parties in an institutional framework that presents the rights bearer with no effective choice. This shift from viewing potentially rights-infringing actions from the perspective of the private party committing those actions to viewing them as components of an institution that accords them their specific salience will be developed further in chapter five, accompanied by a critique of the understanding of power at the heart of the default vertical approach. Here, it is sufficient to flag that the monopoly argument rests upon an individualised account of power, as opposed to a depersonalised or structural one.

Consequently, if the default vertical approach's division of the world into 'public power' (subject to constitutional constraint) and 'private society' (left to its 'free' development, subject to reasonable legislative control) is itself the problem, functional equivalence does nothing to resolve it. It can never account for the exercise of 'private power' that does not sufficiently resemble state power. It therefore remains a limited approach.

IV. INSIGHTS

The 'valuable interests diagnosis' (section IIC) attempts to transcend the limitations discussed above by pivoting away from equating the private party to the state and asking instead whether its ability to impact 'vulnerable valuable interests' is of an order of magnitude similar to that of the state. At first blush,

[68] *Calibre Clinical Consultants (Pty) Ltd v National Bargaining Council for the Road and Freight Industry* [2010] 4 All SA 561 (SCA) [38].

[69] ibid [39]. A similar position was articulated by the Canadian Supreme Court in *McKinney v University of Guelph* [1990] 3 SCR 229, 269.

de-centring the relationship between the private party and the rights holder away from the paradigm of the state appears to resolve the problems highlighted above. One no longer need look for indicia such as control, delegation or monopoly, all of which are bound in different ways to the assumptions underlying default verticality. However, standing alone, this approach under-determines the issue. It cannot explain our persistent intuition that even where valuable interests (Thomas) or basic goods (Barak-Erez) are concerned, state legislation rather than a constitutional bill of rights is the appropriate method of dealing with rights infringement. For instance, bare life is undoubtedly a valuable interest and a basic good. However, we do not think of murder as a constitutionally remediable violation of the right to life of the victim by the murderer. At best, a state that fails to put in place a minimal legislative and police arrangement to protect its citizens' lives may be guilty of a breach of its positive obligations to protect the right to life; however, that is not what we are concerned with here.[70] Consequently, as Thomas points out, the vulnerable valuable interests hypothesis takes us to a place where there remains 'no principled limitation for the applicative scope of these rights'.[71]

Therefore, even if shifting the lens of focus from the state to the rights bearer – as Barek-Erez does – presents us with a good starting point for liberating ourselves from the assumptions of default verticality, further work needs to be done. In particular, the shortcomings of the vulnerable valuable interests diagnosis remind us that we must pay attention to the nature of the specific relationship between the private party and the rights bearer in any given situation. A straightforward transplantation of the rights framework from the 'public' to the 'private' is as unconvincing as a model that concentrates on drawing 'equivalences' between the two. This further work shall be done in chapter five.

[70] In any event, by its very nature, the concept of positive obligations continues to centre the state, and – as we shall see in the next chapter – requires analysis of rights violations to go *through* the state in all cases, an approach that is not always satisfying.

[71] Thomas, *Public Rights, Private Relations* (n 1) 17.

3

Indirect and Direct Horizontality

I. INTRODUCTION

IN CHAPTER ONE of this book, I set out three conceptual assumptions that underlie the default vertical approach to constitutional bills of rights: sovereignty, freedom and individual responsibility. In chapter two, I examined one archetypal model that exemplifies a 'departure' from verticality, namely, 'state action', or the 'functional equivalence' approach, and pointed out its shortcomings. In this chapter, I will address a second archetypal model of departure (indirect horizontality), which holds that the state's pervasive presence within a territory implicates it in 'private' transactions, whether through its legal order or through its acquiescence or inaction. Consequently, rights are to be applied to the 'private' domain, with principles such as proportionality being used to adjudicate situations where both private parties invoke (competing) rights. I argue that this approach continues to characterise private relationships through the paradigm of the contract between individual parties situated in the same horizontal plane – a characterisation that creates difficult problems. Now, one intuitively plausible response to the problems presented by this approach is to erase the distinction between state and non-state parties altogether ('direct horizontality') and apply constitutional rights across the board regardless of the nature of the putative rights violator. However, I argue that this does not resolve all existing issues. Furthermore, it throws up new issues of its own. Direct horizontality, then, must be supported by a principled framework that both defines and limits its scope and application. I conclude by arguing that elements of the two existing archetypes discussed in the last chapter and in this one – a focus on the impact upon rights by private bodies from functional equivalence and a focus on the background framework that enable private acts from indirect horizontality – provide important insights that can assist in developing the principled framework flagged above. What that framework might look like will be the subject of chapters four and five.

* * * * *

In chapter two, I discussed the 'state action doctrine' as one approach that departs from default verticality and imposes constitutional obligations upon non-state parties in certain circumstances. It was found, however, that whatever form it took, the state action doctrine remained committed to the founding assumptions of default verticality. Its central questions – whether and when actions of a private party can be 'attributed' to the state – continued to place the state at the normative heart of the constitutional rights framework. Thus, it entrenched – rather than displaced – the ideas of sovereignty, abstract freedom and individual responsibility, which were critiqued in chapter one.

In this chapter, I shall engage with a second set of contemporary responses to the problems of default verticality, broadly grouped under the heading of 'horizontality'. I shall begin with a typology of horizontal rights frameworks, setting out the concepts of indirect horizontality and direct horizontality. While indirect horizontality imposes constitutional obligations upon existing legal regimes (and thereby indirectly reaches private conduct governed by those legal regimes), direct horizontality makes private conduct itself subject to the constitutional framework (section II).

I then take each approach in turn. Indirect horizontality can take two forms: the 'third party effect', which originated in German constitutional law and was subsequently exported elsewhere; and the US legal realists' argument about the pervasive presence of the state in private orderings. I argue that these approaches – which seek to impose constitutional obligations on private parties by going *through* the state – suffer from a number of problems. These include issues such as vagueness, infringement upon the separation of powers, and 'transplanting' a rights framework from a state–individual relationship to one between private parties, without accounting for the difference between the two (section III).

If indirect horizontality is an insufficient response to the problems of default verticality, then why not simply prescribe that *all* rights shall apply horizontally, leaving the courts to determine when and how to balance competing concerns in concrete cases ('direct horizontality')? I argue that while direct horizontality resolves some of the problems with indirect horizontality, in other respects, it suffers from the very issues that indirect horizontality is designed to address: in particular, an overlap with existing regimes of private law and a persistence of the transplant problem. For this reason, courts and scholars that have had an occasion to engage with direct horizontality have been forced to limit its scope and application (section IV).

I conclude with observing that certain insights that underlie both the state action approach and indirect horizontality can be put to use in constructing a principled limited model of direct horizontality. These include focusing upon the ability of the private actor to violate rights (as discussed in the last chapter), as well as the background that structures the private relationship in question. What such a model or approach might look like will be discussed in chapters four and five (section V).

II. INDIRECT AND DIRECT HORIZONTALITY: A TYPOLOGY

Horizontal application is defined simply as 'binding private parties to constitutional requirements'.[1] For the purposes of this chapter, as indicated above, I shall exclude from consideration the state action doctrine (and its variants). While these are technically forms of horizontal application, the central role of the state sets them apart. For this reason, they were discussed separately in chapter two.

Broadly, horizontal application is of two types: indirect and direct. In both cases, private parties are subjected to a specific constitutional rights framework. The manner in which that happens, however, differs. Indirect horizontality refers to a situation in which a rights framework is imposed on private parties through (non-constitutional) *law*. Direct horizontality, on the other hand, involves subjecting private *conduct* to constitutional rights and obligations.

A. Indirect Horizontality

The word 'indirect' with regard to horizontality indicates that 'there is normally a layer of non-constitutional law mediating between the Constitution and the individual dispute'.[2] In other words, private parties are not themselves bound to comply with constitutional obligations or authorised to enforce constitutional rights against each other. Rather, the law that already governs or structures the relationship between those (private) parties – and which defines their legal rights and obligations vis-à-vis each other – is what is tested for constitutional compliance. The word 'law' here refers both to statutory and common or judge-made law.

For example, in the famous *New York Times v Sullivan* decision, the US Supreme Court found that the common law of defamation – as applied by the Alabama courts to impose heavy damage upon the *New York Times* for libel – violated the constitutional right to freedom of expression.[3] In this case, the Alabama courts, following the common law, had granted damages to the Police Commissioner of Montgomery County, who, in his capacity as a plaintiff, had sued the *New York Times* for libelling him. The Supreme Court found that common law defamation doctrine was inconsistent with the First Amendment. It modified the doctrine to make it sufficiently protective of the freedom of

[1] C Unseld, 'Horizontal Application' in *The Max Planck Encyclopedia of Comparative Constitutional Law*, https://oxcon.ouplaw.com/view/10.1093/law-mpeccol/law-mpeccol-e308?prd=MPECCO.

[2] ibid.

[3] *New York Times v Sullivan* 376 US 254 (1964); see also *Khumalo v Holomisa* 2002 (8) BCLR 771 (CC), where the South African Constitutional Court did the same.

speech and expression. In other words, it was not the Police Commissioner of Montgomery County – the claimant against the *New York Times* – who was held to be in breach of constitutional obligations, but the law that he relied upon to pursue his claim. The result was that his claim failed once the law was modified to bring it into compliance with the constitutional guarantee. In this way, the Constitution applied 'indirectly' to the legal dispute between two private parties – the Police Commissioner and the *New York Times* – and, through a modification of the common law, negated the Police Commissioner's libel claim.

Indirect horizontality can itself take different forms, arrayed along a spectrum. Under a regime of 'strong indirect horizontality', the law that governs the private parties' relationship can be modified – or even struck down – by the courts if it fails to meet constitutional standards.[4] A regime of 'weak indirect horizontality', on the other hand, only authorises courts to 'develop' or 'interpret' the law (most often, common law) in accordance with constitutional provisions, but not necessarily to invalidate it.[5] The difference is often one of degree, and in many cases – where, for example, abstract 'general clauses' are the route through which constitutional rights percolate into private law (as in Germany) – the distinction is almost non-existent in practical terms.

B. Direct Horizontality

Direct horizontality, by contrast, imposes constitutional rights and obligations upon private parties and private conduct without any mediation by any other legal framework. For example, the Thirteenth Amendment to the US Constitution prohibits 'slavery and involuntary servitude'.[6] Article 15(2) of the Indian Constitution proscribes discrimination in, inter alia, access to 'shops' and 'hotels'.[7] Both these provisions restrain private parties from doing something (owning slaves or barring individuals from entering their shop, for example, on racial grounds). Section 8(2) of the South African Constitution sets out direct horizontality in more general terms. It stipulates that 'a provision of the Bill of Rights binds a natural or a juristic person if, and to the extent that, it is applicable, taking into account the nature of the right and the nature of any duty imposed by the right'.[8] Yet another model is that of the Constitution of Kenya, which simply provides that 'the Bill of Rights applies to all law and binds all state organs and all persons'.[9] In other words, the constitutional rights

[4] S Gardbaum, 'Where the (State) Action Is' (2006) 4 *International Journal of Constitutional Law* 760.

[5] See, eg *RWDSU v Dolphin Delivery Ltd* [1986] 2 SCR 573 (Supreme Court of Canada).

[6] Constitution of the United States 1787, Thirteenth Amendment.

[7] Constitution of India 1949, Art 15(2).

[8] Constitution of the Republic of South Africa 1996, s 8(2).

[9] Constitution of Kenya 2010, s 20.

framework applies both to the state and to non-state parties, with the text of the Constitution (at least) making no difference between the two.

These provisions indicate three possible approaches that Constitutional texts can take towards direct horizontality, arranged along a spectrum. We may call the first 'bounded direct horizontality': it picks out specific rights (for example, against involuntary servitude or against non-discrimination in access to certain spaces) and makes them applicable directly (the presumption with respect to all other rights remains that of default verticality). In chapter five, I shall study the Indian case further by arguing that these concrete rights ought to be understood – and interpreted – in the context of the institutional framework within which they are claimed and enforced. The second approach may be called 'bounded interpretive direct horizontality'. It makes it clear that direct application is to be limited in scope, but articulates that limitation in generic terms (with phrases such as 'nature of the right' or 'where applicable'), and leaves the determination of its extent and boundaries to judicial interpretation. This additional caveat maintains the presumption that, unlike default verticality, if a constitution intends to extend the bill of rights to non-state parties, an additional burden of justification must be discharged. The distinction between the two approaches, however, is that in 'bounded direct horizontality', the range of situations to which the horizontal rights framework applies is spelt out in the constitutional text. On the other hand, in 'bounded interpretive direct horizontality', it is the judiciary that is charged with both articulating the principles on the basis of which horizontal rights will be invoked and then applying them to concrete situations.

Finally, the third approach may be called 'unbounded direct horizontality'. Arrayed at the opposite end of the spectrum to bounded horizontality, it straightforwardly applies the bill of rights to state and non-state parties without any distinction or presumption. As we shall see in this chapter, however, much like interpretive horizontality, unbounded horizontality – if it is to be workable – must also be subjected to judicial interpretation that delineates its scope and ambit.

C. Positive Obligations

For the sake of completeness, it is necessary to briefly address another approach to rights and obligations, which is not formally horizontal but which, in effect, will sometimes yield similar results. The theory of positive obligations holds that rights against the state are violated not only when the state actively interferes with their enjoyment, but also through its omission or inaction.[10] Positive

[10] For an elaboration of the concept, see S Fredman, *Human Rights: Transformed Positive Rights and Positive Duties* (Oxford University Press, 2008).

obligations require that, on occasion, the state must act 'positively' in order to fulfil the content of a right. As Stephen Gardbaum points out, there is 'significant analytical and practical overlap'[11] between positive obligations and indirect horizontality. For example, a finding that a clause in the law of contract insufficiently protects the rights of weaker parties may take either form. It may be argued that contract law, in its existing shape, does not comply with the constitutional right to equality (indirect horizontality); but it may also be argued that the state has failed in its positive obligation to protect the right to equality by not amending the law. Gardbaum points out, therefore, that in many situations, positive obligations can even serve as a 'source of indirect horizontal effect'.[12]

It is thus important to clarify that the arguments and the model presented in this book do not seek to displace positive obligations or to substitute them. The following discussion proceeds independently of the positive obligations approach, while acknowledging that at times – but not always – the two approaches operate in the same terrain, and may lead to similar results.

III. INDIRECT HORIZONTALITY: FORMS AND LIMITS

In the previous chapter, while considering the state action doctrine, I argued that the central purpose of the 'functional equivalence approach' is to prevent the state from evading its obligations by removing itself from the sphere of action. The consequential focus, therefore, as Jean Thomas labels it, is on the 'inadequate constraints' placed upon private actors due to a retreating state. Thomas provides an equally useful label for understanding the underlying basis of indirect horizontality: 'a failure of constitutional scrutiny'.[13] In other words, the focus here is on situations where the state is actually present, but the prevailing legal framework does not regard that presence as normatively significant. The 'failure of constitutional scrutiny' is the failure to grasp the presence of the state in an ostensibly 'private' transaction or relationship, and the failure (thereby) to subject it to constitutional scrutiny.

There are two archetypal solutions that claim to address this failure. The first is the 'third-party effect', which has its origins in post-war German constitutional doctrine. The third-party effect understands a constitution as an 'objective order of values' that pervades the private legal realm. The second solution flows from the scholarship of the US legal realists. It holds that the state itself constitutes the public/private divide, and it therefore remains present in the private legal realm. While both these approaches go through the state to get to the private relationship at issue (and are therefore variants of 'indirect' horizontality), there

[11] Gardbaum, 'Where the (State) Action Is' (n 4) 769.
[12] ibid.
[13] J Thomas, *Public Rights, Private Relations* (Oxford University Press, 2015) 11.

are nonetheless important conceptual differences between the two.[14] I consider each in turn.

A. The Third-Party Effect

The third-party effect (*mittelbare Drittwirkung*) – which is the dominant form of indirect horizontality – originated with the German Federal Constitutional Court. *Drittwirkung* is rooted within German legal culture's conceptualisation of state and society.[15] It arose in the context of the institutional relationships between different wings of the German judiciary.[16] Its articulation, interpretation and present status have been subjected to intense judicial as well as scholarly debate both within and outside Germany.[17] And it remains most strongly associated with that jurisdiction, although it now enjoys global influence.[18]

It is not my task here to add to this substantial body of literature by presenting a fresh analysis of the third-party effect. My limited objective is to examine indirect horizontality as an archetypal departure from the default vertical approach, in light of the conceptual assumptions that I set out in chapter one. Consequently, I shall focus on the form of the legal reasoning employed by the Federal Constitutional Court in the *Lüth* judgment,[19] where the third-party effect was first articulated, and which remains the point of departure for any conceptual exploration of the doctrine.

Erich Lüth was a German writer and film director. In the aftermath of World War II, Lüth protested against the effective rehabilitation of Veit Harlan, also a film director as well as a former Nazi propagandist, by calling for a public boycott of Harlan's new film. Harlan sued Lüth. Relying upon German civil law, a lower court injuncted Lüth from making any further calls for a boycott. The Federal Constitutional Court set aside the injunction, on the basis that the

[14] Van der Walt insists, however, that the two approaches are the same. J van der Walt, *The Horizontal Effect Revolution and the Question of Sovereignty* (De Gruyter, 2014) ix.

[15] See, eg RE Quint, 'Free Speech and Private Law in German Constitutional Theory' (1989) 48 *Maryland Law Review* 247; B Markesinis and S Enchelmaier, 'The Applicability of Human Rights as between Individuals under German Constitutional Law' in B Markesinis (ed), *Protecting Privacy* (Oxford University Press, 1999) 191.

[16] J Mathews, *Extending Rights' Reach: Constitutions, Private Law, and Judicial Power* (Oxford University Press, 2018) chs 2 and 3.

[17] For an analysis of important case law, see S Oeter, 'Fundamental Rights and their Impact on Private Law – Doctrine and Practice under the German Constitution' (1994) 12 *Tel Aviv University Student Law Journal* 7.

[18] It has, for example, been adopted in South Africa. For one of many examples, see the discussion in A van Aswegen, 'The Implications of a Bill of Rights for the Law of Contract and Delict' (1995) 11 *South African Journal on Human Rights* 50. For an early piece dealing with its influence in Europe, see A Drzemczewski, 'The European Human Rights Convention and Relations between Private Parties' (1979) 26 *Netherlands International Law Review* 163.

[19] BVerfGE 7, 198 (1958) (*Lüth*) (German Federal Constitutional Court) https://law.utexas.edu/transnational/foreign-law-translations/german/case.php?id=1369.

lower court had not taken into account Lüth's constitutional free speech rights vis-à-vis Harlan in its application of the relevant private law provisions. But what was the relevance of the Constitution to a dispute between two private parties, which turned upon the existing provisions of the civil code? According to the Court:

> The Constitution erects an objective system of values in its section on basic rights, and thus expresses and reinforces the validity of the basic rights. This system of values, centring on the freedom of the human being to develop in society, must apply as a constitutional axiom throughout the whole legal system: it must direct and inform legislation, administration, and judicial decision. It naturally influences private law as well; no rule of private law may conflict with it, and all such rules must be construed in accordance with its spirit.[20]

At the first instance, this analysis – where the rules of private law were to be infused by constitutional values – was to be performed by the lower courts that were seized of the private dispute. If, however, the lower courts failed to do so, or did so in a patently incorrect fashion, then the Federal Constitutional Court could review the decision and set it aside.

The holding of *Lüth*, therefore, was that as a 'system of values', constitutional principles 'radiate' into 'existing and older [private law] rules',[21] which 'receive from it a definite constitutional content which thereafter determines their construction'.[22] At the same time, this does not mean that existing private law rules are subsumed into constitutional law and thereby effaced in their own right. The Constitutional Court was careful to note that 'it is private law which is interpreted and applied even if its interpreters must follow the public law of the constitution'.[23] This interpretive technique relies primarily upon pre-existing 'general clauses' in the civil code – for example, the duty of good faith in contract law – and aims to achieve the 'deliberate interpretation [of these provisions] … in ways that render them substantially compliant with the norms of [the Constitution]'.[24] As an illustration: in the *Burghschaft* case, the German Constitutional Court invoked the good faith and good morals clauses (that were part of the civil code); these clauses were then interpreted in light of the Constitution's 'objective order of values', in order to justify refusing the enforcement of an onerous personal guarantee that had been entered into between unequal parties (a bank and a 21-year-old woman, the daughter of a businessman who had defaulted on his debts).[25]

[20] ibid.
[21] ibid.
[22] ibid.
[23] ibid.
[24] Van der Walt, *The Horizontal Effect Revolution* (n 14) 112.
[25] BVerfGE 89, 214, NJW 1994, 36 (Burgschaft). See the discussion in C Mak, *Fundamental Rights in European Contract Law* (Wolters Kluwer, 2008) 75–82; JM Smits, 'Private Law and Fundamental Rights: A Sceptical View' in T Barkhuysen and S Lindenbergh (eds), *Constitutionalisation of Private Law* (Martinus Nijhoff, 2006) 9.

Thus, as Matthias Kumm writes, the teaching of *Lüth* (and the third-party effect) is that 'constitutional principles radiate to affect the rights and duties of all actors within the jurisdiction'. More specifically, for example:

> [I]n the course of private litigation … [an individual] C could insist that the court, within its jurisdiction, is required to do what is in its power to ensure that freedom of contract, as guaranteed as an instantiation of the general constitutional right to liberty, is adequately protected. In that sense the basic value commitments underlying constitutional rights 'radiate' throughout the legal order to also establish requirements for the interpretation of private law by civil courts … this means that private law is to be interpreted so as to reflect an adequate balance between the respective constitutional interests at stake.[26]

The underlying theory, as Kumm notes, is that of absolute constitutional sovereignty, or the 'total Constitution'.[27] The constitution is deemed to exercise complete normative sovereignty over the entire legal domain, so that there is no transaction or relationship that remains untouched by the 'objective order of values'.

For the sake of completeness, it is important to note that the doctrines of *Lüth* have been advanced in two different (although unopposed) directions. *Lüth* has been invoked in evolving a framework of positive obligations that are enforceable against the state.[28] As indicated above, however, this book does not engage with the important and much-debated topic of positive obligations. The second direction – with which I am concerned here – is that of indirect horizontality and the third-party effect, summed up by Kumm in the quote above.

In order to set up the framework of the critique that will follow later in this section, the following observation is important: conceptually, the third-party effect retains the idea of the public/private divide as it is. That is, the distinction between the public and the private spheres is first taken as pre-existing and given, and it is within this framework that public values 'radiate' into the private sphere.[29] This is marked by how – as pointed out above – the primary vehicles of this form of indirect horizontality are meant to be the general clauses of the (private) civil codes – a fact that has been remarked upon by numerous scholars[30]

[26] M Kumm, 'Who Is Afraid of the Total Constitution? Constitutional Rights as Principles and the Constitutionalization of Private Law' (2006) 7 *German Law Journal* 341, 355–56, 357.

[27] ibid.

[28] M Kumm, 'Constitutional Rights as Principles: On the Structure and Domain of Constitutional Justice' (2003) 2 *International Journal of Constitutional Law* 574, 585–86.

[29] E Engle, 'Third Party Effect of Fundamental Rights (Drittwirkung)' (2009) 5 *Hanseatic Law Review* 165, 171–72.

[30] A Barak, 'Constitutional Human Rights and Private Law' in D Friedmann and D Barak-Erez (eds), *Human Rights and Private Law* (Hart Publishing, 2001) 13, 22; in the same volume, see A Heldrich and GM Rehm, 'Importing Constitutional Values through Blanket Clauses', 113, 115; R Ellgar, 'The European Convention of Human Rights and Fundamental Freedom and German Private Law', 161, 166. See also O Gerstenberg, 'Private Law and the New European Settlement' (2004) 10 *European Law Journal* 766, 773–74.

and has been influential in other jurisdictions (such as South Africa[31]). In effect, therefore, as Benson points out, the 'horizontalisation' of private relations is accomplished '*through* private law'[32] (emphasis added).

B. The Ubiquity of the State

As discussed above, the third-party effect leaves the public/private divide untouched. A second manifestation of the 'failure of constitutional scrutiny' approach, however, comes at the problem from the opposite side. According to this view, it is the state itself that constructs the public/private divide.[33] Any a priori distinction between public and private fails because every private act or private ordering necessarily exists against the backdrop of state action. As Larry Alexander puts the point, 'private power is the product of public laws'.[34]

This argument takes two further, overlapping, albeit not identical, forms. According to one, every private act derives its legal validity from the background legal landscape – which, in turn, is the creation of the state. This fact was judicially recognised by Mahomed DP in his concurring opinion in *Du Plessis v De Klerk*, a judgment of the South African Constitutional Court that dealt with the horizontal application of rights in the absence of specific textual authority for the same. Mahomed DP observed that:

> It is, I believe, erroneous to conclude that the law operates for the first time only when [a] sanction is invoked. The truth is that it precedes it and is indeed the ultimate source for the legitimation of any conduct ... Inherently there can be no 'right' governing relations between individuals *inter se* or between individuals and the state the protection of which is not legally enforceable and if it is legally enforceable it must be part of law.[35]

Mahomed DP's articulation had a long intellectual lineage. It was most forcefully articulated by the US legal realist thinkers in the mid-twentieth century.[36] Taking up the language of sovereignty and delegation (which was discussed in

[31] See, eg J van der Walt, 'Progressive Indirect Horizontal Application of the Bill of Rights: Towards a Co-operative Relation between Common-Law and Constitutional Jurisprudence' (2001) 17 *South African Journal on Human Rights* 341, 351–52.

[32] Benson, 'Equality of Opportunity and Private Law' in Friedmann and Barak-Erez, *Human Rights and Private Law* (n 30) 201, 205.

[33] K Klare, 'The Public/Private Distinction in Labor Law' [1982] *University of Pennsylvania Law Review* 1358, 1415–17; Mathews, *Extending Rights' Reach* (n 16) 5; S Woolman and D Davis, 'The Last Laugh: *Du Plessis v De Klerk*, Classical Liberalism, Creole Liberalism and the Application of Fundamental Rights under the Interim and the Final Constitutions' (1996) 12 *South African Journal on Human Rights* 361, 399.

[34] L Alexander, 'The Public/Private Distinction and Constitutional Limits on Private Power' (1993) 10 *Constitutional Commentary* 361, 377.

[35] *Du Plessis v De Klerk* (1996) 5 BCLR 658, [79] (Mahomed DP, concurring).

[36] It has spread beyond the USA. In the Canadian context, see, eg D Gibson, 'The Charter of Rights and the Private Sector' (1982–83) 12 *Manitoba Law Journal* 213, 219.

the previous chapter), these thinkers argued that 'much of the private power over others is in fact delegated and that all of it is "sanctioned" in the sense of being permitted'.[37] For example, contract law, acting 'through judges, sheriffs, or marshals puts the sovereign power of the state at the disposal of one party to be exercised over the other party. It thus grants a limited sovereignty to the former.'[38] In other words, state action is not limited to situations where the 'traditional or exclusive prerogative of the sovereign' is delegated to a private party; rather, every time a private act is grounded within (state-made) law, the private actor is vested with 'temporary sovereignty' as a 'delegate' of the sovereign itself. In sum: 'All rights of property and contract are governed and protected by law; the state is responsible for them and, therefore, for discrimination which is perpetrated under the authority of these "rights".'[39]

A slightly different version of the argument points out that the existing legal order is as much the product of active state choice as is any 'departure from' or 'intervention into' it. As Robert Hale argued, 'when a state passes certain social legislation, there is a necessity of making a choice between the preservation of one kind of property right and liberty and another'.[40] At all times, the very existence of the legal order reflects the state's choices to privilege certain rights at the cost of others. Any 'private act' within that framework, therefore, can only be understood as a product of that choice, and inseparable from it.[41]

Both these arguments – ie that the state is implicated by virtue of having created the private legal landscape and that both action and inaction count equally as an 'intervention' into the private law status quo – come together in Louis Henkin's reinterpretation of the famous *Shelley v Kraemer* judgment. In *Shelley*, the US Supreme Court held that a racially restrictive covenant was unenforceable, on the ground that the judiciary was a wing of the state. Therefore, its involvement in enforcing a discriminatory contract would effectively amount to state action.[42] Articulating a different justification of the outcome, Henkin argues that *Shelley* ought to be understood as a case where there was a clash between the Fourteenth Amendment right to equal treatment of the Shelleys (the Black buyers of the property) and the freedom-of-contract rights of the objecting property holders in the neighbourhood. Note that, first, the property regime was a creation of the state; and secondly, the Court was required to prioritise one right over the other, where either option would have required an intervention, whether it took the side of the Shelleys in setting aside the covenant

[37] R Hale, 'Force and the State: A Comparison of "Political" and "Economic" Compulsion' (1935) 35 *Columbia Law Review* 149, 199.

[38] M Cohen, 'The Basis of Contract' (1933) 46 *Harvard Law Review* 553, 586.

[39] L Henkin, '*Shelley v Kraemer:* Notes for a Revised Opinion' (1962) 110 *University of Pennsylvania Law Review* 473, fn 24.

[40] Hale, 'Force and the State' (n 37) 200–01.

[41] For an extended discussion, see G de Almeida Ribeiro, *The Decline of Private Law: A Philosophical History of Liberal Legalism* (Hart Publishing, 2019) ch 5.

[42] *Shelley v Kraemer* 334 US 1 (1948).

or the side of the property owners in allowing for its enforcement. The Court confronted the choice before it, and prioritised equal treatment in view of the greater constitutional sanctity enjoyed by it at the time.[43] Perhaps unsurprisingly, this argument involves the same kind of 'balancing' test that is the hallmark of the third-party effect. This suggests, in turn, that when it comes to application, the two approaches will require something similar from the courts.

C. Critique

(i) Individual Responsibility and Abstract Freedom

The critique of indirect horizontality has been dominated by concerns about its 'vagueness and unpredictability',[44] and the vast amounts of discretion it offers up to judges.[45] As Matthias Kumm concedes in his defence of the approach, indirect horizontality only provides us with the form of the analysis: it does not tell us *how* the balance is to be struck.[46] Scholars draw a distinction between the (relatively) more clear-cut question of whether state infringement of constitutional rights is justifiable and the 'open-ended and unwieldy process of "balancing" competing fundamental rights … in the absence of detailed and specific legislative guidance'.[47] Any balancing analysis, therefore, runs the risk of being labelled as ideologically driven.

While I am not focusing upon the mechanics of indirect horizontality here, the critique reveals a deeper issue with this archetypal approach towards departing from default verticality. Indirect horizontality, in practice, has often come to be identified with the enterprise of 'balancing' clashing individual rights because it effectively 'transplants'[48] the rights framework from the vertical/public domain to the horizontal/private domain, without considering the different types of relationships that exist between private parties and the state on the one hand and *inter se* between private parties on the other.[49]

[43] Henkin, '*Shelley v Kraemer*' (n 39) 494. For a similar argument in the context of the Canadian Charter of Rights and Freedoms, see D Gibson, 'Distinguishing the Governors from the Governed: The Meaning of Government under Section 32(1) of the Charter' (1983) 13 *Manitoba Law Journal* 505, 515.

[44] Oeter, 'Fundamental Rights and Their Impact on Private Law' (n 17) 15; Mathews, *Extending Rights' Reach* (n 16) 19, quoting German legal experts.

[45] KM Lewan, 'The Significance of Constitutional Rights for Private Law: Theory and Practice in West Germany' (1968) 17 *ICLQ* 571, 599, quoting the opinion of the German scholar Leisner. D Oliver, 'Introduction' in D Oliver and J Fedtke (eds), *Human Rights and the Private Sphere: A Comparative Study* (Routledge, 2007) 20.

[46] See generally Kumm, 'Constitutional Rights as Principles' (n 28).

[47] Gerstenberg, 'Private Law and the New European Settlement' (n 30) 769.

[48] H Collins, 'Utility and Rights in Common Law Reasoning: Rebalancing Private Law through Constitutionalization' (2007) LSE Law, Society and Economy Working Papers 6/2007, http://www.lse.ac.uk/law/working-paper-series/2007-08/WPS06-2007Collins.pdf.

[49] ibid.

This transplant is based on two presumptions. The first presumption is that, as far as the rights framework is concerned, it can be applied in the same manner to a private relationship as it is to a state-private party relationship. Secondly, as Jean Thomas observes, 'in moving from the "vertical" to the "horizontal" [indirect horizontality approaches] effectively make the legal presumption that non-state actors are all the same, so far as rights are concerned'.[50] We may change this to 'rights and duties': a clash of rights arises because duties are imposed upon private parties to respect the rights of other private parties. In other words, in line with the third underlying conceptual assumption of the default vertical approach that was discussed in chapter one ('individual responsibility'), these two assumptions continue to operate on the premise that parties in the private domain are located in the same 'horizontal' plane with respect to each other, where they remain *formally* equal.

The balancing requirement then comes to dominate indirect horizontality because one of the parties to the relationship (the state), against which rights were unilaterally enforceable, has been simply and directly substituted by a private party, with the only relevant difference being that this private party now has rights of its own that must be taken into account.[51] It is in this sense that the passing observation made above – that indirect horizontality 'retains the idea of the public/private divide as it is' – assumes significance. Instead of asking *what* it is about certain presumptively 'private' relationships that justifies the application of a bill of rights, these approaches take private relationships as they are already characterised (ie between two formally equal, rights-bearing private parties) and then engage in a 'balancing test' between the rights putatively possessed by both parties.[52]

This leads us to a further insight: as the 'balancing' is conducted within the overarching framework of private law, it encounters resistance in taking into account the social and economic background that structures private relationships (it thus reproduces the second underlying assumption discussed in chapter one – 'abstract freedom'). This is evident when we look at the illustrations provided by the defenders of indirect horizontality. In a much-discussed article, for example, Aharon Barak notes that:

> My intuition tells me that the restaurant owner has an obligation to give service, that is, to make a contract, without discriminating on the basis of gender, race or

[50] Thomas, *Public Rights, Private Relations* (n 13) 39.

[51] For this assumption in the context of German indirect effect, see, eg FFVR Von Prondzynski, 'Protection of Constitutional Rights: Comparisons between Ireland and Germany' (1980) 2 *Dublin University Law Journal* 14, 22; J Van der Walt, 'Rethinking the Fundamental Structures of the State with Reference to the Horizontal Application of Fundamental Rights' in M Sachs et al (eds), *Der grundrechtsgeprägte Verfassungsstaat. Festschrift für Klaus Stern zum 80. Geburtstag* (Duncker & Humblot, 2012) 627; and in the context of South African constitutional law, see C Sprigman and M Osborne, 'Du Plessis Is *Not* Dead: South Africa's 1996 Constitution and the Application of the Bill of Rights to Private Disputes' (1999) 15 *South African Journal on Human Rights* 25, 42.

[52] Van der Walt, *The Horizontal Effect Revolution* (n 14) Introduction.

> religion. By contrast, the same intuition tells me that the private party renting out a room in his apartment is entitled to choose a lodger as he sees fit. This intuition is based primarily on the *proper balance* between the freedom to make a contract of the restaurant owner and apartment owner and the right of the persons seeking the service (food or dwelling) not to be discriminated against. I accept that the restaurant owner and apartment owner have the constitutional freedom to decide with whom to contract. Similarly, I accept that the person wishing to dine in the restaurant or rent the room is entitled *not to be discriminated against* (whether by the state or by private parties) and that if he is refused on the basis of gender, religion or race, this constitutes discrimination. (emphasis added)[53]

Barak's intuition about the 'balance' between competing rights is, of course, not shared by the many jurisdictions that consider housing discrimination (in situations involving commercial renting) to be illegal. Indeed, in chapter five, I shall offer an alternative model that argues, contrary to Barak, that, at least in some cases, housing discrimination should be considered a straightforward violation of constitutional rights. What is interesting, however, is that Barak's distinction between the two situations is based entirely on his intuition about the 'balance' between the rights of two abstract parties to a private relationship. In the succeeding paragraph, Barak explains that the basis for his intuition is that a contractual right is 'stronger' when it relates to personal privacy and 'weaker' when it is 'directed against the public at large'.[54] The argument, therefore, simply shifts from one right (freedom of contract) to another (privacy), until the intuition feels adequately grounded. What it misses – or treats as irrelevant – however, is the 'relational context'[55] between the parties to the relationship.

By 'relational context', I mean that often the parties whose rights are to be balanced will be in different positions vis-à-vis each other. For example, social practices based on the denial of letting or selling property to members of an oppressed minority, with the express intention of forcing them into segregated ghettoes, are well known in history.[56] A case where a landlord who acts to advance such a practice with respect to a particular tenant appears, therefore, to be distinct from a case where the denial occurs in the absence of any institutionalised practice (for example, I refuse to let out my flat to a rival, out of professional or personal jealousy). Barak's analysis – focused solely on balancing the competing 'rights' at play – is unable to distinguish between these two situations.

[53] A Barak, 'Constitutional Human Rights and Private Law' in Friedmann and Barak-Erez, *Human Rights and Private Law* (n 30) 13, 39.

[54] ibid.

[55] Thomas, *Public Rights Private Relations* (n 13) 19. For an extended critique that makes this point in the context of the horizontality jurisprudence of the European Court of Justice, see E Frantziou, *The Horizontal Effects of the Charter of Fundamental Rights of the European Union* (Oxford University Press, 2019).

[56] See, eg the discussion of the Ontario High Court in *Re Drummond Wren* (1945) OR 778 (Ont HC).

Something similar is also at work in Matthias Kumm's distinction between a bigoted dinner party host deciding whom to invite home for dinner on the basis of their political views (discrimination permitted) and an employer deciding whom to employ on the same basis (discrimination not permitted).[57] Tellingly, the discussion only arises because Kumm is anxious to allay the concerns of critics that applying the rights framework to private relationships will destroy personal freedom (the second assumption, once again).[58] Kumm argues that the issue is essentially about the '*delimitation* of respective spheres of autonomy' (emphasis added) of the parties.[59] He then claims that the 'competing autonomy interests balance out very differently'[60] in the employment context, but says nothing further.

Barak and Kumm's examples demonstrate implicitly what Peter Benson makes explicit. Citing Barak's article, Benson argues that indirect horizontality is subsumed within the 'normative idiom'[61] of private law, which is to 'specify fair and reasonable terms for voluntary and involuntary interactions between individuals'[62] located within a relationship of 'formal or abstract … equality'.[63] This is, of course, a direct invocation of the third assumption discussed in chapter one, and with which I began this argument: that parties in the private domain are located in the same 'horizontal' plane with respect to each other, shorn of their respective structural or institutional locations, which may make such a description inapposite.

It is important to clarify that the above issues have arisen in the course of how the indirect horizontality has been applied in practice, and in the accounts of some of its prominent defenders. Notwithstanding Benson's point about the 'normative idiom' of private law, indirect horizontality need not be conceptually committed to ignoring the material dimensions of private relations and the relational context that I have highlighted above.[64] Indeed, in the labour law context, it could be argued that cases such as *Wilson v United Kingdom* have, indeed, taken the relational context into account while applying indirect horizontality.[65]

It is therefore true that in its strongest form, indirect horizontality can accommodate the concerns outlined in this section (although, as the arguments advanced above demonstrate, there is often resistance to its doing so). However,

[57] Kumm, 'Who Is Afraid of the Total Constitution?' (n 26) 362.

[58] ibid.

[59] ibid 363.

[60] ibid.

[61] P Benson, 'Equality of Opportunity and Private Law' in Friedmann and Barak-Erez, *Human Rights and Private Law* (n 30) 201, 208.

[62] ibid 209.

[63] ibid 209. See also Heldrich and Rehm, 'Importing Constitutional Values through Blanket Clauses' (n 30) 113, 129.

[64] I do not have space here to discuss the fascinating history of the 'socialisation' of private law in the early 20th century, or the achievements and limitations of those efforts. Interested readers may consult De Almeida Ribeiro, *The Decline of Private Law* (n 41) ch 4.

[65] *Wilson v The United Kingdom* [2002] ECHR 552.

there are two reasons why, even in this strongest form, indirect horizontality will not always be enough.

The first is that indirect horizontality still depends upon the existence of private law as a trigger for its application. There are a range of situations, however, where unequal power relations between parties – and the horizontal violation of rights – will simply not be mediated by existing law. There will thus be nothing that can be suitably interpreted or modified by deploying indirect horizontality. I will consider some of those examples in greater detail in chapter five, and in the case studies in part II of this book.

The second reason is that indirect horizontality remains bound to at least one of the assumptions of default verticality (that of normatively undivided and absolute sovereignty). This leads to indirect horizontality seeing a horizontal violation of rights not as a problem involving power relations between two parties, but as a problem of insufficient state action. I will consider this in more detail in the following section.

(ii) Sovereignty

As I have flagged above, much like the functional equivalence approach, indirect horizontality operates within the same understanding of sovereignty that undergirds default verticality (although it comes at the issue from the opposite direction). Rather than attempting to discern when the state is impermissibly abdicating from its role as the sovereign, indirect horizontality – whether through the third-party approach or the ubiquity-of-the-state approach – holds that, conceptually, the state can never abdicate, because it is always present. This argument, however, rests upon the same idea of sovereignty as being (normatively) absolute and indivisible within a single territory. Only on the basis of that assumption can it be argued that no legally founded action takes place without, in some way, normatively implicating the state.[66] This, to use a familiar term, makes constitutional protection effectively 'gapless'.[67]

There are two corollaries that follow. First, indirect horizontality appears to mischaracterise its very framing of the problem. Instead of focusing upon how *private actors* violate constitutional rights, it focuses instead on how the *state* is responsible for those violations, through its implied acquiescence (either through the existing legal order or otherwise) or inaction. This is what is meant by Jean Thomas's expression that indirect horizontality needs to 'go through' the state in order to get at the private act(s) at issue.

The point is conceded by Kumm, who argues that the only difference between indirect horizontality and direct horizontality is a difference of form: ie whether the case is brought against the public authority (arguing that the state has failed

[66] See, eg Van der Walt, *The Horizontal Effect Revolution* (n 14) ch 2.

[67] See Mathews, *Extending Rights' Reach* (n 16).

to strike the appropriate balance between private rights, or has otherwise failed in its duties) or against the private actor.[68] That difference in form, however, matters.[69] To start with, it appears to exempt the private actor from normative scrutiny of their conduct by asking, instead, whether the *state* has failed to discharge its duties (although, of course, the private party continues to face a potential curtailment of its freedoms). More importantly, it does not seem to be consistent with our intuitions about the issue. When we think about the classic controversies involving horizontality – denial of service on racial grounds and control over employees' conduct, to take just two evergreen examples – we think about them in terms of the relationships between the private parties, and not in terms of whether the state has achieved a successful balancing of the competing interests.

The second corollary – which needs to be considered in some detail – is this: the form of the argument bleeds into the question of adjudication. By going 'through' the state, as pointed out above, the focus is not so much on subjecting the impugned private act or transaction to fundamental rights scrutiny, but on whether the *state* (in this case, the legislator) has achieved a correct balance. What the court is doing, in other words, is not reviewing the act, but how the state has dealt with it. What follows from this – as scholars have noted – is that, at the first instance, the state is accorded a degree of judicial deference.[70] Kumm, for example, takes the example of credit card companies charging exploitative interest rates, and argues that judicial review of the practice will be consistent with allowing the legislature a range of options for deciding where and how to draw the line in order to balance freedom of contract against personal liberty interests in not being subjected to burdensome contracts.[71]

Now, it is important to note that this, by itself, is not a criticism. Indeed, as Kumm's very specific example (fixing interest rates) suggests, in a range of cases, this serves as a strength of the approach.[72] In *Du Plessis*, Ackermann J took the view that 'direct application should take place at the law-making level, so that all laws which are being applied by the courts do already comply with the basic rights, obviating the need for direct horizontal application by the courts'.[73]

[68] Kumm, 'Who Is Afraid of the Total Constitution?' (n 26).

[69] Certain scholars also argue that there is a difference in substance. For an argument focused on the reliance interests of the (freshly adjudicated) duty bearers, for example, see G de Almeida Ribeiro, 'The Effects of Fundamental Rights in Private Disputes' in H Collins (ed), *European Contract Law and the Charter of Fundamental Rights*, vol 2 (Intersentia, 2017) 219.

[70] See, eg C O'Cinneide, 'Ireland: Irish Constitutional Law and Direct Horizontal Effect – A Successful Experiment?' in Oliver and Fedtke, *Human Rights and the Private Sphere* (n 45) 213, discussing Irish jurisprudence. See also Kumm, 'Who Is Afraid of the Total Constitution?' (n 26) 363, discussing Germany. For a summary of the views on this point, see Thomas, *Public Rights, Private Relations* (n 13) 38–40.

[71] Kumm, 'Who Is Afraid of the Total Constitution?' (n 26) 356–57.

[72] See the arguments in De Almeida Ribeiro, 'The Effects of Fundamental Rights in Private Disputes' (n 69) 219.

[73] *Du Plessis v De Klerk* (n 35) [97].

This is true, and the precise nature of the interaction between constitutional horizontality and legislation shall be addressed in greater detail in chapter five.[74] Here, however, I wish to flag a different concern. As Ackermann J observed immediately before the passage cited above:

> [U]ncertainty is aggravated by the fact that (in contrast to a dispute between citizen and state) in a dispute between two private individuals both sides can invoke the basic rights, calling for a difficult balancing of conflicting rights which could reasonably lead different courts to different decisions.[75]

We therefore see a return of the 'transplant problem' at the stage of formulating remedies: the same assumption of formally equal private parties facing each other across a 'horizontal' plane, responsible for constructing the contours of their relationship.

To reiterate, as pointed out at the end of the previous section, this is not a necessary corollary. Indeed, and furthermore, in chapter five of this book, and subsequently in part II, I will argue that in cases where the subject matter of horizontal rights is covered by an existing statutory (or another kind of legislative) scheme, that scheme should be given priority. However, in litigation around that statutory scheme, including litigation that takes the form of constitutional or horizontal rights claims, judicial interpretation should be informed by the institutional approach towards horizontality, especially when the statutory scheme (and private law) is not.

IV. DIRECT HORIZONTALITY: WHAT IT SOLVES (AND WHAT IT DOESN'T)

The above section has demonstrated that while indirect horizontality is useful in some respects, it nonetheless remains tied to some of the founding assumptions of the default vertical model. It also generates additional problems, both conceptual as well as in its application. The question might then arise: if default verticality is no longer fit for purpose, and if both the state action doctrine and indirect horizontality are unsatisfactory substitutes, then why not simply apply constitutional rights directly (direct horizontality)? Some constitutions do bite this bullet. As discussed above, Article 20 of the Kenyan Constitution, for example, stipulates that 'the Bill of Rights applies to all law and binds all state organs *and all persons*'[76] (emphasis added) (what I labelled 'unbounded direct horizontality', and will refer to simply as 'direct horizontality' in this section).

In three respects, direct horizontality straightforwardly solves the concerns discussed above. First, by displacing the state entirely from the picture, it is no

[74] For the strongest articulation of the claim, see G Webber et al, *Legislated Rights* (Cambridge University Press, 2018).

[75] ibid.

[76] Constitution of Kenya 2010, Art 20. This is considered in greater detail in ch 8.

longer tied to sovereignty as a necessary precondition for the application of the rights framework. Secondly, by treating the relationship between the two private parties as the relevant subject of constitutional concern, direct horizontality avoids the mischaracterisation problem involved in going through the state to get at the private relationship and the private parties. And thirdly, it allows courts to adjudicate upon the rights and obligations of the private parties directly.

The third aspect indicates, however, that direct horizontality suffers from problems that indirect horizontality is explicitly set up to avoid. Traditionally, we think that it is the regimes of private law – tort and contract, to name just two – that regulate rights and obligations between private parties. If constitutional rights are made horizontally applicable per se, widespread overlap will be inevitable, and questions of normative priority will arise.[77] For example, if the 'right to life and personal liberty' is directly applicable between private parties, where does that leave the regime of criminal law, which is concerned with precisely the question of preventing people from depriving each other of their life or personal liberty? As we have seen, indirect horizontality seeks to resolve the question of overlap by limiting its own intervention in two ways: first, through interpretation, by using the wide scope provided by 'general clauses' in private law codes to enforce a rights framework between private parties; and secondly, through modification, by subjecting aspects of the private law regime to constitutional scrutiny and modifying or striking them down if required (with due deference to the first-order legislative balance that has already been struck).

But neither of those two options is open to a model of direct horizontality, as it requires constitutional rights to be applicable to private parties and private relationships without mediation through private law. In other words, overlap, rather than reconciliation, is a necessary consequence of direct horizontality.[78] This, in turn, raises a separation of powers issue, in a much starker fashion than in indirect horizontality. As both scholars[79] and courts[80] have pointed out, balancing private rights and obligations appears to require the kind of granular judgement that legislatures are better positioned to make. Furthermore, as we shall see in greater detail in subsequent chapters, such a balance can be struck in a range of ways, all within the spectrum of reasonableness. A complete judicial takeover of the 'horizontal domain', then, raises serious concerns about institutional competence (again, a concern that indirect horizontality attempts to address through norms of deference, but which is not open to direct horizontality).

[77] C Saunders, 'Constitutional Rights and the Common Law' in A Sajo and R Uitz (eds), *The Constitution in Private Relations* (Eleven International Publishing, 2005) 183.

[78] D Leczykiewicz, 'Horizontal Application of the Charter of Fundamental Rights' (2013) 4 *EL Rev* 479. For a discussion in the context of the Irish approach to direct horizontality – the 'constitutional tort' – see W Binchey, '*Meskell*, the Constitution and Tort Law' (2011) 33 *Dublin University Law Journal* 339.

[79] J Thomas, *Public Rights, Private Relations* (n 13); Webber et al, *Legislated Rights* (n 74).

[80] *Du Plessis v De Klerk* (n 35).

It is therefore evident that limiting the scope and reach of direct horizontality *in some form* is necessary. The law of the European Union, for example, provides for direct horizontality within certain domains (such as equal pay).[81] The South African Constitution predicates it upon the 'nature of the right' and the 'nature of the duty'.[82] But that, of course, raises the question: what is the principled basis for restricting horizontality to certain domains, and how is one to decide the basis on which the 'nature' of rights and duties necessitates the application of the rights framework to private conduct?

The debate about direct horizontality, therefore, cannot avoid engaging with the delineation of its limits and boundaries. This delineation has been the focus of both courts and scholars that have had occasion to engage with direct horizontality. The approach of prominent courts, however, has been unsatisfactory. I will briefly flag two examples where direct horizontality has been entrenched within the constitutional landscape for a while and, therefore, where courts have had some time to work out its contours. Note that, in the discussion that follows, the limited point I will consider is the existence – or lack thereof – of a fleshed out normative framework that determines both the scope and the boundaries of direct horizontality.

The first example is the Court of Justice of the European Union (CJEU), which is admittedly something of a *sui generis* case, given the interplay between different levels of law-making, different types of legal instruments, and tensions between the supranational court and the municipal courts. It is not my aim here to encapsulate the long-standing debate within the EU pertaining to the relationship between national and EU law, or the role of direct horizontality in shaping that relationship. Therefore, for the limited purposes of this section, the following snapshot should suffice: the CJEU began by limiting the application of direct horizontal effect to measures that are 'precise', 'clear' and 'unconditional' enough, so that no further legislative intervention – either by the states or by the EU – is required to effectuate the right in question.[83] Subsequently, in later judgments, the CJEU referred to Treaty intent (preventing 'discrimination on the labour market'[84]) and to Treaty guarantee of the freedom of movement as 'fundamental objectives of [the European] Community'.[85] These, it held, were justifications for expanding the reach of direct horizontal effect in cases of discrimination on grounds of nationality. In situations where private parties were in a position to impose conditions that 'adversely affect the exercise of fundamental freedoms guaranteed under the Treaty',[86] they would be subjected

[81] For the most comprehensive discussion of horizontality under EU law, see Frantziou, *The Horizontal Effects of the EU Charter of Fundamental Rights* (n 55).

[82] Constitution of the Republic of South Africa, s 8(2). This is considered in greater detail in ch 8.

[83] See, eg Case 26/62 *Van Gend en Loos v Nederlandse Administratie der Belastingen* [1963] ECR 1; Case 43/75 *Defrenne v SABENA (No 2)* [1976] ECR 455.

[84] Case C-281/98 *Angonese v Cassa di Risparmio di Bolzano SpA* [2000] ECR I-04139.

[85] Case 36/74 *Walrave and Koch v Association Union Cycliste International* [1974] ECR 01405.

[86] Case C-411/98 *Angelo Ferlini v Centre Hospitalier de Luxembourg* [2000] ECR I-08081.

to the horizontal rights framework. Still more recently, further expansion of direct horizontal effect has been justified on the grounds of ensuring 'full effectiveness'[87] of general principles (such as non-discrimination). Sometimes these tests are used in a complementary fashion. For example, in June 2021, the CJEU handed down a preliminary ruling in a case concerning an application from the Watford Employment Tribunal, with respect to the question of equal pay for female and male workers at Tesco Stores.[88] The CJEU held that Article 157 of the Treaty of the Functioning of the European Union had direct effect both because the obligation was clear and precise, and because full effectiveness had to be given to the commitment – set out in the Treaty of the European Union and in the Charter of Fundamental Rights – to promote equality between women and men in all spheres.[89]

As is evident from the above, and as many scholars have pointed out, in the cases under discussion, the 'foundation of the horizontal direct effect is barely explained'.[90] In effect, while the CJEU's jurisprudence informs us of when rights may be applied horizontally (including the well-known distinction between horizontally applicable treaty obligations and inapplicable directives[91]), the underlying normative basis – or, at least, a normative basis internal to the question of horizontality – remains unexplored.[92] The upshot of this is that while there exist 'technical rules' determining the application of horizontal rights on a case-by-case basis, they lack any deeper 'constitutional coherence'[93] (of course,

[87] Case C-144/04 *Walter Mangold v Rudiger Helm* [2005] ECR I-09981 [78].

[88] Case C-624/19 *K and Ors v Tesco Stores* 2nd Chamber, 3 June 2021.

[89] ibid [23], [35].

[90] M de Mol, 'The Novel Approach of the CJEU on the Horizontal Direct Effect of the EU Principle of Non-Discrimination: (Unbridled) Expansion of EU Law?' (2011) 18 *Maastricht Journal of European and Comparative Law* 109, 119.

[91] See P Craig, 'The Legal Effect of Directives: Policy, Rules and Exceptions' (2009) 34 *EL Rev* 349. See also C-176/12 *Association de médiation sociale v Union locale des syndicats CGT and Others* ECLI:EU:C:2014:2 Opinion of AG Villalon.

[92] See, eg the extensive discussion in the Opinion of Advocate General Lenz, discussing the merits and demerits of the direct horizontal application of EU Directives without any engagement with the question of when rights should apply horizontally: Case C-91/92 *Paola Faccini Dori v Recreb Srl* [1994] ECR I-3325 Opinion of AG Lenz.

[93] See Frantziou, *The Horizontal Effects of the EU Charter of Fundamental Rights* (n 55) for this point and an extended bibliography on the subject. Frantziou also points out that the underlying basis of horizontality under EU law – to the extent that it can be discerned – was originally a concern with market integration. That concern has constituted an unarticulated major premise of horizontal rights decisions, including the balancing of rights and duties in right-to-strike cases, as well as limitations upon horizontal rights application. ibid ch 5. See also E Frantziou, 'Case C-176/12 Association de Médiation Sociale: Some Reflections on the Horizontal Effect of the Charter and the Reach of Fundamental Employment Rights in the European Union' (2014) 10 *European Constitutional Law Review* 332; CC Murphy, 'Using the EU Charter of Fundamental Rights against Private Parties after Association De Médiation Sociale' (2014) *European Human Rights Law Review* 170. In addition, see Case C-282/10 *Maribel Dominguez v Centre informatique du Centre Ouest Atlantique* ECLI:EU:C:2011:559 Opinion of AG Trstenjak [118], [119], where the AG began by noting theoretical justifications for horizontal effect (such as uneven power relations), before retreating to the principles of effectiveness and coherence of the EU legal order – again, normative reasons that are external to the question of horizontal application itself.

it is important to flag that the constitutional status of the Treaties is itself a contested issue).

As a second example, the Irish doctrine of constitutional tort – a unique approach to horizontality – also suffers from unclear scope and boundaries. The Irish Constitution does not specifically provide for horizontal application. However, in *Byrne v Ireland*[94] and *Educational Company of Ireland Ltd v Fitzpatrick (No 2)*,[95] the Supreme Court held that constitutional rights cast correlative duties of non-interference on citizens. Consequently,

> a right guaranteed by the Constitution or granted by the Constitution can be protected by action or enforced by action even though such action may not fit into any of the ordinary forms of action in either common law or equity and that the constitutional right carries within it its own right to a remedy or for the enforcement of it.[96]

There is a substantial body of scholarly work around the constitutional tort doctrine.[97] Most scholars agree, however, that it is not grounded within a principled, constitutional theory. In one of the more recent studies, for example, Colm O'Cinneide points out that the doctrine of constitutional tort has been uneven in the application, with 'a serious lack of conceptual clarity as to when and how horizontal effect should be given to fundamental rights'.[98] This is because, inter alia,

> the case-by-case basis on which the Supreme Court has adjudicated constitutional tort claims has meant that no overarching test has been established to determine whether a constitutional right will be given horizontal effect, and if so, to what degree and extent.[99]

For instance, many of the initial constitutional tort cases involved imposing obligations on trade unions (vis-à-vis individuals who wish to opt out of collective bargaining schemes, or those who are affected by industrial action). However, they contained very little analysis of how constitutional rights such as the freedom of association are to be applied when transplanted from the public to the private context, specifically when it comes to historically specific formations such as trade unions.[100]

[94] *Byrne v Ireland* [1972] 1 IR 241.

[95] *Educational Company of Ireland Ltd v Fitzpatrick (No 2)* [1961] IR 345.

[96] *Meskell v CIE* [1973] IR 121. See also *Murtagh Properties v Cleary* [1972] IR 330; *Hayes v INTO* [1987] ILRM 651.

[97] See, eg J Temple Lang, 'Private Law Aspects of the Irish Constitution' (1971) 6 *Irish Jurist* 237; AS Butler, 'Constitutional Rights in Private Litigation: A Critique and Comparative Analysis' (1993) 22 *Anglo-American Law Review* 1; F Von Prondzynki, 'The Protection of Constitutional Rights: Comparisons between Ireland and Germany' (1980) 2 *Dublin University Law Journal* 14; T Kerr and T Cooney, 'Constitutional Aspects of Irish Tort Law' (1981) 3 *Dublin University Law Journal* 1.

[98] O'Cinneide, 'Irish Constitutional Law and Direct Horizontal Effect' (n 70) 213, 215, citing other scholars, such as Michael Forde, for this proposition.

[99] ibid 229.

[100] ibid 236. See also G Whyte, 'Industrial Relations and the Irish Constitution' (1981) 16 *Irish Jurist* 35.

In some of its judgments, the Irish Supreme Court has hinted that constitutional rights will apply horizontally (via constitutional tort) in cases only where existing private law is 'plainly inadequate' to deal with the issue.[101] This, ostensibly, solves the separation of powers issue that I have outlined above. As O'Cinneide points out, however, such a clean-cut separation of private law and horizontal constitutional rights has had the effect of walling off private law regimes from constitutional scrutiny[102] – and also, as a corollary, lacks the interpretive tools for engaging in that kind of constitutional scrutiny.

Furthermore, at a more conceptual level, the argument that horizontal rights will apply where private law does not exist is insufficient. The absence of legislation is as much a function of legislative choice as is its existence. Consequently, it can easily be argued that the absence of a private law regime represents legislative intention *not* to regulate a certain domain, and judicial intervention via horizontal application is unjustified.[103] In the Irish context, this is exemplified by the Supreme Court's 'abortion cases', where, in the absence of common law proscriptions, the Court injuncted private health clinics, student unions and other bodies from providing advice on obtaining abortions in the UK, on the basis that the right to life of the unborn child took priority over the freedom of expression.[104] O'Cinneide and Forde both point out that the abortion cases do not engage in any analysis of issues around the scope of application and balancing of constitutional rights and obligations between the private parties.[105] It is therefore clear that the 'inadequacy' formulation does not obviate the need for a theory that tells us when horizontal rights are applicable to private relationships.

The CJEU and Irish examples highlight the need for a normative framework that can be applied to adjudicating questions of direct horizontality. In the concluding chapter of this book, I will also demonstrate how the case law of more recent constitutional courts – such as those of Kenya and South Africa – reveals a similar need.

[101] *W v Ireland (No 2)* [1997] 2 IR 141 (HC); *Hanrahan v Merck Sharp and Dohme* [1988] ILRM 629 (SC).

[102] O'Cinneide, 'Irish Constitutional Law and Direct Horizontal Effect' (n 70) 240; for exactly the same point, see also BME McMahon and W Binchy, *Irish Law of Torts*, 2nd edn (Butterworth (Ireland), 1990) 10. For a very similar critique in the context of horizontal rights as applied under the Constitution of Cyprus, see P Konstantinidis, 'The Horizontal Effect of Fundamental Rights in the Jurisprudence of the Supreme Court of Cyprus' (2018) 30(1) *The Cyprus Review* 145, 157.

[103] See eg *Hosford v John Murphy & Sons Ltd* [1988] ILRM 300 (HC), discussed in McMahon and Binchy, *Irish Law of Torts* (n 102) 11; M Forde, 'Who Can Remedy Human Rights Abuses? The "State Action" Question' in KD Ewing, CA Gearty and BA Hepple (eds), *Human Rights and Labour Law: Essays for P Higgins* (Mansell Publishing, 1994) 220, 235; for a similar argument in the US context, see eg RS Kay, 'The State Action Doctrine, the Public–Private Distinction, and the Independence of Constitutional Law' (1993) 10 *Constitutional Commentary* 329.

[104] *Attorney General [SPUC] v Open Door Counselling Ltd* [1988] IR 593; *SPUC v Grogan* [1989] IR 760.

[105] O'Cinneide, 'Irish Constitutional Law and Direct Horizontal Effect' (n 70) 234; Forde, 'Who Can Remedy Human Rights Abuses?' (n 103) 231–34.

Contemporary scholarly models, too, recognise and respond to this need. In the next chapter, I shall examine two recent models, by Johan van der Walt and Jean Thomas. While a full consideration of these models is a subject for the next chapter, it is sufficient to note here that both van der Walt and Thomas emphasise the requirement for a principled, domain-based limitation on the operation of direct horizontality, for many of the reasons discussed above. The crucial questions that then arise are: what is the underlying principle, and what does it mean in terms of a concrete model for conceptualising and applying a framework for direct horizontal rights?

V. CONCLUSION

In the previous chapter and this, I have discussed two archetypal models that depart from default verticality and apply constitutional rights to non-state parties. I have argued that both these models remain wedded to one or more of the foundational assumptions underlying default verticality.

The first model – functional equivalence – is focused upon how to 'attribute' a private party's composition or conduct to that of the state. In doing so, it continues to operate under the framework of the unitary, centralised conception of sovereignty that has characterised how we understand the state.

The second model finds state action – through commission or omission – within private law and private orderings. In doing so, however, it leaves the structure of private law or orderings untouched, and simply substitutes the state with the private rights violator. In practice, this means that it continues to view these private parties as operating within the same horizontal plane, where they face each other as abstract equals (and therefore have competing rights that need to be balanced against each other). This is known as the 'transplant problem'. Furthermore, and separately, as the state does not have rights that need to be 'balanced' against that of the private party, the principles used in determining when a state has (or has not) justifiably limited a right are fundamentally distinct from those that apply to a relationship between two private parties, both possessing rights and responsibilities of their own.

While the 'transplant problem' is not insurmountable, there are other issues – such as the mischaracterisation of the private relations, and a continued attachment to default verticality's account of sovereignty – that suggest that even in its strongest form, indirect horizontality might not be the complete answer to the problem that I have identified. It may, then, seem intuitively attractive to respond to these issues by simply dissolving the distinction between state and non-state parties altogether, and applying constitutional rights across the board ('direct horizontality'). This, however, comes with its own set of problems (including overlap with existing private law regimes), and does not even resolve some of the existing problems with the above approaches. What this reveals is that there must be a principled basis underlying when, where and how 'direct horizontality' will be applicable.

It is here that both the archetypal models that I have discussed, for all their shortcomings, also provide valuable insights. As discussed in the previous chapter, on the one hand, one manifestation of functional equivalence asks whether the private body is capable of affecting rights in a relevantly similar fashion to the state. Importantly, this places the rights bearer and her interests at the centre of the story. On the other hand, indirect horizontality's insistence that putatively 'private' relationships always have an element of state involvement, as well as the 'transplant problem', alerts us to the importance of analysing such relationships against the background context that gives them their force and meaning.

As we shall see, both these insights form a crucial part of contemporary scholarly accounts of bounded horizontality, the subject of chapter four. While arguing that those existing models fall short in certain important respects, I also intend to use both the above insights as building blocks to develop the institutional approach towards horizontality (chapter five). The institutional approach argues that often, the character of 'private' relationships cannot be understood without understanding that they are embedded within social structures and institutions. Private parties' respective locations within these structures take them out of the 'horizontal plane' that is the basis of default verticality, and place them instead in positions of enduring and entrenched advantage or disadvantage. These institutional locations then place some private parties at the risk of having their core interests and rights harmed by other private parties. It is this unique relationship, which is not reducible either to the classical understanding of the 'vertical' equation between state and private parties or (as observed above) to the horizontal equation *inter se* between private parties, that justifies the application of constitutional bills of rights to certain 'private relationships'.

4

Two Models of Bounded Horizontality

I. INTRODUCTION

IN CHAPTER ONE of this book, I identified three assumptions that underpin the default vertical approach towards constitutional rights. In chapters two and three, I argued that existing judicial (and scholarly) models that attempt to depart from default verticality nonetheless remain tied to one or more of its underlying assumptions. This is because, in different ways, these models (state action and indirect horizontality) continue to treat the state as the primary normative site for applying the constitutional rights framework. This led to the question – asked at the end of chapter three – whether the problems with default verticality could be resolved by jettisoning the vertical/horizontal divide altogether, and applying constitutional rights in the 'private sphere' in exactly the same manner as we apply them against the state. Unbounded direct horizontality, however, brings problems of its own. The structure of the rights framework resists any direct transplantation from state to non-state entities. The attempt to do so raises issues that are both conceptual (what do we do when the subject of horizontal rights obligations is also a rights bearer?) and pragmatic (the collapsing of all existing private law domains into the constitutional rights framework). Consequently, any model that advocates direct horizontality would necessarily have to be a bounded, or a limited model: that is, it would have to set principled constraints upon direct horizontality, in terms of both which rights apply horizontally and which 'private' relationships they apply to. In the jurisdictions that I have surveyed in this book – including jurisdictions where the constitution does make provision for direct horizontal application – courts have (so far) been hesitant to develop a principled account of bounded direct horizontality. In this chapter, therefore, I will turn to contemporary scholarly accounts. In particular, I will study the models developed in Johan van der Walt's *The Horizontal Effect Revolution and the Question of Sovereignty* (2014) and Jean Thomas's *Public Rights, Private Relations* (2015).

* * * * *

This chapter considers the bounded horizontality models of Johan van der Walt and Jean Thomas. I examine these two contemporary authors because, like the arguments developed in this book, they too reject both default verticality as well as the existing models of departure from it. Furthermore, they too articulate a comprehensive model of bounded horizontality that attempts to delink itself from some or all of the assumptions underlying default verticality. This chapter, thus, aims to set out their respective accounts, and examine whether and to what extent they are successful in setting out a plausible model of bounded horizontality on the lines indicated above. This, in turn, will set the stage for chapter five, where I will articulate my own institutional approach towards horizontality that – I will argue – incorporates the insights of both Van der Walt and Thomas, while avoiding some of the weaknesses of their respective models.

This chapter will begin with an account of Van der Walt and Thomas's respective models. It will not, however, be a simple summary. Rather, I will attempt to *reconstruct* their arguments from the perspective of the three assumptions of default verticality discussed in chapter one and examine the approach that these scholars take towards those assumptions (section II).

Next, I will examine the strengths and weaknesses of each model. I will argue that Van der Walt correctly recognises that the key to the application of the horizontal rights framework lies in how certain private relationships are nested within institutional structures that lend them peculiar salience. Van der Walt, however, insists on limiting these institutional structures to the interactions between 'social majorities and minorities' – a limitation that (I will contend) is misplaced.

On the other hand, Thomas correctly argues that the horizontality enquiry ought to focus on questions of power and vulnerability, and how these attributes frame certain private relationships. Thomas, however, goes on to argue that horizontal rights in the 'private domain' must retain the structure of established public law rights, and that therefore the (private) subject of horizontal obligations must exercise state-like power (for example, by holding a monopoly over access to a basic good). This, I will suggest, is unduly limiting. In many cases that appear intuitively fit for applying the rights framework, it is not that a private actor *individually* exercises a monopoly (such as the racist house owner or landlord in a racist society), but that the background social institutions (in this case, racism) accord to their individual action a salience that goes beyond the concrete power that they exercise (section III).

Combining the core insights of Van der Walt (relevance of background institutions) and Thomas (focus on power and vulnerability), however, yields the basis for the institutional model. I will conclude this chapter by briefly flagging this point, before articulating and developing the model in chapter five (section IV).

II. TWO CONTEMPORARY ACCOUNTS OF BOUNDED DIRECT HORIZONTALITY

A. Van der Walt

In *The Horizontal Effect Revolution and the Question of Sovereignty*, Johan van der Walt develops an account of horizontality that is founded on a root-and-branch critique of the assumptions underlying the default vertical approach.[1] To begin with, recall the third assumption underlying default verticality, according to which individuals in the 'private sphere' face each other on terms of abstract equality (ie within the same 'horizontal plane'). They are therefore deemed equally responsible for shaping the terms of their relationship, with the rights framework playing no supervisory or regulatory role.[2] Van der Walt explicitly rejects this assumption, noting that the public/private divide – and, by extension, default verticality – incorrectly 'look[s] upon public law relations as vertical power relations (between superiors and inferiors) and upon private law relations as horizontal relations (between equals)'.[3] Once it is understood, however, that private law relations are not 'horizontal' in this sense, it follows that the application of the rights framework to such relations is 'a move towards the horizontalisation or re-horizontalisation of private law relationships, and not as a move towards applying constitutional demands to horizontal relations'[4] (because these relations were never truly horizontal in the first place). In other words, the default vertical approach asks: in what circumstances do we apply the rights framework – originally designed for the vertical public law relationship between state and individual – to horizontal private relationships? Van der Walt, on the other hand, asks: 'given that private relationships were never horizontal to start with, in which circumstances should we apply the rights framework in order to "horizontalize" them?'

Default verticality's assumption that private relationships are horizontal is accomplished, Van der Walt points out, through the conscious 'erasure of baseline questions'[5] (that is, questions relating to the distribution of economic and social power) from the legal enquiry. This speaks to the second assumption underlying default verticality – that of abstract freedom. It is only after those baseline questions have been shorn off that we get the abstract legal subject, whose freedom is protected through the application of (vertical) rights

[1] J van der Walt, *The Horizontal Effect Revolution and the Question of Sovereignty* (De Gruyter, 2014).

[2] See ch 1 of this book.

[3] Van der Walt, *The Horizontal Effect Revolution* (n 1) 6.

[4] ibid 7.

[5] ibid 40.

against the state; and it is through an equal protection of such de-contextualised freedom that we construct the private domain as a set of 'horizontal' (equal) relationships between equal subjects.

A combination of these two assumptions – abstract freedom and individual responsibility – yields a situation where actually existing inequalities and hierarchies within the 'private' domain are deemed normatively irrelevant for the application of the constitutional rights framework. Thus, for Van der Walt, what horizontality is really about is 'the restriction and even the undoing of private hierarchies. It concerns the constitutionally required levelling and horizontalisation of these hierarchies.'[6]

This framing is important, because it suggests that the key challenge for horizontality is not about how best to 'transplant' constitutional rights from the public to the private sphere (the problem that, as we saw, indirect horizontality struggles with[7] and something that Van der Walt expressly criticises it for), but rather, how to determine which forms of power relations or inequalities within the 'private' sphere are normatively significant with respect to the application of the rights framework ('re-horizontalisation'). Because, as Van der Walt himself concedes, some form of principled limitation is required, so that the 'the practice of constitutional review [does not turn into] the higher review of all private law disputes'.[8]

What principle does Van der Walt adopt? He argues that there are certain private relationships and transactions where 'disputes between individuals … have social-political significance that extends beyond the *relations of those directly involved*' (emphasis added).[9] Drawing upon the work of Gunther Teubner and other systems theorists, he defines the purpose of horizontality as to 'thematise conflicts in which human rights of individuals are asserted against structural violence',[10] because in certain 'individual forms of action'[11] what is actually implicit is 'institutional conflict'.[12]

As an example, Van der Walt takes the famous instance of *Shelley v Kraemer*[13] and the constitutional validity of racially restrictive covenants in a society that is itself scarred by racial domination and subjugation. In the *Shelley* context, Van der Walt argues, 'private conduct that seeks to perpetuate *wide scale racial segregation* becomes "governmental". Such private conduct can no longer claim

[6] ibid 83.

[7] See ch 2 of this book.

[8] Van der Walt, *The Horizontal Effect Revolution* (n 1) 150.

[9] ibid 22.

[10] G Teubner, 'Societal Constitutionalism beyond the Nation State' in P Dobner and M Loughlin (eds), *The Twilight of Constitutionalism* (Oxford University Press, 2010) 339, referred to in Van der Walt, *The Horizontal Effect Revolution* (n 1) 288.

[11] Teubner, 'Societal Constitutionalism beyond the Nation State' (n 10).

[12] ibid.

[13] *Shelley v Kraemer* 334 US 1 (1948).

to be private' (emphasis added).[14] Thus, the collective refusal of white property owners to sell to Black homebuyers is no longer simply a private decision about how an individual intends to dispose of their property, but, rather, should be understood as a set of 'private endeavours to promote or sustain *public inequality*' (emphasis added).[15] Van der Walt does not explain what he means here by 'public inequality', but presumably it is inequality that goes beyond the specific private relationship at issue. This is evident from the fact that Van der Walt goes on to refer to disputes between individuals that have a 'social-political significance that extends beyond the *relations of those directly involved*' (emphasis added).[16] Van der Walt draws upon Laurence Tribe's insights in his analysis of *Shelley* which Tribe describes as the subjugation thesis: private discrimination is permitted except where it has an 'overall effect of confining minorities to their current disadvantaged positions in society'.[17]

While *Shelley* and racially restrictive covenants present straightforward examples, Van der Walt still needs a final argument to complete his account: how do we identify *in general* those private relationships that 'thematise … an institutional conflict'? Van der Walt answers this question in two parts. He begins by identifying the first assumption underlying default verticality: the idea of undivided sovereignty. As long as there continues to exist 'an oppositional monopoly as far as threats to liberty are concerned',[18] departures from default verticality will continue to have to go through the state (whether through state action or indirect horizontality) in order to get to the private relationship at issue. Van der Walt thus proposes what he calls 'differantial sovereignty' (*sic*), which frames the relationship between 'social majorities and minorities' in a society. This brings him to the final prong of his model: relevant 'private disputes' to which the horizontal rights framework should apply, he argues, are those that embody conflict between social majorities and minorities (such as racially restrictive covenanting).

As we can therefore see, Van der Walt's model of horizontality turns upon three axes: (i) a rejection of the three assumptions underlying default verticality; (ii) locating horizontality in those private transactions or disputes that reflect not simply the two (or more) private parties involved, but embody 'institutional conflict … within individual forms of action'; and lastly (iii) specifying that this 'institutional conflict' is that which exists between 'social majorities and minorities' at any given time.

[14] Van der Walt, *The Horizontal Effect Revolution* (n 1) 191.

[15] ibid 180.

[16] ibid 22.

[17] L Tribe, *American Constitutional Law*, 2nd edn (Foundation Press, 1988) 1718, referred to in Van der Walt, *The Horizontal Effect Revolution* (n 1) 177.

[18] Van der Walt, *The Horizontal Effect Revolution* (n 1) 199, translating a line from Nicklas Luhmann.

B. Thomas

Thomas's starting point is similar to Van der Walt's.[19] She begins by noting that default verticality is a historically contingent phenomenon, whose origins lie in the unique form of power that was once vested in the state.[20] However, the existence of other power structures in the modern world – many of which are themselves the products of private law – that are capable of violating rights to an extent and a degree that is not all that dissimilar to what the state can do, requires a clear departure from default verticality.[21]

Thomas's priority, therefore, is the *rights bearer*. Thus, the first question relevant for an application of the rights framework is to ask which entities are capable of violating rights, and how. Like Van der Walt, however, Thomas also concedes that this may be a necessary, albeit insufficient, condition for horizontality, as it would mean that 'the potential applicative scope of those [horizontal] rights expands exponentially'.[22] In such a situation, 'each right generates a number of duties, such as non-interference, protection against violation by third parties, and possibly also positive measures to diminish the likelihood that rights will be violated'.[23]

Thomas is also concerned with the 'transplant problem', noting, as I argued in chapter three, 'the legal presumption that non-state actors are all the same, so far as rights are concerned'.[24] Thus, much like Van der Walt, Thomas clarifies that the purpose of the horizontal rights framework is 'not to apply public law rights to private relations directly',[25] but to articulate a principled basis for determining which private entities are subject to horizontal obligations and which private relationships ought to be brought within the framework.

To arrive at this basis, Thomas begins by asking herself what it is that characterises the rights framework in the vertical context (ie between the individual and the state). Superficially, this might simply sound like a return to default verticality, with its focus upon the state. There is, however, a crucial distinction: unlike default verticality, which takes the normative priority of the state for granted, Thomas makes no such assumptions, at least at the beginning. The question that she asks is: what is normatively distinctive about the relationship between the rights bearer and the duty bearer (which happens to be the state)? This, of course, necessarily involves focusing upon the character of the state as well. However, the reason for that is only that the state is one of the parties to

[19] See J Thomas, *Public Rights, Private Relations* (Oxford University Press, 2015).
[20] ibid Introduction.
[21] ibid Introduction.
[22] ibid 17.
[23] ibid 17.
[24] ibid 39.
[25] ibid 18.

the vertical relationship, and not that the pre-defined attributes of the state are being taken as the starting point for the existence of the rights framework.

This is evident from how Thomas develops her argument. First, she examines what it is that is being protected (a set of core enumerated interests). Next, she argues that what characterises rights is their 'relational context'[26] – ie they depend upon the specific relationship between the two parties in question. In other words, they 'cannot be understood exclusively in reference to the interests of individual subjects'.[27] This relationship, Thomas claims, is that of 'interpersonal dependency'.[28] 'Dependency', she argues, 'involves an increased vulnerability of one party to another … it is a relational structure that links power and need, or power and vulnerability, so that the vulnerability of one person is specific *to* the influence of another.'[29] We may notice here that the condition of dependency addresses the 'transplant problem' that we identified with indirect horizontality in the previous chapter. Instead of simply 'transplanting' the rights framework to the private context and then engaging in an intuitive 'balancing' of rights and duties between two formally equal parties, the condition of dependency links the application of the rights framework to the specific nature of the relationship between the private parties.

Thomas refines this idea further by noting that dependency must be specific, both in terms of who one is dependent on and for what. In particular, a relationship of interpersonal dependency exists where 'one party substantially controls the goods of another' (emphasis added).[30] Drawing once again from the example of the vertical rights framework, evidence of such control can be found, for example, in the existence of a monopoly (akin to the state's monopoly over legitimate coercion), the state's ability to affect the 'dignitary status' of everyone in its territory because (in part) of the absence of feasible exit options, and so on. This, according to Thomas, is

> the moral context of the vertical relationship between the individual and state … [which] means that the special protection associated with that relationship can be replicated on a principled basis within the private sphere so that not all relational contexts within that sphere are treated as though they were the same.[31]

The last bit, of course, speaks to the principled limitations of the model: only those relationships within the 'private sphere' that replicate the 'moral context' of the individual–state relationship will be subject to the rights framework.

Finally, while the existence of a dependency relationship is necessary for constitutional horizontal rights to apply, it is not a sufficient condition. Thomas

[26] ibid 19.
[27] ibid 118.
[28] ibid 19.
[29] ibid 189.
[30] ibid 223.
[31] ibid 23.

still needs a reason for why obligations ought specifically to attach to the private duty bearer; the mere existence of dependency appears not to be enough. Consequently, she argues that this dependency must, in addition, arise in the course of an 'undertaking' – ie a course of action that the more powerful party must have voluntarily undertaken, which provides the background context to the existence of dependency (eg the act of hiring an employee). This provides the last link in the chain, justifying not only the application of the rights framework, but also ensuring that it is that specific private party who is bound to it. Thus,

> the more powerful person's obligations will be limited in two main ways. First, they will arise only in respect of those vulnerable persons whose vulnerability arises in respect of the undertaking itself. This means that we cannot extend the obligations to say that the more powerful supervisor [ie a supervisor on the factory floor] will owe all the obligations in question (protection, aid, etc.) to everyone he passes on the street at the end of the workday. Second, the more powerful party's obligations will arise only in virtue of those interests in respect of which the other person's vulnerability is caused or significantly exacerbated by the undertaking itself. The dependency analysis, therefore, operates within a sphere of the undertaking that is the nexus or fulcrum of the relational structure.[32]

In sum, therefore, Thomas's horizontality model depends upon (i) identifying that an individual's access to a core good is at stake; (ii) identifying the existence of a relationship of 'dependency' between the two parties, where the dominant party exercises substantial control over the weaker party's access to the good; and (iii) demonstrating that that relationship has arisen within the context of an 'undertaking' involving both the parties.

What unites Van der Walt's and Thomas's bounded horizontality accounts is a prima facie rejection of the three assumptions underlying default verticality. Like that of Van der Walt, the basis of Thomas's model lies in the understanding that default verticality's 'flattening' of the 'private sphere' – so that all 'private relationships' are deemed to take place within the same 'horizontal plane' between equally free individuals – is deeply flawed. And this visualisation of the private sphere and the horizontal plane is linked to the unitary conception of sovereignty, which forms the basis of limiting rights claims to the individual–state relationship. Thomas addresses this constraint by arguing that it is not sovereignty that is the normatively significant factor in the rights framework, but a specific kind of power difference ('dependency') – a difference that is also found in relationships that do not involve the state and its sovereign power. Thus, while Van der Walt propounds a new idea of sovereignty that exists in the 'private' domain, Thomas displaces the concept of sovereignty from the rights framework itself.

There is also, however, a more significant difference between the two. Van der Walt and Thomas differ on the question of how to identify the private

[32] ibid 193.

relationships that will be subjected to the rights framework. For Van der Walt, the key lies in locating an *institutional* background that frames an individual dispute. This, in turn, he defines as conflicts involving social majorities and minorities. For Thomas, on the other hand, what matters most is the relative position of the two *parties* vis-à-vis each other: what is crucial, apart from an 'undertaking', is the existence of a specific form of power and control (over basic goods) by the stronger party, and the existence of vulnerability or dependency on the part of the rights bearer, in a manner that approximates the 'moral context' characterising the relationship between the individual and the state.

III. STRENGTHS AND WEAKNESSES: AN ANALYSIS

A. Thomas

Let us begin with Thomas's model. There are two central concerns that underpin her approach: the transplant problem, and placing principled limits upon the application of the rights framework in the private domain. Thomas attempts to solve both problems through her 'extrapolative' methodology. In the words of Grellette:

> [Thomas] looks at the basic structure and context of our public law practices, and the basic tenets of modern rights theory. From these sources, she sets out to develop an account of public law rights that is sufficiently abstract as to be *institutionally translatable* from public to private law, but which is also precise enough to provide judges with meaningful guidance in identifying and deciding cases grounded in those norms. (emphasis added)[33]

Both the application and the limits of horizontality flow from this extrapolation. Therefore, at the heart of Thomas's model lie two choices: (i) her identification of the 'basic structure and context of our public law practices'; and (ii) the level of abstraction at which they are identified (before being 'transplanted' into the private sphere).

For Thomas, then, the public law relationship between the state and private parties is characterised by the ideas of control, dependency and the undertaking. What makes the vertical relationship subject to the rights framework, according to her, are: (i) the control exercised by the state over basic goods; (ii) the dependence of individuals upon the state for the continued enjoyment of those goods; and (iii) that this control and dependency are functions of the 'state's undertaking to coercively govern'.[34] Having identified these salient features at a sufficient level of abstraction, Thomas is then able to 'translate' them into the horizontal

[33] M Grellette, 'Review: *J Thomas,* Public Rights, Private Relations' (2016) 79(5) *MLR* 924, 925.

[34] AR Reeves, 'Book Review: J Thomas, *Public Rights, Private Relations*' (2016) 35 *Law and Philosophy* 529, 533.

context. Therefore, in a situation where (i) a private party controls a basic good, (ii) other private parties depend upon it for the continued enjoyment of that good and (iii) the relationship between the parties is a function of an undertaking, rights will apply.

However, the ideas of 'control' and 'undertaking' require one further step of elaboration, in the 'transplant' process. To do this, Thomas once again looks to the public law context. Control, therefore, is understood as a state-like 'monopoly' over access to a basic good;[35] and through the vehicle of the 'undertaking', Thomas draws a distinction between goods that are *independently* enjoyed by the rights holder and those that are *created* by the (private) duty bearer in the course of the undertaking. In the former case, she argues that substantive horizontal rights apply (ie the good cannot be taken away), while in the latter, only procedural rights apply. This completes the model.

There are, however, two crucial issues with this second move in the 'transplant' process. The first is the assumption that the monopolistic aspect of the state's control must accompany the transplantation to the private sphere. Recall that some of the problems with the concept of monopoly were discussed in chapter two: in particular, that ideas of monopoly continue to be bound to default verticality's conception of sovereignty as unitary and undivided.[36] It is true, of course, that the state does exercise a monopoly over legitimate coercion, and that the existence of that monopoly appears – intuitively – to be a relevant factor in the application of the rights framework. It does not necessarily follow, however – as Thomas appears to believe – that in the process of transplant, the existence of the monopoly must shift from the state to the individual duty bearer at issue.

Consider, for example, one of the classic cases where there exists a strong intuitive case for the application of horizontal rights: racially restrictive covenanting, of the *Shelley v Kraemer* variety. As discussed before, it is not the case that the individual house owner who refuses to sell or rent their property to a person on account of their race has a monopoly over the housing market. What seems to be at play here is something different: controversies around racially restrictive covenanting tend to arise in racist societies, where covenants of this form become tools of upholding racial segregation and exclusion.[37] Therefore, the salient aspect of racially restrictive covenants that attracts rights-based scrutiny is not what form of control the individual private house owner exercises upon basic goods, and the dependency of the buyer or renter upon that house owner; rather, dependency and control structure the relationship between the two private parties because of their relative locations of power and powerlessness within the social institution of race (and racism). In this context, racially restrictive covenants both reflect and entrench that institutional difference in power.

[35] Thomas, *Public Rights, Private Relations* (n 19).

[36] See ch 2 of this book.

[37] This is Tribe's justification of the judgment in *Shelley v Kraemer* quoted by Van der Walt, discussed above.

To put it another way, using the language of monopoly: the distinctive feature of a monopoly is that those who are subject to it have no feasible exit option. In the case of racially restrictive covenanting in a racist society, those at the receiving end – the putative rights bearers – also lack a feasible exit option (ie exiting from the structures and institutions of racism that are manifested in specific forms, such as restrictive covenants). However, the fact that the rights holder lacks a feasible exit option does not mean that an individual duty bearer exercises a monopoly. Rather, the individual duty bearer's acts are constitutive of a social institution, which is where the monopoly (if any) rests.

The flaw in Thomas's approach, therefore, lies in the assumption that when the 'transplant' happens from public to private sphere, the structure of the relationship between the individual and the state must be replicated between the two private parties, whose relationship is being made subject to the rights framework. It is this assumption that compels her to insist that the duty holder must exercise a form of control – and correspondingly, that the rights bearer must be in a situation of dependency, which structurally resembles the vertical individual–state relationship. As I have argued, however, the dependency of the rights bearer need not correspond to the exercise of control by the duty holder in a one-to-one relationship. The locus of that power and control may lie elsewhere.

The second issue with Thomas's transplant is her distinction between goods that have an 'independent existence' and goods that are 'created' by the private duty holder. Recall that in the former case, Thomas argues that there are substantive obligations upon the private duty holder, while in the latter case, there are only procedural obligations. For instance, a private corporation that has set up a plant in a particular area cannot divert the local water supply to that plant and deprive the local villagers of access to drinking water.[38] However – Thomas argues – a drug company that has developed an anti-HIV vaccine has no substantive obligation to make it available at affordable prices to those that need it.

As multiple critics have pointed out, though, Thomas ignores the fact that private duty holders cannot 'create' basic goods without a supporting legal structure, enacted by the state. Tushnet observes, for instance, that Thomas's argument remains vulnerable to the legal realist critique discussed in chapter three:

> [T]he [legal realist] analysis treats those relations of dependency as the result of *the distribution of the rights of property, contract and tort that have the cumulative effect* of making it difficult for some to live decent lives without becoming dependent – at the very least, upon those willing to offer them employment on terms dictated by the employer. (emphasis added)[39]

In the case of the drug company, for example – leaving aside the factual point that, historically, drug research and development has been heavily underwritten

[38] Thomas, *Public Rights, Private Relations* (n 19) Introduction.

[39] M Tushnet, 'A Review of J Thomas, *Public Rights, Private Relations*' (2016) 7 *Jurisprudence* 355, 362.

by the state – the controversy only arises because the law of patents entitles the company to prohibit the rest of the world from making that same drug – on the pain of state coercion. Thomas, therefore, appears to be making the same mistake that the US Supreme Court made in *Jackson v Metropolitan Edison Co*,[40] as discussed in chapter one: the assumption that there exist 'natural monopolies', where the rights framework does not apply because the morally salient acts cannot be traced back to a specific, individual agency.

It is important to understand that these two objections stem from the same source. As indicated above, in her 'transplant' from the public to the private sphere, Thomas wants to 'extrapolate' the structural features of the state–individual relationship to the private relationship at issue. This is where the problem arises. First, Thomas is compelled by the logic of her argument to invest the private duty holder with at least some state-like characteristics – leading us back into the difficult terrain encountered in chapters two and three. And secondly, she limits herself to analysing the formal private relationship between the two parties, and not the context within which those relationships are embedded. This obviously remains tied to some of the lingering elements of default verticality.

At a deeper level, Thomas's approach is constrained by a personalised understanding of power. Her analysis of dependency, control and the undertaking is informed by viewing power as exercised through individual acts. Under this framework, for example, the power exercised by a monopolist is normatively salient when it comes to the application of the horizontal rights framework. In the case of a non-monopolistic labour market (for example), on the other hand, substantive horizontality would not apply. What this ignores, however, as I have argued previously, is that the exercise of power can be both personalised and depersonalised (ie structural, or exercised through institutions). In both cases, the impact upon the rights bearer – and her rights – is significant. A complete understanding of horizontality (as will be developed in the next chapter) must take both cases into account.

B. Van der Walt

It is precisely these weaknesses that Van der Walt manages to steer clear of. This is because Van der Walt's starting point is different. Thomas, as we have seen, seeks to extrapolate from the vertical state–individual relationship the structural features that can be transplanted into private relationships. Van der Walt, on the other hand, rejects the transplantation process altogether. His starting point is that the existence of hierarchy attracts the rights framework. Hitherto, that has been relevant primarily in the vertical context because, as I argued in

[40] *Jackson v Metropolitan Edison Co* 419 US 345 (1974).

chapter one, it is the hierarchies that persist in the individual–state relationship that have been deemed to be morally salient, while most hierarchies in the 'private' domain are regarded by default as the 'natural outcomes of virtuous diligence and natural talent'.[41] For Van der Walt, consequently, the task is not to derive the structural features of the state–individual relationship, which are then applied to private relationships; rather, it is to establish that the non-application of the rights framework to what he calls 'private hierarchies' is unjustifiable.[42]

The manner in which he does that has been demonstrated in the previous section. What is important to note here is that as Van der Walt is not committed to extrapolating from the structure of rights in the public sphere, he does not need to invest his private duty bearers with state-like characteristics, even in the abstract. Like Thomas, however, what Van der Walt *does* need to do is to provide the principled framework within which the scope and limits of horizontal rights can be articulated. It is here that Van der Walt appears to hit upon the insight that eludes Thomas, along the lines of what we have discussed above. Not *all* private hierarchies will be subjected to the rights framework, he argues; rather, only those where a violation of rights 'comes from social "institutions" and not just from individual actors'.[43] While the form of the legal action remains individual (ie one private party against another), the relevant private relationship 'thematises' institutional conflict.

As we have seen above, Van der Walt recognises that this argument will not work under default verticality's assumption of undivided sovereignty that vests within the state, and its corollary: the vision of personalised power. His argument, therefore, rests upon an explicit abandonment of the normative salience of sovereignty. For this reason, the requirement of monopoly – or other aspects resembling sovereignty – are not necessary prerequisites to the application of the horizontal rights framework to private relations.

Van der Walt's model brings us closer to our intuitive understanding of the paradigmatic case of racially restrictive covenanting, as discussed above. That said, two issues arise. First, if we argue that rights scrutiny is attracted not by the private relationship itself, but by what it 'thematises', ie institutional conflict, then the question, as framed by Dagan and Dorfman, arises: how do we 'justify to the defendant why *she* should be forced to be the agent of remedying the plaintiff's unjustified harsh predicament' (emphasis added)?[44] In Thomas's model, as we have seen, the roles played by control, dependency and the undertaking are to ensure that there exist good reasons not just to apply the horizontal rights framework to a private relationship, but also to saddle that specific private party with obligations under that framework. Van der Walt, on the other hand,

[41] Van der Walt, *The Horizontal Effect Revolution* (n 1) 6.

[42] ibid 83.

[43] Teubner, 'Societal Constitutionalism beyond the Nation State' (n 10) 339.

[44] H Dagan and A Dorfman, 'Interpersonal Human Rights' (2018) 51 *Cornell International Law Journal* 361, 368.

does not establish why or how 'institutional conflict' is best resolved through an individual suit against a specific private defendant.

Secondly, 'institution' and 'institutional conflict' are not self-defining terms. As we have seen in the previous section, Van der Walt further elaborates this by articulating 'institutional conflict' in terms of conflict between 'social majorities' and 'minorities'.[45] However, he does not, in my view, explain *why* this should be the axis around which the horizontality framework turns. Indeed, the one example that he picks to articulate the point obscures more than it clarifies. Van der Walt spends a significant amount of time discussing the parallel abortion litigations in the USA and in Germany.[46] Both those cases, however, involved challenges to laws, and therefore concerned the vertical relationship between state and individual in its classical sense. Thus, even if the concept of 'social majorities and minorities' (here, the anti- and pro-abortion factions in society) emerges out of these examples, it is unclear what role it is expected to play in the horizontal context.

For these reasons, while Van der Walt's central insight into how individual private relationships can characterise institutional violations of rights is a highly promising one, its development raises questions that he does not answer.

IV. CONCLUSION: TOWARDS THE INSTITUTIONAL MODEL

Default verticality is founded upon the public/private divide. In particular, default verticality requires two moves: first, drawing a normative distinction between the state/individual relationship on the one hand and 'private' relationships on the other; and secondly, demonstrating that this distinction warrants presumptively applying the constitutional rights framework to the first set of cases, but not to the second. These moves are justified by the three underlying assumptions of default verticality: unitary sovereignty, abstract freedom and individual responsibility (discussed in chapter one).

Judicial attempts to depart from default verticality (discussed in chapters two and three) have accepted these moves to different degrees, primarily because they continue to subscribe to the underlying assumptions. At the same time, unbounded direct horizontality, which effectively rejects both moves and denies that the rights framework bears any relation to the nature of the relationship between the rights holder and the duty bearer, creates problems of its own. The models discussed in this chapter attempt to take a different path. They acknowledge that a particular relationship must fulfil certain conditions before the constitutional rights framework applies (conditions that, by definition, are present in the state/individual relationship, but not in *all* private relationships).

[45] Van der Walt, *The Horizontal Effect Revolution* (n 1) 180.
[46] ibid ch 8.

At the same time, the starting point need not be an acceptance of the state as the default duty bearer. The question is: what are those conditions and how do we identify them?

Jean Thomas answers the question by examining the state/individual relationship and 'extrapolating' its normatively significant features. Her analysis focuses upon a difference in power between the parties to a private relationship. This difference is a necessary, but not sufficient, condition for the rights framework to apply. In addition, flowing from her extrapolative approach, differences in power must reach a certain degree (tantamount to one party exercising 'control' over the other party's access to a basic good, thus creating a situation of 'dependency') and must arise in a certain context (an 'undertaking'). As we have seen, however, even though Thomas's extrapolative approach appears to decline the two moves of default verticality highlighted at the beginning of this section, at the point at which she articulates her model in concrete terms, she goes back to (at least partially) anchoring it within some of the assumptions of default verticality. This leaves her model arguably struggling with addressing what appear to be intuitively paradigmatic instances for the application of direct horizontality.

Van der Walt, on the other hand, is more explicit about rejecting the two moves. He notes that the purpose of the constitutional rights framework is to address hierarchy – whether 'public' or 'private'. But, like Thomas, Van der Walt also accepts that not every 'private' hierarchy is or ought to be subjected to that framework. He therefore argues that it is in those private relationships where the hierarchy 'thematises' a broader institutional conflict, that the rights framework will apply. Van der Walt's attempt to flesh this out in more concrete terms, however, is unsatisfactory. His articulation of it in terms of 'social majorities and minorities' is neither clearly defined nor adequately justified.

Nonetheless, both Thomas and Van der Walt demonstrate, through their respective models, the issues that direct horizontality must address, and indicate a path forward for how it might do so. In the next chapter, I will articulate and develop a model of bounded horizontal rights that will attempt to take this path. In particular, I will argue that: (i) it is correct that the constitutional rights framework applies to private relationships in cases where there exists a 'private hierarchy', or a difference of power; (ii) that the relationship in question is nested, or embedded, within an institution, and that the difference in power flows from the parties' relative locations within that institution; and (iii) the private relationship and the institution are mutually constitutive: the institution persists because of an aggregation of similar private relationships, while the private relationships themselves derive their force and salience from the institution. This, among other things, is what justifies placing the obligation upon the duty bearer. The institutional model, thus, is founded on a rejection of the three assumptions of default verticality, as well as a refusal to take the public/private divide as a normatively significant starting point for the application of the rights framework.

5

The Institutional Approach

I. INTRODUCTION

IN CHAPTER ONE, I discussed the three conceptual assumptions underlying the default vertical approach to constitutional rights. However, it is almost trite to observe that contemporary conditions do not resemble those under which the default vertical approach emerged. The emergence of 'new power centres and mechanisms of oppression'[1] has necessitated departures from default verticality and triggered the application of constitutional rights to relationships involving non-state parties. In chapters two and three, therefore, I discussed some of the archetypal ways in which courts have accomplished this. I argued that each of the dominant archetypes is unsatisfactory, as it remains bound to one or more of the three underlying assumptions of default verticality: sovereignty, abstract freedom and individual responsibility. In concluding chapter three, I argued that, nonetheless, two important insights from the existing archetypes could form the basis of an alternative approach. The first is that default verticality leaves certain crucial human interests unprotected, in cases where the state is uninvolved. The perspective of the rights bearer, thus, ought to be central to any approach that departs from the default (Jean Thomas calls this the 'vulnerable valuable interests' diagnosis[2]). The second, related insight is that the background relationship between the rights bearer and the (putative) rights violator is an important factor in determining whether and, if so, how the rights framework is to be applied to the impugned conduct or practice. In chapter four, I explored two contemporary models – proposed by Johan van der Walt and Jean Thomas – that use these insights (to different degrees), to articulate versions of bounded direct horizontality that are no longer tied to the assumptions of default verticality. I argued that individually, Van der Walt and Thomas's accounts represent promising approaches to the problem, but also fall short in certain respects. However, Thomas's focus on the relational structure between the private parties and Van der Walt's insight about understanding private relationships contextually are both integral elements in a successful

[1] D Grimm, *Constitutionalism: Past, Present, and Future* (Oxford University Press, 2016) 129.
[2] J Thomas, *Public Rights, Private Relations* (Oxford University Press, 2015) 15.

account of bounded horizontality. In this chapter, drawing upon those insights, I will develop the institutional model of horizontality.

* * * * *

The institutional model of bounded horizontality examines (allegedly rights-violating) acts or practices between two parties in the context of the background institutional relationship between them (ie the parties' relative locations within social, economic or cultural institutions). It argues that where there exists a difference in power between the parties, enabling one to violate certain constitutional rights of the other, and where such difference flows from the parties' relative locations within the institution, then those rights should be horizontally enforced.

Therefore, an account of the institutional approach requires the following: first, a working understanding of what constitutes an 'institution' for our purposes; and secondly, the link between the institutional differences in power on the one hand and the nature of the rights and remedies that are enforced on the other.

Let me, at the outset, offer a tentative articulation of the concept of an 'institution', which I will attempt to refine in the course of this chapter. I begin by noting that there is extensive philosophical and sociological literature that discusses the idea of an institution.[3] Drawing from these accounts, I suggest that there are three salient features that constitute an 'institution' in general. First, there must be convergence of behaviour, by multiple actors, over a sustained period of time (creating what might be understood as 'norms', 'patterns of conduct' or 'conventions'). Secondly, an institution is not simply an aggregate of individual converging practices, but has a 'coherence' and 'unity' of its own. And thirdly, an institution assigns roles, functions and powers to individual actors, often in a hierarchical fashion. Derek Layder's articulation perhaps sums up the concept best: a set of '(reproduced) social relations which have an ongoing, organised and relatively enduring quality to them'.[4]

A quick caveat: while these three features indicate that an institution is not reducible to individuals and individual acts, it is nonetheless constituted by individuals. Thus, when, in the succeeding pages, I discuss the concept of impersonal institutional power, it is important to keep in mind that this does not entail anthropomorphising or reifying abstract social structures. As succinctly observed by Moishe Postone, institutional power can be best understood as the 'domination of people by abstract social structures that people themselves

[3] For a bibliography and an account, see S Miller, 'Social Institutions', *The Stanford Encyclopedia of Philosophy*, https://plato.stanford.edu/entries/social-institutions/.

[4] D Layder, 'Power, Structure, and Agency' (1985) 15 *Journal for the Theory of Social Behaviour* 131, 133.

constitute';[5] or, to put it even more clearly, 'power is implicated in the enduring structural relations that characterize a society and is *exercised* by intentional human agents who *participate* in these relations'. (emphasis added)[6]

Now, while these three characteristics are sufficient for us to intuitively grasp the meaning of the term 'institution', there are two additional features that are necessary in considering which institutions are relevant for the purpose of applying a horizontal rights framework. The first is that an individual does not ordinarily have the ability of exiting from an institution. So, for example, a particular school or hospital might be an 'institution' in the sense that sociological theory understands it. However, it is not an institution for the purposes of the horizontal rights framework. On the other hand, as we shall see below, race, or caste, does constitute an 'institution' in the relevant sense.

The second, linked feature is that the hierarchies of domination and subordination created by and through institutions are permanent, enduring and – again – features that a particular individual cannot ordinarily overcome. This point is articulated by Derek Layder, who uses the term 'structural power', but broadly refers to the same phenomenon that this book calls 'institutional power':

> structural power is relatively independent of agency, but that agency, for example in the form of exercises of power, is always subject to the influence of structural power. Power structures are relatively independent of agency in the sense that although they are social products, and thus the outcome of human action at specific historical junctures (in the form of individual or collective struggles, conflict, diplomacy, reform etc.), once established, such structures develop over *time to attain an existence which sediments them as constraints on future agency*. (emphasis added)[7]

Thus, the primary concern of the institutional approach revolves around differences in power that exist within and because of institutions, how these differences in power enable some private parties to violate the rights of others and how that can be mitigated or addressed through a horizontal rights framework. However, it is not any and every difference in power that attracts the horizontal rights framework. The individual's inability to exit from, or overcome, these power differences because of the manner in which they are embedded in certain kinds of institutions is also a key determining factor in the application of horizontal rights.

The concept of the institution, therefore, serves as a *boundary condition* for triggering the application of horizontality. At this stage, let me flag two possible preliminary objections: *vagueness* and *width*. I shall address both objections briefly here, with the caveat that a more complete response will take the form of demonstrating how the institutional approach will work in practice, in this chapter as well as in part II of this book.

[5] M Postone, *Time, Labor, and Social Domination* (Cambridge University Press, 1993) 31.
[6] JC Isaac, *Power and Marxist Theory: A Realist View* (Cornell University Press, 1987) 9.
[7] Layder, 'Power, Structure, and Agency' (n 4) 133.

The first objection might be that the concept of the institution is too vague for practical application (and, relatedly, creates challenges for the rule of law and legal certainty if courts are called upon to determine such definitional questions on a case-to-case basis). To this, a brief answer may be made: I believe that the elements of an institution, as outlined above, are no more vague than concepts that courts do apply on a regular basis – such as 'personal liberty' and 'equality' – and whose content they flesh out through precedent, incrementally and over time. Indeed, Langille and Davidov make a very similar point about the labour law category of the 'employment contract' (which I shall discuss at some length in the next chapter). Responding to criticism that courts have failed to adequately define what constitutes an employment contract, Langille and Davidov rely on Wittgenstein's concept of family resemblances to argue that 'not all definitions have to be of the analytical variety'.[8] Indeed, 'institutions', as set out above, do fall within the concept of 'family resemblances', which – Wittgenstein notes, in the context of the concept of 'games' – are best understood as 'network(s) of similarities overlapping and criss-crossing'.[9] Langille and Davidov go on to point out that in legal reasoning, context gives colour to the meaning of terms.[10] The task of this chapter, and the succeeding ones, will be to provide that context while demonstrating how the content of the concept of an institution can be moulded through adjudication.

With respect to concerns around the rule of law and legal stability, as we shall see in this chapter as well as part II, the institutional approach does not seek to supplant private law or legislation, or to turn all legal disputes into 'higher constitutional law review'. The institutional approach acknowledges that there can be reasonable differences when it comes to the specific contours of a right, which are to be resolved, in the first instance, by legislation. The institutional approach steps in when there are gaps, or when legislation is evidently insufficient to protect rights. One of its important roles is to inform judicial approaches towards interpreting existing legal frameworks. We shall see this in practice in part II, when considering the application of the institutional approach to specific legal problems.

Secondly, in addition to the problem of vagueness, it may be objected that, notwithstanding the definitional stipulations set out above, the concept of the institution is a wide one, and takes in a broad swathe of human relationships. This is true. The initial threshold for attracting the institutional approach – ie the existence of an institution – is a relatively low one. However, a few things

[8] BA Langille and G Davidov, 'Beyond Employees and Independent Contractors: A View from Canada' (1999) 21(7) *Comparative Labor Law & Policy Journal* 7, 11. See also C-176/12 *Association de médiation sociale v Union locale des syndicats CGT and Others* ECLI:EU:C:2014:2 Opinion of AG Villalon, acknowledging the critique of uncertainty, but arguing that courts can develop horizontality incrementally and over time.

[9] L Wittgenstein, *Philosophical Investigations* (MacMillan, 1953) [97].

[10] Langille and Davidov, 'Beyond Employees and Independent Contractors' (n 8) 13.

ought to be noted about the width of the concept. The first is that while the existence of an institution is a necessary condition for horizontal rights application, it is not a sufficient one. It still needs to be shown that the (private) duty bearer exercises power over the rights holder, that the difference in power flows from their relative institutional positions, and that it enables the former to violate the rights of the latter (indeed, as we shall see, the two enquiries – the existence of the institution and the existence of structural power hierarchies – are often bound up with each other, making the threshold not quite so low as it may initially seem).

For example, in the next chapter, it shall be argued that the labour market is an institution for our purposes. It does not follow, however, that *every* constitutional right is *ipso facto* applicable between the worker and the employer. Rather, the institutional approach limits itself to a set of discrete rights and remedies, flowing from the power differential between the parties, and the horizontal application of each of these rights needs to be separately justified.

Indeed, such an approach, where the *necessary-but-not-sufficient* threshold for triggering the application of rights is a low one, is familiar to constitutional adjudication.[11] It is important to reiterate that the satisfaction of the threshold condition, ie the existence of an institution, is only a first step. The identification of power differences, the rights at issue and, of course, the question of whether remedies are justified in a specific case (taking into account the rights of the other party as well) all remain to be answered.

Secondly, concerns around the width of the concept are mitigated when we consider the role that the institutional approach will play in adjudication. As pointed out above, the institutional approach exists to complement existing law, not supplant it. The width of the concept, therefore, does not necessarily translate into width of *adjudication*, where a vast new area of human relations is brought within the scope of regulation for the first time. This will be demonstrated in the final section of this chapter and in part II.

Finally, it ought to be reiterated that the width of the concept does not mean that it lacks analytical purchase, or that it cannot serve a useful role in adjudication. Once again, this chapter and part II will be dedicated to showing how the institutional approach – with the concept of the institution as an integral element – is both theoretically sound and practically useful.

To sum up my overview of the institutional approach: an 'institution' for the purposes of the horizontal rights framework has a conglomeration of characteristics. Consequently, it might not always be possible to define and identify institutions in advance. Rather, the presence – and combination – of the characteristics discussed above will often serve as evidence that practices that initially appear to be individualised rights violations are actually embedded in an institutional relationship, and require the application of horizontal rights. Indeed,

[11] See, eg R Alexey, *A Theory of Constitutional Rights* (Oxford University Press, 2010).

as I shall argue in this chapter, the concrete resolution of both issues – the articulation of an 'institution' and the question of rights and remedies – must be context- and jurisdiction-specific. My task here is to develop the contours of the approach and illustrate its working in one specific jurisdiction.

I attempt to accomplish this in the following manner. I begin in section II with some context setting, identifying a broader legal and philosophical tradition that explores the nature of institutional power, and the relationship between questions of justice on the one hand and the role of institutional power on the other. The institutional approach, I shall show, takes this enterprise forward by drawing a conceptual connection between institutional argument and direct horizontality (section II).

I then move on to doctrine. Section III of this chapter demonstrates how, in some of the jurisdictions that we have considered in detail in chapters two and three – the USA, South Africa and Germany – judges have, at various times, articulated the beginnings, or proto-versions, of the institutional approach. The purpose of sections II and III, therefore, is to show that the ideas underlying the institutional approach have not come out of the blue (either in legal theory or in legal doctrine), but have been part of an undercurrent in judicial discourse across jurisdictions (section III).

In the heart of this chapter, I shall then consider the judicial development of the institutional approach under the Indian Constitution in some detail. The Indian Constitution has three relevant horizontal rights provisions – Article 15(2) (non-discriminatory access to shops), Article 17 (prohibition of 'untouchability') and Article 23 (prohibition of 'forced labour'). I shall look at three court cases where an allegedly rights-violating practice was at issue, but which did not appear to fall within a strict understanding of these provisions (discrimination in schools, gender-based exclusion of entry to temples and non-payment of minimum wages, respectively). However, by understanding the practices in question as both constitutive and reflective of institutionally mediated differences in power (the institutions in question being caste, patriarchy and the labour market), and by understanding the constitutional provisions as targeting precisely these institutions, the Indian Supreme Court brought them within the ambit of the horizontal rights framework. The Court's interpretation, I shall argue, is justified in the context of Indian constitutional history, where the power of economic, social and cultural institutions has long been viewed as a threat to rights, and resistance to which has been framed in the language of rights. I will end this part of the chapter by reflecting on how these decisions help us to understand the application of the institutional approach in practice (section IV).

Having grounded the institutional approach in both judicial doctrine and legal philosophy, I then move on to consider two issues: first, the ways in which the institutional approach succeeds where the alternatives discussed in chapters two and three failed, by successfully jettisoning the underlying assumptions of default verticality. The institutional approach does not depend upon a unitary idea of sovereignty. Rather, it relies upon an embedded concept of freedom, which takes into account the background socioeconomic situation of the parties. It also understands that in situations where there exist abiding and pervasive differences of institutional power between parties, they should not be treated as existing on the same 'horizontal' plane, equally responsible for shaping the contours of their relationship (section V).

Secondly, I shall address the relationship between the institutional approach and existing regimes of private law, by examining three possible interfaces between the two. The first, and most common, situation is where there exists a constitutional right that is to be applied horizontally, as well as an existing legislative or common law regime. The constitutional right, in such a situation, complements and informs the interpretation of the legislative regime, and in certain circumstances acts as a touchstone upon which the constitutionality of private law may be tested (if required). The second situation is where a private law regime that imposes obligations upon private parties is challenged by those very parties, on the basis that it curtails their (primarily autonomy-based) rights and freedoms. The institutional approach, through its horizontal rights provisions, will play a role in determining whether the legislature has successfully 'balanced' the competing rights at play in regulating a set of private relationships and practices. The final situation is where there is a legislative vacuum, or where private law simply does not exist. I shall show that in such cases, where possible, constitutional right can be enforced directly (section VI).

II. THE INSTITUTIONAL APPROACH: PHILOSOPHICAL FOUNDATIONS

The institutional approach, with its insistence that questions of rights, freedom, power and justice must be addressed through an institutional lens, has deep-rooted philosophical antecedents. For instance, in the writings of Marx – and of his interlocutors – there are long-standing arguments against viewing the relationship between capital owners and the labour force in atomistic terms, or in terms of individual acts of oppression by the former against the latter. Instead, it is crucial to understand 'the power of individuals as something they are endowed with by a certain social structure … [and how] social power becomes the private power of private persons'.[12]

These scholars have advocated, thus, for the necessity of taking into account the structural, or impersonal, 'constraints'[13] emanating from the market economy

[12] S Mau, *Mute Compulsion: A Marxist Theory of the Economic Power of Capital* (Verso, 2023) 25, quoting Marx's *Capital, Volume 1* and *The Grundrisse*. Mau's book represents the most recent – and most comprehensive – treatment of the concept of 'economic power' within the Marxian approach. See also M Heinrich, *An Introduction to the Three Volumes of Karl Marx's Capital* (Monthly Review Press, 2012) ch 3.

[13] See K Marx, 'On the Jewish Question' (1844) www.marxists.org/archive/marx/works/1844/jewish-question/; see also the analyses in EM Wood, *Democracy Against Capitalism: Renewing Historical Materialism* (Cambridge University Press, 1995) 43; I Shoikhedbrod, *Revisiting Marx's Critique of Liberalism: Rethinking Justice, Legality and Rights* (Palgrave Macmillan, 2019) 61.

and understanding that what is at issue is subordination that flows from 'institutional conditions ... ie the capital–labour relation, private property, market exchange'.[14] Exploitation, thus, is a function of 'institutional power', which flows from ownership and control over capital (which, in turn, translates to control over the labour and production process).[15] These scholars argue, therefore, that 'the nominally free exchange of labour power in the labour market [ie through the legal device of the contract] conceals a *deeper form of social coercion*' (emphasis added).[16]

It is important to note that the argument does not involve anthropomorphising artefacts such as the labour market. What it does involve is understanding that relationships between private parties are not completely defined by their formal characteristics (such as the labour contract, which both parties have entered into on formally free and equal terms). Rather, as indicated above, a complete understanding requires taking into account the different locations of the parties within institutional structures, and how that affects the nature of the relationship.[17] In other words, Marx and his interlocutors draw a distinction between the *formal* relationship between the capitalist and the labourer (which is characterised by abstract equal freedom, manifested through the device of the contract) and the *substantive* relationship between them (which cannot be understood without taking into account their relative institutional locations as members of the capitalist and labour classes, respectively).[18]

One necessary corollary of this is a theory of power that involves human action but does not 'presuppose human agency'.[19] As Søren Mau argues in some detail, an account of institutional power must necessarily depart from mainstream, 'dyadic' understandings, which limit power to 'a relation between A and B';[20] instead, on this view of power, it is understood that 'the power dyad is itself situated in the context of other social relations through which it

[14] JE Elliott, 'Social and Institutional Dimensions of Marx's Theory of Capitalism' (1979) 37 *Review of Social Economy* 261, 266; see also WC Roberts, *Marx's Inferno: The Political Theory of Capital* (Princeton University Press, 2016); J Wolff, 'Marx and Exploitation' (1999) 3 *Journal of Ethics* 105; GA Cohen, 'The Structure of Proletarian Unfreedom' (1983) 12 *Philosophy and Public Affairs* 3, 6.

[15] Elliott, 'Social and Institutional Dimensions' (n 14) 268.

[16] See K Marx, *Grundrisse* (first published 1861; M Nicolaus trans, Penguin Books, 1973); see also the analysis in JE Elliott, 'The *Grundrisse* as Social Theory: Link between Young Marx and Mature Marx' (1978) 59 *Social Science Quarterly* 239. For similar arguments paying 'attention to the roots of unfreedom in patterns of social organisation' in the English radical tradition, see S Marks, *A False Tree of Liberty: Human Rights in Radical Thought* (Oxford University Press, 2019) 240.

[17] Mau, *Mute Compulsion* (n 12).

[18] For a detailed analysis, see Shoikhedbrod, *Revisiting Marx's Critique of Liberalism* (n 13) ch 2. It is important to note, however, that this concept of institutional economic power is not reducible *only* to the relationship between the members of the capitalist and labour classes, but is more pervasive, and affects relationships *inter se* within the classes as well. In other words, institutional power is *not* reducible merely to class domination. This will become relevant in Part II of this book. For an analysis, see Mau, *Mute Compulsion* (n 12).

[19] Mau, *Mute Compulsion* (n 12) 27, quoting Steven Lukes.

[20] ibid 34.

is actually constituted as a power relationship', and that 'the very A-ness of A [in our context, this means A's location within an institution] might be at least partly the result of a power relationship'.[21] I shall come back to these ideas through the course of this chapter and the succeeding ones; for now, it is important to note that an account of power is woven into the warp and weft of the institutional approach, and is integral to it.

In recent times, the argument has been made most strongly by Iris Marion Young. In *Justice and the Politics of Difference*, Young articulates an account of justice that moves away from questions of 'distribution' and focuses instead on issues of 'domination and oppression'.[22] These concepts, she argues, cannot do without an understanding of institutional context:

> [Institutional context] includes any *structures or practices*, the rules and norms that guide them, and the language and symbols that mediate social interactions within them, in institutions of state, family, and civil society, as well as the workplace. These are relevant to judgments of justice and injustice insofar as they condition people's ability to participate in determining their actions and their ability to develop and exercise their capacities. (emphasis added)[23]

Following from this, Young defines 'domination' as consisting 'in institutional conditions that inhibit or prevent people from participating in determining their actions or the conditions of their actions'.[24] Oppression, in turn, is defined as a set of 'systematic institutional processes which prevent some people from learning and using satisfying and expansive skills in socially recognised settings',[25] whose causes 'are embedded in unquestioned norms, habits, and symbols, in the assumptions underlying institutional rules and the collective consequences of following those rules'.[26]

Young's account of justice, therefore, eschews the requirement of intentionality and of 'direct causal agency' (ie locating it within a single identifiable action).[27] So, for example, and as I shall discuss in the next section, racially restrictive covenanting is not so much about one individual declining to sell her property to another as about the leveraging of the institutional hierarchies of racism in order to deny, through ghettoisation and exclusion, one class of people the opportunity for full and flourishing participation in society. Such an example constitutes, for Young, an instance par excellence of 'structural injustice':

> Structural injustice is a kind of moral wrong distinct from the wrongful action of an *individual agent* or the repressive policies of a state. Structural injustice occurs as a

[21] ibid.
[22] IM Young, *Justice and the Politics of Difference* (Princeton University Press, 1990) 3.
[23] ibid 22.
[24] ibid 38.
[25] ibid 38.
[26] ibid 41.
[27] S Parekh, 'Getting to the Root of Gender Inequality: Structural Injustice and Political Responsibility' (2011) 26 *Hypatia* 672, 676–77.

> consequence of *many individuals and institutions acting to pursue their particular goals and interests*, for the most part within the limits of accepted rules and norms. (emphasis added)[28]

Completing the argument, Young further points out that institutions place individuals in different 'locations'. It is their relative locations that determine the range of possible actions open to them, and it is those actions that, in turn, 'reproduce' those institutions.[29] In Young's account, therefore, we have: (i) an articulation of the relevance of institutions in adjudicating questions of justice; (ii) an understanding that the manner in which formally 'private' relationships are mediated by institutions is integral to this determination; (iii) a theory of power that is depersonalised; and (iv) a two-way mutually reinforcing link between institutions on the one hand and private relationships on the other.

For the sake of completeness, however, it is important to note that Young believes that the concept of legal responsibility is too constrained to capture relationships mediated by institutional injustice (instead, she develops a broader idea of 'political responsibility'[30]). For her, therefore, it would not be easy to fit institutional relationships within the rights framework. This reflects Thomas's concern (discussed in the last chapter) about drawing a close enough link between the private rights holder and the duty bearer to justify attributing legal responsibility for the rights violation to the duty bearer. Drawing upon the work of Sandra Fredman, amongst others, I shall return to the question of how to address the question of responsibility within the institutional approach in section V of this chapter.

Building upon Young's insights, Sharon Kruse argues that philosophical accounts of freedom and non-domination that focus on differences in power will nonetheless fall short if they continue to assume that domination is a function of 'intentional decisions by discrete human beings'.[31] Like Young, Kruse advances an alternative understanding that focuses on 'patterns of social interaction that systematically thwart the agency of particular classes of persons, however unintentionally'[32] (she takes racism and sexism as examples). The argument is based on what Kruse calls the 'non-sovereign, distributed character of human agency'.[33] The use of the term 'non-sovereign' should alert us to the manner in which, at a philosophical level, this account runs counter to the assumptions of default verticality (a point that shall be explored in greater detail later in this chapter): in particular, in its refusal to locate rights or freedom-infringing

[28] IM Young, *Responsibility for Justice* (Oxford University Press, 2013) 52.
[29] ibid.
[30] ibid.
[31] SR Kruse, 'Beyond Non-Domination: Agency, Inequality and the Meaning of Freedom' (2013) 39(2) *Philosophy and Social Criticism* 187, 191.
[32] ibid 204.
[33] ibid 188.

agency within a single, central point (whether that is the figure of the sovereign or intentional and discrete individual action[34]).

Legal scholars have drawn upon this philosophical apparatus. Let us take three illustrative examples. In the feminist legal tradition, for instance, Fredman draws upon Young to note that women's 'access to goods is powerfully mediated both by the power relations within a household, and by their responsibilities for children and other dependents'[35] (the latter, of course, is itself the product of patriarchal institutions and structures). Fredman therefore argues for a gender-sensitive conceptualisation of socioeconomic rights, which moves away from questions of distribution, and addresses issues surrounding 'facilitating agency and promoting equal participation'.[36] This framing, in turn, allows Fredman to, for example, advocate for the recognition of unpaid work, and for the framing of concrete legal policies such as 'social security and pensions … [recognising] the social contribution of those who devote their time and skills to these activities … through regarding nongainful employment in the same way as gainful employment for the purposes of calculating pensions'.[37]

Importantly, this is framed as part of a broader understanding of the right to work. In other words, an institutional understanding of the right to work yields a set of concrete entitlements, such as the legal recognition of housework, implemented through pensions or social security. I shall consider similar issues in chapter seven of this book.

Similarly, in the domain of labour law, Virginia Mantouvalou argues for an understanding of the legal concept of 'exploitation' in terms that shift away from 'individual wrongdoers'[38] and focuses instead on 'the role of institutions that create structural injustice'.[39] As she points out, for example, 'when it comes to the labour market, a *system* of private property places employers in a position of power, and workers in a position of dependency' (emphasis added).[40] Within this context, she examines whether specific rules or laws – ie the legal structure – entrench or mitigate this imbalance of power.[41]

[34] Readers will note that the account of power and freedom discussed thus far also bears certain similarities with the work of Foucault, especially his critique of sovereignty and his insistence that 'Power relations are rooted in the whole network of the social'. See M Foucault, *The Will to Knowledge: The History of Sexuality I* (Penguin, 1976) 89. For reasons of space, I shall only note the existence of overlaps, and shall not discuss Foucault in depth in this book.

[35] S Fredman, 'Engendering Socio-Economic Rights' (2009) 25 *South African Journal on Human Rights* 410, 423.

[36] ibid.

[37] ibid 427.

[38] V Mantouvalou, 'Legal Construction of Structures of Exploitation' in H Collins, G Lester and V Mantouvalou (eds), *Philosophical Foundations of Labour Law* (Oxford University Press, 2018) 188, 188.

[39] ibid.

[40] V Mantouvalou, 'Welfare to Work, Structural Injustice and Human Rights' (2020) 83 *MLR* 929, 943.

[41] ibid.

While Mantouvalou's focus is on legal institutions that facilitate domination (especially in the context of labour law), her method is of broader significance: to study specific practices in order to determine their exploitative character by looking at the 'preexisting social institutions that underwrite and encourage the transaction'.[42] In similar terms, Zwolinski describes how 'identification of structural injustice [may be used] in order to determine which particular interactions are to count as instances of exploitation'.[43] It is this specific method – focusing on specific interactions or practices, but understanding and characterising them in terms of their institutional context in order to determine whether and how the rights framework is applicable – that constitutes the heart of the institutional approach.

It is not my purpose here to defend the views advanced by these scholars. My purpose is more modest: it is simply to situate the institutional approach, and the conceptual apparatus that it relies upon, within an existing tradition of legal thinking and within an established philosophical tradition more broadly. For this reason, I limit myself here to a schematic account of the thinkers discussed above, and do not go further.

The third, and final, example is perhaps the most intuitively obvious one: in scholarly literature, the concept of 'structural' and 'institutional' discrimination is now firmly established as a facet of discrimination law: it acknowledges that discrimination is not just caused by individual acts, but is the result of practices and behaviour that is embedded within institutions.[44] It is, in fact, this idea that has also found maximum purchase in judicial doctrine, to which I now turn.

III. THE JUDICIAL ANTECEDENTS OF THE INSTITUTIONAL APPROACH

I shall begin this section by returning to the judgment with which I initiated my discussion in chapter one, and which marks the origins of the 'state action' doctrine and the public/private divide in contemporary constitutionalism: the *Civil Rights Cases*. Recall that the Civil Rights Act guaranteed non-discriminatory access to inns, theatres and other public conveyances. The constitutionality of the Civil Rights Act was challenged on the grounds that the federal Congress lacked the competence to regulate interpersonal relations between private actors. In response, the government argued, inter alia, that the Act was saved by the Thirteenth Amendment to the US Constitution. The Thirteenth Amendment prohibited 'slavery' and 'involuntary servitude', and

[42] V Mantouvalou, 'Legal Construction of Structures of Exploitation (n 38) 195.

[43] M Zwolinski, 'Structural Exploitation' (2012) 29(1) *Social Philosophy & Policy* 154, 159.

[44] See, eg A Altman, 'Discrimination' *The Stanford Encyclopedia of Philosophy*, https://plato.stanford.edu/entries/discrimination/; FL Pincus, 'Discrimination Comes in Many Forms: Individual, Institutional, and Structural' (1996) 40 *American Behavioural Scientist* 186; S Fredman, 'Substantive Equality Revisited' (2016) 14 *International Journal of Constitutional Law* 712.

authorised the federal Congress to enforce this prohibition through appropriate legislation. The Civil Rights Act, so the government argued, was an example of 'appropriate legislation'.

How did the government draw the link between 'slavery' and 'involuntary servitude' on the one hand and non-discriminatory access to public facilities on the other? The answer can be found in Solicitor-General Phillips's submissions to the Supreme Court, which are summarised at the beginning of the judgment:

> Granting that by involuntary servitude, as prohibited in the Thirteenth Amendment, is intended *some institution, viz., custom*, etc., of that sort, and not primarily *mere scattered trespasses* against liberty committed by private persons, yet, considering what must be the *social tendency* in at least large parts of the country, it is 'appropriate legislation' against such an institution to forbid any action *by private persons* which in the *light of our history may reasonably be apprehended* to tend, on account of its being incidental to quasi-public occupations, *to create an institution*. (emphasis added)[45]

I want to pay close attention to the highlighted words. First, Solicitor-General Phillips argued that the term 'involuntary servitude' referred to an 'institution'. The word 'institution' was defined in both positive and negative terms. In positive terms, the Solicitor-General drew an analogy with 'custom', which the dictionary defines as a 'a mode of behaviour … which is widely practised and accepted … in a particular society'.[46] In negative terms, he distinguished it from 'mere scattered trespasses' – that is, individual acts that could not accurately be classified as components of 'a traditional and widely accepted way of behaving'. Now, how was one to tell the difference? The Solicitor-General advocated for a historical examination that would ask whether these private acts constituted a 'social tendency' towards creating an institution. In other words, historical context and the social backdrop were the glue that bound together a collection of seemingly 'individual private acts' and gave them their 'institutional' power.

This proto-articulation of an 'institution' tracks the tentative definition that I offered at the beginning of this chapter. 'Involuntary servitude', as understood by the Solicitor-General, was constituted by a pattern of behaviour, but was not simply reducible to an aggregate of individual, convergent practices (what the Solicitor-General referred to as a 'social tendency'). Its effect was to construct a hierarchy of power between white and Black people, which put the former in a position to violate the rights of the latter. And importantly, the pervasive character of the institution made individual exit unviable.

However, we saw in chapter one that the majority of the Supreme Court did not take up the Solicitor-General's invitation to interpret the Thirteenth Amendment in this way. As Nerken points out, through its distinction between the 'invasion' and the 'impairment' of rights, the majority in fact 'atomize[d]

[45] *The Civil Rights Cases* 109 US 3 (1883) 7.
[46] *Oxford English Dictionary* (Oxford University Press, 2020) www.oed.com/.

the problem of Black civil rights, portraying violations as discrete, isolated, individual transactions, the outcome of which was determined by the individual circumstances and initiative of the Black participant in each transaction'.[47] In other words, the majority believed that civil rights violations were, indeed, nothing more than 'mere scattered trespasses … committed by private persons'.

Justice Harlan disagreed. And he, at least partly, adopted the institution-focused language of the Solicitor-General, noting that the '*institution* [ie of slavery and involuntary servitude] rested wholly upon the inferiority, as a race, of those held in bondage' (emphasis added).[48] The denial of equal civil rights was an integral manifestation of institutional inferiority, a component of the 'practical subjection'[49] of one class by another.

While advancing a proto-version of the institutional approach, however, the pull of the public/private binary was too strong to be resisted entirely. Solicitor-General Phillips found himself slipping back into it at the very end, making reference to 'quasi public occupations';[50] Justice Harlan did as well, by noting that innkeepers were, in a sense, 'public servants'.[51] Even in dissent, therefore, the institutional approach remained only partially imagined, at best.

The language of the institutional approach, nonetheless, would reappear on more than one occasion in subsequent decades, often as an undercurrent to the dominant reasoning in a judicial opinion. In *Shelley v Kraemer*, which was discussed in chapter two, the Supreme Court refused to enforce a racially restrictive covenant on the basis that judicial enforcement would amount to impermissible 'state action' in contravention of the Fourteenth Amendment. At the very beginning of its judgment, however, the Court observed that what was at issue was 'the particular *patterns of discrimination*' (emphasis added) caused by 'terms of agreement among private individuals'.[52] Similarly, in *Reitman v Mulkey*, where the Supreme Court struck down a Californian constitutional amendment that would have authorised racially restrictive covenants, Justice Douglas observed that the case presented a 'zoning problem'.[53] Both the *Shelley* majority and Justice Douglas viewed racially restrictive covenants not as an aggregate or a collection of private decisions by property owners and buyers, but as components of a 'pattern' of discriminatory conduct (constitutive of the institution of racism) that, essentially, was aimed at reshaping or maintaining spatial demographics.

[47] I Nerken, 'A New Deal for the Protection of Fourteenth Amendment Rights: Challenging the Doctrinal Bases of the Civil Rights Cases and State Action Theory' (1977) 12 *Harvard Civil Rights-Civil Liberties Law Review* 297, 321.

[48] *The Civil Rights Cases* (n 45) 36 (Harlan J, dissenting).

[49] ibid 62 (Harlan J, dissenting).

[50] ibid 7.

[51] ibid (n 45) 41 (Harlan J, dissenting).

[52] *Shelley v Kraemer* 334 US 1 (1948), 13.

[53] *Reitman v Mulkey* 387 US 369 (1967), 385 (Douglas J, concurring).

A year after that, in *Jones v Alfred H Mayer*, a majority of the Supreme Court came close to revisiting the Solicitor-General's arguments in the *Civil Rights Cases* and accepting them. The Court held that a federal law that mandated equal property rights across the USA, regardless of race, was directly applicable to private parties by virtue of the Thirteenth Amendment. A majority of the Court observed that the law reflected a legislative understanding that property rights 'might be infringed not only by "state or local law" but also by "*custom, or prejudice*"' (emphasis added).[54] The Court referred to the 'imposing body of evidence pointing to the mistreatment of Negroes (*sic*) by *private individuals and unofficial groups*, mistreatment unrelated to any hostile state legislation' (emphasis added),[55] but which had the sanction of 'local prejudice'.[56] It was the operation of this systematic prejudice that brought the 'private acts' in question within the ambit of the Thirteenth Amendment:

> Just as the Black Codes, enacted after the Civil War to restrict the free exercise of those rights, were substitutes for the slave system, so the exclusion of Negroes from white communities became a substitute for the Black Codes. *And when racial discrimination herds men into ghettos and makes their ability to buy property turn on the color of their skin, then it too is a relic of slavery.* (emphasis added)[57]

This judicial undercurrent continues to surface, on occasion, in contemporary US Supreme Court jurisprudence. In 2015, for example, a narrowly divided Supreme Court held that disparate impact claims were cognisable under the Fair Housing Act.[58] Disparate impact claims focus on the consequences or results of allegedly discriminatory acts, rather than on the intention or motives of allegedly discriminatory actors. The structure of disparate impact analysis, it should be obvious, bears a family resemblance to the institutional approach, as it acknowledges that discrimination can arise out of the impact of practices and patterns of behaviour that cannot be reduced to individual transactions by malicious actors.[59] This is evident in the judgment of the Court: while the question raised was one of statutory interpretation, and therefore did not involve issues of horizontality, in its examination of the historical context leading up to the enactment of the Fair Housing Act, the Court had this to say:

> [In the mid-twentieth century] various practices were followed, sometimes *with governmental support*, to encourage and maintain the separation of the races: Racially

[54] *Jones v Alfred H Mayer Co* 392 US 409 (1968) 423.

[55] ibid 427.

[56] ibid 433.

[57] ibid 441–43; Douglas J made the point more explicitly, noting that while one had ceased to be a slave to an individual, one had become 'in some sense the slave of society'. ibid 447 (Douglas J, concurring).

[58] *Texas Department of Housing and Community Affairs v Inclusive Communities Project* 576 US 519 (2015).

[59] See, eg the discussion in the Supreme Court's judgment in *Griggs v Duke Power Co* 401 US 424 (1971) and its progeny, interpreting Civil Rights Act 1964, Pub L 88-352 (Title VII).

> restrictive covenants prevented the conveyance of property to minorities; steering by real-estate agents led potential buyers to consider homes in racially homogenous areas; and discriminatory lending practices, often referred to as redlining, precluded minority families from purchasing homes in affluent areas ... By the 1960's, *these policies, practices, and prejudices* had created many predominantly black inner cities surrounded by mostly white suburbs. (emphasis added)[60]

As the italicised portions show, a majority of the Court was keenly aware that segregation and housing discrimination were caused by an agglomeration of private acts that had constituted themselves into 'policies, practices, and prejudices' – a result that justified imposing disparate impact-based non-discrimination obligations on both state and private parties (albeit, in this case, statutorily). As the majority also observed – by flagging the point about governmental support – institutions of the kind that are the subject of this discussion rarely exist without the background support of, or at least facilitation by, legal structures (a point I shall come back to later in this chapter).

Unsurprisingly, all of these judgments spoke to the most obvious fault line in US society, and the most visible, institutionally mediated social hierarchy: that of race. What these judges understood was the simple fact that white property owners and (potential) Black property buyers (for example) did not stand as two formally equal parties in a transaction that they were equally free and responsible for shaping. Rather, their social locations were defined by and through the structures and institutions of race (and racism), which shaped what actions they were effectively free to take (or not to take). It was this social institution of race, and the manner in which it constituted permanent and abiding hierarchies of power, that the Thirteenth Amendment's prohibition of 'slavery' and 'involuntary servitude' was intended to address. It was through this institutional logic that judges drew a connection between the 'private' act of (for example) entering into a racially restrictive covenant and the constitutional prohibition of slavery and involuntary servitude.

As we have also seen, however, the development of the idea was partial, at best. A similarly partial account was provided by the South African Constitutional Court in *Du Plessis v De Klerk*, as discussed in chapter three. Recall that in *Du Plessis*, ultimately, the Constitutional Court decided against the application of direct horizontality in the interim Constitution, because of the absence of a specific enabling constitutional provision (a defect that was remedied in the final Constitution, in the form of section 8(2)). However, a plurality of the judges expressed significant unease with this conclusion, precisely because a Constitution limited to the vertical application of rights remained oblivious to the fact that apartheid as a social institution would continue to linger even after it was legally dismantled.

[60] ibid 5–6 (internal citations omitted).

So, for example, in his concurring opinion, Mahomed DP warned that 'to leave individuals free to perpetuate advantages, privileges and relations, quite immune from the discipline of chapter three [of the South African Constitution], would substantially be to allow the *ethos and pathology* of racism effectively to sustain a new life' (emphasis added).[61] 'Ethos' ('the characteristic spirit of a culture … as manifested in its attitudes'[62]) and 'pathology' ('social abnormality'[63] in this context) are both terms redolent of institutions and systems, a point made explicit a little later by Mahomed DP, when he lamented the 'private and institutionalised desecration of [constitutional] values', and insisted that the Constitution was not intended to permit 'the privatisation of apartheid'.[64] The use of the words 'private' and 'institutional' in the same sentence is particularly significant as, much like Solicitor-General Phillips in the *Civil Rights Cases*, it provides the principled basis for determining which private acts ought to be subjected to constitutional scrutiny and why. The fear of 'privatising' apartheid was echoed by Ackermann J, who specifically referred to the 'freedom of contract and other devices of the common law'[65] – quintessentially private transactions (underpinned by legal structures), as discussed in chapter one – that could be (ab)used to accomplish this.

Moreover, in his dissenting opinion, Madala J expressly distinguished the circumstances that had led to the creation of the South African Constitution from the contexts that framed the US, Canadian and German charters. For Madala J, the key distinction lay in the fact that:

> The extent of the oppressive measures in South Africa was not confined to government/individual relations but equally to individual/individual relations. In its effort to create a new order, our Constitution must have been intended to address these oppressive and undemocratic *practices* at all levels … our Constitution starts at the lowest level and attempts to reach the furthest in its endeavours to restructure the *dynamics* in a previously racist society. (emphasis added)[66]

Quoting a previous opinion of Justice Froneman, Madala J went on to note that South Africa had been marked by 'a history of *structural* inequality and injustice on racial and other grounds, gradually filtering through to virtually all spheres of society'.[67] Thus, the principled case for horizontality was based upon a link between oppressive practices in all spheres (including the private sphere), reflective and constitutive of institutional inequality and injustice.

However, these initial articulations – marking the first groping towards an institutional approach – were stillborn. As we saw in chapter three, a majority

[61] *Du Plessis v De Klerk* 1996 (5) BCLR 658 (15 May 1996) [75] (Mahomed DP, concurring).
[62] *Oxford English Dictionary* (n 46).
[63] ibid (n 46).
[64] *Du Plessis v De Klerk* (n 61) [85] (Mahomed DP, concurring).
[65] ibid [110] (Ackermann J, concurring).
[66] ibid [163] (Madala J, dissenting).
[67] ibid [164] (Madala J, dissenting).

of the South African Constitutional Court decided that the implementation and balancing problems with direct horizontality (an issue that shall be addressed later in this chapter) meant that it was a question better left to Parliament, to address through legislation. While the framers of the Constitution disagreed with this conclusion by introducing a horizontal rights provision into the final text, the proto-articulation of the institutional model is yet to be taken further by the South African Court.[68]

Much like in the USA, the social institution that the Court evidently had in mind when considering the problem of horizontality was that of race (manifested in the form of slavery in the USA, and apartheid in South Africa). Analytically, the manner in which race operates as an oppressive institution is relatively straightforward to parse. There are other cases, however, where the institutions in question, and their effects, are more difficult to identify, especially in the scope of a judicial enquiry. Courts have, nonetheless, attempted to do so on occasion. The Federal Constitutional Court of Germany presents an instructive example. As we saw in chapter two, Germany follows the indirect model of horizontality, where constitutional norms 'radiate' into private law through statutory general clauses. In *Handelsvertreter*, the Court was concerned with the enforcement of a non-competition clause in a contract between an entrepreneur and a commercial agent. Among other things, the statutory provision allowed entrepreneurs to impose up to a two-year non-compete requirement in their contracts, with no compensation payable if the agent was culpable for terminating the contract.

The German Constitutional Court noted that what was at issue was a contractual term which, in theory, had been negotiated through 'the exercise of individual freedom'[69] of the contracting parties, on the basis of their 'private autonomy'[70] and their 'own responsibility'[71] (note the explicit references to the default verticality's assumptions of abstract freedom and individual responsibility). In practice, however, the Court observed that

> because private autonomy is based on the principle of self-determination, that is, it presupposes that the conditions of free self-determination actually exist … If one of the contract parties has such a *strong preponderance* that it can in fact set contractual provisions unilaterally, this will result in the other contract part being determined differently. Where there is *a lack of balance of power* between the parties involved, the means of contract law alone can not guarantee an appropriate balance of interests. (emphasis added)[72]

The Court then found that, as a class, commercial agents had 'hardly any room for negotiation. This is especially true of so-called single-company

[68] See ch 8 of this book.
[69] *BVerfGE* 81, 242, 7 January 1990 (*Handelsvertreter*).
[70] ibid.
[71] ibid.
[72] ibid.

representatives who put all their workforce in the service of a single company.'[73] Indeed, various provisions of the Civil Code themselves recognised that '*the majority* of commercial agents are economically dependent and therefore do not have sufficient bargaining power to freely negotiate their rights and obligations with the entrepreneurs' (emphasis added).[74] It was therefore the task of legislation to rebalance the skewed power relations, something that it failed to do when it incorporated a blanket exclusion of compensation for agents whose contracts were terminated *and* who were subject to a two-year non-compete requirement if the termination was caused by their own culpability. The exclusion, therefore, was struck down.

It is important to draw attention to the fact that the Court was not considering, in this case, the specific contract between the employer and the agent, who were the parties to the case. This was not a case where the 'imbalance of power' was individual, based upon the positions of the two contracting parties (a classic 'contract of adhesion'[75]). Rather, the imbalance was structural: it arose out of the relative bargaining power possessed by entrepreneurs and agents as members of economic classes, and was based upon their relative locations within the institution of the marketplace, within which they were interacting. Indeed, this fits within one of the foundational reasons for the introduction of indirect horizontality into German constitutional law, which both Lewan and Clapham describe as the recognition that individuals need to be protected not only from state power, but also from 'social power'.[76]

While *Handelsverteter* provides us with a strong proto-statement of the institutional approach beyond the institution of race, the German commitment to indirect horizontality ensures that its reach – and the reach of other judgments based on similar reasoning[77] – remains limited. For an application of the institutional approach to direct horizontality as well, we must look elsewhere. And that brings us to the Indian Constitution, the subject of the next section.

[73] ibid.

[74] ibid. For similar findings in the context of the 'platform economy' (specifically, with regard to the relationship between Uber and its drivers), which I shall examine in some detail in Part II of this book, see, eg *David Heller v Uber Technologies* 2019 ONCA 1 (Court of Appeal for Ontario); *Uber BV v Aslam* [2018] EWCA Civ 2748 (Court of Appeal of England and Wales); the discussion in S Fredman and D Du Toit, 'One Small Step Towards Decent Work: *Uber v Aslam* in the Court of Appeal' (2019) 48 *Industrial Law Journal* 260.

[75] For an interesting account of the difficulties inherent in using the adhesion doctrine to mitigate the imbalance of power between contracting parties, see F Kessler, 'The Contract of Adhesion – Some Thoughts about Freedom of Contract Role of Compulsion in Economic Transactions' (1943) 43 *Columbia Law Review* 629.

[76] KM Lewan, 'The Significance of Constitutional Rights for Private Law: Theory and Practice in West Germany' (1968) 17 *ICLQ* 571, 572; A Clapham, *Human Rights in the Private Sphere* (Oxford University Press, 1996), 182. The term is borrowed from the German labour law scholar, Nipperdey.

[77] See, eg 25 *BVerfGE* 256 (1969) (*Blinkfuer*).

IV. THE INSTITUTIONAL APPROACH IN INDIA

I will begin with the plain text of the horizontal rights provisions of the Indian Constitution. Article 15(2) stipulates that:

> No citizen shall, on grounds only of religion, race, caste, sex, place of birth or any of them, be subject to any disability, liability, restriction or condition with regard to … access to shops, public restaurants, hotels and palaces of public entertainment; or … the use of wells, tanks, bathing ghats, roads and places of public resort maintained wholly or partly out of state funds or dedicated to the use of the general public.

Article 17 provides that '"Untouchability" is abolished and its practice in any form is forbidden. The enforcement of any disability arising out of "Untouchability" shall be an offence punishable in accordance with law.' Article 23, in relevant part, states that 'Traffic in human beings and *begar* and other similar forms of forced labour are prohibited and any contravention of this provision shall be an offence punishable in accordance with law'.

The discussion so far enables a few important inferences to be drawn from the text itself. The first is that, compared to its counterparts in South Africa, Kenya and elsewhere, the Indian Constitution's horizontal rights provisions operate at a greater level of specificity. There is no omnibus clause that allows for the horizontal application of rights where appropriate, leaving the courts to work it out on a case-by-case basis. Rather, the Constitution delineates the specific domains where horizontality shall apply.

Secondly, two out of three provisions refer to social institutions. 'Untouchability' is a 'system'[78] where a class of people in society are treated as 'permanently and hereditarily impure',[79] the consequences of which include territorial segregation and social separation.[80] *Begar* is a system of (often inter-generational) debt-bondage,[81] which was (and in some cases continues to be) widespread in certain parts of India. Both Articles 17 and 23, after using the specific words 'untouchability' and '*begar*', follow up by prohibiting them in 'any' or 'similar' forms, suggesting that the core elements of the institution in question manifest themselves in different ways.

And thirdly, the terms used are specific to India, suggesting that it was the concrete historical experience of how certain social institutions operated that prompted the framers of the Constitution to subject them to the constraints of horizontal rights application.

The text, therefore, reveals certain important elements of the institutional approach: a focus on social practices (or, as in the case of Article 15(2), as we

[78] BR Ambedkar, *The Untouchables: Who Were They and Why They Became Untouchables?*, http://drbacmahad.org/Speeches/the-untouchables-who-were-they-and-why-they-became.pdf.

[79] ibid.

[80] ibid.

[81] *S Vasudevan v SD Mital* AIR 1962 Bom 53 (High Court of Bombay).

shall see, a set of acts representative of those practices); and furthermore, specific identification of those practices, based upon a concrete historical understanding of how, in that jurisdiction, they functioned in a manner so as to facilitate or enable the violation of the rights of some individuals by other private parties.

In that context, I will now turn to the judicial interpretation of these provisions, with the following caveat: Indian constitutional jurisprudence on horizontality remains underdeveloped. The three cases that I shall now discuss, therefore, are not reflective of a long-standing or developed judicial tradition, but, rather, are three specific examples of how the Indian Supreme Court has understood and articulated horizontality in its institutional sense.

A. Article 15(2) and Shops

Indian Medical Association v Union of India is a 2011 decision, delivered by a two-judge bench of the Supreme Court of India, dealing with access to educational establishments.[82] The Army College of Medical Science (ACMS) was a formally private educational institution that admitted only children of army personnel, based upon their scores in an entrance examination. The ACMS's admissions policy was challenged before the Supreme Court on numerous grounds. While the factual matrix of the case is extremely complex, the following summary is adequate for our purposes here: it was argued, inter alia, that the government exercised enough control over the ACMS's structure and functioning for it to be classified as an instrumentality of the 'state', and therefore subject to the fundamental rights chapter of the Indian Constitution. In any event, it was argued that the ACMS's admissions policy violated the existing statutory and doctrinal framework, which limited the freedom of private educational institutions to restrict admissions in this fashion.

The Court accepted the second argument, finding that the ACMS's admissions policy violated the parent statute. However, the ACMS then raised a second argument: the statute in question required private educational institutions to reserve a certain quota of seats for socially and educationally disadvantaged sections of society. This, in turn, traced its validity to Article 15(5) of the Constitution, which authorised the state to introduce legislation of this kind. The ACMS argued, however, that Article 15(5) violated the Indian Constitution's 'basic structure',[83] and therefore, as it had been introduced into the Constitution as an amendment, it was void. This argument, if accepted, would have implied that the parent statute – which prohibited the ACMS's admissions policy – was also void.

[82] *Indian Medical Association (IMA) v Union of India* (2011) 7 SCC 179.

[83] Under Indian jurisprudence, constitutional courts can invalidate constitutional amendments if they 'damage or destroy' the Constitution's 'basic structure' – a set of abstractly framed values such as democracy, the rule of law, secularism, federalism, judicial independence and so on.

The Supreme Court marshalled a range of arguments to reject the ACMS's challenge to Article 15(5) of the Constitution. One of the Court's arguments was that Article 15(5) was consistent with the vision of substantive social justice that was advanced by the Constitution through a number of its provisions, and in the field of education by Article 15(2), whose text we have seen above. Article 15(2), however, made no mention of educational institutions. How, then, did the Court bring colleges within the scope of this horizontal, anti-discrimination provision?

The Supreme Court did so by looking to the Constituent Assembly Debates – the *travaux* of the Indian Constitution. It found that during those debates, the head of the Constitution's Drafting Committee, BR Ambedkar, was specifically asked about the meaning of the word 'shops'. Ambedkar's response was that Article 15(2) used the word in a 'generic sense',[84] referring to any situation where:

> [An] owner is prepared to offer his service to anybody who is prepared to go there seeking his services ... the word 'shop' used here is not used in the limited sense of permitting entry. It is used in the larger sense of requiring the services if the terms of the service are agreed to.[85]

The Court latched upon Ambedkar's statement to hold that

> as education ... is a service that is offered for a fee ... and is offered to all those amongst the general public, who are otherwise qualified, then such educational institutions would also be subject to the discipline of clause (2) of Article 15.[86]

In doing so, the Court evidently announced a horizontal anti-discrimination of substantial scope: all service providers – in other words, participants in economic transactions – were bound not to discriminate in the provision of services on grounds of caste, race, sex, religion or place of birth.

As a concept, this is not unique: civil rights legislation that accomplishes the same goal has been enacted in many jurisdictions, and often in a sectoral manner (for example, the Fair Housing Act in the USA, discussed above). The Court's interpretation of Article 15(2) in *IMA v Union of India*, however, went two steps further: first, it located the horizontal anti-discrimination guarantee within the Constitution, and it was therefore, by implication, directly enforceable at the instance of private parties. Secondly, it did not stop at limiting the scope of the provision to 'public places' (or to 'public accommodations'[87] – the term used in other jurisdictions), which would have implicitly resuscitated the public/private divide even in the realm of horizontality. Instead, it expanded it to cover economic transactions (provision of services in exchange for consideration) in

[84] Parliament of India, *Constituent Assembly Debates: vol VII, 29 November, 1948*, https://indiankanoon.org/doc/1464664/.

[85] ibid.

[86] *IMA v Union of India* (n 82).

[87] In the USA, see, eg Civil Rights Act 1964, Title II – Public Accommodation, 42 USC 2000.

general. The provision, then, would not cover intimate, non-economic transactions, which I discussed in chapter three. However, the basis for that would not be that such interactions took place in a 'private domain', but that they did not involve the provision of services.

To understand the underlying basis of the Court's interpretation, it is important to go back to the Indian Constituent Assembly Debates. On the same day (29 November 1948) that BR Ambedkar clarified the 'generic' scope of Article 15(2), his close associate, Shri S Nagappa, framed it as a clause that would provide independence to 'the class'[88] for which it was intended. Nagappa went on to clarify that by 'independence' he meant 'social freedom'[89] (as opposed to 'political freedom', which had been secured by formal independence from British rule) and the grant of 'social rights'.[90] In the discussion that followed, members of the Constituent Assembly highlighted some of the injustices that had prompted the inclusion of the provision. These included the owners of private rest houses refusing accommodation to travellers on the basis of their caste,[91] placing village wells off-limits to members of certain castes[92] and the refusal of eating establishments to serve food on the basis of religion.[93] In Ambedkar's concluding speech – an extract from which was cited by the Supreme Court in *IMA* – he clarified that the scope of the provision extended to addressing precisely these kinds of injustices.

It is therefore clear that the framing of Article 15(2) of the Constitution was drawn from the concrete historical experience of caste-based subordination in Indian society (which sometimes spilled over into the religious domain as well) and the specific form it took: dominant castes leveraging their economic as well as social power in order to exclude non-dominant castes from equal participation in the economic and social life of the community. Indeed, the framing of Article 15(2) was the culmination of a long period of political activism that asked for legal protection from this kind of subordination.[94] In 1928, the Government of Bombay commissioned a report into the status of what were then known as the 'Depressed Classes'. In its report, the Government Committee explained the mechanism by which this manner of group subordination was accomplished:

> We have heard of numerous instances where the orthodox classes have used their economic power as a weapon against those Depressed Classes in their villages, when the latter have dared to exercise their rights, and have evicted them from their land, and stopped their employment and discontinued their remuneration as village servants. This boycott is often planned on *such an extensive scale* as to include the

[88] Parliament of India, *Constituent Assembly Debates, vol VII* (n 84).
[89] ibid.
[90] ibid.
[91] ibid.
[92] ibid.
[93] ibid.
[94] For a more detailed historical account, see G Bhatia, *The Transformative Constitution* (HarperCollins India, 2019) ch 4.

> prevention of the Depressed Classes from using the commonly used paths and the stoppage of sale of the necessaries of life by the village Bania. According to the evidence, sometimes small causes suffice for the proclamation of a social boycott against the Depressed Classes. Frequently it follows on the exercise by the Depressed Classes of their right to use the common well, but cases have been by no mean rare where a stringent boycott has been proclaimed simply because a Depressed Class man has put on the sacred thread, has bought a piece of land, has put on good clothes or ornaments, or has carried a marriage procession with a bridegroom on the horse through the public street. (emphasis added)[95]

What is striking about this passage is its observations about the manner in which the systematic and structured violation of rights was accomplished. It was accomplished without any visible state intervention, and primarily on the basis of the relative economic and social power of the two sets of private parties. This power flowed from their relative locations within the institutions and structures of caste. It is for this reason that Ambedkar labelled this phenomenon a 'social boycott', and originally proposed a detailed constitutional clause (borrowed from existing legislation in Burma) that would have outlawed it:

> A person shall be deemed to boycott another who –
>
> (a) Refuses to let or use or occupy any house or land, or to deal with, work for hire, or do business with another person, or to render to him or receive from him any service, or refuses to do any of the said things on the terms on which such things should commonly be done in the ordinary course of business, or
>
> (b) Abstains from such social, professional or business relations as he would, having regard to such existing customs in the community which are not inconsistent with any fundamental right or other rights of citizenship declared in the Constitution, ordinarily maintain with such person, or
>
> (c) In any way injures, annoys or interferes with such other person in the exercise of his lawful rights.[96]

While the final constitutional provision – Article 15(2) – did not go into the issue with this level of detail, the discussion above makes it clear that its underlying basis remained the same.

I can now use *IMA v Union of India*, and its interpretation of Article 15(2) of the Indian Constitution, to flesh out the contours of the institutional approach and address the questions that I spelt out in section I. First, *IMA*'s interpretation of Article 15(2) rested upon identifying an 'institution': this was the institution of caste, comprising a range of practices, patterns of behaviour and social norms. Secondly, an individual's relative location within the institution of caste brought with it relative economic and social power, or the lack thereof.

[95] This statement is extracted from BR Ambedkar, *What Congress and Gandhi Have Done to the Untouchables*, http://guruprasad.net/wp-content/uploads/2014/06/What-Congress-and-Gandhi-have-done-to-the-Untouchables.pdf.

[96] ibid.

Thirdly, this difference in economic and social power was utilised to enforce 'social boycotts', through which dominant castes excluded others from participation in economic and social life, through physical segregation, deprivation of the use of facilities, and exclusion from commerce and economic transactions. And finally, the remedy was a constitutional provision that, applied horizontally, would prohibit the practices that were characteristic of this institutional violation of rights. In the case of Article 15(2), this took the form of an enforceable, non-discrimination guarantee.

B. Article 17 and 'Untouchability'

In *Indian Young Lawyers Association v State of Kerala*, a constitutional challenge was mounted to the Sabarimala Temple's practice of excluding women between the ages of 10 and 50 from accessing the temple's precincts.[97] As in *IMA v Union of India*, the constitutional and statutory framework was complex, and an added layer of complexity was added by the Indian Supreme Court's intricate and complicated religious freedom jurisprudence. The exclusion of women was justified on the basis that it was part of an ancient temple custom, and that such a custom was specifically authorised by rules framed by the government under the Kerala Hindu Places of Worship (Authorisation of Entry) Act. While there was – and still remains – deep controversy over the precise basis of the custom, two arguments were advanced in court: the 'celibate' character of the temple deity and that the 10-to-50 age cap was a necessarily blunt instrument to keep out menstruating women.[98]

The petitioners argued, however, that the disputed statutory rule was ultra vires the parent enactment, which guaranteed equality of entry to all 'classes' (and that gender constituted a 'class' under the meaning of the Act). A straightforward acceptance of the petitioner's argument would have limited the case to a pure question of statutory interpretation; if the answer was 'no', however, it would require the Court to consider the question of what the Constitution had to say about the matter. This entailed reading together, and reconciling, a number of constitutional provisions, such as the freedom of religion (Article 25(1)), the rights of religious 'denominations' to manage their own affairs (Article 26(b)) and the rights to equality and non-discrimination (Articles 14 and 15).

By a 4:1 majority, the Supreme Court held that the exclusion of women was unconstitutional. The majority judges wrote separately, and employed different, albeit overlapping, reasoning. For the purpose of the institutional

[97] *Indian Young Lawyers' Association v The State of Kerala*, Writ Petition (Civ) No 373 of 2006 (Supreme Court of India). The judgment of the Court was subsequently 'reviewed' by a larger bench in highly dubious circumstances. It remains pending at the time of writing.

[98] ibid.

approach, however, I will limit myself here to one concurring opinion – that of Chandrachud J – and one specific argument in his opinion, ie the invocation of Article 17 of the Constitution.

As we have seen above, Article 17 is directly horizontally applicable, and prohibits 'untouchability'. In the concrete historical context of India, 'untouchability', as also noted above, refers to a caste-based practice of subordination, accomplished through social exclusion and permanent physical segregation, founded upon ritual ideas of purity and pollution. Now, how exactly did Chandrachud J extend this concept of 'untouchability' to cover the situation of the exclusion of women from the Sabarimala Temple? Much like the Supreme Court did in *IMA v Union of India*, he held, on the basis of the Constituent Assembly Debates, that the scope of the provision was meant to be broader than what its concrete wording indicated at first blush. It also included situations that bore a 'family resemblance' to classic, caste-based untouchability: ie situations where ritual ideas of purity and pollution were employed in service of maintaining an abiding and permanent institutional hierarchy (in this case, based on gender). This hierarchy was characterised by excluding the subordinated individuals from full and equal participation in social life, and banning their access to cultural goods.

Chandrachud J began with the text of the Constitution, noting that what was prohibited was 'untouchability' 'in any form'.[99] He then progressed to the Constituent Assembly Debates, observing that the framers deliberately refrained from specifically defining or further concretising the meaning of 'untouchability'.[100] Surveying the writings of the most prominent anti-untouchability activists in the years leading up to the framing of the Indian Constitution, Chandrachud J concluded that the purpose of Article 17 was to combat 'social norms, which subjugated individuals into stigmatized hierarchies'.[101] As the caste system, and caste-based untouchability, enforced these hierarchies through a ritual 'order of purity and pollution',[102] the prohibition under Article 17 could be extended to other situations where 'social exclusion of the worst kind has been *practiced and legitimized* on notions of purity and pollution' (emphasis added).[103]

This framing of the meaning of 'untouchability' allowed Chandrachud J to take the crucial next step, which was the heart of his argument: applying Article 17 to the exclusion of menstruating-age women from the Sabarimala Temple. Chandrachud J noted:

> The notion of 'purity and pollution' stigmatizes the menstruation of women in Indian society. In the ancient religious texts and customs, menstruating women have

[99] ibid [71] (Chandrachud J, concurring).
[100] ibid [72] (Chandrachud J, concurring).
[101] ibid [75] (Chandrachud J, concurring).
[102] ibid [76] (Chandrachud J, concurring).
[103] ibid [79] (Chandrachud J, concurring).

been considered as polluting the surroundings. Irrespective of the status of a woman, menstruation has been equated with impurity, and the idea of impurity is then used to justify their exclusion from *key social activities*. (emphasis added)[104]

These 'key social activities' included the freedom of movement, the right to education, the right to entry into places of worship and 'eventually ... access to the public sphere',[105] which together constituted 'systemic humiliation, exclusion and subjugation faced by women'.[106]

As Chandrachud J was careful to note, the argument did not turn upon the finding that women had a pre-existing constitutional *right* to enter religious spaces that was being denied to them.[107] This was not, therefore, akin to cases that have arisen in other jurisdictions where courts have deferred to the internal autonomy of religious groups.[108] Rather, what attracted the horizontal constitutional right against 'untouchability' in this case was that the invocation of menstruation in order to exclude women from equal access to social and cultural goods (in this case, access to religious spaces) was just one instance nestled in a set of practices that sought to establish and reinforce gendered social hierarchies by invoking ideas of purity and pollution. This point was driven home with particular clarity by KM Pannikar, a member of the Constituent Assembly, during the debates on 'untouchability', in a passage that was also cited by Chandrachud J in his judgment:

If somebody says that he is not going to touch me, that is not a civil right which I can enforce in a court of law. [But] there are certain complex of disabilities that arise from the *practice* of untouchability in India. (emphasis added)[109]

In line with the institutional model, the point that Pannikar and Chandrachud J were making was that the 'private acts' at issue – the refusal by one person to touch another, or the refusal to allow a class of people access into a temple – attained constitutional salience when they could be understood to be integral, or constitutive, elements of practices of social subordination that served to exclude people from basic social goods.

Like I did with *IMA v Union of India*, I will now go back and examine how Chandrachud J's interpretation of Article 17 fits within the institutional approach, whilst also illuminating it.[110] In *IMA*, the institution identified

[104] ibid [81] (Chandrachud J, concurring).
[105] ibid.
[106] ibid.
[107] ibid [82] (Chandrachud J, concurring).
[108] See, eg the discussion of the 'ministerial exception' in *Hosanna-Tabor Evangelical Lütheran Church and School v Equal Employment Opportunity Commission* 565 US 171 (2012).
[109] *Indian Young Lawyers' Association* (n 97) [72] (Chandrachud J, concurring).
[110] It is worth clarifying that this argument is not intended to dilute the seriousness of caste oppression, draw any equivalences or displace caste from the centre of Art 17. There is no doubt that the prohibition of caste-based untouchability remains at the heart of Art 17; what this argument seeks to do is to use the logic of the institutional approach to extend its application beyond its core.

by the Supreme Court was that of caste. In the *Sabarimala Case*, although Chandrachud J did not spell it out in so many words, it is clear that the institution in question was that of patriarchy: which, in its simplest terms, is defined as 'a system of society … in which men hold the power and women are largely excluded from it'.[111] Secondly, as the definition itself suggests, patriarchy mediates an abiding and pervasive difference of power, where gender determines one's location within the institution.

Like 'caste', however, 'patriarchy' in itself is too abstract a concept to be meaningful in the context of constitutional adjudication. As the third prong of the institutional approach, therefore, what was needed was an indication of the 'range of practices, patterns of behaviour, and social norms' that constituted the institution. This was provided by the text and drafting history of Article 17: at the core of Article 17 was caste-based untouchability, where ritual ideas of purity and pollution were employed to create and sustain social hierarchies. The extended understanding of Article 17 moved beyond the core of caste to encompass gender as well in cases where an analogous set of practices prevailed. Concretely speaking, the arguments employed to justify the exclusion of women from the Sabarimala Temple exemplified this set of practices in two crucial respects: in the invocation of menstruation, which was used across the board to deny women equal moral status in society, and in women's exclusion from a basic cultural good (access to a religious place of worship). This brought the specific practice of exclusion within the ambit of Article 17. Therefore, and lastly, the Court fashioned the appropriate remedy: striking down the practice as unconstitutional and issuing a declaration that women could not be denied entry to the Sabarimala Temple.

A reading of Chandrachud J's concurring opinion reveals one further point about the institutional approach. By its very nature – dealing with how institutions interact with specific relationships and acts, and how those relations and acts are shaped by institutional locations – it must move between different levels of the abstract and the concrete, and bring them into reflective equilibrium (this, incidentally, addresses the worry about the threshold for triggering the institutional approach being too low, by virtue of the breadth of 'institutions': in practice, as we can see, this is just the beginning of the enquiry).

In *IMA*, the Supreme Court was faced with the concrete and specific language of Article 15(2) ('access to shops …'). It read this language as identifying the institution of caste (at its highest level of abstraction), and proscribing a set of practices revolving around the social boycott (more concrete than simply identifying caste, but more abstract then 'access to shops'). It then used this logic to cover the example of access to schools (back to the concrete). This is shown diagrammatically in Figure 1.

[111] *Oxford English Dictionary* (n 46).

Figure 1 Reasoning with the institutional approach in *IMA vs Union of India*

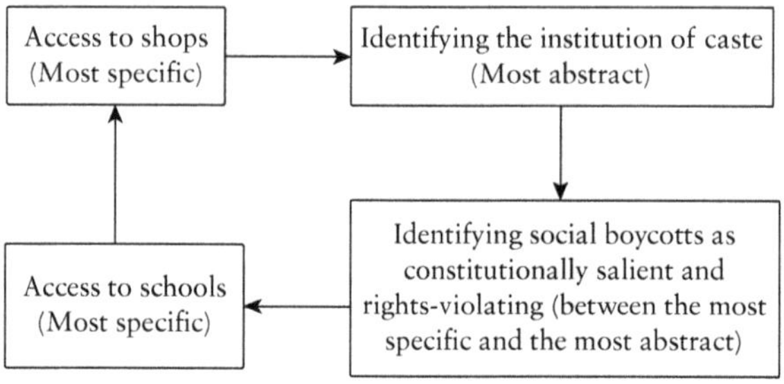

In the *Sabarimala* case, the process of reasoning was somewhat more complex (Figure 2).

Figure 2 Reasoning with the institutional approach in the *Sabarimala Case*

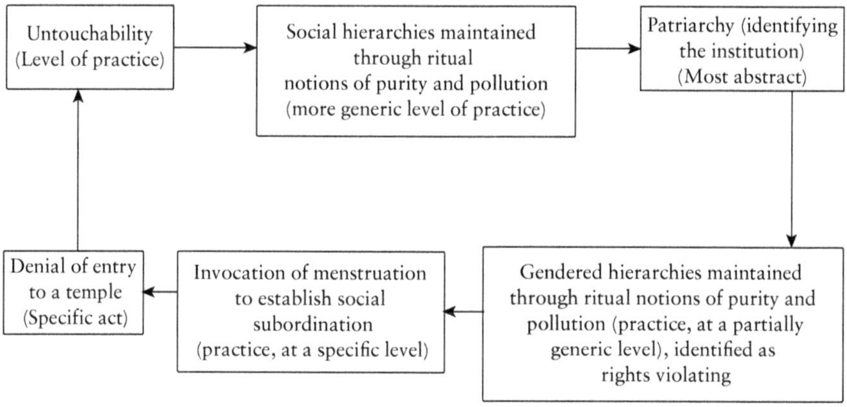

C. PUDR and 'Forced Labour'

In the context of the institutional approach towards horizontal rights, both *IMA* and *Sabarimala* were relatively easy cases. This is because, at their root, they both involved issues of discrimination: the one area of law where (as we have seen above) the role of institutions has been the subject of detailed and long-standing scrutiny, both by courts and by scholars. Furthermore, and much like race, how caste and gender operate as institutions in the manner discussed at the beginning of this chapter (convergence of practices, a unique identity and the existence of hierarchies) has been studied intensively within the context of discrimination law. In terms of both rights and remedies, therefore, these cases, despite their creative reasoning and reference to institutions, to some extent followed a known path.

Consequently, if the reach of the institutional approach was confined to the domain of discrimination law, its contribution would be limited: it would only justify taking rights-conferring legal provisions that already exist in the form of statute law in many countries, and are widely accepted as legitimate, and constitutionalising them under a direct horizontality model. This is why the third case on the list is particularly important, as it takes us away from the familiar territory of discrimination law and theory, and demonstrates the potential of the institutional approach.

PUDR v Union of India involved allegations of multiple labour law violations during the construction of a Games Village for the 1982 New Delhi Asian Games.[112] As the petition was filed to enforce fundamental rights under Part III of the Indian Constitution, the state raised a preliminary objection that it was not maintainable. It argued that the claim involved violations of specific statutory provisions, and not constitutional rights.[113] The Supreme Court rejected this argument, finding, for example, that the treatment of contract and migrant workers violated Article 21 of the Indian Constitution (the right to life and personal liberty).[114] With respect to one claim, however, there did not seem to be any applicable constitutional provision: this was the claim for payment of minimum wages. The Supreme Court, nonetheless, was not deterred. It turned to Article 23, which, as we have seen above, prohibits the practice of forced labour.

The Court began by (correctly) noting that Article 23 was among those rights in the Fundamental Rights chapter that were designed 'to protect the individual not only against the state but also against other private citizens'.[115] It then turned to the text of the provision, observing – akin to (future) observations in *IMA* and *Sabarimala* – that the scope of the provision was very wide, as it prohibited 'traffic in human beings and *begar* and *other similar forms* of forced labour' (emphasis added).[116] More specifically, the Court pointed out that 'begar' was a word of Indian origin, which referred to a compulsion to work without remuneration.[117]

Considering, then, the question of what constituted 'other similar forms' of forced labour, the Supreme Court observed that at the heart of the provision was the idea of 'exploitation': in particular, the exploitation practised by 'socially or *economically* powerful sections of the community' (emphasis added)[118] upon those not so powerful. And the vehicle of this exploitation, according to the Court, was the labour contract:

> in a country like India where there is so much poverty and unemployment and there is *no equality of bargaining power*, a contract of service may appear on its face voluntary but it may, in reality, be involuntary, because while entering into the contract,

[112] *PUDR v Union of India* (1982) 3 SCC 235.
[113] ibid [8].
[114] ibid [11].
[115] ibid [12].
[116] ibid.
[117] ibid [13].
[118] ibid.

> the employee, by reason of his *economically helpless condition*, may have been faced with Hobson's choice, either to starve or to submit to the exploitative terms dictated by the powerful employer. (emphasis added)[119]

This structural difference of bargaining power, the Court held, was the difference between labour being genuinely 'free' or 'forced':

> It is not unoften that in *capitalist society economic circumstance exert much greater pressure on an individual in driving him to a particular* course of action than physical compulsion or force of legislative provision. The word 'force' must therefore be constructed to include not only physical or legal force but also force arising *from the compulsion of economic circumstance* which leaves no choice of alternatives to a person in want and compels him to provide labour or service even though the remuneration received for it is less than the minimum wage of course, if a person provides labour or service to another against receipt of the minimum wage, it would not be possible to say that the labour or service provided by him is 'forced labour' because he gets what he is entitled under law to receive.[120]

Now, the problem of structurally unequal power between the owners of capital on the one hand and labour on the other is not a new one (see section II of this chapter). Nor is the argument that the formal freedom of contract masks a deeper, social *unfreedom*.[121] What was new, however, was that the Supreme Court elected to constitutionalise this relationship through the language of 'freedom' and 'compulsion', both of which were institutionally mediated. This explained the Court's reference to the 'compulsion of economic circumstances' in a 'capitalist society' – two phrases that together constitute a reference to the market/contract mechanism for distributing rights and liabilities. Until now, the issue had been framed in one of two dominant ways: first, as not involving a rights violation, since both parties to the contract were formally free – even though one party was too weak to make effective use of its freedom; or secondly, by carving out a set of exceptional circumstances where an individual relationship between the two parties was so evidently unequal that the formal equality between the parties could be overridden by their actual inequality.[122] In *PUDR*, however, the Court articulated a different approach: the institutional location of the parties *did* define the 'freedom' (or, in Shri Nagappa's words, the 'social freedom') that they had to set the terms of their contracts. Furthermore, this relative difference in power between the parties, in terms of their institutional location within the marketplace, was a constitutive feature of such relationships.

It is particularly important to note how the Court's analysis here directly takes issue with two of the three assumptions of default verticality that I discussed in

[119] ibid.

[120] ibid [14].

[121] For an excellent summary of the history of the debates around the meaning of freedom in the context of wage labour, see J Banaji, *Theory as History: Essays on Modes of Production and Exploitation* (Brill, 2010) ch 5.

[122] For a summary of the philosophical views, see Bhatia, *The Transformative Constitution* (n 94) ch 7.

chapter one: abstract freedom and individual responsibility. The Court's articulation of a different – *institutionally grounded* – understanding of freedom,[123] the infringement of which triggered the application of horizontal rights, demonstrates how the institutional approach departs from default verticality. I shall discuss this in greater detail in section V of this chapter.

Now, of course, it may be immediately objected that not all contractual relationships involve institutionally salient differences in power. There are many contracts between parties with equal power, and there are employment contracts in highly specialised professions where it is the employee who has the greater power to dictate the terms of the contract. How, then, does one identify that this specific contract merits the application of the rights framework? The Supreme Court's answer was: the existence of the minimum wage. In other words, if one party to the contract was unable even to negotiate the statutorily determined minimum wage, then it was evidence of an institutionally asymmetric contract, which ought to attract constitutional scrutiny. In other words, the minimum wage played two roles in the Court's analysis: one, as a heuristic device to identify situations where institutional power structures were at work; and two, as a remedy: it was the instrument of the minimum wage that ultimately mitigated that inequality of power, at least to a small extent. Consequently, the non-payment of minimum wage was a direct horizontal rights violation, because it could be presumed that in such a contract one party had violated the freedom of the other.

It may further be objected that in *PUDR* the Court effectively took a position on one side of a long-standing and controversial economic debate; and that it did so without even acknowledging that a controversy existed, let alone engaging with it in any satisfactory manner. The effect of legal intervention in the marketplace upon employment – especially through mechanisms such as wage-fixation – has been debated for two centuries, and continues to be debated today.[124] There are those who argue that the inevitable consequence of wage-fixation is a depression of employment in the long-term, thus ensuring that even on *PUDR*'s substantive understanding of 'freedom', reading an enforceable right to a minimum wage into Article 23 of the Indian Constitution would have

[123] For a deeper treatment of institutional freedom and unfreedom in the context of wage labour, see J-P Sartre, *A Critique of Dialectical Reason*, vol 1 (A Sheridan-Smith trans, New Left Books, 1976) 207. Notably, Sartre subsequently uses the phrase 'liberal atomism', which also appears in my discussion of default verticality's assumption of individual responsibility.

[124] See, eg the debates around the Speenhamland System, discussed in K Polanyi, C Thomasberger and M Cangiani (eds), *Economy and Society: Selected Writings* (Polity Press, 2018). For a summary of what different economic theories say, see H Herr, M Kazandziska and S Mahnkopf-Praprotnik, 'The Theoretical Debate about Minimum Wages' (International Labour Organisation) Global Labour University Working Paper No 6, www.econstor.eu/bitstream/10419/96384/1/glu-wp_no-6.pdf. For recent empirical work on the issue showing that (i) firms are price-setters and (ii) a minimum wage has no appreciable negative impact on employment, see B Zipperer, 'Turnover, Prices, and Reallocation: Why Minimum Wages Raise the Incomes of Low-Wage Workers' (2022) 3(1) *Journal of Law and Political Economy* 160.

the long-term effect of decreasing freedom rather than increasing it (by erasing jobs). This distinction between 'static' and 'dynamic' efficiency is familiar across multiple legal domains (such as that of intellectual property). Advocates of rights-based approaches have had to contend with the objection that the (relatively) unregulated market – as opposed to enforceable obligations upon market actors – is the most efficient, long-term guarantor of rights. How, then, could *PUDR* apply the institutional approach to the market and to the labour contract in such a facile manner?

A close reading of *PUDR* reveals, however, that the Supreme Court believed that this decision had already been made in the Constitution itself. In particular, the Court pointed to Part IV of the Indian Constitution, titled the Directive Principles of State Policy (the DPSPs). The DPSPs are not directly enforceable in court, but are 'fundamental to the governance'[125] of the country and have been held, over time, to act as interpretive aids to determining the content of enforceable fundamental rights. And the DPSPs include a host of social-democratic labour rights that envisage intervention in the marketplace based upon the same underlying principles as the institutional approach. Thus, even though those labour rights themselves are not enforceable, they are meant to inform the interpretation of the rights that are – one of which is the right against forced labour under Article 23. Indeed, provisions against the concentration of economic wealth and the means of production, for a living wage and for industrial democracy (for example) all signal recognition that imbalances of power within the institution of the market are constitutionally salient in the Indian context. And it was these provisions that the Court used to inform its argument about the institutionally determined meaning of the word 'forced' in 'forced labour' (and therefore, by extension, the meaning of 'freedom').

The Court's view was buttressed, once again, by the framing debates. In a striking document that set out a blueprint for the fundamental rights chapter of the Constitution, BR Ambedkar made it clear that the Indian Constitution was not going to be a market-agnostic document, and that it would recognise the 'connection between individual liberty and the shape and form of the *economic structure* of society' (emphasis added).[126] More specifically, Ambedkar then noted that a market economy effectively facilitated the abdication of state power to 'private persons to *govern* others' (emphasis added)[127] (he later referred categorically to 'private employers'[128]). Consequently, discarding the structure of 'existing Constitutions',[129] which sought to limit state power constitutionally

[125] Constitution of India 1949, art 37.

[126] BR Ambedkar, 'Memorandum and Draft Articles on the Rights of States and Minorities, 24 March 1947' in B Shiva Rao (ed), *The Framing of India's Constitution: Select Documents*, vol II (Universal Law Publishing, 1968) 100.

[127] ibid.

[128] ibid 102.

[129] ibid 100.

and regulate labour relations legislatively, Ambedkar proposed instead a constitutional plan to constrain:

> more powerful individuals or to be more precise to eliminate the possibility of the more powerful having the power to impose arbitrary restraints on the less powerful by withdrawing from *the control he has over the economic life* of the people. (emphasis added)[130]

Ambedkar freely admitted that this was a new understanding of constitutional law, one that sought a deeper democratisation of both political and economic life, which would prevent the '*economic structure* [from] tak[ing] the shape given to it by those *who are in a position to mould it*' (emphasis added).[131]

Close attention to Ambedkar's words, which are strikingly similar to his closing speech in the Constituent Assembly summarising the final version of the draft Constitution,[132] reveals a nuanced articulation of the institutional approach, as applied to the market. Ambedkar identified a specific problem: the ability of private persons – private *employers* – to 'govern' others (the use of a term that so strongly suggested the individual–state relationship was not accidental[133]). This ability, or power, flowed from the employer's relative location within the (market-based) economic structure, facilitating their 'control' over economic life and the capacity to (unilaterally) 'mould' it, ie to set and change the terms and conditions of market relationships. And the remedy for this was to be constitutionally encoded. Although Ambedkar began with a far more ambitious plan for mandating state socialism within the Constitution, he, and the constitutional framers, eventually settled for enshrining this vision in the form of horizontal rights and the Directive Principles of State Policy.

A summary of the interpretive structure of *PUDR*'s approach to Article 23 is provided in Figure 3.

Figure 3 Reasoning with the institutional approach in *PUDR*

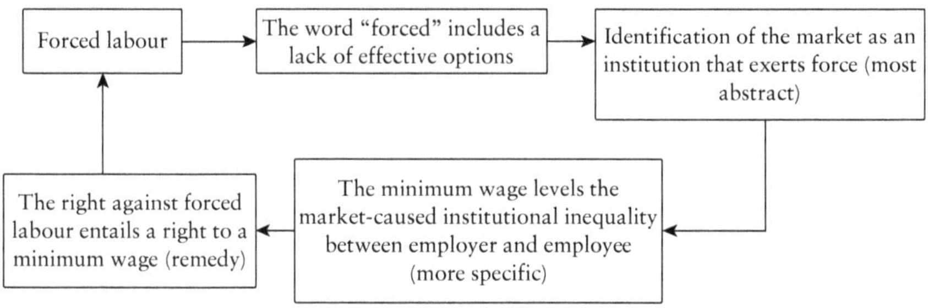

[130] ibid.

[131] ibid 101.

[132] Parliament of India, *Constituent Assembly Debates, vol XI, 25 November 1949*, https://indiankanoon.org/doc/792941/.

[133] For a more recent iteration of this, see E Anderson, *Private Government: How Employers Rule Our Lives (and Why We Don't Talk about It)* (Princeton University Press, 2017).

In short, the institution identified was that of the labour market. It was constituted by a convergence of individual practices (ie contracts between employers and employees). Individuals' relative location within the marketplace (in terms of access to and control over capital) generated abiding and pervasive differences of power. These differences were leveraged through the mechanism of the labour contract, which denied to one set of parties any effective freedom to participate in the setting of the terms and conditions of their relationship with the dominant parties. The remedy for this was a constitutionalisation of the right to a minimum wage, which was deemed to be an (admittedly imperfect) substitute for this deprivation of freedom.

The last part of the reasoning is particularly important because it demonstrates the manner in which the institutional approach travels beyond the otherwise similar reasoning process employed by the German Constitutional Court in *Handelsverter*. Both courts arrived at the conclusion that existing market conditions subordinated one class of individuals to another, at an institutional level. However, as the German Constitutional Court was constrained by the framework of indirect horizontality, it was compelled to find a remedy within the structures of contract law (in this case, setting aside the relevant contractual clause). The Indian Supreme Court, on the other hand, was employing direct horizontality, and was therefore not required to limit itself to contractual remedies. It was, instead, able to speak the language of enforceable rights (in this case, the right to a minimum wage).

There remains a final point to be noted. In all of the above cases – but particularly so in *PUDR* – there existed a background legal structure that provided the framework within which the institution existed and took its specific form. For example, in the case of *PUDR*, the institutional power exercised by employers flowed from their control over capital, which itself is enforced by property law. The point that I discussed in chapter three, therefore – that even in practices and relationship that seem purely 'private', there is always the presence of the state (even if it is through non-intervention) – remains valid. The shape and form of the institutions that I have discussed in this chapter is non-trivially influenced by the background legal framework. That framework, therefore, cannot be ignored in the analysis.

D. The Mechanics of the Institutional Approach

What do the above three examples reveal about the mechanics of the institutional approach, as it might be deployed in practice? I wish to make a few points, in light of some of the issues that were raised at the beginning of this chapter.

First, at the beginning of the chapter, for ease of understanding, I set out the institutional approach in somewhat schematic terms: the analysis began with teasing out the concept of an 'institution', then went on to discuss institutional power differences, before finally ending with the question of remedies.

This raised the question of whether the first 'step' – the identification of the 'institution' – was doing any meaningful substantive work, given the broad articulation of the concept and the correspondingly low threshold for triggering the approach.

I responded to this question on its own terms at the beginning of the chapter. Having now examined the workings of this approach, here is a further response: as we have seen, in a concrete case, the analysis does not follow the clean-cut chronology of *first* identifying an institution (the 'low' threshold) and *then* looking at power differences, *followed* by the remedy. Rather, as we have seen, there is an ongoing, reflexive process where the Court, when faced with a situation where a private party has putatively violated the rights of another, asks whether the violation is *embedded* within an institutional relationship, and within a hierarchy of power flowing from that relationship. This, in turn, is not a one-step process, but requires the Court to go back and forth between the private relationship and the institution, refining its understanding of both the relationship (and the rights violation) in question and the level of abstraction at which the institution is understood. Once the two are brought into a form of reflective equilibrium, the Court is in a position to consider the question of remedies. It is this process of reasoning that distinguishes the institutional approach from other approaches towards horizontality.

In effect, therefore, the concept of the institution plays the role of situating the structural analysis of power. In that sense, we will find that the questions of power and the existence of the institution are not always cleanly separable, even though they play distinctive roles. Take, for example, the most straightforward example of racially restrictive covenants. A court, when faced with a refusal to sell or loan property and asked to find a violation of horizontal rights, will ask whether the refusal has taken place in an institutional context (such as that of race). Identifying the institution (race) and the power differences (racial hierarchies) that together justify an application of the institutional approach will be a connected enquiry. On the other hand, the court may find that there is a power difference (stemming, for example, from the fact that one of the parties is a property owner and the other is not), but that it is not embedded within the institution of race (for example, consider a situation where an individual refuses to sell their property to a personal rival). Thus, even though the analysis does not necessarily proceed in the clean-cut chronology of *first* identifying an institution and *then* examining power differences, one can still see that the existence of the institution is not irrelevant (of course, there may be examples where there is no power difference at all, such as an owner of multiple properties seeking to add another to his collection).

It may finally be asked: does this approach ask the courts to do too much? Indeed, does it amount to an expansion of judicial power in an arena where courts have often demonstrated problematic tendencies: ie the analysis and consideration of structural power relations? There is force to this critique. While a full response is not possible within the scope of this book, I suggest that the Indian example discussed above provides some instruction: horizontality that is articulated through specific constitutional rights – and where the analysis of power is, to an extent, already present in the constitutional text – sets constraints upon the interpretive discretion that is granted to courts, and also provides valuable signposts. This is opposed to broad and open-ended horizontal rights provisions (some of which I shall consider in the concluding chapter) that leave it entirely up to the courts to determine when, where and how horizontality will apply. The Indian constitutional text, thus, might provide something of an answer to scepticism about the ability and willingness of judiciaries to deploy the institutional approach.

V. THE INSTITUTIONAL APPROACH AND THE ASSUMPTIONS OF DEFAULT VERTICALITY

In this section, I consider the relationship between the institutional approach and the assumptions underlying default verticality. By demonstrating how the institutional approach departs from these assumptions, I also aim to further clarify and refine the content of the institutional approach itself, as it emerged from the previous section.

Recall that in chapter one, I discussed how unitary sovereignty, abstract freedom and individual responsibility are the three pillars upon which default verticality rests.[134] Existing forms of horizontality, as noted in chapters two and three, are unsatisfactory at least in part because they fail to liberate themselves from these assumptions. Admittedly, a more comprehensive critique of the assumptions forms part of the accounts of Van der Walt and Thomas, which were discussed in chapter four. This section, therefore, will also engage with the similarities and differences in how the institutional approach and the approaches of Van der Walt and Thomas deal with these issues.

A. Sovereignty

The concept of unitary sovereignty plays a central role in the construction of the default vertical approach. The state's monopoly over law-making powers – and thus, over the exercise of normatively sanctioned authority and coercion – enables the default vertical approach to posit it as a uniquely significant threat to core individual interests. It thereby justifies the limited application of the rights framework to the individual–state relationship.

In the previous chapter, we saw how Jean Thomas attempts to displace sovereignty by asking what it is that is normatively significant about the relationship between the state and the individual that could be replicated in private relationships. We also saw, however, that by limiting herself to looking at the formal

[134] See ch 1 of this book.

features of the state–individual relationship, such as the existence of a monopoly, Thomas's approach ends by partially collapsing back into the state action paradigm, where the enquiry returns to asking how much, or how closely, the private rights violator appears to formally resemble the state.[135]

The institutional approach shares Thomas's intuition that for a horizontal rights framework to be successful, it must grasp what is normatively significant about the state–individual relationship and limit the application of horizontal rights to private relationships that share those normatively significant features. To begin with, there are two candidates: the ability of the rights violator to significantly infringe a core individual interest[136] (this is also Thomas's starting point) and, relatedly, a difference in power between the rights bearer and the rights violator.

The institutional approach, however, takes a specific lens to the question of power. It is not every difference of power that attracts the rights framework (for example, a difference in physical strength that allows person A to assault person B, an offence under criminal law). Rather, the institutional approach considers salient those power differences that flow from the parties' relative locations within an institution. These power differences are characterised by the fact that they are structural and depersonalised, by their entrenched and enduring nature (which therefore goes beyond the individual characteristics of the private parties) and by the fact that the comprehensive nature of the institutions under discussion makes an effective 'exit' from the unequal relationship effectively impossible (or extremely difficult).

So, for example, in the first two cases discussed in the previous section, the institutions at issue were casteism and patriarchy (manifested through discriminatory access to schools and temples respectively). Both these institutions are 'comprehensive'[137] in the sense that they are not restricted to individual or one-off relationships, voluntarily entered into by otherwise unrelated parties, but are constitutive elements of contemporary society. Indeed, they affect all relationships between individuals of different castes, or women and men, as the case may be. Something similar is at work in our classic example of racially restrictive covenants as manifestations of the institution of racism: while racism, casteism and patriarchy can be mitigated and potentially overcome through a long process of structural change (primarily in the domain of politics and society), an individual private party whose rights are violated because of an institutional difference in power can neither remedy the violation nor (feasibly) exit the institution.

[135] See ch 4 of this book.

[136] See D Barak-Erez, 'Civil Rights in the Privatized State' (1999) 28 *Anglo-American Law Review* 503; the discussion in ch 2(I)(C) of this book.

[137] I do not here use the word 'comprehensive' in the same manner as John Rawls's conception of a 'comprehensive doctrine', but draw from it to suggest that in their respective spheres, these institutions cover a totality of experience.

This, therefore, allows us to note the crucial distinction between the institutional approach on the one hand and default verticality and Thomas's approach on the other. Thomas, following default verticality, treats monopoly and no-exit as two sides of the same coin: ie people cannot exit because of the existence of a monopoly, and that is the crucial, normatively significant feature of the state–individual relationship from the perspective of the rights framework. The institutional approach recognises, however, there may be no feasible exit option even *without* any one private party exercising a monopoly. So, as we saw in the previous chapters, it is not as though the racist homeowner (or home-owning society party to the restrictive covenant) exercises a monopoly over the sale and purchase of all the homes that might be available to the buyer. Indeed, through some luck and the right contacts, some buyers may well find a non-racist home-owner in an equally 'good' neighbourhood, from their perspective.[138] However, for the institutional approach, that is not the point; what is the point is that the racially restrictive covenant both manifests and is constitutive of the institution of racism, and the permanent subordination of one group to another, from which there is no individual exit.

The radical break that the institutional approach makes with default verticality's monopoly-based idea of sovereignty is visible most sharply in the final case that I discussed: *PUDR*. This is because ideas of monopoly are discussed primarily in the economic domain. Indeed, the US cases discussed in chapter two primarily turned upon the question of whether a particular firm or corporation enjoyed a monopoly over the production and distribution of a good.[139] But in *PUDR*, it was nobody's case that an individual employer exercised a monopoly over hiring. Formally, therefore, workers were free to go elsewhere and bargain with any other employer for better wages. However, as a number of scholars – most famously, GA Cohen – have pointed out, the 'unfreedom' under a capitalistic labour market is best understood not as a constraint on individual action, but as *class* unfreedom;[140] that is to say, wage-workers in an unregulated marketplace are *collectively unfree* to bring about changes in the conditions and structure of work. This unfreedom flows from the institutional differences of power between capital owners and wage workers in a capitalist economy.[141] As Dieter Grimm notes, after specifically relying upon the language of class:

> Considered in formal terms, both parties [ie the labourer and the capitalist] were merely exercising their contractual freedom. Considered materially, one side was in

[138] Although a very common effect of restrictive covenanting – seen across countries and recognised by the US Supreme Court – is the 'private zoning' and the construction of ghettoes, that lock in communities into existing structures of advantage and disadvantage.

[139] See ch 2 of this book.

[140] Cohen, 'The Structure of Proletarian Unfreedom' (n 14).

[141] ibid. As Cohen writes elsewhere, 'each [labourer] is free only on condition that the others do not exercise their similarly conditional freedom'. GA Cohen, *History, Labour, and Freedom: Themes from Marx* (Oxford University Press, 1989) 263.

> a position to arbitrarily dictate terms, while the other could only accept these or perish. By this means, instead of a just reconciliation of interests, *private terms of rule* developed in the sphere freed from state rule, thereby enabling one part of society to exploit the other. (emphasis added)[142]

Grimm's use of the phrase 'private terms of rule' is particularly interesting, as it recalls the vocabulary of sovereignty while specifically discussing actions in the 'private sphere'. Nor is Grimm the only one to draw this specific link: as I discussed in section IV, during the drafting of the Indian Constitution, BR Ambedkar specifically referred to 'government' by private employers.[143] More recently, Elizabeth Anderson's work – the appropriately titled *Private Government* – draws an analogy between the forms and extent of control exercised by states and employers from the perspective of the individual citizen or the employee, as the case may be.[144] In other words, the concept of unitary – or monopolistic – sovereignty does not necessarily exhaust the range of features that make the individual–state relationship normatively significant from the perspective of the rights framework.

We are now in a position to understand how the institutional approach departs from default verticality's normative construction of unitary sovereignty. According to default verticality, the rights framework applies to the state–individual relationship because of (inter alia) the monopolistic powers that unitary sovereignty grants to the state. This has sent courts and scholars in multiple jurisdictions on a hunt for private parties exercising monopolies as a necessary (although not always sufficient) component of horizontal rights application. The institutional approach, on the other hand, flips the focus from the formal characteristics of the state to the rights bearer, and asks (in the words of Ira Nerken) for a 'review of the real options before the bindee'.[145] Thus, under the institutional approach, while neither of the private parties to a relationship may be a 'monopolist' (in the formal sense of the term), it is the institutional background that structures the relationship that is responsible for the absence of feasible exit options for the rights bearer. Corey Robin and Alex Gourevitch put the point pithily when they observe, in a discussion about the concept of freedom in the market, that although workers 'are free to exit *this* workplace, they are not free to exit *the* workplace'.[146] In other words, workers are essentially subjected to a monopoly without the existence of a monopolist.[147]

[142] Grimm, *Constitutionalism* (n 1) 189.

[143] Ambedkar, 'Memorandum' (n 126) 100.

[144] Anderson, *Private Government* (n 133). Anderson specifically considers – and rejects – the 'exit option' argument albeit for different reasons.

[145] Nerken, 'A New Deal' (n 47) 375; see also H Lessard, 'The Idea of the "Private": A Discussion of State Action Doctrine and Separate Sphere Ideology' (1956) 10 *Dalhousie Law Journal* 107.

[146] C Robin and A Gourevitch, 'Freedom Now' (2020) 52 *University of Chicago Law Journal* 384, 388.

[147] The origins of this argument are Marxian. In *Wage Labour and Capital*, Marx notes that 'the worker leaves the capitalist to whom he hires himself whenever he likes, and the capitalist discharges

Thus, insofar as there exists a 'monopoly' with respect to the rights bearer's vital interests, it exists at the level of the institution, and not at the level of the private relationship. That is to say, the institutional approach accommodates an impersonal, or depersonalised, understanding of power.[148] It is in this manner that it liberates itself from the default vertical assumption of unitary sovereignty (and identifiable monopolies), which, in the final instance, rests on a personalised understanding of power. This also distinguishes it from Thomas's model, and brings it closer to Van der Walt's articulation of 'différantial sovereignty' (diffused throughout the horizontal domain), albeit without committing to this account of 'social majorities and minorities'.

B. Abstract Freedom

As was the case with ideas of 'monopoly' and 'exit', the institutional approach articulates a broader conception of freedom. Grimm calls this 'constituted freedom', and defines it as freedom that 'can only be exercised within the context of social or state institutions'[149] (as opposed to freedom 'whose exercise depends solely on the individual's act of will'[150]). Similarly, as part of his theory of 'societal constitutionalism', Sciulli lays an affirmative duty upon the state to guarantee autonomy within private institutions.[151]

This idea of 'constituted freedom', as articulated by the institutional approach, has two elements. The first is that it departs from default verticality's idea of abstract freedom, where the specific contexts within which private parties operate is deemed irrelevant. The institutional approach, therefore, makes common cause with the long-standing critique of the abstract 'disembodied individual', which has been at the centre of much legal thinking. As we saw in each of the three examples discussed above, markers of ascriptive identity such as gender, caste and class directly determine whether the rights framework will apply or not. In other words, an individual's socioeconomic status, which speaks to their institutional location(s), must be taken into account in determining whether freedom has been infringed in a normatively significant way.

Secondly, the institutional approach also adopts a broader understanding of the flip side of freedom, ie coercion or compulsion. As I showed in the discussion in the previous sub-section, the coercive character of the rights-violating acts at issue is obscured if we treat these acts in isolation (for example, person

him whenever he thinks fit, as soon as he no longer gets any utility out of him, or not the anticipated utility. But the worker, whose sole source of livelihood is the sale of his labour cannot leave the whole class of purchasers, that is, the capitalist class, without renouncing his existence'. *cf* Mau, *Mute Compulsion* (n 12) 136.

[148] Mau, *Mute Compulsion* (n 12) 136.

[149] Grimm, *Constitutionalism* (n 1) 190.

[150] ibid.

[151] D Sciulli, *Theory of Societal Constitutionalism* (Cambridge University Press, 1992).

'A' exercises their right over property to refrain from letting their house to person 'B'). Consequently, the locus of the violation shifts from the actor to the institutional context. Once again, this phenomenon was initially articulated by Marx, who memorably referred to 'the dull compulsion of *economic relations*' (as opposed to 'direct force') that characterised the 'subjection of the labourer to the capitalist' (emphasis added).[152] More recently, as discussed in section II of this chapter, we find an analogy in contemporary discrimination law, which consciously eschews intentionality as a necessary feature of discrimination, focusing instead on discriminatory effect as a product of institutions, structures and norms.

C. Individual Responsibility

The manner in which the institutional approach departs from default verticality's assumption of individual responsibility can be straightforwardly understood: the institutional approach rejects the vision of private individuals facing each other as abstract wills, who are presumptively equally responsible for shaping the terms of their relationship. Instead, like Thomas and Van der Walt's models, the institutional approach denies that the private sphere is 'horizontal' in any normatively significant way, and takes seriously differences in power between private parties who face each other on formally equal terms.

The institutional approach seeks to go behind that formal equality and examine whether it masks a deeper 'social coercion', which flows from impersonal, institutional differences in power. In deciding which private relationships ought not to be classified as putatively 'horizontal', the institutional approach thus adopts a method that resembles Van der Walt's model. It looks for situations where 'disputes between individuals … have social-political significance that extends beyond the relations of those involved'.[153] In other words, the institutional approach resists what Nerken calls the 'atomisation' of private relationships.[154] Of course, where the institutional approach departs from Van der Walt's horizontal rights model is that it takes relative institutional location as the salient factor instead of the existence of social majorities and minorities.

The institutional approach's departure from the assumption of individual responsibility resembles Laurence Tribe's subjugation thesis, which I have already discussed.[155] Recall that Tribe justified the judgment of the US Supreme Court in *Shelley v Kraemer* by arguing that racially restrictive covenants constituted acts

[152] K Marx, *Capital: Volume One* (1867) www.marxists.org/archive/marx/works/1867-c1/ch28.htm.

[153] J van der Walt, *The Horizontal Effect Revolution* (DeGruyter, 2014) 22.

[154] Nerken, 'A New Deal' (n 47).

[155] See ch 3 of this book.

that were part of a broader pattern of keeping certain communities and groups in positions of subjugation. Later judgments would point out specifically – as discussed previously in this chapter – how racially restrictive covenants essentially amounted to private zoning, creating segregated neighbourhoods, where access to civic amenities was often also cleaved along racial lines. The basic insight remains the same: it is the institutionally mediated power difference between the two private parties that takes their relationship out of the formally 'horizontal' domain, where each party is deemed individually responsible for shaping the terms of the relationship, primarily through the mechanism of contract. Instead, it requires, in the words of Van der Walt, a 're-horizontalisation'[156] through the rights framework.

Tribe's argument brings us back to the difference between permanent and enduring hierarchies of power, which are mediated by structures and institutions (and which, in Tribe's account, are identified by the 'subjugation' that they cause), and individualised differences in power, which are dealt with by various domains of private law (and therefore, as already seen, tend to have a knock-on effect on the practical application of indirect horizontality). The case of physical assault has been discussed before; consider now the contract of adhesion, which authorises courts to rewrite or invalidate terms of a contract where a specific individual party is deemed to have exercised an unconscionable degree of power over another. This distinction operates as a principled limitation upon the horizontal rights framework under the institutional approach: not only must there be, as Jean Thomas points out, a valuable interest at stake (ie a right that the private duty bearer has the capacity to impact); but also, only those private relationships that are structured through an institutionally mediated difference of power are subjected to the horizontal rights framework.

A few corollaries follow. The first (which shall be explored more fully in the next section) is that the existence of an institutional background affects how competing rights between private parties are to be 'balanced' in a horizontal rights analysis. Recall that one of the criticisms of both direct and indirect horizontality has been how, in making the 'transplant' from the state as a duty bearer to a private party that is both a rights holder and a duty bearer, they ultimately require adjudicators (whether courts or legislative bodies) to perform an arbitrary 'balancing' exercise between the rights of both parties, by assigning relative weights to the competing rights at issue.[157] The institutional approach both sets a limit upon the situations in which this exercise is required to be carried out (not every case of competing rights needs to be adjudicated within a horizontal rights framework), and affects the nature of the exercise itself. To go back to Aharon Barak's example of the racist house owner, the exercise now no longer requires balancing the right to privacy with the right not to be subjected to racial

[156] Van der Walt, *The Horizontal Effect Revolution* (n 153) 7.
[157] See ch 3 of this book.

discrimination (which Barak resolves in favour of the former); rather, the very structure of the analysis is altered. Both the house owner's duty and the renter's right flow from their relative institutional locations vis-à-vis each other, in the context of their relationship.[158]

Now, this account raises the immediate question: if the private duty bearer is not herself a monopolist, and if the normatively significant factor in affixing liability is institutional location (and not the individual action itself), then how do we justify pinning duties on the private party in question? In other words, if it is the institutional location, and not the private party themself, that is 'responsible' for the rights violation, why must that private party bear the burden of the obligation in question? We have seen that Thomas attempts to address this problem by linking two private parties in a voluntary 'undertaking'. For Thomas, the more powerful private party is deemed to have (in some way) consented to assuming certain obligations to the institutionally weaker party.[159] In the previous chapter, however, this formulation was criticised as being too restrictive, and it is not one that is open to the institutional approach. In this context, it should be noted that existing human rights law has already begun to depart from the notion of strict individual responsibility discussed above. For example, Fredman points out how the Public Sector Equality Duty under section 149 of the UK Equality Act shifts the focus from which party is morally responsible for a wrong to which party is in the best position to remedy it.[160]

The institutional approach takes a similarly broad view of responsibility (noting, for example, that ultimately institutions are constituted by individual acts, even though they are not reducible to the sum of those acts), but also draws upon Fredman's insight. So, to return to the old example of the racially restrictive covenant: constitutional obligations are imposed upon the house owner in order to even out the institutional inequality that exists between him and the buyer. In other words, the obligation does not track individual moral culpability, but is designed to equalise the relationship between the parties, so that they can be genuinely said to face each other on a horizontal plane. This also frames, and limits, the remedies that can be enforced against private parties. These remedies (in this book's examples, the invalidation of restrictive covenanting, the prohibition of denial of access to services, the obligation not to restrict the entry of women into the temple and the obligation to pay the minimum wage) all closely track the reason why the horizontal rights framework is applicable to the private relationship in the first place (the institutional imbalance of power). They are themselves limited to correcting for that imbalance.

[158] ibid.

[159] See ch 4 of this book.

[160] S Fredman and D Du Toit, 'Breaking the Mold: Equality as a Proactive Duty' (2012) 60 *American Journal of Comparative Law* 265.

VI. THE INSTITUTIONAL APPROACH AND PRIVATE LAW REGIMES

As discussed in chapter one, the public/private divide, in its classical sense, limits the application of the rights framework to the relationship between individuals and the state. The set of rights that private parties possess against each other is a subject for legislation (or the common law, as the case may be). Any account of bounded direct horizontality, therefore, will necessarily create overlaps between the horizontal rights framework and existing regimes of private law. The precise nature of the overlap must then be clarified. As both Van der Walt and Thomas acknowledge, for instance, 'the practice of constitutional review … [cannot become a] higher review of all private law disputes'.[161] This is closely linked to the separation of powers problem as well: private disputes raise the kind of granular questions that, as we saw in chapter three, are believed to be best settled by legislatures rather than courts in adversarial litigation.[162] Indeed, the broader question of how constitutional rights interact with existing regimes of private law has been a vexed issue in multiple jurisdictions. It is argued, for example, that indirect horizontality evolved in Germany precisely in order to make space for constitutional rights in private relationships, while preserving the autonomy and internal coherence of private law itself.[163]

What does the institutional approach have to say about this? At the outset, it is important to note that the question becomes relevant only when the preconditions for the application of the horizontal rights (discussed above) are in existence: ie there must exist an institution in the relevant sense, and the parties to the impugned relationship must occupy different institutional locations that enable one to violate the rights of the other. This immediately shrinks the borders of possible overlap. It would, for example, leave a significant amount (although not all) of criminal law and tort law unaffected.

Where the conditions for the application of the institutional approach *are* in existence, it is important to reiterate – as I argued at the beginning of this chapter – that the role of the institutional approach is to complement private law, not to supplant it. In this context, there are three possible scenarios that arise. The first, and most frequent, scenario is where there does exist legislation (or common law). In this case, as noted above, the statutory scheme will be given analytical primacy. The institutional approach recognises, in the words of Webber and Yowell, that:

> [W]ithin a zone demarcated, on one side, by what reason requires and, on the other, by what reason prohibits, the legislature must make choices in settling which

[161] Van der Walt, *The Horizontal Effect Revolution* (n 153) 5; for a contrary perspective, see M Kumm, 'Who's Afraid of the Total Constitution: Constitutional Rights as Principles and the Constitutionalization of Private Law' (2006) 7 *German Law Journal* 341.

[162] See ch 3 of this book.

[163] OH Cherednychenko, 'Fundamental Rights and Private Law: A Relationship of Subordination or Complementarity?' (2007) 3(2) *Utrecht Law Review* 1, 5.

> relationships between persons will realise the commitment [to the set of constitutionally guaranteed rights].[164]

The role of the institutional approach in this scenario is complementary to legislation, and can take the following forms. First, the existing legal regime may be patchy, fragmented or subject to multiple possible interpretations. Consider an example that I shall discuss in greater detail in the next chapter: the application of the labour law framework to platform workers. Platform work – a recent product of the digital economy – sits uneasily between the traditional binary of 'employment' and 'contract work'. Employment status, however, is a key determinant of what rights platform workers have under labour law. Courts around the world have twisted themselves into knots attempting to fit platform work within the traditional labour law framework, and have often concluded their judgments by calling upon legislatures to amend the law in order to reflect the reality of this work. This, then, is a classic example of a situation where rights are at stake but the legislative framework may be patchy or yet to catch up. Here, the institutional approach can play an important interpretive role. As I shall show in the next chapter, for example, the institutional approach provides strong reasons for courts to hold that, in many cases, platform workers *are* employees under existing law.

Furthermore, as discussed in section IV, while it may be possible to apply an existing legal framework to the private relationship (as many courts have done in platform litigation), there may still exist a gap in terms of the remedies offered. In other words, a constitutional right to a minimum wage (derived from the institutional approach to direct horizontality) may apply to the relationship between drivers and their platforms regardless of whether 'intermediate status' under the relevant law (for example) provides for such a remedy or not. Such situations may often arise, for example, in cases where courts do set aside contracts of adhesion but are not able to go any further, as they are limited by remedies under contract law.

Secondly, it may be the case that the legislation in question does not take into account institutional differences in power when setting out a scheme of rights and remedies, or does so insufficiently. In such a scenario, institutional horizontality – expressed in the form of constitutional rights – can serve as a touchstone for adjudicating the constitutional validity of the legal framework that is in place. Notably, this is similar to the methods and processes of indirect horizontality. Recall, for example, the *Handelsverter* case, which was discussed in section III of this chapter. A non-compete clause, as part of contract legislation, was struck down as it failed to adequately take into account institutional differences in power between the bargaining parties. *Handelsverter* is a good

[164] G Webber and P Yowell, 'Introduction: Securing Human Rights through Legislation' in G Webber et al, *Legislated Rights* (Cambridge University Press, 2018) 1, 19. For a very similar statement, see *Du Plessis v De Klerk* 1996 (5) BCLR 658 (CC) (Sachs J, concurring).

example of what can broadly be described as indirect horizontality within the institutional rights framework.

It is important to note that this does not mean that indirect horizontality and the institutional approach collapse into each other. In the previous section, I discussed some of the ways in which the institutional approach differs from indirect horizontality at the conceptual level. Difference, however, need not mean antagonism: while there are circumstances (see below) where the institutional approach will apply directly, here the institutional approach can also inform the application of indirect horizontality, in a framework where a legislative scheme that settles the rights and obligations of private parties already exists. The institutional approach to horizontality is not zero-sum, seeking to displace other approaches; rather, it seeks to complement and complete our understanding of horizontality, and the manner in which it is deployed is, therefore, context-dependent.

To reiterate, the role of the institutional approach is not limited to striking down legal provisions. As pointed out above, it can play an equally significant role in interpreting private law. Consider, for example, the US Supreme Court judgment in *Texas Department of Housing and Community Affairs v Inclusive Communities Project*,[165] also discussed previously in this chapter. To recap, the question in this case involved statutory interpretation: whether disparate impact claims were cognisable under the Fair Housing Act. The US Supreme Court held that they were, and referred, at the beginning of its judgment, to the institutional character of the housing segregation ('policies, prejudices, and practices') that the Act was intended to remedy. In other words, the institutional approach necessarily entails that any discrimination law statute must recognise both direct and indirect discrimination claims. In case of ambiguity in the statutory text, it thus allows the Court to interpret it in a manner that would bring it in line with the institutional approach.

In the same context, a second possible situation arises when a private law regime exists and the private duty holder challenges it on the grounds that it impermissibly encroaches upon their constitutional rights. For example, a housing discrimination law may be challenged on the twin grounds of the right to property and the right to privacy. This would, of course, take the form of vertical litigation against the state, as it is a law that is under challenge. In chapter three, I showed how scholars such as Barak and Kumm advocated a form of proportionality analysis in order to adjudicate such cases involving clashes of private rights and to decide on the basis of the relative intensity of the rights involved. I also identified certain problems with this analysis.

The institutional approach alters the adjudicatory structure that courts may apply in cases like this. Instead of examining the case as a straightforward clash between the private rights of parties – the homebuyer (not to be

[165] *Texas Department of Housing and Community Affairs v Inclusive Communities Project* (n 58).

discriminated against) and the homeowner (property and privacy) – who are deemed to be formally equal and in the same position, a court will have to ask, instead, whether, in imposing obligations upon a private party, the impugned legislation has identified, and sought to remedy, a rights violation arising out of institutional differences in power. If that is indeed the case, then there is a strong reason to uphold the constitutional validity of the law. Naturally, this may not always be true: the remedy might be grossly disproportionate (for example, life imprisonment for a restrictive covenant), or the violation might be *de minimis*. The institutional approach, to reiterate, seeks not to entirely supplant the existing structure of adjudication in such cases, but to add a crucial additional factor to it.

The final, and most straightforward, scenario is when there is a clear 'gap', ie when the relationship between the private parties is not covered by existing law (and where, therefore, indirect horizontality cannot, by definition, apply). This was the case in both *IMA* and *PUDR*, which were discussed in section IV of this chapter. In *PUDR*, there was no minimum wage law that bound the private employer. In *IMA*, there was no civil rights law (along the lines of US Civil Rights Act) that imposed obligations of non-discrimination upon private service providers. In both cases, then, the Supreme Court was able to apply the constitutional provision to the private relationship (and, in the case of *PUDR*, fashion the relevant remedy, ie the payment of minimum wage). Another example of such gaps is the US Civil Rights Act, whose horizontal non-discrimination provisions operate only in some domains. In cases like these, the institutional approach can justify extending a legislative regime of rights protection to those excluded from it. In other words, the framework of rights and remedies already exists in legislation, and the adjudicatory process extends its ambit. Thus, even in cases where legislation does not govern the specific private relationship at issue, it does not follow that the courts will need to operate in a vacuum. Indeed, on a closer analysis, this was what happened in *PUDR*: there already existed a minimum wage legislation. It did not directly apply to the employers in question. The Supreme Court, thus, was not called upon to create a minimum wage from scratch (an enterprise that would have raised serious separation of powers issues when it came to questions such as quantification), but to simply direct that the employees in the case were covered by it. Note that there is no bright line between such cases, or in cases where the institutional approach plays an interpretive role: while the typology outlined here remains helpful, there will be cases that arguably fall into more than one category.

To sum up: we are now in a position to appreciate how the institutional approach addresses key concerns around the overlap between direct horizontality and existing private law regimes. The institutional approach is a model of bounded horizontality. Its application, in the first instance, is limited to private relationships where a rights violation flows from an institutional difference in power. Secondly, the application of direct horizontality under the institutional approach varies depending on whether and to what extent the private relationship at issue is covered under existing law. Courts will first look for an existing legal regime. Where it is present, the rights framework plays a background and complementary role, similar to (and sometimes reinforcing) indirect horizontality: it acts as a standard against which the legal structure can be measured, and interpreted or altered if the circumstances require. In this way, the institutional approach remains responsive to separation of powers-based concerns, effectively ensuring that elected bodies continue to have 'the first bite at the cherry'. Furthermore, the institutional approach plays a role in justifying the imposition of obligations upon private parties, should these obligations be challenged on traditional constitutional grounds. And lastly, it is, of course, in the absence of law that the private relationship may be subjected directly to the constitutional horizontal rights framework ('bounded direct horizontality').

Finally: this remains a theoretical overview. The best way to understand the relationship between the institutional approach to bounded horizontality and the existing regimes of private law is to examine how it might play out through the practice of adjudication. That is the task of part II of this book.

Part II

Application

PART II OF this book will consider the application of the institutional approach to certain contemporary, real-world legal problems, to test how well the concepts evolved in part I can work in practice.

Before I begin, however, the following preliminary observation is in order: the manner in which the institutional approach is deployed will depend on the nature of the constitutional system under consideration. In chapter five, I considered three case studies from India, a jurisdiction that (i) has a single written constitution, (ii) explicitly guarantees a set of concrete horizontal rights and (iii) provides for judicial review of legislation for constitutional compliance. For these reasons, the Indian example is perhaps the most straightforward illustration of how the institutional approach can be deployed in practice and the distinctive role that it can play in constitutional adjudication.

Other situations are more complex. In many constitutions, as we have seen, horizontal rights provisions are open-ended, thus placing a significantly greater burden upon courts when it comes to developing an account of horizontal rights adjudication. In the concluding chapter, I shall consider, in particular, the examples of Jamaica, South Africa and Kenya, where courts have recently been called upon to interpret their constitutions' horizontal rights provisions in cases involving significant institutional power disparities between parties. We shall see how the institutional approach can make a difference in those contexts.

The final set of situations is the most complex, and will be discussed in (a part of) the next two chapters: jurisdictions where there is no single written constitution, with a judicially enforceable bill that can serve as a hook for the institutional approach (this could also apply to constitutions which have no provisions for horizontality at all). In these circumstances, legislation necessarily plays a dominant role in articulating and concretising rights and obligations within private relationships, and consequently indirect horizontality (or various forms of it) will be the method through which a court might enforce horizontal rights. In these situations, the institutional approach will play a subordinate and complementary role.

What might this role be? In considering some of the case law around platform work and labour law in the UK (chapter six, section V) and domestic relationships in New Zealand (chapter seven, section III), I shall show that there are two kinds of roles the institutional approach can play. The first is to complement existing judicial analysis of private relationships by adding the element of institutional power differences. The second is to (potentially) fill in gaps within the existing legislative framework, to the extent that the court is empowered to do so. In this way, in such contexts, the institutional approach can play a distinctive role in adjudication.

6

Application I: Platform Work

I. INTRODUCTION

THIS CHAPTER WILL study the application of the institutional approach to one specific domain: the legal regulation of platform work. Platform work is of different types, and takes different forms.[1] For the purposes of this chapter, I adopt Fredman and Du Toit's definition: platform work is 'work which is digitally mediated, in that work and worker are brought together through the platform or digital base'.[2] For the most part, platforms serve 'a flexible workforce that cycles through a variety of part-time or precarious and temporary jobs to make ends meet'.[3] For this, as Prassl points out, platforms depend upon a 'near instant recourse to a large pool of on-demand workers'[4] – a characteristic feature of the platform economy (and, indeed, of the labour market in general[5]).

In section II of this chapter, I will lay out the reasons why platform work has been selected as a case study for the institutional model. The legal regulation of platform work ostensibly constitutes a branch of labour law (although this is denied by some platforms, which portray themselves as technology companies). However, across jurisdictions, legal frameworks to address issues around platform work are at different stages of development. In some jurisdictions, courts have articulated relatively sophisticated arguments, grounded in existing legislative arrangements that have, to an extent (but not fully), captured the reality of

[1] J Prassl, *Humans as a Service* (Oxford University Press, 2018) 8. This can also happen within the same platform. See Alex Rosenblatt's classification of Uber drivers into 'hobbyists', 'part-timers' and 'full-timers'. A Rosenblatt, *Uberland: How Algorithms are Rewriting the Rules of Work* (UC Press, 2018).

[2] S Fredman and D Du Toit, 'One Small Step Towards Decent Work: *Uber v Aslam* in the Court of Appeal' (2019) 48 *Industrial Law Journal* 260, 260; for a more granular taxonomy, see Prassl, *Humans as a Service* (n 1) 13.

[3] Rosenblatt, *Uberland* (n 1).

[4] Prassl, *Humans as a Service* (n 1) 13. For the mechanics of how this works, see R Schein, 'From Free Time to Idle Time: Time, Work-Discipline, and the Gig Economy' in P O'Connell and U Ozsu (eds), *The Research Handbook on Law and Marxism* (Edward Elgar, 2021) 400, 407: 'Uber's service model relies on fast pick-up times, which means more idling drivers. Drivers' uncompensated time waiting for a ride is essential to Uber's capacity to meet riders' expectations for quick response times.'

[5] For a discussion, see S Mau, *Mute Compulsion: A Marxist Theory of the Economic Power of Capital* (Verso, 2023) ch 6.

platform work.[6] Courts have also played an incremental role in extending these arrangements to sectors that might have been left out.[7] In other jurisdictions, however, legal frameworks are either missing or, as courts have pointed out, have large gaps and are unequipped to account for the specific features of the platform economy. The case of platform work provides us with an example, therefore, of a situation in which the application of the institutional approach can be observed over the range of contexts identified at the end of the last chapter: absence of legislation, inadequate legislation, and the interaction between legislation and the constitutional framework.

In section III, I will engage with existing arguments for constitutionalising labour and employment rights in general, as advanced by both courts and scholars. I will show that different aspects of the institutional approach – that is, a focus on institutional power differences, and the use of the vocabulary of rights to mitigate them – have been articulated by scholars such as Virginia Mantouvalou, Alan Bogg and Alex Gourevitch. I will use these arguments – and the idea of 'workplace constitutionalism', which envisages that the governance of the workplace be informed by constitutional principles – to segue into the institutional approach, and examine how it applies to the domain of labour law and the labour market.

In section IV, drawing upon and taking forward the insights of the *PUDR* judgment in chapter five, I will argue that: (i) the labour market is an 'institution', as it is comprehensive (exercising a pervasive influence over an individual's everyday life), and does not allow for an effective exit; and (ii) the ownership of capital (and the means of production) creates an institutionally mediated difference in power between employers and workers. This power difference is masked by the legal form of the contract, but enables the former to violate the rights of the latter. It therefore justifies the application of the institutional approach.

In section V, I will apply these arguments to the specific issues that arise out of platform work. The existing approach asks whether workers are 'employees', 'independent contractors' or, in some jurisdictions, 'workers'. Employment or worker status serves as a legal gateway to access a range of labour rights. Traditional tests of employment, however, ask questions such as whether a worker is bound to work only for a single party (thus replicating the flawed 'monopoly' framework discussed above), whether the worker has their own equipment, and so on. It is here that the institutional approach is useful. I shall argue that the institutional approach correctly disentangles the question of an exit option from that of a specific monopoly. Furthermore, the institutional

[6] See, eg *Uber BV v Aslam & Farrar* [2018] EWCA Civ 2748 (Court of Appeal of England and Wales).

[7] *The Independent Workers' Union of Great Britain v The Secretary of State for Works and Pensions* [2020] EWHC 3050 (Admin).

approach allows one to focus on how the difference in power between platforms and workers stems from the former's ownership and control of the 'app' and the uses to which the 'app' is put (control over entry and exit, surveillance of behaviour, control over the manner of work, a 'ratings' system). The role of the 'app' in the relationship between the platform and the worker, therefore, will also help to distinguish between situations where there is an institutionally mediated difference in power (which attracts constitutional rights) and where the 'contract' is actually between equal, autonomous parties.

Finally, in section VI, I will turn to which specific rights are applicable through the institutional approach. These will include rights at the point of entry (that is, entry into the relationship between the platform and the worker) and rights during the relationship. They will include both collective rights (such as the right to collective bargaining, drawn from the freedom of association) and individual rights (such as the right to a minimum wage, drawn from the right against forced labour), as well as rights against discrimination and rights to safe working conditions. It is in this manner that the application of the institutional approach, in concrete form, will be demonstrated.

It is important, however, to qualify the claims made on behalf of the institutional approach. It is not my case that the institutional approach requires the articulation of a detailed constitutional charter, which will set out a comprehensive labour code for dealing with platform work in the form of constitutional rights; nor do I advocate for 'a judicially created labour code'[8] based on direct application of a bill of rights. Legislation is, and will continue to be, the primary vehicle for addressing labour rights, including in the context of platform work. Indeed, the granular adjustment of rights and obligations in the context of labour law, as well as the fact that the specific contours of labour rights are subject to reasonable disagreement,[9] would make constitutional resolution of all labour law questions an undesirable outcome.

The significance of the institutional approach, however, lies in the forms of its engagement with existing labour law frameworks. These could include, for instance, declaratory judgments in cases of legislative vacuum. For example, as we saw in the last chapter, a court may declare the existence of a horizontally enforceable constitutional right to a minimum wage. Needless to say, the details of implementing the minimum wage must necessarily be laid out in legislation, with the state subsequently being found in breach of its obligations by the courts if it fails to comply. These could also include (as section VI shall show) providing a rationale for extending existing labour rights to platform work in cases of dispute, as well as providing a stronger, doctrinal basis for courts to bring platform workers within the ambit of labour rights. Here, courts can use the

[8] B Langille, 'The Freedom of Association Mess: How We Got into It and How We Can Get out of It' (2009) 54 *McGill Law Journal* 177, 180.

[9] See, eg the essays in G Webber et al, *Legislated Rights* (Cambridge University Press, 2018).

constitution, along with directly applicable horizontal constitutional rights, to fill in gaps within legislation (dealing with situations where, in Langille's words, a set of people have been 'excluded from the statutory regime that instantiates a fundamental freedom open to others'[10]). They can also use it to interpret legislation (following the procedures of indirect horizontality, as discussed in the previous chapter) so that it conforms with the constitution (indeed, as this chapter considers case law from the UK, this will be its primary focus).

The Conclusion will bring together the different strands of this chapter. In sum: questions of institutional power. and the rebalancing of power differentials have always been central to the idiom of labour law. However, this rebalancing has (primarily) taken legislative form, and been limited to the contract of employment. The utility of the institutional approach lies, first, in locating labour rights within the constitution (thus making them applicable in the absence of legislation, or leading to generative engagement with legislation that might be partial, inadequate or require further buttressing) and applying them horizontally; and secondly, in mitigating the overriding salience of the contractual configuration that determines the relationship of the parties. The institutional approach, in other words, shifts the focus from the nature of the contract towards treating workers as rights bearers, whose rights are applicable against other private parties, within the institution of the labour market. Because of the reasons discussed above, platform work provides a particularly useful terrain upon which the application of the institutional approach can be worked out in practice. This is why this chapter takes platform work, within the broader context of labour law and the labour market, as the subject of its study.

For the sake of completeness, a final caveat is necessary before I start. Workers' rights involve specific forms of state intervention in the labour market. Consequently, economic theory invariably constitutes the background within which discussions around workers' rights take place. Neoclassical economics, for example, advocates for minimal interference with the labour contract. Labour rights theories, thus, are often at odds with the claims of neoclassical economics. While that debate is important, and has been addressed elsewhere,[11] I intend to bracket it in this chapter. This is because the institutional

[10] Langille, 'The Freedom of Association Mess' (n 8) 204.

[11] For an account of what different economic theories and labour rights theories say about the legal regulation of the labour market in general and about specific rights in particular, see, eg ACL Davies, *Perspectives on Labour Law* (Cambridge University Press, 2004). See also S Deakin and F Wilkinson, 'Rights v Efficiency? The Economic Case for Transnational Labour Standards' (1994) 23 *Industrial Law Journal* 289, especially 310: 'The case for fundamental employment rights must rest, in the final analysis, on factors which lie beyond any purely economic calculus; but it is equally clear that an assessment of the economic consequences of social legislation, whether at national or transnational level, should form a part of the process of *social policy making*.' For a stronger version of the argument, see ND Zatz, 'The Minimum Wage as a Civil Rights Protection: An Alternative to Antipoverty Arguments?' (2009) 2009 *University of Chicago Law Forum* 1. For an opposite view, arguing that

approach helps to determine which horizontal rights will be applicable to a particular private relationship and when. In the context of this chapter, questions of economic theory may come in at a prior point (for example, in law reform and social policy debates over which rights should exist in the constitution, or in legislation, in the first place). Alternatively, they may come at a later point, in arguments around the overriding of certain labour rights on the basis of economic reasoning. The concern of this chapter, however, is to justify the application of existing constitutional rights horizontally to the labour market, by using the institutional approach.

Additionally, in most of the examples that I shall consider in this chapter, labour codes already exist: the institutional approach thus does not bear the burden of articulating a first-principles defence of the existence of labour law itself. Rather, the controversies are about who should be included, and how horizontality will inform the interpretation of those labour codes, where there are gaps or ambiguities.

II. WHY PLATFORM WORK?

Through the late nineteenth and twentieth centuries, it became clear to legislators and courts across jurisdictions that pure contract law was insufficient to govern the relationship between capital and labour, or to regulate the labour market.[12] Broadly, responses to this insight took two forms: labour legislation that granted employment rights on the basis of an 'employment relationship' and collective *laissez faire*. Different jurisdictions adopted a combination of these two responses, to different degrees.[13]

While scholars have cautioned against viewing the platform economy as an entirely novel form of work that has no roots in previous, atypical working relationships,[14] it is also true that platform work presents a fresh set of challenges to existing labour law frameworks. Predominantly, labour legislation framework is based upon the concept of 'employment', which, in turn, is drawn

constitutions (and constitutional rights) should abstain from wealth distribution and redistribution – an argument addressed in ch 3 of this book – see J Jowell, 'Is Equality a Constitutional Principle?' (1994) 47(2) *Current Legal Problems* 1; for a response on this point, see B Hepple, 'Four Approaches to the Modernisation of Individual Employment Rights' in R Blanpain and M Weiss (eds), *Changing Industrial Relations and Modernisation of Labour Law: Liber Amicorum in Honour of Professor Marco Biagi* (Kluwer Law International, 2003) 181, 184.

[12] See, eg K Klare, 'Judicial Deradicalization of the Wagner Act and the Origins of Modern Legal Consciousness 1937–1941' [1977–78] *Minnesota Law Review* 265.

[13] For a brief history of the trajectory of labour law in the UK, see, eg Davies, *Perspectives on Labour Law* (n 11) ch 1.

[14] J Prassl and M Risak, '*Uber, TaskRabbit, and Co:* Platforms as Employers? Rethinking the Legal Analysis of Crowdwork' (2015–16) 37 *Comparative Labor Law & Policy Journal* 619; V de Stefano, 'The Rise of the "Just-in-Time Workforce": On-Demand Work, Crowdwork, and Labor Protection in the "Gig Economy"' (2016) 37 *Comparative Labor Law & Policy Journal* 471.

from twentieth-century dominant models of work. As Fredman and Du Toit point out, these models come under strain in the case of platform work, 'where technology permits a radical dispersal of the functions of traditional employers and a multiplicity of work relationships'.[15] In other words, the 'flexibilisation' that characterises platform work – where workers can switch between different platforms, have no defined hours of work, are often asked to bring their own equipment, and so on – no longer resembles the (briefly) classic twentieth-century figure of the 'employee', working 'for a single employer; on an indefinite contract; at the employer's premises; and regularly for that employer, whether or not the firm is busy'.[16]

Thus, platform workers neither fall cleanly within the category of employees nor appear to be 'independent contractors', who are placed outside the labour legislation framework. This is reflected in judicial decisions across jurisdictions: different courts have come to different conclusions in 'misclassification' lawsuits (where platform workers approach the court arguing that they have been wrongly classified as independent contractors, and ask the court to hold that they are employees[17]). However, what unites these decisions is the often explicit acknowledgement that the court is being forced to pick between 'two square pegs' for a round hole.[18] Unsurprisingly, these decisions often end with exhortations to the legislature to create a statutory framework that will take into account the specific features of platform work.[19] In some cases, there exist

[15] Fredman and Du Toit, 'One Small Step Towards Decent Work' (n 2) 260–61; M Doherty and V Franca, 'Solving the "Gig-Saw"? Collective Rights and Platform Work' (2020) 49 *Industrial Law Journal* 352. See also Schein, 'From Free Time to Idle Time' (n 4) 403, noting that the 'fragmented, episodic, and atomised' nature of work has been more the norm than the exception in the history of capitalism.

[16] Davies, *Perspectives on Labour Law* (n 11) 76. It is also important to reiterate that while this is a constitutive feature of platform work, it is not unique to it. For similar arguments in non-platform work context – dealing with the 'segmentation' of worker rights – see H Collins, 'Independent Contractors and the Challenge of Vertical Disintegration to Employment Protection Laws' (1990) 10 *OJLS* 353. For an account of developments in Canadian labour law that attempted to respond to this changing character of work, see BA Langille and G Davidov, 'Beyond Employees and Independent Contractors: A View from Canada' (1999) 21(7) *Comparative Labor Law & Policy Journal* 7.

[17] *Douglas O'Connor v Uber Technologies* No C-13-3826 EMC, 11 March 2015 (Northern District of California); *Dynamex v The Superior Court of Los Angeles County* Ct App 2/7 B249546 (Supreme Court of California); Case C-320/16 *Uber v Bensalem*, Case (10 April 2018) (Grand Chamber of the CJEU); *M Kaseris v Rasier Pacific, VOF* [2017] FWC 6610 (Australian Fair Work Commission); *Pallage v Rasier* [2018] FWC 2579 (Australian Fair Work Commission); *Razak v Uber* CA No 16-573 (11 April 2018) (District Court for the Eastern District of Pennsylvania); *Lawson v Grubhub* Case No 15-cv-05128-JSC (8 February 2018) (District Court of the Northern District of California); *Vega v Postmates* 2018 NY Slip Op 4610 (21 June 2018) (Appellate Division of the Supreme Court of New York); *Inake v Deliveroo*, 6622665 CV EXPL 18-2673 (23 July 2018) (Court of First Instance, Amsterdam); *Uber v Aslam & Farrar* EWC (Civ) 2748 (2018).

[18] *Cotter v Lyft* 13-cv-04065-VC (11 March 2015) (District Court for the Northern District of California).

[19] For efforts to do so, see, eg Assembly Bill 5, the State of California.

'wider' statutory frameworks – such as the concept of a 'worker' in EU law or that of a 'limb B employee' in the UK – with a limited set of rights. However, there as well, as shall be seen in section VI, the interface between labour law and platform work remains controversial, and the subject of litigation. The legal regulation of platform work, therefore, provides a terrain on which the working of the institutional model can be clearly visible.

Secondly, labour law has devised different methods to protect the interests of (less powerful) workers against (more powerful) employers. As mentioned above, one dominant method, popularised under the term 'collective *laissez faire*' by scholars such as Kahn-Freund, has been to strengthen the bargaining power of bodies such as trade unions, so that the interaction between employers and trade unions can take place in a more genuinely 'horizontal' domain, where two equal contracting partners work out the terms of their relationship.[20] Collective laissez-faire was particularly characteristic of labour law in the UK in the mid-twentieth century, and was based upon a regime of immunities: that is, the process of collective bargaining (including strikes and picketing), conducted through trade unions, was immunised from common law claims that employers might make (such as the tort of inducement to breach of contract), and which could therefore legally cripple the association rights of workers ('negative law').[21] The underlying vision, therefore, was that of an autonomous norm-making framework that was buttressed by law (through the regime of immunities), but not governed by it. Rather, the primary role was to be played by the balance of collective forces that, in an ideally working system, would place employers and workers in a roughly equal position when bargaining.

However, collective laissez-faire as a stand-alone norm-generating regime, which could adequately protect the rights and interests of workers, has come under strain in recent years, with the worldwide decline of trade unions. More specifically, as scholars have pointed out, the segmented and transnational character of platform work makes this a particularly difficult solution. As Alex Wood et al argue, for example, the

> organisational form experienced by remote gig workers is a product of the confluence of technology that facilitates the *detachment of work from place* (labour platforms and their platform-based rating and ranking systems) and the power relations, especially individual marketplace bargaining power in the form of skills and reputation. (emphasis added)[22]

[20] R Dukes, *Labour Constitution: The Enduring Idea of Labour Law* (Oxford University Press, 2014).

[21] See, eg P Davies and M Freedland, *Kahn Freund's Labour and the Law*, 3rd edn (Stevens & Sons, 1983).

[22] A Wood, M Graham, V Lehdonvirta and I Hjorth, 'Good Gig, Bad Gig: Autonomy and Algorithmic Control in the Gig Economy' [2018] *Work, Employment and Society* 1, 15; see also Prassl, *Humans as a Service* (n 1) 66.

While collective organisation remains important and efforts to that end within the platform economy have been documented,[23] there is a case to be made that the alternative method – a substantive rights-based model that goes beyond protecting the bargaining process[24] – may be necessary, at the very least, to supplement the results of collective bargaining. This, it is important to stress, does not mean the removal of protection for collective bargaining, whether through immunities or otherwise. Rather, as sections V and VI will show, the institutional approach requires effective constitutional protection of collective bargaining as a horizontally applicable instantiation of the right to free association.

For these reasons, the rest of this chapter will focus on the constitutionalising of labour rights via the institutional approach, its application to the specific case of platform work and its engagement with the labour law framework.

III. CONSTITUTIONALISING LABOUR AND EMPLOYMENT RIGHTS

This section will consider existing judicial and theoretical justifications for the constitutionalisation of labour rights, in order to appropriately locate and contextualise the institutional approach. The constitutionalisation of labour and employment rights – that is, grounding labour law in 'fundamental rights that possess peremptory or constitutional force within the legal order'[25] – is not unknown to constitutional law (at least in its vertical form). The rationale for this is set out by Hugh Collins et al, who point out that the idea of human rights at work stems from the insight that

> the employment relation resembles the power relation of an authoritarian state over its citizens. If workers' rights can be viewed as fundamental or human rights, these are stringent entitlements with an increased moral and legal force. They can therefore be a countervailing legal force against an employer's power based on ownership of private property. They may also ensure that workers' essential interests are not sacrificed in the political compromises of legislation.[26]

The Canadian Supreme Court held in 2007, for instance, that the Canadian Charter's freedom of association clause explicitly protects the right to collective

[23] Doherty and Franca, 'Solving the "Gig-Saw"?' (n 15).

[24] H Collins, G Lester and V Mantouvalou, 'Introduction' in H Collins, G Lester and V Mantouvalou (eds), *Philosophical Foundations of Labour Law* (Oxford University Press, 2018).

[25] H Collins, 'Theories of Rights as Justifications for Labour Law' in G Davidov and B Langille (eds), *The Idea of Labour Law* (Oxford University Press, 2011) 138, 140.

[26] Collins et al, 'Introduction' (n 24) 9. For the most recent analysis – empirical and conceptual – of the differences in power within the workplace, see the essays in (2022) 3(1) *Journal of Law and Political Economy*.

bargaining, and prohibits the legislature from 'substantially interfering' with that right.[27] The Court reasoned that

> the right to bargain collectively with an employer enhances the human dignity, liberty and autonomy of workers by giving them the opportunity to influence the establishment of workplace rules and thereby gain some control over a major aspect of their lives, namely their work.[28]

It held that, furthermore, 'one of the fundamental achievements of collective bargaining is to palliate the historical inequality between employers and employees'.[29] The Court also relied upon US judgments interpreting the Wagner Act, where the right to collective bargaining had been termed a 'fundamental right' because of the structural imbalance of power between employers and employees.[30]

Other constitutions categorically encode labour and employment rights, while allowing for a substantial degree of interpretation at the instance of the judiciary. In Europe, these include the Constitutions of France, Greece, Italy, Portugal and Spain.[31] The South African Constitution guarantees a right to strike, and a right against unfair labour practices, available to all workers, under section 23.[32] The case of the South African Constitution is an important one because, as we saw in the previous chapter, section 8 of the Constitution extends the application of constitutional rights to private relationships *where appropriate*.[33] A combination of sections 8 and 23, therefore, creates the possibility of a set of constitutionally enforceable, horizontally applicable employment and labour rights – albeit complementary to South Africa's existing labour law regime[34] and the principle of subsidiarity developed by its courts.[35] The question of which rights will be horizontally applicable, and in what contexts, depends, of course, on the underlying theory of horizontality. It is here that the institutional model can prove useful.

27 *Health Services & Support v British Columbia* 2007 2 SCR 391 (Supreme Court of Canada). I cite the case here for the limited purpose of stating the proposition of law; for a detailed critique, and a critique of Canadian constitutional labour law jurisprudence more generally, see Langille, 'The Freedom of Expression Mess' (n 8); for a more optimistic reading, see R Adams, 'The Revolutionary Potential of *Dunmore*' (2003) 10 *Canadian Labour and Employment Law Journal* 117.

28 *Health Services & Support v British Columbia* (n 27) 439.

29 ibid 440.

30 *NLRB v Jones & Laughlin Steel Corp* 301 US 1 (1937).

31 J Fudge, 'The New Discourse of Labor Rights: From Social to Fundamental Rights' (2007) 29 *Comparative Labor Law & Policy Journal* 29.

32 Constitution of the Republic of South Africa 1996, s 23; for an extended application of this provision in the domain of labour law (albeit vertically), see *Murray v Minister of Defence* 2009 (3) SA 130 (CA) (Supreme Court of Appeal).

33 Constitution of the Republic of South Africa, s 8(2).

34 See, eg Labour Relations Act 1995; Employment Equity Act 1998; Basic Conditions of Employment Act 1997.

35 The principle of subsidiarity precludes reliance on a constitutional right where legislation exists, unless the constitutionality of the legislation is being challenged. See *South African National Defence Union v Minister of Defence* 2007 (8) BCLR 863 (CC).

The constitutionalisation of labour and employment rights exists at the international and transnational level as well. The International Labour Organisation's 1998 Declaration encodes a 'core'[36] set of primarily procedural labour standards titled 'Fundamental Principles and Rights at Work', which it enjoins member states to respect and protect.[37] Similarly, the 2000 European Charter of Fundamental Rights requires member states to guarantee collective bargaining rights, rights to fair working conditions and rights against unjust dismissal.[38] There is also a historical tradition underlying such an articulation: as Jessica Whyte notes, during the framing of the Universal Declaration of Human Rights, a majority agreed 'that a 20th century rights declaration must offer protection from the "dependence and *economic subjugation*" of a capitalist market' (emphasis added)[39] (although that did not, finally, take detailed form in the Declaration).

It is therefore evident that setting out labour and employment rights in constitutional documents – or reading such rights into constitutional documents by courts – is not new. In keeping with the default vertical approach, however, these rights are primarily directed against the state. For this reason, as mentioned above, the task remains to flesh out a theory that will justify the horizontal application of these rights, in constitutional documents.

What of theory? The institutional approach, as has been articulated in the previous chapter, focuses upon questions of power of a very specific kind (institutional power). It is therefore important to locate it within, but also to distinguish it from, other theories that have also made power central to their analysis, especially in the context of the labour market. The distinction I seek to draw here is between *structural* accounts of power (including the institutional approach) and *interpersonal* accounts of power (from which the institutional approach seeks to distinguish itself).

Examples of contemporary interpersonal theories of power include, most prominently, the republican theories expounded by Philip Pettit, Frank Lovett and other such scholars.[40] Republican scholars are particularly concerned by relationships in which one party can wield *arbitrary power* (domination) over another.[41] Republican scholars note that the context of the labour market is one in which domination is of particular concern. Importantly, however, republican theories of rights and domination continue to insist that the source of arbitrary power must be located within specific, identifiable agents (such as individual employers).

[36] RJ Adams, 'From Statutory Right to Human Right: The Evolution and Current Status of Collective Bargaining' (2008) 12 *Just Labour* 48, 53.

[37] ILO Declaration on Fundamental Principles and Rights at Work (1998) www.ilo.org/declaration/thedeclaration/textdeclaration/lang-en/index.htm.

[38] Charter of Fundamental Rights of the European Union 2000 (2000/C 364/01).

[39] J Whyte, *The Morals of the Market: Human Rights and the Rise of Neoliberalism* (Verso, 2019) 78.

[40] For a genealogy of the term, and its contemporary usage, see F Lovett, 'Republicanism', *The Stanford Encyclopedia of Philosophy*, https://plato.stanford.edu/entries/republicanism.

[41] See, eg P Pettit, *Republicanism: A Theory of Freedom and Government* (Oxford University Press, 1997).

This affects republican theories in two distinct ways: first, prominent republican theorists hold that as long as there exists a viable avenue of exit from a specific employment relationship, nothing more is required. This takes the form of the right to a threshold-level of basic income, which allows an individual to leave a specific employment relationship but not exit the labour market entirely.[42] And secondly, republican theorists hold that in a well-functioning competitive market, supplemented by a right to basic income, there is no further need for employment rights, as no individual employer can dominate workers.[43] In other words, it is their argument that 'a 'property system or distribution will not be inimical as such to freedom' to the extent that 'it is the cumulative, unintended effect of people's mutual adjustments' via free market exchange'.[44]

While republican theorists, therefore, operate with the same insight as the institutional approach – that is, conceptualising a horizontal rights framework based upon differences in power – the key distinction lies in how power is imagined. Recall how, in the previous chapter, when discussing the *PUDR* judgment, a distinction could be observed between exiting *a* workplace and exiting *the* workplace; or the possibility of being subject to a *monopoly* without being subject to a *monopolist*.[45] To deepen the point here, as Alan Bogg points out,

> it is not clear how the empowered exit mobility of workers will modify the structural constituents of domination in labour markets, such as hierarchical firm organization bureaucracy, and widespread employer control of the labour process. This may constitute a situation of what Lovett has described as 'decentralized domination', whereby workers simply enjoy a choice between dominating agents. While more competitive labour markets could improve working conditions, kindly masters are still masters.[46]

For this reason, therefore, thinkers who identify as 'labour republicans' argue that it is important to expand the definition of power to include impersonal, or structural power. As Alex Gourevitch argues:

> The labor republican view is that a form of domination arises when there is an unequal *structure of control* over productive assets. Specifically, this domination appears when this structure is so unequal that some group of owners privately

[42] R Taylor, *Exit Left: Markets and Morality in Republican Thought* (Oxford University Press, 2017).

[43] F Lovett, *General Theory of Domination and Justice* (Oxford University Press, 2010); see also the concerns voiced in Collins et al, 'Introduction' (n 24).

[44] K Breen, 'Non-Domination, Workplace Republicanism, and the Justification of Worker Voice and Control' (2017) 33 *International Journal of Comparative Labour Law & Industrial Relations* 419, 424.

[45] In these, as in so many other things, we owe the first articulation of the idea to Marx. In *Capital*, Marx notes that labour power 'cannot get free from capital, and whose enslavement to capital is only concealed by the variety of individual capitalists to whom it sells itself'. K Marx, *Capital: Volume 1* (Penguin, 1976) 763–64.

[46] A Bogg, 'Republican Non-Domination and Labour Law: New Normativity or a Trojan Horse?' (2017) 33 *International Journal of Comparative Labour Law & Industrial Relations* 391, 402; see also Klare, 'Judicial Deradicalization of the Wagner Act' (n 12).

> controls all of society's productive assets. Those who do not own are economically dependent on employers for jobs, wages, and thus their livelihoods … a reason for calling this *structural domination* is that the unfreedom of the laborer is not a product of his situation vis-à-vis a specific employer, but rather of his dependence on *some employer* or another for livelihood … that absence of alternatives is created by the distribution of control over productive assets, a distribution that is secured by legal protection of private ownership. (emphasis added)[47]

This structural argument, indeed, has not been made only by labour-republican theorists. In their introduction to the recently published volume, *Philosophical Foundations of Labour Law*, Collins et al point out that the 'asymmetry in the labour market arises in general because only one party, the employer, owns substantial property, *the means of production*, which places *structural constraints* on the freedom of the other party, the employee, to refuse offers of employment' (emphasis added).[48]

Other scholars, like Gilabert, are more direct, and call it 'the relative power that agents have by virtue of their class positions within a class system'.[49] At the heart of the argument lies the understanding that the difference in power – the 'asymmetry' – flows from existing institutions and structures, and cannot be understood without reference to the private parties' relative locations within those structures.[50]

For the purposes of the institutional approach, the next step after articulating an account of structural power as applied to the labour market is to articulate remedies to protect labour from the vagaries of such power. Importantly, there is indeed a specific version of the labour republican argument that holds that the form labour protection should take ought to include a constitutional form (titled 'workplace constitutionalism'). As Breen notes:

> Insofar as regulation provides a *constitutional framework* for enterprise government akin to the constitutional framework for political government, the regulatory approach for combating *employer domination* is vitally important from a republican perspective … it sets the acceptable terms of employment relationships, limits managerial power and discretion, provides modes of redress, allows for accountability, and backs all these up with sanctions. (emphasis added)[51]

[47] A Gourevitch, 'Labor Republicanism and the Transformation of Work' (2013) 41 *Political Theory* 591, 602. See also KS Rahman, *Democracy against Domination* (Oxford University Press, 2016).

[48] Collins et al, 'Introduction' (n 24) 5; see also Klare, 'Judicial Deradicalization of the Wagner Act' (n 12) 304, referring to 'inequalities of bargaining power arising from the unequal social distribution of property ownership'. For more contemporary assessments, see L Michel, 'The Goliath in the Room: How the False Assumption of Equal Worker–Employer Power Undercuts Workplace Protections' (2022) 3(1) *Journal of Law and Political Economy* 4.

[49] P Gilabert, 'Dignity at Work' in Collins, Lester and Mantouvalou, *Philosophical Foundations of Labour Law* (n 24) 79.

[50] Mau, *Mute Compulsion* (n 5).

[51] Breen, 'Non-Domination, Workplace Republicanism, and the Justification of Worker Voice and Control' (n 44) 434.

It should be clear that this framing of the issue – and, in particular, the understanding of power as being located not in individual acts and agency, but in structures, which is then expressed through individual acts and agency – is very close to the conceptualisation offered by the institutional approach. In other words, the institutional approach belongs to the family of theories that place structural accounts of power at the heart of their analysis of the labour market and visualise constitutional rights as (one of) the vehicles that can mitigate structural imbalances in power. Drawing upon these insights, together with the insights offered in chapter five, the next section will therefore consider the application of the institutional approach to the labour market in general. The following section will then consider its application to the specific features of platform work.

IV. THE INSTITUTIONAL MODEL AS APPLIED TO THE LABOUR MARKET

In chapter five, I discussed the Indian Supreme Court's judgment in *PUDR v Union of India*. Recall that in *PUDR*, the Court found a horizontally enforceable constitutional right to a minimum wage, which it derived from the (horizontal) right against forced labour. To do that, however, the Court had to locate an element of compulsion in the employment relationship, notwithstanding the existence of an ostensibly free contract between the parties. This the Court did by pointing to the structural features of the modern capitalist economy, which left ordinary workers with little effective choice but to accept the terms upon which they were offered employment. While the Court did not develop the theoretical argument further (stopping at this understanding of 'force'), it was pointed out in chapter five that this approach reflected the beginnings of the institutional approach.[52]

Here, I will recap and develop the argument further. The fundamental proposition is as follows: the institution of the labour market is constituted by a difference in power between capital owners and workers. The purpose of constitutionally guaranteed, horizontally applicable labour rights is to mitigate this institutional power imbalance.

The first step of the institutional approach is to identify the existence of an institution: in this case, the labour market. The labour market fulfils the indicative criteria that were outlined in chapter five. First, it is comprehensive, in the sense that it exercises a pervasive influence over individuals' daily lives. Participation in the labour market – through the wage-bargain, as Karl Klare puts it – is an essential prerequisite for survival.[53] For most individuals,

[52] For a deeper analysis of what 'compulsion' might mean in this context, see 'Who Are the Workers?' in M Van Der Linden, *Workers of the World: Essays Toward a Global Labor History* (Brill, 2011).

[53] As Marx notes, 'the free worker can … only satisfy his vital needs to the extent that he sells his labour'. *cf* Mau, *Mute Compulsion* (n 5) 132.

participation must be both continuous (spread out over years) and intensive (multiple hours a day). Indeed, because of this very pervasiveness, work through the labour market is often a gateway to 'other primary goods such as self-respect, and can be a way of developing other capacities through dialogue and social interaction'.[54] Thus, as Ellen Wood puts it:

> Material life and social reproduction in capitalism are universally mediated by the market, so that all individuals must in one way or another enter into market relations in order to gain access to the means of life; and the dictates of the capitalist market – its imperatives of competition, accumulation, profit maximization, and increasing labor productivity-regulate not only all economic transactions but social relations in general.[55]

The institutional character of the labour market is further buttressed by the absence of effective exit (a point briefly alluded to in the previous section, while discussing republican theories). In other words, while it is (on occasion) possible to exit a specific workplace,[56] it is not (or is only very rarely[57]) possible for an individual to exit the labour market itself: 'non-owners of capital can[not] afford to absent themselves from markets for their labor'.[58] Thus, as Gilabert observes,

> capitalists may not directly force or coerce workers to work, but they shape the circumstances faced by workers *so that they have no good alternative to working under capitalists*, and they fail to offer better terms at the points of hire, a better treatment at work, or support the creation of a better social environment in which workers' power increases over time. (emphasis added)[59]

Furthermore, while it is theoretically possible, on occasion, for an individual worker to 'escape' their situation by leveraging upward mobility, as GA Cohen demonstrates at some length, this freedom is dependent upon the collective compulsion that ensures that the mass of workers remain tied to their institutional location. This fits well with the discussion of exit in the previous chapter: an institution does not make exit impossible, but it is a characteristic feature that individuals cannot ordinarily exit or eschew their institutional locations.[60]

Indeed, this effective inability to exit, as indicated in the previous section, was invoked by the Canadian Supreme Court in *Health Services and Support*.

[54] Collins, 'Theories of Rights as Justifications for Labour Law' (n 25) 149.

[55] EM Wood, 'From Opportunity to Imperative: The History of the Market' [1994] *The Monthly Review* 14, 15.

[56] For an empirical analysis of how the difficulties in quitting even specific workplaces, under conditions of a reasonably competitive market, allow firms to be 'wage-setters', see S Naidu and M Carr, 'If You Don't Like Your Job, Can You Always Quit? Pervasive Monopsony Power and Freedom in the Labor Market' (2022) 3(1) *Journal of Law and Political Economy* 131.

[57] GA Cohen, 'The Structure of Proletarian Unfreedom' (1983) 12 *Philosophy and Public Affairs* 3.

[58] R Hunter, 'Critical Legal Studies and Marx's Critique: A Reappraisal' (2021) 31 *Yale Journal of Law and the Humanities* 389, 410.

[59] Gilabert, 'Dignity at Work' (n 49) 83.

[60] GA Cohen, *History, Labour, and Freedom: Themes from Marx* (Oxford University Press, 1989).

Relying, in turn, upon US case law, the Canadian Supreme Court used this reasoning to justify a constitutional right to collective bargaining.

And finally, once in the labour market, as Elizabeth Anderson explains, in general, 'employers' authority over workers … is *sweeping*, arbitrary, and unaccountable … it is a form of private government' (emphasis added).[61] Thus, as Collins points out in summarising GA Cohen's argument:

> It is possible to argue that no coherent distinction can be drawn between the fundamental institutions that must satisfy theories of justice and core institutions of civil society such as the family and *contracts of employment* that need not meet those standards. (emphasis added)[62]

The labour market thus fulfils the characteristic features of an institution: pervasiveness and the absence of a feasible exit option from the institution itself (although individuals may be able to move within the institution, ie swap employers). It equally fulfils the second condition of the institutional approach, which is a difference in power flowing from parties' institutional location. In the case of the labour market, the difference in power stems from the employers' ownership of capital (ie the means of production) and the workers' ownership (only) of labour power qua individuals.[63] This is masked by the legal mechanism of the contract, 'which presupposes that both parties are equal before law'.[64] The relative difference is explained (again) by Gilabert:

> Workers have some power as owners of their labour force. They may not be put to work without their formal consent. Capitalists in turn have power as owners and controllers of the means of production … on the other hand, both workers and capitalists can form associations to increase their relative power. In the case of workers, the generation of associational power is very important given *that their structural power as individuals* is comparatively weak. (emphasis added)[65]

It is important to note that this difference in power exists both at the point of entry into the relationship and in the content of the relationship itself. The institutional approach thus provides the basis for collective rights (such as the right to collective bargaining), which aim to mitigate the power imbalance at the point of entry. As this is impossible to ever fully address, however, the institutional

[61] E Anderson, *Private Government: How Employers Rule Our Lives (and Why We Don't Talk about It)* (Princeton University Press, 2017) 105–06. However, note that Anderson's model of the workplace has come under sustained criticism. For an assessment, see C Cetty, 'Talking about *Private Government*: A Review of the Economic Claims Made to Rebut Anderson's Analysis' (2022) 3(1) *Journal of Law and Political Economy* 28.

[62] H Collins, 'Is the Contract of Employment Illiberal?' in Collins, Lester and Mantouvalou, *Philosophical Foundations of Labour Law* (n 24) 65.

[63] For an account, see M Heinrich, *An Introduction to the Three Volumes of Karl Marx's Capita* (Monthly Review Press, 2012) ch 4. For a more complex view of power configurations that operate in different kinds of work beyond wage labour, see Van Der Linden, *Workers of the World* (n 52).

[64] Collins, 'Is the Contract of Employment Illiberal?' (n 62) 61.

[65] Gilabert, 'Dignity at Work' (n 49) 78.

approach also provides grounds for individual labour rights (such as the right to a minimum wage, as discussed in the previous chapter). This shall be developed more fully in section VI.

V. THE INSTITUTIONAL MODEL AS APPLIED TO PLATFORM WORK

I will now examine how the institutional approach might be applied to the case of platform work. As discussed in section II of this chapter, traditional labour law is founded upon the employment relationship/independent contractor binary, which determines which set of workers are entitled to avail of the panoply of labour rights. Over the years, courts around the world have made clear that in considering this issue, they will not limit themselves to the formal or the express terms of the contract between the parties, but will consider the substantive content of their relationship.[66]

To do this, courts have evolved a set of indicators, which are remarkably similar across jurisdictions. However, as pointed out above, these indicators do not always take into account the features highlighted by the institutional approach. Relevant to our purposes, for example, one significant factor across jurisdictions is whether the worker is free to work for more than one putative 'employer' or is contractually bound to offer their services only to a single employer. The logic of this test harks back to the 'traditional employment relationship', where an employee worked in a single factory or upon a single shop-floor, as opposed to the freelancer, who would perform many different contracts with different contracting partners. And as is evident, the test presupposes the personalised vision of power, located within a single, specific entity, which is precisely what the institutional approach seeks to displace; as Bogg's observations (in the previous section) make clear, '*decentralised* domination' is no less a form of domination.

When applied to platform work, where the existence of multiple platforms and 'decentralised domination' are more features than exceptions, this indicator is particularly inapposite. Indeed, it is reminiscent of the old 'monopoly argument' in deciding when to enforce rights against non-state parties. As we have seen, however, the institutional approach specifically rejects the monopoly argument by disentangling the absence of an exit option from the existence of an identifiable monopoly. The inability to exit is an inability to exit the institution, not an inability to exit from an unequal relationship with any specific actor. Consequently, the fact that an individual worker can transition between different platforms ought not to have any bearing upon the rights that they are entitled to claim against the (institutionally) more powerful platforms.

[66] For examples, see Prassl, *Humans as a Service* (n 1) 97.

Another indicator invoked by courts is whether the worker's equipment is provided by the putative employer or whether they are expected (or required) to use their own equipment (such as the car in the case of ride-hailing services such as Uber).

In the case of platform work, however, a focus on equipment potentially diffuses attention from the source of platforms' institutional power. As Rosenblatt observes in the context of Uber:

> The company determines the type of cars that are eligible on its platform, and it sometimes modifies the list of acceptable types at will; sets and changes the pay rates as it wishes; controls the dispatch; targets drivers unevenly with its incentives; retains full power to suspend or fire drivers without recourse; and mediates and resolves conflicts at its discretion, ranging from issues of passenger disputes to wage theft. An *algorithmic manager* enacts its policies, penalises drivers for behaving in a manner unlike what Uber 'suggests', and incentivizes them to work at particular places in particular times. (emphasis added)[67]

Central to the functioning of what Rosenblatt calls this 'algorithmic boss' is the 'app'. As Vincenzo Pietrogiovanni points out:

> Uber's activity is essentially based on the *applications* that connect drivers and passengers. The 'ride' follows and it is followed by other several important steps: creating an account; reserving the ride; rating the driver; checking information relating to drivers (eg their driving licence or the condition of their cars) – all of which is completely owned and directly managed by Uber, *without any participation or direct access to the process by the drivers*. Moreover, *the algorithm that creates the match between the driver and the customer is probably the largest part of the entire production process*. Indeed, it is through the 'app' that the drivers get their information about each 'ride'. Once the journey has commenced, the 'app' provides the driver with turn-by-turn directions – which are not obligatory on paper, but if drivers fail to follow them, they may encounter negative results … (emphasis added)[68]

Similarly, Prassl and Risak point out that:

> The platform is fully in control of the existence of the relationship. Drivers have to sign up with Uber to use its app; but the process is significantly more intensive than mere registration: the company will vet drivers' cars, check their licences and demand proof of relevant insurance for the jurisdiction in question. Uber is similarly in charge of terminating its driver's access to the platform.[69]

Prassl and Risak further point out that the 'ratings system' employed by the platform is used as a gateway for access to the 'app' (workers whose ratings slip below a certain level can be 'booted' from the 'app') and, in some cases,

[67] Rosenblatt, *Uberland* (n 1) 92.
[68] V Pietrogiovanni, 'Between *Sein* and *Sollen* of Labour Law: Civil (and Constitutional) Law Perspectives on Platform Workers' (2020) 31 *King's Law Journal* 313, 320–21.
[69] Prassl and Risak, '*Uber, TaskRabbit, and Co*' (n 14) 638.

provides privileged access within the 'app'.[70] This, then, effectively serves as a form of performance appraisal[71] (with consumers of the service playing the role of 'middle managers'[72]).

It is therefore clear that the institutional difference of power between the platform and the worker is sustained and entrenched by the 'app', which is exclusively owned and controlled by the platform. Depending upon the platform in question, the 'app': (i) serves as a gateway to entering the work relationship; (ii) is used to surveil and control behaviour during the course of the work relationship (for example, determined routes in the case of ride-sharing services); (iii) is used to determine remuneration for work (through algorithms that, again, are designed by the platform), including the unilateral slashing of rates, which workers must accept in order to keep accessing the platform;[73] and (iv) through its ratings system, is used to discipline and exclude workers. As Alex Rosenblatt sums up the point, when referring to the case of Uber: 'algorithms manage how much drivers are paid, where and when they work, and the eligibility requirements for their employment'.[74] In addition, as Rosenblatt correctly notes, mediating work through the 'app' puts workers at 'an informational disadvantage, and so it is harder for them to make full and informed decisions as *independent contractors*' (emphasis added).[75]

Control and ownership of the 'app', therefore, serves the analogous purpose that control of capital and the means of production did in the traditional labour market, which we discussed in the previous sections: 'the labour process is embedded in the company's proprietary software, and the company programs the software to design, direct, and surveil the worker'.[76] Control and ownership over the equipment used for the work, by comparison, pales into insignificance (as Brishen Rogers puts it, the 'relative investment' of the platform remains of a far greater order, because of the 'app'[77]). Rebecca Schein puts the point most eloquently, and in the language of the institutional approach, when, in the context of disputes over working time, she notes that 'drivers who dispute the company's time-keeping accuracy are confronted – via ostensibly powerless

[70] ibid.

[71] See, eg T Slee, *What's Yours Is Mine: Against the Sharing Economy* (OR Books, 2015) 100–01.

[72] Rosenblatt, *Uberland* (n 1) 149.

[73] See, eg ibid 90.

[74] ibid 18.

[75] ibid 92.

[76] The argument that the 'app' – and not material equipment – serves as 'means of production' in such cases appears to have been explicitly accepted by the Spanish Court in its ruling of 25 September 2020, holding a delivery rider to be an employee. AT Signes, 'Notes on the Spanish Supreme Court Ruling that Considered Riders to be Employees' [2020] *Comparative Labor Law & Policy Journal* Dispatch No 30 – Spain 1, 5. See also J Tomasetti, 'Rebalancing Worker Rights and Property Rights in Digitalised Work', https://papers.ssrn.com/sol3/papers.cfm?abstract_id=3345808.

[77] B Rogers, 'Employment Rights in the Platform Economy: Getting Back to Basics' (2016) 10 *Harvard Law & Policy Review* 479, 494; see also Pietrogiovanni, 'Between *Sein* and *Sollen* of Labour Law' (n 68).

service reps – with *the objective, impersonal authority* of Uber's software' (emphasis added).[78]

At the same time, however, as pointed out at the beginning of this chapter, platform work is of different kinds, and there exist situations where the platform itself genuinely serves as little more than as an intermediary facilitating workers to enter into independent contracts with those in need of their services. This includes a range of circumstances where neither the platform nor the user (of the service) occupies an institutional position of power that enables them to violate the rights of the worker in question. It is evident that the nature of the relationship between the parties in such cases will not justify the application of the horizontal rights framework.

Admittedly, therefore, boundary questions – of the kinds presented by the employment/independent contractor binary – will remain. The nature of the boundary questions will, however, alter: instead of focusing upon the traditional indicia distinguishing between employers and employees, and the contractual configuration – which have hamstrung courts in their examination of platform work – focus will shift to institutional differences of power and the precise manner in which the 'app' is put to use by the platform.[79]

An added benefit of this approach is that, in certain instances, the institutional relationship might apply to some rights, but not to others. For example, a skilled freelancer may be able to set their own wages (thus obviating the need for a horizontal constitutional right to a minimum wage), but the location of the workplace for that service – say, the service-user's home – might still require the enforcement of the right to safe working conditions. The institutional approach is thus flexible enough to account for situations where, within the labour market, private parties might occupy different locations, depending upon the right at issue.

Now, an objection may be raised here that this approach is too flexible, and presents rule-of-law problems by undermining certainty in adjudication. Indeed, as ACL Davies points out, the rule-of-law-based objection to horizontal application, which was discussed in chapter five, carries particular salience in labour law, as 'workers' rights are likely to be violated by employers, most of whom are private individuals or firms'[80] (and therefore have rights of their own, as well as an entitlement to a clear understanding of their obligations).

[78] Schein, 'From Free Time to Idle Time' (n 4) 400, 411.

[79] A judgment by the Palermo Tribunal in November 2020 appears to have adopted just such an approach. See A Aloisi, 'Demystifying Flexibility, Exposing the Algorithmic Boss: A Note on the First Italian Case Classifying a (Food-Delivery) Platform Worker as an Employee' [2021] *Comparative Labor Law & Policy Journal* Dispatch No 35 – Italy 1, 8. For an approach that bears a family resemblance to this analysis, see Alan Bogg's analysis of the European Committee of Social Rights' decision in *ICTU v Ireland*. A Bogg, 'Economic Coordination as Freedom of Association' in S McCrystal, E McGaughey and S Paul (eds), *Labour in Competition Law* (Cambridge University Press, 2021) http://www.labourlawresearch.net/sites/default/files/papers/Competition%20Law%20and%20FOA-4-1.pdf.

[80] Davies, *Perspectives on Labour Law* (n 11) 47.

In response to this, first, one may note that in many cases, there will be an existing labour law framework (which may or may not incorporate the insights of the institutional approach) that will set out the rights and obligations of the parties to a platform contract. The likely shape of constitutional litigation, in such a scenario, will be around the adequacy of this legislative framework (it might, for example, deny non-employees the right to unionise). A constitutional court may then invoke the institutional approach to return a finding on the law, necessitating legislative change – which, in turn, will allow employers the time to bring their own practices into line with the (changed) law. This addresses, at least to some extent, Davies's concern that 'individuals should be able to understand the law and use it to plan their lives … [consequently] individuals should be able to comply with human rights *simply* by acting lawfully'.[81]

For example, in many jurisdictions, there now exists an 'intermediate category' of 'workers', which is defined more broadly than 'employees', and which is granted a reduced catalogue of labour rights. As I shall show with a few illustrations in the next section, the institutional approach can be useful in order to both justify the inclusion of platform workers within the intermediate category and critique the situations in which this category is incomplete or insufficient. By contrast, in the context of labour law, constitutional litigation of the kind discussed in chapter five, where legislative vacuum required the declaration of an immediately enforceable, horizontal constitutional right upon private parties, is more likely to be an exception (albeit, a necessary exception) rather than the rule.

Secondly, it is important to reiterate that the purpose of the institutional approach is to assist in determining what rights workers have against employers (and, specific to this chapter, against platforms). This is the role that is currently played by the employer/employee binary, and the traditional indicia to distinguish between the two. The historical record shows that the employee/contractor framework has been, and continues to be, the subject of extensive litigation. As cases around the world indicate, this is especially true of platform work, where the employee status of platform workers is consistently brought to court, often with differing verdicts being handed out. Indeed, as Davies notes in the context of the UK,

> the tests applied by the courts to decide who is a typical employee and who is not are so ambiguous that researchers may not be able to classify people with any certainty even when presented with the details of their employment relationship.[82]

In this context, I would argue that the application of the institutional approach, in the manner that has been spelt out so far in this chapter, would not raise significantly fresh challenges for adjudicatory bodies, or present a radical

[81] ibid. See also C-176/12 *Association de médiation sociale v Union locale des syndicats CGT and Others* ECLI:EU:C:2014:2 Opinion of AG Villalon [78], responding to the same argument in the specific context of applying the right to consultation horizontally.

[82] Davies, *Perspectives on Labour Law* (n 11) 78.

departure from the kinds of issues they are already dealing with, within this domain. Indeed, in the context of platform work, the application of the institutional approach, with its focus on the 'app', may bring greater clarity than presently exists.

It can be seen, therefore, that the institutional approach provides a strong theoretical foundation for the indicative factors set out above. These factors are based upon an understanding of what may constitute a genuinely horizontal relationship between two parties. Or, in terms of the institutional approach, they help identify situations where the relevant institutional locations of the two parties within the labour market do not place one in a position of power over the other. In the circumstances outlined above, the 'app' plays a relatively marginal role in determining entry into, conditions of and exit from the work relationship. Instead, the ability of the worker (because of factors of skill, specialisation and ownership of business) places them in a position where, arguably, the contract no longer masks an institutional imbalance of power, but is a genuine reflection of a substantively equal relationship.

I will now sum up the argument. The institutional approach provides us with a set of conceptual arguments to justify the application of horizontally applicable, constitutionally guaranteed labour rights. It does so by identifying the labour market as a relevant institution. Further, it operates upon the premise that within this institution there exists a difference in power between employers and workers that flows from the former's ownership and control over capital. This argument then applies with equal force to platform work, along with the following advantages.

First, it provides an overarching constitutional standard that can engage productively with existing labour law frameworks (especially in cases where individuals have been excluded from protection under existing statutory labour law regimes); and, in the absence of an available legislative framework, it makes the case for direct horizontal application of certain labour rights within the platform economy.

Secondly, the institutional approach critically interrogates the employer/independent contractor binary that has structured traditional labour law, and as proven to be specifically problematic in its extension to platform work. This is a suggestion that has been made by other scholars. In a similar formulation, Alan Supiot (along with many others) suggests replacing the employer/contractor binary with concepts of 'dependent' and 'independent' work, focusing specifically on 'digital tools that allow owners to control the work of others without giving them orders',[83] something that I have discussed above. The institutional

[83] A Supiot, 'A Labour Code for the 21st Century' (27 May 2018) *Green European Journal*, www.greeneuropeanjournal.eu/a-labour-code-for-the-21st-century/. See also S Deakin, 'Decoding Employment Status' (2020) 31 *King's Law Journal* 180; the discussion in Davies, *Perspectives on Labour Law* (n 11) 82; for an overlapping, but distinct, approach, see G Davidov, 'The Three Axes of Employment Relationships: A Characterization of Workers in Need of Protection' (2002) 52 *University of Toronto Law Journal* 357.

approach does not use the same vocabulary as Supiot, but the overlaps between concepts of institutional power and dependency – both of which, in the context of platform work, place the role of the 'app' at the centre – are evident.

And thirdly, because of its focus on how power relations are structured, the institutional approach is able to capture the core features of the platform economy (such as the central role of the 'app'), and can also dispense with features that are irrelevant (such as the ability to switch between multiple platforms, and ownership of equipment). It is thus in a position to explain when labour rights should apply – as constitutional, horizontal rights – to the relationships between workers and platforms and, likewise, when, and to what extent, they should not.

VI. APPLYING RIGHTS ACCORDING TO THE INSTITUTIONAL MODEL

This section begins by setting out a number of labour rights that flow from an application of the institutional approach. At the outset, it is important to reiterate that I do not propose to replace existing labour codes with a set of constitutional rights that will be subject to direct, horizontal litigation between workers and employers. Indeed, the rights discussed below are already a part of labour codes across jurisdictions. There exists, however, a legislative vacuum in some cases, as we saw with minimum wage rights for contract workers in the previous chapter. In the case of platform workers, there also exist legislative gaps that are interpreted by platforms to exclude them from labour rights that are enjoyed by that sector of the workforce that unambiguously falls within the definition of employees (or workers[84]). The role of the courts, therefore, is primarily envisioned as *declaratory* (that is, declaring that a certain party has a certain right, the contours of which are already set out in legislation) and *incremental* (extending the scope of coverage of legislative rights), and not as fashioning or implementing concrete, fully fleshed out rights.

Indeed, scholars such as Langille see this as the primary manner in which constitutional rights (such as the freedom of association and the right to equality) should interact with statutory labour codes.[85] I do not disagree; that is not to say, however, that the institutional approach *never* goes beyond the boundaries of legislation. As we shall see, in some cases, such as the scope of collective bargaining, the institutional approach does do so.

It is also important to keep in mind that – as pointed out in the preface to part II – the arguments below will be shaped by the constitutional background: a constitution could have specifically articulated horizontal rights; it could have

[84] See, eg *The Independent Workers Union of Great Britain v The Central Arbitration Committee* [2021] EWCA Civ 952.

[85] Langille, 'The Freedom of Association Mess' (n 8).

a general horizontal rights clause that empowers courts to decide which rights to apply it to, and when; or it could restrict courts to interpreting and developing only existing statutory law. As we proceed through this section, it should be self-evident that certain arguments would be applicable to only one or two of the above contexts, while others might be applicable across the board.

Let us now proceed to the discussion. Once it is determined that one private party exercises institutional power over another in a manner that can enable the former to violate the rights of the latter, the institutional approach then asks: which are the rights that are vulnerable to being infringed by virtue of superior institutional power? Scholars of horizontality will recognise that this is a formula often used by courts: in determining when a particular right applies horizontally, courts have often asked whether the duty bearer is in a position to threaten the exercise of the said right. In the specific context of employment, Collins observes that:

> In exercising their disciplinary power over employees, for instance, should we not require private employers to respect civil liberties, for their disciplinary powers pose a threat to freedoms such as freedom of speech and association that seems to be as equally grave as that presented by a powerful state?[86]

While the institutional approach eschews direct analogies with the state, the point is well taken. Now, more specifically, in the case of platform work (and the labour market more generally), as indicated above, these rights apply both at the point of entry into the work relationship and through the work relationship. As Collins points out, borrowing from Kahn-Freund's vocabulary, the former can be understood as *submission*, while the latter is *subordination*:

> Submission occurs when a person enters a contract of employment on terms dictated entirely or almost entirely by the employer and where there may be no reasonable alternatives to earn an income but to take this job … the concept of subordination differs from submission, because it concerns the daily experience of an employee being subject to the hierarchical control of the employer or manager.[87]

In more specific terms:

> First, workers face capitalists within the sphere of exchange, notably in the labour market, to negotiate the terms of labour contract (stating, for example, workers' salary). They also encounter each other in the sphere of production, where many issues not codified in the labour contract arise regarding the control of production (such as the pace of work, the introduction of labour saving technology, technical division of labour, and decision-making about daily workplace activities).[88]

The rights in question, therefore, would include collective rights, which aim to mitigate the institutional imbalance of power so that both parties are in a

[86] Collins, 'Is the Contract of Employment Illiberal?' (n 62) 65.
[87] ibid 51; see also Gilabert, 'Dignity at Work' (n 49).
[88] Gilabert, 'Dignity at Work' (n 49) 78–79.

position to shape the terms of their relationship. They would also include individual rights that constitute a threshold beneath which these terms cannot go.

On the individual front, the institutional approach takes familiar vertically enforceable rights found in most constitutions, and applies them in a horizontal framework. The first is the right to a minimum wage, which flows from a right that is often found in constitutions: the right against forced labour.

The justification for holding that the right to a minimum wage is a subset of a horizontally applicable right against forced labour was set out in the previous chapter, in the examination of the *PUDR* judgment. Here, I recapitulate the argument briefly. The minimum wage serves as a heuristic to determine situations in which it can be said that the structural constraints of the labour market essentially make workers 'unfree'. Workers who 'agree' to a wage that goes below even the minimum wage (which is assumed to be the threshold remuneration allowing for a basic, dignified life) are deemed to have been coerced or forced into the agreement, borne out of the differences in institutional power between employers and workers. Thus, as Collins et al frame the argument:

> workers' inequality of power, understood in this way, leads them to accept wages that they would not accept if the risks were distributed equally. Capitalism gives the opportunity to exploit systematically workers' aversion to risk … the right to a fair wage should be understood as a right to address the risk imbalance that is inherent in capitalism.[89]

The extension of the right against forced labour to the horizontal context, therefore, translates into an enforceable right to a minimum wage (and, indeed, can arguably be extended to working hours limits and holiday pay, which cleave to the same logic).

Indeed, in the context of platform work, scholars have pointed out how the oversupply of labour[90] – a characteristic feature of platforms – is directly responsible for depressing wages, often to below minimum wage levels.[91] While concerns have been raised about how this might be enforced in cases where workers switch between platforms, as ACL Davies's scholarship on working time demonstrates, this difficulty is not insurmountable within the existing legislative framework.[92]

When it comes to the question of remedy, once again, the *PUCL* judgment indicates the way forward. Many jurisdictions will have a minimum wage, encoded in a statute, that applies to at least some sets of workers or employees. Litigation, thus, will normally take the form of challenging the exclusion of

[89] Collins et al, 'Introduction' (n 24) 25.

[90] The availability of a reserve supply of labour as a characteristic feature of the platform economy has led scholars like Prassl to draw continuities with older forms of work, such as the 19th-century putting-out system. Prassl, *Humans as a Service* (n 1) 80.

[91] ibid 59.

[92] ACL Davies, 'Wages and Working Time in the "Gig Economy"' (2020) 31 *King's Law Journal* 250; Prassl, *Humans as a Service* (n 1) 106.

certain categories of workers from minimum wage laws (as was the case in *PUCL*); the institutional approach, as we have seen, provides a court with good reasons to extend the coverage of those laws to those excluded from them (as opposed to having to *judicially* fix a minimum wage). A court could do this (as the Indian Supreme Court did) by interpreting an existing, horizontal right against forced labour to derive a horizontal right to a minimum wage; in a constitution where there is only a vertical right against forced labour but a generic horizontal rights clause, the institutional approach would give a court a reason to hold why, in this context, applying the constitutional right horizontally is appropriate. Finally, where there is neither, but there is a statute that makes a minimum wage dependent on employment status (a plausible scenario), the institutional approach (as discussed above and as shall be shown below) could contribute to a court finding that the putative workers before it belong to the categories that are granted statutory labour law protections.

The second right that could be applied in the horizontal framework is the right to a fair trial (also found in many constitutions, and a general facet of the rule of law). In the previous section, I discussed the centrality of the 'app' to the platform economy. Recall that through its 'ratings' system, the 'app' serves as a gateway – or, alternatively, a drawbridge – into the working relationship or out of it. Based upon their 'app' ratings, workers can find themselves locked out of more remunerative work, or locked out of the platform altogether. In essence, therefore, this amounts to dismissal without due process (or any process whatsoever). It is evident that principles of the right to fair trial are applicable here (at the very least, the right to a notice and hearing before coercive action), as extended into the horizontal domain,[93] including the right to access a forum where these decisions can be effectively challenged.[94] In constitutions that have a right against unfair labour practices,[95] courts can also invoke that right and apply it to the horizontal domain.

The manner in which this could be done in adjudication – across different constitutional contexts – largely follows my discussion about the right to minimum wages above: where a direct horizontal right exists, workers could invoke it. Where there is a vertical constitutional right to a fair trial or against unfair labour practices, the institutional approach would help make the case for its horizontal application; and where there is only statute, the institutional approach would inform an assessment of which parties are entitled to invoke the statutory protections on offer.

Thirdly, and closely linked, are issues of discrimination. It was famously documented, for example, that Uber cited the 'independent contractor' status of its drivers to justify its refusal to comply with US anti-discrimination law, which

[93] See, eg KD Ewing, 'Democratic Socialism and Labour Law' (1995) 24 *Industrial Law Journal* 103.

[94] H Collins, 'Market Power, Bureaucratic Power, and the Contract of Employment' (1986) 15 *Industrial Law Journal* 1.

[95] See, eg *Murray v Minister of Defence* (n 32).

would have required it to 'provide wheelchair-accessible transit'.[96] Under the institutional approach, platforms would no longer be able to avoid constitutionally mandated non-discrimination obligations (the analysis in specific contexts would, again, be similar to the discussions around the right to minimum wages and the right against unfair labour practices).

Furthermore, staying with the issue of discrimination, as discussed above, platform 'apps' are proprietary, non-transparent and algorithm-based. In this context, there exists a swathe of contemporary scholarship dealing with issues around algorithmic bias and algorithmic discrimination. The central role of algorithms in creating and maintaining the institutional difference in power between platforms and workers thus makes a clear case for the extension of the rights to equal treatment, and against non-discrimination, into the horizontal domain.

These issues also extend to other areas. For example, as Rosenblatt points out, 'through ratings systems, consumers can directly input their biases into worker evaluation systems in ways that companies cannot do on their behalf'.[97] This has many potential consequences: if, on the basis of the institutional approach, the right to non-discrimination would be held to apply *inter se* between platforms and their workers, there would then be a corresponding burden upon platforms to demonstrate that the 'apps' do not function in a discriminatory way, or with discriminatory effects. Thus far, platforms have resisted scrutiny of such issues by invoking their proprietary rights to the 'apps'; such an argument would no longer be available – or at least, would be severely weakened – if the workings of these 'apps' were subjected to the obligations of non-discrimination.

Indeed, this argument would not be limited to non-discrimination. It would apply wherever the 'app' was used to violate a putative right (including the right against unfair labour practices). Recall Schein's description of the 'objective, impersonal authority of Uber's software'. Once it is understood that the 'app' is a crucial site of the institutional difference in power between the worker and the platform, a set of guarantees against algorithmic decision-making, as well as, crucially, the right to algorithmic transparency – which exist, for example, in EU law – can be applied horizontally, *inter se*, between the two parties.

Finally, there is substantial controversy over safe working conditions in platform work. The issue of safe working conditions may complicate the platform/worker binary, and bring into the equation a third party: the individual who is the direct recipient of the worker's services, through the platform. For certain kinds of platform work (such as services provided in the domestic context), the institutional approach may require a shift from the platform as the duty bearer (because the platform's institutional power does not, in fact, place that

[96] Rosenblatt, *Uberland* (n 1) 202.
[97] ibid 155.

particular right at threat) to the consumer (who, in that specific context, occupies the position that the platform otherwise would). This may, of course, not always be the case: as the platform continues to control the terms on which both the worker and the end user can utilise it, it retains the power to make use of its services conditional upon the fulfilment of certain obligations by the end user (these could include, for example, non-discrimination obligations as well as the health and safety obligations referred to above). Responsibility in such cases may well be joint in nature.

As indicated in the previous section, the flexibility of the institutional approach is key to accommodating the heterogeneity of platform work. By placing the rights bearer at the centre of its enquiry, the institutional approach is alive to situations where, within the institutionally mediated work relationship, different private parties may be in position where their institutional location enables them to violate different rights. It is important to note that there exist similar arguments in this direction: this 'splitting' of rights and obligations has also been suggested by Prassl and Risak (and before them, by Davies and Freedland[98] and by Langille and Davidov[99]), who advocate a 'functional' approach to various features of the employment relationship and argue for placing obligations based upon which party is performing a specific functional aspect of employment.[100] As indicated above, the responsibility may also be joint, and 'splitting' the work relationship into its functional components, under the institutional approach, does not necessarily entail silos as far as rights and obligations are concerned. The institutional approach provides the underlying theoretical justification that buttresses Prassl and Risak's functional argument, as applied to platform work (it is important to note that in certain jurisdictions, such as the UK, this is no longer a serious problem or issue).

Moving on, the institutional approach applies with at least as much force to the collective aspect of labour law, guaranteeing the right to collective bargaining (flowing from the freedom of association). The logic of this is straightforward, and has been specifically recognised, inter alia, by the Supreme Court of the USA: the right to collective bargaining is required to offset the institutional power enjoyed by employers, on account of their ownership and control over capital and the means of production.[101]

The associational rights argument, however, goes beyond the simple question of mitigation of power imbalances at the point of entering the bargaining process, and demonstrates one domain where the institutional approach goes significantly beyond existing approaches. One of the fundamental purposes

[98] P Davies and M Freedland, 'Changing Perspectives on the Employment Relationship in British Labour Law' in C Barnard, S Deakin and GS Morris (eds), *The Future of Labour Law: Liber Amicorum Sir Bob Hepple QC* (Hart Publishing, 2004) 129.

[99] Langille and Davidov, 'Beyond Employees and Independent Contractors' (n 16).

[100] Prassl and Risak, '*Uber, TaskRabbit, and Co*' (n 14).

[101] See s III of this chapter.

of the right to freedom of association in the vertical domain is to ensure the participation of citizens in governance (in other words, substantive democracy). The institutional approach provides us with a reason to extend that logic to the domain of 'social institutions'.[102] In practical terms, that translates to granting workers (through collective bargaining) an 'opportunity to play a part in the rule-making process of the enterprise'.[103]

This is something that has traditionally been argued to be beyond the ambit of collective bargaining, which traditionally is limited to questions of wages, working hours and so on,[104] or to the 'sphere of exchange … rather than … the sphere of production'.[105] In other words, the scope of collective bargaining has traditionally been curtailed by invoking concepts such as 'managerial prerogative'[106] and entrepreneurial control. Thus,

> most management rights are never challenged by collective bargaining or legislated mandates on employer behavior … under collective bargaining, 'management has the right to determine what work shall be done; to determine what kinds of services and business activity to engage in; and to determine the techniques, tools, and equipment by which work on its behalf shall be performed'.[107]

By contrast, the institutional approach justifies a more extensive and deeper role for collective bargaining (again, flowing from the freedom of association, and its governing logic in the vertical domain) than might otherwise be allowed. It affirms Karl Klare's proposition that 'those whose collective efforts make social production possible should have a decisive say in the decisions that affect the process, that they pose themselves morally and institutionally as the authors of their own destinies in the workplace'.[108]

[102] Ewing, 'Democratic Socialism and Labour Law' (n 93) 116.

[103] ibid 118. See also Bogg, 'Republican Non-Domination and Labour Law' (n 46); A Bogg and C Estlund, 'Freedom of Association and the Right to Contest: Getting Back to the Basics' in A Bogg and T Novitz (eds), *Voices at Work* (Oxford University Press, 2014) 142.

[104] LA Compa, 'Labor's New Opening to International Human Rights Standards' (2008) 11(1) *WorkingUSA: The Journal of Labor and Society* 99.

[105] Klare, 'Judicial Deradicalization of the Wagner Act' (n 12) 320.

[106] Tomasetti, 'Rebalancing Workers' Rights' (n 76); see also Klare, 'Judicial Deradicalization of the Wagner Act' (n 12). While this introduces an additional party – the trade union – into the equation, it is important to note that for the purposes of the institutional approach, a trade union lacks the features that characterise an 'institution' for the purpose of *inter se* horizontal rights application.

[107] Michel, 'The Goliath in the Room' (n 48) 15. See also Chamber of Commerce Brief in *First National Maintenance Corp v NLRB* 452 US 666 (1981); *cf* S Jager, S Noy and B Schoefer, 'Codetermination and Power in the Workplace' (2022) 3(1) *Journal of Law and Political Economy* 198, 199.

[108] Klare, 'Judicial Deradicalization of the Wagner Act' (n 12) 321. Note that a (weaker) version of this is instantiated through workers' councils, whom the employer has a duty to consult. See, eg European Social Charter (Revised), Strasbourg, 3.V.1995, Art 21; see also the discussion in Davies, *Perspectives on Labour Law* (n 11) ch 10. For a longer bibliography, see the references in N Hsieh, 'Rawlsian Justice and Workplace Republicanism' (2005) 31 *Social Theory and Practice* 115. For a critical analysis of the history of 'codetermination' in European law, see Jager et al (n 107); LS Zakson, 'Worker Participation: Industrial Democracy and Managerial Prerogative in the Federal Republic of

In the specific context of platform work, therefore, this would arguably extend to not just subjecting the working of the 'apps' to obligations of non-discrimination, but also subordinating the platform's proprietary claims over the 'apps' to the democratic process of collective bargaining over how, when and in what manner the 'apps' are to be deployed in regulating work. Additionally, the institutional approach here would reinforce the claims for algorithmic transparency that we have discussed previously, in the non-discrimination context: as long as the functioning of the 'app' (including, for example, the source code) are kept confidential by the platform, it is obvious that the asymmetry of information will preclude any effective bargaining on the lines discussed above.

Thus, under the institutional approach's understanding of the scope of the right to collective bargaining, platforms can no longer claim blanket immunity from subjecting the 'app' to scrutiny by invoking corporate confidentiality or competition law concerns; at the very least, the institutional approach provides strong countervailing arguments against such claims.

While arguments for greater worker voice and participation are generally made within the framework of industrial democracy, what is significant here is that the institutional approach can help constitutionalise those arguments, and substantially push the boundaries of existing law. The claims outlined above would normally be excluded from collective bargaining agreements on the grounds that they pertain to managerial prerogative. The institutional approach provides us with constitutional reasons to challenge any such exclusion.

Finally, it is important to note that collective bargaining can take many concrete forms, and, as the Canadian Supreme Court and the European Court of Human Rights have both correctly observed, a constitution cannot stipulate the specific regime that it must take[109] (for example, Article 27 of the Charter of Fundamental Rights of the European Union guarantees to workers the right 'to information and consultation',[110] which is then provided a concrete form by the European Works Council Directive[111]). What it can do, however, is invalidate any substantive interference or undue burden that the state may seek to place upon the right (as informed by the institutional approach, in the manner discussed above), including – as discussed in section II of this chapter, in the

Germany, Sweden, and the United States' (1984) 8(1) *Hastings International and Comparative Law Review* 93.

[109] *Swedish Engine Drivers' Union v Sweden* [1976] ECHR 2; *Health Services & Support v British Columbia* (n 27); indeed, as Alex Rosenblatt points out, collective bargaining efforts will need to take into account the different forms of platform work within the same platform. Rosenblatt, *Uberland* (n 1) 54. But see *Fraser v Ontario (Attorney General)* (2008) 92 OR (3d) 481 (Supreme Court of Ontario); the critique in B Langille, 'Why Are Canadian Judges Drafting Labour Codes – and Constitutionalising the Wagner Act Model?' (2010) 15 *Canadian Labour and Employment Law Journal* 101.

[110] Charter of Fundamental Rights of the European Union (2012/C 326/02), Art 27.

[111] Directive 2009/38/EC of the European Parliament and of the Council, of 6 May 2009.

account of collective laissez-faire – restrictions under existing common law.[112] This would also extend to legal burdens, such as anti-trust and competition laws, that have been used to defeat efforts at collective bargaining, especially where rights are available only to employees but not to other workers (for example, as of 2002, more than 30 million US workers were excluded from exercising their associational rights[113]). Thus, the advantage of the institutional approach, as applied horizontally, is that it precludes employers from invoking anti-trust or competition laws against the right to collective bargaining, and also precludes arguments predicated upon the non-employee status of workers to do so.[114]

The role of the institutional approach in such situations can be illustrated through a set of recent examples. In *R (on the application of Independent Workers Union of Great Britain) v Central Arbitration Committee and Roofoods Ltd t/a Deliveroo*,[115] the UK High Court (and subsequently the Court of Appeal) ruled that, because of the existence of a substitution clause, Deliveroo riders were not 'workers' within the meaning of section 296(1)(b) of the Trade Union and Labour Relations Act 1992, and were not in an 'employment relationship' in the context of EU law. The consequence of this, as Bogg points out, is that Deliveroo workers were deprived of their right to unionise, and Deliveroo was entitled to invoke competition law against them in case they attempted to do so, along with potential discrimination and blacklisting.[116] Bogg argues that the dispositive weight given to the substitution clause by the High Court was incorrect in view of ILO Recommendations on the employment relationship, which had been incorporated into EU law by the European Court of Human Rights' Grand Chamber.[117] For the reasons advanced in the previous section, the institutional approach provides strong theoretical ballast to supplement Bogg's argument that substitution clauses ought not to be dispositive in determining the question of employment status: the logic underlying the substitution clause argument – that it negates any personal obligation to perform work – has little bearing upon the institutional power differences that structure the contract. Thus, much as the institutional approach justifies giving less weight (for example) to the traditional 'employment' test of whether the worker can switch between different putative

[112] J Fudge, 'Labour Rights as Human Rights: Turning Slogans into Claims' (2014) 37 *Dalhousie Law Journal* 602; K Banks, 'The Role and Promise of International Law in Canada's New Labour Law Constitutionalism' (2012) 16 *Canadian Labour Law and Employment Journal* 233.

[113] Compa, 'Labor's New Opening' (n 104).

[114] See Bogg, 'Economic Coordination as Freedom of Association' (n 79), also for warnings about how the freedom of association may be used as a deregulatory tool against a collective bargaining system. As Bogg notes, however, a contextualised understanding of this right – as the institutional approach attempts to provide – can mitigate this risk.

[115] [2018] EWHC 3342, upheld on appeal in *The Independent Workers Union of Great Britain v Central Arbitration Committee and Roofoods Ltd t/a Deliveroo* [2021] EWCA Civ 952, albeit on the limited point of the scope of Art 11 of the European Convention on Human Rights.

[116] A Bogg, 'Taken for a Ride: Workers in the Gig Economy' (2019) 135 *LQR* 135.

[117] *Sindicatul 'Pastorul Cel Bun' v Romania* [2014] 58 EHRR 10.

employers, it also justifies giving less weight to the existence of a substitution clause in determining what rights a worker ought to enjoy.

To add to this, if, hypothetically, the institutional approach was accepted as providing interpretive guidance to courts (in the manner outlined previously in this chapter), the High Court would be required to interpret the word 'worker' in a manner that *protected* Deliveroo workers' right to association, instead of negating it (an argument Bogg himself makes, in view of the fact that Article 11 of the European Convention on Human Rights is a 'fundamental right'). This would be done by holding that Deliveroo workers fall within the definition of 'worker', and it would then follow – without a court having to do more – that they do have the right to unionise, as already provided by the statute. It is in this way that, acting in lockstep with existing legislation, the institutional approach can articulate a background framework of constitutional, horizontal rights that provide the context within which labour laws can be interpreted so as to protect the rights of platform workers.

However, there are also examples where the institutional approach's role is not towards the evolution or modification of the law, but is an explanatory one. This is equally important. For instance, in this chapter, I have discussed at some length the example of ride-sharing platforms as a central case in considering the application of the institutional approach to platform work. In *Uber v Aslam and Ors*, the question of whether Uber drivers were 'workers' within the wider 'Limb B' definition under section 230(3)(b) of the Employment Rights Act of 1996[118] (which goes beyond the requirement of an employment relationship and only requires that an individual 'perform personally any work or services for another party') came up for decision. Both the Employment Tribunal and the Employment Appellate Tribunal held that the drivers were workers. This conclusion was affirmed by the Court of Appeal, which considered 13 indicators (originally set out by the Employment Tribunal) in support of its finding.

Looking at these indicators closely, it is clear that what specifically weighed with the Court of Appeal, among other things, were: information asymmetry (and control over passenger data); Uber's power to 'log off' drivers for not accepting trips; the algorithmic rating system, which 'amounts to a performance management/disciplinary procedure';[119] and Uber's power to unilaterally amend terms. It will be noticed that each of these indicators was discussed in the previous section as an instance of the institutional power wielded by platforms such as Uber, which enables the violation of rights. While the Court of Appeal did not frame its analysis in terms of institutional power, it did note that in labour law, the concept of a 'sham' contract had evolved to take into account:

> [T]he convoluted, complex and artificial contractual arrangements, no doubt formulated by a battery of lawyers, unilaterally drawn up and dictated by Uber to tens of

[118] Employment Rights Act 1996, s 230(3)(b).
[119] *Uber BV v Aslam & Farrar* (n 6) [96].

> thousands of drivers and passengers, not one of whom is in a position to correct or otherwise resist the contractual language.[120]

Notably, the holding of the Court of Appeal was upheld, in relevant part, by the UK Supreme Court, applying similar reasoning. Specifically, the Supreme Court noted that, through the indicators that it had set out, the Court of Appeal had correctly demonstrated that the elements of subordination and dependency were fulfilled in this case.[121]

I submit that, for the reasons advanced above, a close reading of the judgments in the *Uber* case reveals a shift from the interpersonal view of power to the structural or institutional view of power in the context of labour law. Indeed, the judgments can be best explained and justified from this framework of analysis. This is particularly evident in the 13 factors discussed by the Employment Tribunal and the Court of Appeal, which shifted away from the old indicia of 'employment' to indicia more suited for the decentralised, institutional power at issue between platforms and workers. While the UK courts did not, of course, call what they were doing 'the institutional approach' (locating it, rather, within a shift towards a more purposive understanding of the labour contract), as pointed out above, the institutional approach serves as a better explanatory basis for the judgment(s), as well as providing theoretical support for the courts' approach, given that this is still contested terrain. According to the institutional approach, therefore, the judgments in the *Uber* case were rightly decided, their best justification lies in reasoning that takes into account institutional power imbalances and, finally, this form of reasoning should be extended to other cases involving the platform economy as well.

It is also important to note that an important ancillary question in the *Uber* case involved the question of when the drivers qualified as workers. The Employment Tribunal held that the drivers were 'working' from the moment that the 'app' was switched on, and this finding was affirmed by the Employment Appellate Tribunal, the Court of Appeal and the Supreme Court. Of particular interest is the Employment Tribunal's observation that 'it is essential to Uber's business to maintain a pool of drivers who can be called upon as and when a demand for driving services arises'.[122] As noted previously in the chapter, the existence of a 'reserve pool of labour' is central to institutional power within the labour market, and particularly central to the platform work model. Consequently, the finding that drivers were 'workers' – and therefore entitled to Limb B rights from the time the 'app' was switched on – flows directly from the structure of argument set out in the previous section: it is the institutional difference in power that enables more powerful parties to violate the rights of

[120] ibid [105].
[121] *Uber BV v Aslam* [2021] UKSC 5 [93]. I focus here on the Court of Appeal's reasoning, as it demonstrates more clearly the overlap with the institutional approach.
[122] *Uber BV v Aslam & Farrar* (n 6) [101].

the less powerful. The purpose of the institutional approach is to accurately identify the nature of this difference in power and apply the rights framework to mitigate it.

A final, illustrative example is that of *The Independent Workers' Union of Great Britain v The Secretary of State for Work and Pensions*.[123] In this case, the UK High Court held that certain EU Directives pertaining to the health and safety of workers had not been properly transposed into domestic law by the UK, in contravention of its obligations under the EEC Treaty. The UK's defence turned upon the distinction between 'employees' and 'workers', and the argument that EU law required it to extend those health and safety benefits only to employees and not to 'Limb B' workers. This argument was rejected by the Court, which then went on to find that, on merits, the UK had discharged its obligations in some respects, while in other respects it had not. Importantly, a dichotomy between the rights enjoyed by 'employees', which included 'welfare', and the rights enjoyed by Limb B workers, which were limited to 'health' and 'safety' but did not include welfare, was upheld by the Court, because the overarching EU Directive was itself limited to 'health' and 'safety'. This case reveals that in jurisdictions that have introduced the three-tiered employment law structure, there remain problems with respect to differential treatment that cannot always be resolved by pure statutory construction without reference to overarching normative principles (as in this case).

Could the institutional approach make a difference? Potentially, yes. The institutional approach here would ask what justifies excluding Limb B workers from the same 'welfare' rights that are afforded to full employees (in addition to 'health' and 'safety'). Where no justification can be offered, the institutional approach can become either the basis of law reform proposals or, in jurisdictions where it is possible, the basis for a narrowly tailored constitutional challenge, based on the principles of non-discrimination, that will seek to extend the rights already available to employees under legislation to the more extensive category of 'workers'.

A concluding point: it is important to note that these are only a basic minimal set of constitutional rights that are designed to mitigate the violations that flow from the institutional difference in power that exists in the work relationship. They do not restrict what additional rights might be accorded, whether through statute or through the collective bargaining process.[124] They thus aim at 'collective bargaining from a base of expanding social protection'.[125] Scholars have expressed concerns about the 'juridification' of labour law and how constitutionalisation can inadvertently serve to harm labour rights by taking issues

[123] *The Independent Workers' Union of Great Britain* (n 7).

[124] The either/or is important, as treating legislated rights as exhaustive of the 'floor', beyond which only collective bargaining can secure greater rights, has been subjected to criticism. See Davies, *Perspectives on Labour Law* (n 11) 6.

[125] Ewing, 'Democratic Socialism and Labour Law' (n 93) 115.

out of the political domain and into the realms of courts.[126] This concern is justifiable. That is why it is important to stress that the role of the institutional approach is not to supplant or substitute for either private law or collective bargaining, but to provide for a threshold of rights that workers can resort to in the absence of statutory labour law (one of which, as we have seen, includes the right to collective bargaining).

VII. CONCLUSION

In its application to labour law in general and to platform work in particular, the institutional approach does not seek to radically depart from existing accounts, but to complement them in important ways. From its origins, one of the *raisons d'être* of labour law has been precisely to mitigate the power imbalance between employers and workers. Although this rationale has been critiqued for being both under- and over-determined, it has been endorsed in judicial decisions as well as by the labour law scholarship, and has also been invoked as a theoretical rationale for the employment/contract binary. Furthermore, many scholars and practitioners of labour law (as discussed above) have conceptualised power in structural terms, in a manner that overlaps with the core arguments of the institutional approach.

It may, then, be asked: what is the precise contribution of the institutional approach, and why is it needed? This chapter has attempted to provide three answers to that question. First, the institutional approach is a theory of horizontal constitutional rights. To the extent that the 'inequality of power' justification of labour law is accurate, the institutional approach provides a reason for substantive and procedural employment rights to be constitutionalised. This is relevant in two sets of situations. Primarily, as we have seen, the institutional approach facilitates productive engagement between statutory labour law regimes and constitutional rights. It is also important, however, that the constitutionalisation of labour rights places them beyond the power of legislative majorities to alter (although, as we have seen, the details of implementation must still be worked out through legislation). This becomes relevant in situations such as platform work, where the failure of legislation to 'catch up' to the realities of the work form could lead to a situation where workers are either unprotected or must depend upon an inadequate (and possibly inaccurate) legal framework to enforce their rights. It may also become relevant in

[126] Doherty and Franca, 'Solving the "Gig-Saw"?' (n 15); H Arthurs, 'The Constitutionalisation of Employment Relations: Multiple Models, Pernicious Problems' (2010) 19 *Social & Legal Studies* 403; for how to drive a wedge between using the language of constitutional rights, and relying solely on judicial enforcement, see WE Forbath, 'Constitutional Rights: A History, Critique, and Reconstruction' (2001) 69 *Fordham Law Review* 1821.

situations where legislatures elect to roll back or eliminate basic labour rights. The specific ways in which this could happen – across different constitutional contexts – have also been discussed in the chapter.

Secondly, the institutional approach does not address *all* forms of power imbalance (a common critique against this account of labour law), but a specific kind of imbalance that is grounded within the existence and operation of institutional power. It follows from this that the institutional approach is not tied to the employment/contractor binary, which, as we have seen, has been particularly unsuitable in addressing evolving forms of work, such as platform work. The indicators to determine the existence of an employment (or worker) relationship (which, in turn, serves as a gateway towards labour rights eligibility) are tied to a particular vision of what work looks like, and are not always able to respond to different realities. This chapter has attempted to demonstrate that the institutional approach – at the constitutional level, and at the level of guaranteeing threshold rights – is able to respond to those realities. It has done so by specifically examining the application of the institutional approach to platform work.

Thirdly, in some respects, the institutional approach goes beyond the limits of existing labour law frameworks. To take two specific examples: the institutional approach provides a firmer theoretical foundation to arguments seeking a greater extent of worker 'voice' in managerial decisions by grounding those arguments within a right to political participation, as extended to the domain of employment. And secondly, given that the 'app' is the locus of the institutional difference in power between the worker and the platform, the institutional approach justifies arguments in favour of algorithmic transparency – ie throwing open the functioning and algorithmic decision-making processes of the 'app' for scrutiny, and especially scrutiny by the affected parties (the workers). The institutional approach thus provides powerful counter-arguments against the platforms' property rights-based claims to keep the 'apps' shielded from scrutiny.

Needless to say, it is not the argument of this chapter that the institutional approach can create, replace or constitutionalise labour codes in their entirety, or that, given the plurality and heterogeneity of the platform work, the application of the institutional approach will always be straightforward or non-controversial. Rather, the task of this chapter has been to show that the utility of the institutional approach does not end with its intellectual plausibility (the argument of the previous five chapters). In addition, the institutional approach can be profitably applied to existing, real-world situations, especially those where existing legal frameworks have, or appear to be, non-existent or fall short.

Finally, while the arguments in this chapter have been focused on labour law – and the labour market as the relevant institution – the logic can be extended to other economic domains. It is easy to see, for example, how the arguments in the chapter can be applied to the housing market and to the relationships between landlords and tenants. Indeed, Harry Arthurs has proposed reconceptualising labour law as one element of a broader law of 'economic subordination and private resistance', which is concerned with 'the experience of many groups under capitalism, all of which should have the basic right to be protected from the arbitrary exercise of private economic power'.[127] This language is close to the language of the institutional approach; its extension to other domains, however, is a task for a future day.

[127] HW Arthurs, 'Labor Law as the Law of Economic Subordination and Resistance: A Thought Experiment' (2013) 34 *Comparative Labor Law & Policy Journal* 585, 593–94.

7

Application II: Domestic Relationships and Unpaid Labour

I. INTRODUCTION

IN THE PREVIOUS chapter, I considered the application of the institutional approach to the sphere of production, ie the labour market. In this chapter, I will consider its application to the sphere of (social) reproduction, ie a set of activities that are not formally part of the labour market but the existence of which presupposes the latter.[1] In scholarship, social reproduction is understood to include the following:

> [B]iological reproduction; unpaid production in the home (both goods and services); social provisioning (… voluntary work directed at meeting needs in the community); the reproduction of culture and ideology; and the provision of sexual, emotional and affective services (such as are required to maintain family and intimate relationships).[2]

I will discuss one specific site of the sphere of social reproduction: the family. In many human societies, the family has been, and continues to be, a central social institution, 'an important sphere of distribution of many social goods, from the material to the intangible'.[3] Families are constituted by a number of different relationships. In nuclear families, these include relationships between spouses and between parents and children (if there are children). Extended families encompass a wider range of relationships, depending upon the dominant form that the family takes in a particular society. These relationships involve institutional power and hierarchy, visible most starkly between parents and children, but equally present in the relationships between spouses, between 'heads' of households and members of the households, and so on.

[1] S Mau, *Mute Compulsion: A Marxist Theory of the Economic Power of Capital* (Verso, 2023) 124; C Arruzza, 'Remarks on Gender' (*Viewpoint Magazine*, 2 September 2014) https://viewpointmag.com/2014/09/02/remarks-on-gender/. For the link between the two, see T Bhattacharya, 'Introduction: Mapping Social Reproduction Theory' in T Bhattacharya (ed), *Social Reproduction Theory: Remapping Class, Recentering Oppression* (Pluto Press, 2017); for a critique of Bhattacharya and an argument for a more granular set of links, see K Munro, '"Social Reproduction Theory", Social Reproduction, and Household Production' (2019) 83 *Science and Society* 451.

[2] C Hoskyns and SM Rai, 'Recasting the Global Political Economy: Counting Women's Unpaid Work' (2007) 12 *New Political Economy* 297, 300.

[3] SM Okin, *Justice, Gender, and the Family* (Basic Books, 1989) 135.

Historically, these relationships have been shielded from constitutional scrutiny and from the concerns of justice.[4] For reasons that I shall explore more fully in section II of this chapter, the family has often been treated as a zone of human interactions that ought to remain free from state (ie public) interference. A corollary of this is that power differences and hierarchies within the family remain untouched. Feminist and other critical scholarship has, however, long challenged this paradigm, and (as will be shown below) has advanced a persuasive case for subjecting powerful actors within the family to the claims of justice.

As a social institution whose place in many modern societies is as pervasive as (if not more so than) the labour market, the family is an important site for testing the viability of the institutional approach in its application. Specifically: does the institutional approach give us good reason to apply horizontal rights within the family, and subject institutionally powerful actors to horizontal obligations?

As in the previous chapter, for analytical clarity, the institutional approach requires us to identify a specific set of relationships where its application can be illustrated. Consequently, in this chapter, I shall limit my focus to one specific relationship within the family: the cis-heterosexual domestic relationship. By 'domestic relationship', I mean marital relationships, as well as other legally recognised forms such as civil unions, civil partnerships or domestic partnerships. In many jurisdictions, these relationships now accommodate a range of sexual identities. For the purposes of analysis in this chapter, however, I set as a boundary condition 'cis-heterosexual domestic relationships', ie domestic relationships involving a cis-man and a cis-woman as the two parties, as defined under the laws of a particular jurisdiction.

The reason for this, as I shall argue later in the chapter, is that in many societies, the institutional imbalance of power in such relationships flows from cis-heteropatriarchy (hereinafter 'patriarchy'), which is defined as a male, conforming-to-assigned-sex system of power, or 'a system of relations, both material and cultural, of domination and exploitation of women by men'[5] (and, in such societies, is often at the root of the 'traditional' family structure as well).[6] Furthermore, historically, in modern societies, the cis-heterosexual domestic relationship has been accorded normative primacy in patriarchal structures and within the family. Therefore, the workings of institutional power have been studied in greatest depth when it comes to these relationships. It should, of course,

[4] D Satz, 'Feminist Perspectives on Reproduction and the Family' *The Stanford Encyclopedia of Philosophy*, https://plato.stanford.edu/entries/feminism-family/.

[5] Arruzza, 'Remarks on Gender' (n 1). See also G Lerner, *The Creation of Patriarchy* (Oxford University Press, 1986) 239: 'the manifestation and institutionalisation of male dominance over women and children in the family, and the extension of male dominance over women in society in general'.

[6] See, eg C Card, 'Against Marriage and Motherhood' (1996) 11(3) *Hypatia* 1.

remain possible to extend the insights that the institutional approach brings to bear on cis-heterosexual domestic relationships to other forms of domestic relationships as well, and to other kinds of relationships within the family. That, however, will be a future task.

Consequently, for sake of brevity, the phrase 'domestic relationship', as used in the rest of this chapter, should be taken to refer to cis-heterosexual domestic relationships unless otherwise specified. It is also important to clarify that, as many of the sources referred to in this chapter build their arguments in the context of marriage, the terms 'marriage' and 'domestic relationship' should also be read interchangeably unless the context otherwise requires.

For the purposes of this chapter, I also introduce a second boundary condition. Hierarchies and differences of power within domestic relationships can take many forms, not all of which might be resolvable by a framework of enforceable rights and obligations. For example, certain feminist scholars have argued against the legal mandating of shared domestic responsibilities during the course of a domestic relationship,[7] as opposed to modifying 'external counterweights',[8] such as equal entitlement to spousal earnings or more flexible work. Claims to the freedom of intimate association and arguments for limitations upon state intervention place further obstacles against the direct transplantation of the rights regime into the domain of the domestic relationship, without at least some modifications.[9]

I therefore limit myself to one set of claims: remuneration for unpaid domestic labour, performed during the course of the domestic relationship, which takes the form of enforceable property rights against the male spouse at the time of separation (and which, therefore, raises no concerns about the right to intimate association and the inadequacy of a rights framework to address inequalities within intimate associations[10]). I will argue that the institutional approach allows us to understand unpaid domestic labour as a violation of horizontal constitutional rights and property claims on separation (which exist through legislation in some jurisdictions, but not all) as a remedy. It is important to note that this does not exclude other remedies (whether rights-based or not) that can be taken by spouses both during the course of the relationship and upon separation.

In section II of this chapter ('Contextualising the Issue'), I will argue that historically, within the context of the domestic relationship, housework has first, not been considered 'work' (that merits consideration or remuneration);

[7] J Elshtain, *Power Trips and Other Journeys* (University of Wisconsin Press, 1990).

[8] Satz, 'Feminist Perspectives on Reproduction and the Family' (n 4).

[9] See ch 3 of this book.

[10] I do not here claim that the institutional approach and the horizontal rights framework cannot – or should not – be applied during the existence of the domestic relationship; only that doing so would raise a set of complex issues and concerns that would be beyond the scope of this book to do justice to.

secondly, has been considered to be freely and voluntarily performed, primarily by female spouses; or thirdly, has been treated as an obligation inherent in familial life. Recently, however, each of these assumptions has been challenged. Not only do housework and care work enable the existence of capitalist work cycles by 'freeing up' men to participate in market-mediated work, but they also constitute an independent contribution to the economy. Furthermore, statistics demonstrate that a disproportionate burden of housework and care work falls upon the shoulders of women, including women who participate in the 'formal' workforce – thus suggesting that it is a combination of social norms and cultural expectations that effectively compel women to perform housework and domestic work.[11]

In section III, I will argue that these responses suggest a role for the institutional approach. So far, I have been referring to the family as a social institution. However, for the purposes of my analysis, I will demonstrate that the domestic relationship (whether formally defined as a 'marriage' or not) itself bears the hallmarks of an institution as defined here. The domestic relationship is, of course, embedded within the institution of the patriarchal family, so the distinction may not matter very much. In accordance with the elements of an institution as discussed in chapter five, the institution of the domestic relationship is a 'comprehensive' one: first, it exercises a dominant and pervasive influence upon the lives of those who are a part of it. Secondly, it constructs a hierarchy of power between men and women (as the evidence provided in section II indicates). Thirdly, its centrality in social and cultural life makes the prospect of an individual 'exit' difficult, and (in a non-trivial set of cases) infeasible. In many cases, the inability to exit is a direct function of institutional inequalities within marriage (for example, unpaid housework, which creates an economic imbalance between the spouses).

More specifically, this institutional difference in power is exacerbated by the background legal framework – in particular, marital property rules. Under most legal regimes, domestic work, housework and care work do not vest in the spouse an enforceable right to marital or domestic property (such as the shared marital home). This leads to a predominance of situations where such property is formally under the legal control of the male spouse (often enabled by the fact that the male spouse is the primary earning member of the family). This, in turn, makes exit from the institution more difficult (for economic reasons), and

[11] See, eg UN Women, 'Promoting Women's Economic Empowerment: Reorganizing and Investing in the Care Economy' (May 2018) www.unwomen.org/-/media/headquarters/attachments/sections/library/publications/2018/issue-paper-recognizing-and-investing-in-the-care-economy-en.pdf?la=en&v=2004; see also the statistics in UN Women, 'Redistributing Unpaid Care and Sustaining Quality Care Services: A Prerequisite for Gender Equality' (2016) Policy Brief No 5, www.unwomen.org/-/media/headquarters/attachments/sections/library/publications/2016/un-women-policy-brief-05-redistributing-unpaid-care-en.pdf?la=en&v=2644.

entrenches the institutional differences in power (although this is by no means a universal situation, especially in the twenty-first century).

Moreover, the final precondition of the institutional approach – that the institutionally mediated differences in power between parties enable one to violate the rights of the other – is also present in the case of the domestic relationship. The extraction of unpaid labour constitutes a violation of multiple constitutional rights. The most obvious violation, of course, is of the right to equality and against non-discrimination. Equally important are the rights to property, and to life and livelihood. Next, I will suggest that the right against forced labour (in its expanded sense, as articulated by the *PUDR* judgment discussed in chapter five) is also involved. Each of these rights are already present in vertical form, in some or most constitutions. The institutional approach makes a case for extending them to the horizontal domain of the domestic relationship and the family.

In section IV, I shall consider the remedies that the institutional approach can be invoked to provide. Historically, the most common response, framed in the language of rights, has been a demand for wages for housework. This has taken different forms in different countries. What is common to the different models, however, is that the 'wage' is paid by the state, on the premise that housework and care work constitute contributions to the national economy, which must be recompensed by the state.[12] This makes the issue of wages for housework a somewhat poor example of the institutional approach, as either the right is against the state (which makes it a vertical right) or, at the very least, it is claimed from the state (thus bringing it into the domain of positive obligations).

However, there is another set of remedies that fits better within the scheme of the institutional approach. These remedies revolve around division of income and property at the time of divorce or separation. In many jurisdictions, 'indirect contributions' to marital income and property – which take the specific forms of housework and care work – are considered in the division of assets. These indirect contributions, then, take the form of claims against the (predominantly) male spouse, and are therefore horizontal in character. They also specifically take the form of remedies for the rights violations (in the form of unpaid or forced labour) that are the result of the institutional differences in power between the spouses in a marital relationship. And finally, the nature of the remedy also speaks to the institutional approach's logic: the success of such claims guarantees

[12] See the historical discussion in L Toupin, *Wages for Housework: A History of an International Feminist Movement, 1972–77* (Pluto Press, 2018). In 2021, a promise by a state politician in India to introduce compensation for housework in his manifesto sparked a national debate. See, eg A Sunil, 'Wages of Housework' *The Hindu* (31 January 2021); K Bhat, 'Wages for Housework?' *The Hindu* (21 February 2021); A Chandrasekharan, 'Wages for Housework' *The Indian Express* (20 January 2021).

a partial ability to exit from specific marital relationships at any time, an ability that is often stymied because of a lack of resources due to unequal earning power within the relationship. The institutional approach, therefore, provides a plausible case for such property claims to take the form of a directly enforceable constitutional right, where it does not already exist in legislation; and, as we shall see, it informs legislation where it does exist.

To substantiate how this might work in practice, this section will consider judgments from various jurisdictions that have considered this issue, within the frameworks of the differing constitutional contexts that I discussed in the introduction to this part and in the previous chapter: that is, where enforceable horizontal rights exist in constitutions, and where they do not.

As with the previous chapters, the purpose of examining doctrine is not to provide a comparative overview of case law or to sum up the existing jurisprudence on family law in these jurisdictions. Rather, it is to provide archetypes of judicial and legal reasoning, which demonstrate the possible practical applications of the institutional approach, within existing parameters of constitutional adjudication.

Also as with the previous chapter, it is important to clarify that the concrete adjustment of rights is a task for legislation (indeed, in some jurisdictions, such as New Zealand and Kenya, legislation requires judges to take into account domestic labour and care work at the time of division of assets upon separation[13]). As noted above, the task of the institutional approach is to provide recourse in cases where there is a legislative vacuum or insufficient law. Further, this chapter does not make the argument that such property claims constitute the *only* legal structure that can mitigate the institutional imbalance of power – and the consequent rights violations – that occur in the context of the domestic relationship. More modestly, it argues that such claims constitute one plausible existing structure that can do so. Jurisdictions may settle upon different legal solutions to the problem identified by the institutional approach. The discussion of property claims is to outline one such solution that is consistent with the institutional approach.

There are three caveats that must be set out before I commence with my argument. First, it is important to acknowledge that across the world, domestic relationships – and, indeed, the family – exist in diverse and plural forms. Cis-hetereopatriarchy is not a necessary condition for society to exist, nor is it my claim that the following account of power differences and rights violations within the context of domestic relationships is universally applicable. However, as in the previous chapter, I believe that there exist enough commonalities across jurisdictions for the institutional approach to be useful in addressing and mitigating a range of power differences and rights violations within the institution of domestic relationships. Indeed, as statistics compiled by organisations such

[13] See s IV of this chapter for a discussion.

as UN Women (referred to above) show, the issues identified in this chapter are common to many countries.

Secondly, it is important to note that the arguments advanced in this chapter are not meant to exhaust the domain of constitutional law as applied to the family. In particular, they are not meant to operate to the exclusion of state obligations towards the family form. In other words, this is not an argument for 'privatising' rights inhering within the family, ie shifting obligations from the state to individuals (in our case, the male spouse). As scholars have pointed out, one of the consequences of treating the family as a 'private' domain has been to minimise the state's positive (welfare) obligations to ensure that families can lead a flourishing existence (for example, family rights to welfare, to child support, to ensure an adequate standard of education for children).[14] However, horizontality by definition involves state intervention into the domain of the family (through the vehicle of constitutional rights) and therefore rejects the idea of the family as a 'private' domain. Furthermore, horizontal constitutional obligations (concretised through statute or judge-made law) with respect to property distribution at the time of separation, as explained above, do not detract from or alter the state's positive obligations of material support towards domestic relationships and family units while they continue to be in existence.[15]

This, in fact, also explains that while the rationale for the application of the institutional approach is grounded in a challenge to the historical treatment of family relations as 'private' and outside the realm of justice, the scope of the institutional approach (as developed in this chapter) is limited to one very specific area of family law: the property rules in a domestic relationship at the time of separation. The reason for this (as indicated above) is that many of the injustices that arise from the 'privatisation' of the family involve the abdication of the state from discharging its positive obligations, and therefore require articulating and enforcing claims against the state. By definition, the institutional approach applies to situations involving relative differences in power between private individuals (because of their institutional location), the violation of rights as a result and the application of a remedy against the private rights violator. In these specific terms, the institutional approach identifies men and women in a domestic relationship within the family as holding different degrees of institutional

[14] AL Alstott, 'Neoliberalism in US Family Law: Negative Liberty and Laissez-Faire Markets in the Minimal State' (2014) 77 *Law and Contemporary Problems* 25; for a proposed application of these ideas in mid-20th-century India, see, eg *Women's Role in the Planned Economy*, discussed in G Bhatia, *The Transformative Constitution* (HarperCollins, 2019) ch 7.

[15] For example, Shanley argues for divorce rules that treat the wages of the primary wage earner and primary caregiver as joint property, but that are categorically complementary to the range of state welfare obligations discussed above. ML Shanley, 'Just Marriage' in J Cohen and D Chasman (eds), *Just Marriage* (Oxford University Press, 2004) 1, 25. Similarly, for an analysis of how Indian courts have attempted to quantify unpaid domestic labour not at the time of separation, but in cases involving compensation claims for deaths caused by motor vehicles, see P Kotiswaran, 'An Ode to Altruism: How Indian Courts Value Unpaid Work' (2021) 56(36) *Economic and Political Weekly* 45.

power, the violation of rights due to uncompensated labour performed by the latter within the domestic relationship, and a remedy that takes the form of vested property rights in case of separation. To reiterate, although the remedy applies at the time of separation, its existence makes the possibility of exit more feasible at all times during the continuation of the domestic relationship, thus mitigating (to a degree) the inequality of power.

It is also not the claim of this chapter that the institutional approach can solve all problems even at the time of separation. As scholars have pointed out, equitable divorce rules still assume that there exist resources to divide up. For families that are already in debt or in poverty, counting the female spouse's care work and other labour as granting her a vested right in property is unlikely to benefit her in any significant way[16] (although there may be marginal benefits[17]). While this is undoubtedly true, it only goes to show that the institutional approach cannot resolve all injustices that exist within family relations and the domestic relationship, whether functioning or broken. The institutional approach is meant to mitigate only the rights-violating consequences that flow from the male spouse's relatively greater institutional power, and is ultimately complementary to a range of family and domestic relationship-centred rights that are primarily enforceable against the state.

Finally, it is important to clarify that the choice of the family – and within that, the marital relationship – as the subject of analysis is not intended to 'normalise … in effect the institution of heterosexual marriage to the exclusion of other organisational forms of for the provision of social reproduction'.[18] Nor is it intended to endorse 'a sliding scale of value' that privileges marital relationships over other forms of cohabitation when it comes to considering care work and reproductive labour.[19] Rather, the family and the marital relationship are the focus of this chapter because, as shall be shown in section IV, it helps illustrate the workings of the institutional approach in all the contexts that I have discussed in this book: direct application in the absence of law, supplementing existing private law regimes where there are gaps and providing a background interpretive framework. The insights from this chapter, however, will apply beyond the family and the marital relationship as well, contributing to what Prabha Kotiswaran calls the 'expansion of the reproduction boundary' beyond the family to other domains.[20]

[16] ibid.

[17] See, eg *Bhe v Magistrate, Khayelitsha* 2005 (1) SA 580 (CC) (Constitutional Court of South Africa).

[18] P Kotiswaran, 'The Laws of Social Reproduction: A Lesson in Appropriation' (2013) 64 *Northern Ireland Law Quarterly* 317, 321; KL Quinn, 'Mommy Dearest: The Focus of the Family in Legal Feminism' (2002) 37 *Harvard Civil Rights-Civil Liberties Law Review* 447.

[19] A Barlow, 'Configuration(s) of Unpaid Caregiving within Current Legal Discourse in and around the Family' (2007) 58 *Northern Ireland Law Quarterly* 251.

[20] P Kotiswaran, 'The Laws of Social Reproduction' (n 18) 322. Kotiswaran considers the cases of surrogacy, bar dancing and sex work: social reproduction outside the family and mediated by the market.

II. CONTEXTUALISING THE ISSUE

The investigation of the public/private divide as a social construct has been a central theme of this book. The public/private divide, as considered so far, has drawn its dividing line between the domains of the state and the non-state. The concept itself, however, has had multiple overlapping meanings throughout history. A second, equally consequential distinction has been between the spheres of social production and reproduction[21] – or, as one scholar puts it, between 'the public realm of politics, law, and the market, on the one hand, and the private realm of family, the household, and intimacy, on the other'.[22] The former is deemed to be the province of justice, while the latter is not.

As Carole Pateman, along with many others, has argued at some length, this division is essentially gendered in nature.[23] Its contemporary origins belong to the same historical period (the evolution of capitalism) discussed in chapter one of this book. The concentration of sovereign power within the state, and consequently the imperative to limit the powers of the state, was accompanied by the aforesaid division between the public and the private spheres, with different sets of rules being applied to each.[24] As Seyla Benhabib points out:

> As the male bourgeois citizen was battling for his rights to autonomy in the religious and economic spheres against the absolutist state, his relations in the household were defined by non-consensual, nonegalitarian assumptions. Questions of justice were from the beginning restricted to the 'public sphere', whereas the private sphere was considered outside the realm of justice.[25]

Thus, the political principles (including principles of rights) that were applicable to the public sphere (here, 'public' included everything beyond the domain of the domestic) were deemed not to apply to the private sphere. This was accomplished through 'various versions of a separation between public or civil authority from the private world of the household'.[26]

The arguments for and against excluding the family from the domain of justice have been the subject of extensive debate, and I do not intend to rehearse them here.[27] For the purposes of this chapter, I take it as established that feminist

[21] See, eg S Federici, *Caliban and the Witch: Women, The Body and Primitive Accumulation* (Autonomedia, 2004) 8. Federici distinguishes between the sphere of waged labour (production) and unpaid labour in the home (reproduction).

[22] W Lucy, 'Private and Public: Some Banalities about a Platitude' in C Mac Amhlaigh, C Michelon and N Walker (eds), *After Public Law* (Oxford University Press, 2013) 56, 77.

[23] See, eg C Pateman, *The Sexual Contract* (Polity Press, 1988); Okin, *Justice, Gender, and the Family* (n 3).

[24] SM Okin, 'Women and the Making of the Sentimental Family' (1981) 11 *Philosophy and Public Affairs* 65.

[25] S Benhabib, *Situating the Self: Gender, Community, and Postmodernism in Contemporary Ethics* (Polity Press, 1992) 109.

[26] A Hughes, 'Learning from the Levelers?' in E Anderson (ed), *Private Government: How Employers Rule Our Lives (and Why We Don't Talk about It)* (Princeton University Press, 2009) 75, 87.

[27] For an account, see Satz, 'Feminist Perspectives on Reproduction and the Family' (n 4).

scholarship has displaced any presumption that the family, as a social institution, exists prior to, or outside of, the claims of justice. Needless to say, how and in what form the claims of justice will apply to a particular relationship, or set of relationships, within the family remains to be affirmatively established.

Moving on, the construction and articulation of the public/private divide in this way was both constituted by, and had specific consequences for, work performed within the household in the context of the domestic relationship (excluding domestic work that was contracted out upon a wage-labour basis). Unlike work performed within the formally defined labour market, work performed within the 'private realm of the family' (and predominantly by women), unless contracted out, was unremunerated. As Sandra Fredman points out, various justifications have been advanced for this over time. First, housework – and, in particular, some of its concrete forms, such as care work – was deemed not to qualify as 'work' (Pateman observes that it was articulated in the language of 'nurture'[28]), and therefore not deserving of remuneration. Secondly, such work was deemed to be freely and voluntarily performed (primarily by female spouses), and therefore fundamentally opposed to the wage-work that was performed in the 'public sphere'.[29] And thirdly, such work was deemed to be performed as part of the 'family bargain', where the (predominantly male) spouse who worked in the labour market earned the wages for the sustenance of the family unit, while the work within the domestic relationship, which enabled the (predominantly male) spouse to work in the first place, remained unwaged.[30] The co-constitutive evolution of the public/private divide, and its gendered character in terms of work, is summed by Silvia Federici in the following way:

> With the demise of the subsistence economy that had prevailed in pre-capitalist Europe, the unity of production and reproduction which has been typical of all societies based on production-for-use came to an end, as these activities became the carriers of different social relations *and were sexually differentiated*. In the new monetary regime, only production-for-market was defined as a value-creating activity, whereas the reproduction of the worker began to be considered as valueless from an economic viewpoint and even ceased to be considered as work. Reproductive work continued to be paid – though at the lowest rates – when performed for the master class or outside the home. But the economic importance of the reproduction of labor-power carried out in the home, and its function in the accumulation of capital became invisible, *being mystified as a natural vocation and labeled 'women's labor'*. In addition,

[28] Pateman, *The Sexual Contract* (n 23).

[29] P Kleingeld, 'Just Love? Marriage and the Question of Justice' (1998) 24 *Social Theory and Practice* 261, 262.

[30] S Fredman, *Women and the Law* (Oxford University Press, 1998) ch 4. For a detailed history of the evolution of these ideas through 19th-century liberal capitalism, 20th-century state capitalism and 21st-century neoliberal financialised capitalism, see N Fraser, 'Crisis of Care? On the Social-Reproductive Contradictions of Contemporary Capitalism' in Bhattacharya, *Social Reproduction Theory* (n 1) 21.

> women were excluded from many waged occupations and, when they worked for a wage, they earned a pittance compared to the average male wage. (emphasis added)[31]

This brief history is no doubt reductive in some respects. There is evidence that specifically in the early years of the Industrial Revolution, both the male and the female spouses worked in the labour market (especially in factories, and in paid domestic work), although this did not prevent the primary burden of domestic work from continuing to fall upon the female spouse (with the burden inequitably distributed along class lines as well).[32] Similarly, at the time, wage-work was sometimes performed within the home (such as put-out work, ie work sub-contracted and performed from an individual's home), and often by women.[33] The above history also assumes the predominance of the nuclear family unit, as opposed to larger – or joint – families, where the allocation of domestic work may have followed a different pattern. While it is important to acknowledge these features, I believe that they do not, ultimately, detract from the limited point that I make here: that is, to establish the link between the public/private divide (as articulated in this chapter), and the ubiquity of unwaged and gendered character of domestic work, performed within a domestic relationship.

For quite a few decades, however, these assumptions have been contested. Philosophically, as pointed out above, the concept of the public/private divide upon which unwaged domestic labour rests has been challenged. It has been demonstrated to be historically contingent and socially and legally constructed, rather than 'natural'.[34] Conceptually, it has been argued that it is only domestic work that enables, or 'frees up', male spouses to participate in the labour market. Waged labour, therefore, is in a very basic sense dependent upon the unwaged labour within the domestic relationship.[35] This relationship between gendered household labour and gendered disparity in workforce participation has been demonstrated empirically as well.[36] Also empirically, the contribution of domestic work, in real terms, to countries' gross domestic product has been

[31] Federici, *Caliban and the Witch* (n 21) 75. See also MB McKenna, 'Feminist Materialism and the Laws of Social Reproduction' in P O'Connell and U Ozsu (eds), *The Research Handbook on Law and Marxism* (Edward Elgar, 2021) 283.

[32] Federici, *Caliban and the Witch* (n 21).

[33] Federici, *Caliban and the Witch* (n 21) 72.

[34] See, eg F Olsen, 'The Myth of State Intervention in the Family' (1985) *Journal of Law Reform* 835.

[35] 'The Reproduction of Labour Power in the Global Economy and the Unfinished Feminist Revolution' in S Federici, *Revolution at Point Zero: Housework, Reproduction, and the Feminist Struggle* (PM Press, 2012) 91; M Mies, *Patriarchy and Accumulation on a World Scale* (Zed Books, 1986); it is important to note that these arguments have not been limited to the Global North, nor is it that similar arguments made in the Global South are merely derivative in nature. See, eg S Anandhi, 'Middle Class Women in Colonial Tamil Nadu, 1920–1947: Gender Relation and the Problem of Consciousness' (PhD thesis, Jawaharlal Nehru University, 1992) 204, https://shodhganga.inflibnet.ac.in/handle/10603/14993.

[36] See, eg Chandrasekharan, 'Wages for Housework' (n 12), citing economic studies for India.

estimated to be very substantial.[37] Finally, it has been demonstrated that even in societies where 'traditional' gender roles have begun to break down to greater or lesser degrees, the increased participation of women in the labour market has not led to a more equitable division of work responsibilities within the domestic relationship, leading to what is now commonly known as 'the second shift'.[38] Multiple reasons have been identified for this, which go back to the original 'gendering' of the private sphere, discussed above. As Shanley points out, for example, when considering the social construction of the 'ideal worker':

> Employment practices … [have] developed around the sexual division of labor. Jobs were designated 'male' or 'female', and men's jobs tended to pay higher wages than women's … although discrimination against women in the workplace has diminished, the ideal worker model continues to affect both decisions to marry and the dynamics within marriages … the difference in wage-earning capacity between men and women gives men more resources with which to deal with the world, and this in turn affects dynamics within the family … Because many jobs are sex segregated, and wages for men's jobs are higher than those for women's, it will make economic sense in some families for the husband to work full time and his wife to do the caregiving.[39]

The gendered character of the public/private divide, with the bulk of domestic work continuing to be performed by women, persists worldwide even today.[40] It has also received judicial attention. As the US Supreme Court observed as recently as 2003:

> Because employers continued to regard the family as the woman's domain, they often denied men similar accommodations or discouraged them from taking leave. These mutually reinforcing stereotypes created a self-fulfilling cycle of discrimination that forced women to continue to assume the role of primary family caregiver, and fostered employers' stereotypical views about women's commitment to work and their value as employees.[41]

On the basis of all the arguments advanced above, it is evident that the question of unwaged domestic labour is one of public and political justice: the arguments that would seek to relegate it to a 'private' issue, beyond the scope of the norms of justice, have been proved to be lacking in all relevant respects. For the purposes of this chapter, however, something more needs to be done. It needs to be shown, first, that the domestic relationship is a fit case for the application of

[37] See, eg UNRISD, 'Research and Policy Brief 9: Why Care Matters for Social Development', www.unrisd.org/80256B3C005BCCF9/(httpAuxPages)/25697FE238192066C12576D4004CFE50/%24file/RPB9e.pdf. For a survey of some of the literature, see C Hoskyns and SM Rai, 'Recasting the Global Political Economy: Counting Women's Unpaid Work' (2007) 12 *New Political Economy* 297.

[38] A Hochschild, *The Second Shift: Working Parents and the Revolution at Home* (Viking, 1989); N Folbre, *Who Pays for the Kids? Gender and the Structure of Constraint* (Routledge, 1994).

[39] Shanley, 'Just Marriage' (n 15) 1, 21–22.

[40] For data from more than 90 countries, see, eg The International Labour Organisation, 'Care Work and Care Jobs for the Future of Decent Work', www.ilo.org/wcmsp5/groups/public/---dgreports/---dcomm/--- publ/documents/publication/wcms_633135.pdf.

[41] *Nevada Department of Human Resources v Hibbs* 538 US 721 (2003).

the institutional approach; and secondly, that the political injustice of unwaged domestic work can be mitigated through a coherent and persuasive model of horizontal rights, enforceable within the domestic relationship. That is the burden of the next two sections.

III. THE APPLICABILITY OF THE INSTITUTIONAL APPROACH

The domestic relationship bears all the hallmarks of an 'institution', within the meaning of the institutional approach. As indicated above, it is nested within the social institution of the family, which, as Okin points out, remains 'an important sphere of distribution of many social goods, from the material to the intangible'.[42] The link between the domestic relationship and access to primary goods is, indeed, one of the bases upon which Rawls classified it as one of the institutions that constitutes the 'basic structure of society',[43] and therefore subject to the principles of justice.

It is in this sense that the domestic relationship is a 'comprehensive' institution. As discussed in previous chapters, for the comprehensiveness condition to be met, it is not essential that everyone be mandated to participate in the institution. Rather, the institution's social role in mediating access to basic goods, as well as the degree of influence it does exercise over those who participate in it, are the determining factors. On those parameters, there is little doubt that the domestic relationship qualifies, as a 'social institution … [that] plays a crucial role in serving as an impersonal source of value that can give meaning to personal choice'.[44] Furthermore, as Okin points out, even those who have not yet entered, or will not enter, into a domestic relationship are socialised by the norms and expectations that surround it ('anticipation of marriage'[45]).

Secondly, for the reasons described above, the domestic relationship is characterised by socially and legally created – and reinforced – differences in power: 'gender-structured marriage is a clear case of socially created and reinforced inequality'.[46] As Kleingeld spells out:

> Marriage as a social institution still largely determined by gender ideology as well as by laws, policies, and institutions that reinforce the traditional patriarchal form of marriage. As household labor studies have consistently shown, women continue to perform more housework than men. Even women with full-time paid jobs often work a 'second shift', putting in significantly more hours per week than their male counterparts. This makes it easier for men and harder for women to improve their position in the labor market (by working overtime, taking evening courses, and so on). Moreover,

[42] Okin, *Justice, Gender, Justice, and the Family* (n 3) 135.
[43] J Rawls, *A Theory of Justice* (Belknap Press, 1971).
[44] MC Regan, 'Between Justice and Commitment' in Cohen and Chasman, *Just Marriage* (n 15) 67, 72.
[45] Okin, *Justice, Gender, and the Family* (n 3) 142.
[46] ibid 123.

> women stand to suffer a sharp drop in their standard of living after divorce. The fact that women assume most of the responsibilities for child care – in part as a result of their weaker position economically, educationally, and in the marriage – further affects their potential to be independent through paid jobs, and thus perpetuates this situation of inequality. Clearly, then, elements of gender injustice persist in both the legal and the social reality of marriage.[47]

It is important to note, too, that these differences in power are not temporary in nature or freely chosen, but are enduring in character and constitutive of the institution.[48] They are the consequence of a range of factors beyond the direct control or will of individual parties, such as norms and patterns of behaviour, socialisation and legal structures. They are thus distinct from the temporary, variable and freely chosen positions of authority or dependence that might accompany other relationships.[49] Indeed, Nancy Fraser specifically uses the language of institutions – and the institutional context – to articulate women's vulnerability within a domestic relationship. As Fraser observes, while commenting on the work of Okin:

> [W]omen's traditional responsibility for childrearing helps shape labor markets that disadvantage women; the result is unequal power in the economic marketplace, which in turn reintroduces and exacerbates, unequal power in the family. Women, thus, are rendered vulnerable, first by anticipation of marriage, since the expectation of primary domestic and child-care responsibilities burdens their decisions about education, training, and degree of commitment to employment. Next, women are rendered vulnerable within marriage, since they enter it with inferior labor market opportunities and, hence, with less leverage over their husbands; vulnerability increases in marriage over time, moreover, as the gap in spouses' earning power, and thus in exit options, widens. And finally, women are rendered vulnerable in separation or divorce, which usually brings a precipitous drop in women's and children's standards of living.[50]

Indeed, Fraser's observations come as part of her critique of Carole Pateman's classification of the marriage contract as constituting a set of individual 'master/subject relations'. Fraser's critique is precisely that gender inequality within domestic relationships is better understood as 'a set of impersonal structural mechanisms that are lived through more fluid, cultural forms'.[51] This, it will be noted, is exactly the language of the institutional approach, which specifically seeks to replace the concept of interpersonal domination with an institutional one.

[47] Kleingeld, 'Just Love? Marriage and the Question of Justice' (n 29) 262–63.

[48] See, eg E Brake, *After Marriage: Rethinking Marital Relationships* (Oxford University Press, 2016) 100.

[49] ibid.

[50] N Fraser, 'Beyond the Master/Subject Model: Reflections on Carole Pateman's Sexual Contract' (1993) 37 Social Text 173, 175.

[51] ibid 181.

Furthermore, the 'direct personal economic dependence that results from the division of labour within the average family'[52] has an immediate bearing on another important characteristic of institutions: difficulty – and, in particular, asymmetry – of individual exit.[53] Indeed, dependence *within* the domestic relationship and inability to exit *from* the domestic relationship are mutually reinforcing, ie:

> [W]ithin ongoing marriages, increasing economic inequality between spouses reduces the worse-off party's exit options. This, in turn, leads to power inequality in decision-making, as the less powerful party is less able to protect her interests and consequently becomes even less powerful.[54]

As Fraser pithily puts it, in the domestic relationship, 'voice correlates inversely with opportunities for exit'.[55] Or, to cite a more detailed formulation:

> The gendered division of labor and the fact that 'women's work' is less well-paid than men's together make it more likely that married women, rather than their husbands, will downgrade their careers, choose part-time work, or stay home to facilitate child-rearing or when the spouses' careers conflict. These choices make women 'vulnerable by marriage': economic dependence, and dependence on marriage for benefits such as health insurance, fosters power inequality and makes exit difficult, in turn facilitating abuse.[56]

The domestic relationship, therefore, is an institution that is comprehensive in nature. It creates an enduring hierarchy of power between men and women (located within the larger patriarchal institution of the family). And exit very often carries high costs.

Having established the existence of an institution in all its relevant senses, the next step is to identify the rights at issue. Recall that the institutional approach is a model of bounded horizontality: a private party can enforce rights horizontally against another private party only in those circumstances where both parties belong to the institution, and the duty bearer's institutional location enables them to violate the rights of the rights bearer. It is therefore important to demarcate which rights are sought to be enforced in the context of the domestic relationship.

First, the most obvious right that is violated is that of non-discrimination, on grounds of sex. An important distinction must be drawn here: as scholars have pointed out, it would be both impossible and counter-productive to

[52] Okin, *Justice, Gender, and the Family* (n 3) 122.

[53] A Sen, 'Gender and Cooperative Conflict' in I Tinker (ed), *Persistent Inequalities: Women and World Development* (Oxford University Press, 1991) 123.

[54] Brake, *After Marriage* (n 48) 102, 106.

[55] Fraser, "Beyond the Master/Subject Model' (n 50).

[56] E Brake, 'Marriage and Domestic Partnership', *The Stanford Encyclopedia of Philosophy*, https://plato.stanford.edu/entries/marriage/; see also J Waldron, 'When Justice Replaces Affection: The Need for Rights' (1988) 11 *Harvard Journal of Law and Public Policy* 625.

require intimate and affective relationships to conform to a standard of absolute personal equality in all their dimensions (and, indeed, individuals in such affective relationships might choose otherwise). What we are concerned with here, however, is gendered institutional inequality, whose source is the difference in institutional power held by the members of a domestic relationship. The violation of equality (in its institutional form) has been exhibited above, and I will not reiterate it here.

Secondly, there is a potential infringement of the right to property, which most, but not all, constitutions guarantee in the vertical form. As has been discussed extensively above, the failure to count domestic work as wage-work, coupled with the fact that legal regimes vest formal title in property only on the basis of financial contribution, results in a situation where marital property is predominantly in the name of the male spouse. At the time of separation, this results in the fact that, notwithstanding substantial contributions (in the form of domestic work and care work over the course of the marital relationship), the female spouse has no legal claim to the property (whose purchase would not, in many cases, have been possible without her unwaged contribution). Indeed, on the basis of exactly this reasoning, the Colombian Constitutional Court recognised the female spouse's right of possession *in* marital property, derived directly from the Colombian Constitution (while not going as far as recognising a right *to* property).[57]

Thirdly, the factors pointed out above make it clear that the institutional imbalances of power infringe the right to livelihood. This flows directly from the structural economic dependency that has been discussed previously in this section. Admittedly, the right to livelihood is not present in vertical form in many constitutions. In some jurisdictions, however, such as India (which will be discussed below), the right to livelihood has been 'read into' the right to life, and held to contain, at a threshold level, arbitrary deprivation of livelihood.[58] In such jurisdictions, for the reasons explained above, the right to livelihood is a prime candidate for horizontal application.

Arguably, unpaid domestic work also implicates a fourth right: that against forced labour. Recall that, in chapter five, while discussing the case of *PUDR v Union of India*, it had been argued that the word 'force' need not be limited to direct and individualised coercion (such as an individual putting a gun to another person's head). Force can, and often is, structural and institutional in nature (in the *PUDR* case, it was the 'mute compulsion of economic relations' in a market economy). The three reasons adduced above for why unpaid domestic work within a domestic relationship continues to be unpaid also demonstrate how such work falls within the broader definition of 'forced labour'. Note that

[57] See Sentencia No T-494/92 Corte Constitucional de Colombia (Colombian Constitutional Court).

[58] See, eg *Olga Tellis v Bombay Municipal Corporation* AIR 1986 SC 180.

the compelled character of the work – in the sense that *PUDR* articulated it – does not change by virtue of the fact that the male spouse's income may be used for family subsistence purposes: its cause is a set of norms, patterns and expectations that are themselves constitutive of the social institution of the domestic relationship, and therefore carry an institutional character.[59]

As Shanley points out: 'while marriage and divorce laws themselves are now usually drafted in gender-neutral terms, cultural norms and employment practices perpetuate a division of labor at work and at home that results in a system of gender and racial hierarchy'.[60]

Thus, it is specifically within the context of the institutional approach, with its accounting for impersonal violations of rights, that we can identify unpaid domestic labour within the domestic relationship as forced labour, and propose a horizontal rights framework to mitigate it. Indeed, this argument is not as radical as it might sound. While not using the explicit framing of 'forced labour', Satz nonetheless observes, in the context of domestic work in a domestic relationship: 'It is not enough to allow people to choose if their choices are unfairly constrained by unequal family and workplace structures, unequal pay for equal work, and inadequate social and welfare services which together render so many women vulnerable.'[61] It will be noticed that this idea of 'unfree choice' is, in relevant respects, equivalent to that of 'forced labour'.[62]

As a final caveat, it is important to acknowledge that there do, of course, exist domestic relationships where, by mutual agreement, roles and responsibilities are distributed on a more equitable basis. The presence of exceptions, however, does not undermine the institutional argument. Furthermore, as we shall see in the next section, legal application and remedies in this domain are flexible enough to account for exceptions of precisely this nature.

IV. APPLICATION AND REMEDIES

So far in this chapter, I have argued that (i) the domestic relationship constitutes an institution for the purposes of the institutional approach and (ii) unpaid, gendered domestic work constitutes an infringement of constitutional rights of the institutionally less powerful party by the institutionally more powerful party. This brings me to the final prong of the institutional approach: the questions of application and remedies.

[59] For example, quoting data from India's National Sample Survey, Sirisha C Naidu points out that more than 60% of both rural and urban women stated that they took on domestic duties because 'no other family member was available'. SC Naidu, 'Domestic Labour and Female Labour Force Participation: Adding a Piece to the Puzzle' (2016) LI(44–45) *Economic and Political Weekly* 101, 105.

[60] Shanley, 'Just Marriage' (n 15) 1, 20. Note that 'racial hierarchy' is specific to the USA, but has its equivalents elsewhere. In India, for example, it would be caste hierarchy.

[61] Satz, 'Feminist Perspectives on Reproduction and the Family' (n 3).

[62] This reading is supported by Kotiswaran, 'Wages for Housework' (n 15).

As indicated above, there exists a range of policy-based as well as legal responses designed to mitigate institutional inequalities and rights violations within domestic relationships, including the question of unpaid, gendered domestic labour. The institutional approach, of course, speaks the language of horizontal rights, and therefore seeks to address only one specific form of mitigation. The institutional approach itself may be applied to a subsisting relationship: for example, by treating domestic work as a financial contribution that triggers a joint right in the marital property that may only be legally in the name of the male spouse, and precludes one spouse from disposing of it without the consent of the other. However, for reasons discussed above, in this chapter, I will limit the discussion to the enforceable horizontal rights at the time of separation.

The question of separation or exit – and how it links back to inequalities and rights violations within the domestic relationship – has been discussed in the previous section. To put it schematically: unpaid, gendered domestic labour reinforces and entrenches the differences in institutional power that already exist between the spouses when they enter the domestic relationship. It ensures that the income gap grows larger during the course of the relationship, and that property and assets are more likely to be legally held by the male spouse. This, in turn, both makes exit from the relationship more difficult and, relatedly, causes significantly greater hardship to the female spouse on exit.[63]

At the end of the previous section, I framed this in terms of horizontal rights violations: of equality and non-discrimination, of the right to property, of the right against forced labour and the right to life and livelihood. At its heart is the non-recognition of domestic work as work (and which, therefore, would merit remuneration). One way that the rights framework can mitigate this non-recognition is to deal with its consequences. In case of separation at an abstract level, it would mean a legal regime where non-recognised domestic work would be treated as a contribution to the domestic relationship *on equal terms* with recognised and remunerated 'outside' work. This, in turn, would require that, notwithstanding formal legal title, the female spouse would bear an equal right to marital property as the male spouse (in whose name it might be), that would be enforceable against the male spouse. How this mitigates institutional imbalance of power is evident: it ensures the legal recognition of (unpaid) domestic labour through the means of an enforceable property rights, and crucially facilitates exit from the institution. As I showed in the previous chapter, and as Fraser has specifically pointed out in the context of domestic relationships, there is a direct correlation between ability to exit *from* an institution and having a voice (ie equality) *in* the institution. Thus, in this deeper way as well, this solution addresses (to a limited and partial extent, as indicated

[63] See the discussions in AM Parkman, 'Bargaining over Housework: The Frustrating Situation of Secondary Wage Earners' (2004) 63 *American Journal of Economics and Sociology* 765; K Silbaugh, 'Turning Labor into Love: Housework and the Law' (1996) 91 *Northwestern University Law Review* 1; McKenna, 'Feminist Materialism and the Laws of Social Reproduction' (n 31).

above) institutional differences in power and rights violations within domestic relationships.

This link has been made by theoreticians ('in the event of divorce the wages of both a primary wage earner and a primary caregiver should be treated as joint property'[64]) and by various jurisdictions in legislation (as we shall see below), and also has cross-jurisdictional purchase. As noted in a document issued by multiple United Nations bodies – including, in particular, the Office of the United Nations High Commissioner for Human Rights – 'unpaid work performed by women in households and family enterprises ... should be considered in property distribution upon termination of the marriage'.[65] While these proposals exist at the levels of policy and legislation, as noted in the previous chapter, the purpose and impact of the institutional approach is to put them on a constitutional and interpretive footing.

Two preliminary points: first, as flagged above, it may be argued that with changing work patterns, there now exist a number of domestic relationships that are not adequately characterised in the manner articulated above, ie relationships where both spouses hold equal power, or where the male spouse opts to engage in domestic work and care work. There are also relationships which last for very short durations, and to which (it is widely accepted) default distribution rules ought not to apply. Now, while it is true that relationships exist along a spectrum, recall that, as argued in chapter five, the institutional approach specifically allows for the presence of departures and exceptions, as it stipulates that individuals are not *ordinarily* able to overcome institutional differences in power by dint of their specific or peculiar circumstances. It may then be objected, however, that the solution prescribed above would lead to unjust results. To this it may be answered that legislative regimes and judicial doctrine (as we shall see below) allow judges the discretion to depart from general principles of property distribution at the time of dissolution, depending upon the circumstances. In other words, the law recognises that relationships are structured in complex ways, and that the rules governing separation cannot operate rigidly. The institutional approach, it is important to note, does not deny this flexibility: what it does do is to provide a principled constitutional framework within which such cases ought *ordinarily* to be adjudicated.

This leads to a second, preliminary point. In many jurisdictions, there exists the option of marriage contracts that establish the terms upon which both parties are to enter the domestic relationship, its maintenance, as well as the consequences that will follow upon separation. One significant impact of the institutional approach is to place constraints upon the scope of the contracts: parties ought not ordinarily, for example, be able to 'contract out' of the

[64] Shanley, 'Just Marriage' (n 15) 25.

[65] UNHCR, 'A Practitioner's Toolkit on Women's Access to Justice Programming: Marriage, Family and Property Rights', www.unodc.org/pdf/criminal_justice/WA2J_Consolidated.pdf.

threshold rights framework that will apply on dissolution,[66] much like an individual cannot 'waive' a constitutional right. This is in recognition of the fact that because of institutional differences in power (which the horizontal rights framework is meant to mitigate), such contracts are structurally unequal[67] (here there are similarities with the argument advanced in the previous chapter). Needless to say, as in the last chapter, the institutional approach represents only a threshold base of rights. Through contract, parties can always agree upon more rights being vested in the rights bearer than the institutional approach requires – but they cannot settle for less. This, of course, remains subject to the judicial discretion for 'exceptional cases' discussed above.

I will now present specific examples. Here, I shall consider how different jurisdictions have dealt with the issue of equal property rights upon separation, either through legislation or through adjudication, and how the institutional approach can facilitate generative engagement with private law. As in the previous chapter, it is not my intention here to establish a regime of constitutional family law, available to litigants at the first instance. As in the case of labour law, the issues that arise out of the domestic relationship, and its breakdown, are multifaceted and fine-grained: for instance, just the issues of what ought to count as 'relationship property' and what ought to count as 'separate property', where the marital home falls within this scheme, and how the length of the relationship ought to affect this question, have proven to be hugely controversial, with jurisdictions choosing to address them in a bewildering range of ways.[68] Undoubtedly, many of these issues are best served by a legislative (or, as we shall see, common law) framework taking a first stab at dealing with them. The institutional approach has an important part to play in informing the interpretation of existing legal frameworks, filling gaps and acting as a (preferably temporary) recourse in cases of legislative vacuum.

I will take these different constitutional contexts in turn. First, I will consider situations where the option of enforcing constitutional horizontal rights directly is unavailable, and the only role open to courts is to work in and around the interstices of legislation. Consider New Zealand's Property (Relationships) Act 1976 (as amended in 2001), which establishes a presumption of equal sharing of property at the time of separation.[69] This presumption may be displaced by evidence of differential contributions to the marriage, but is specifically premised on the rejection of the assumption that financial contributions are weightier

[66] For an account of the domestic relationship governed completely by contract, see C Sunstein and R Thaler, 'Privatizing Marriage' (2008) 91 *The Monist* 377.

[67] Sen, 'Gender and Cooperative Conflict' (n 53).

[68] For a flavour, see The New Zealand Law Commission, 'Review of the Property (Relationships) Act 1976', ch 3, www.lawcom.govt.nz/sites/default/files/projectAvailableFormats/NZLC%20-%20PRA%20Review%20Project%20-%20Final%20Report%20R143_0.pdf.

[69] See *Martin v Martin* [1979] 1 NZLR 97 (CA); *Dalton v Dalton* [1979] 1 NZLR 113 (CA); *Williams v Williams* [1979] 1 NZLR 122 (CA); *P v P* [1980] 2 NZLR 278 (CA); *B v B* [2016] NZHC 1201.

than non-financial contributions.[70] One of the founding principles of the Act was to address the consequences of the gendered division of labour within domestic relationships[71] – a division that, notably, persists to this day. Thus, as recently as 2019, in an exhaustive review of the Property (Relationships) Act, the New Zealand Law Commission noted that 'the division of functions within families along traditional gender roles is still common in New Zealand'.[72]

The individual sections of the Property (Relationships) Act have been subject to considerable interpretive dispute (especially on issues regarding what constitutes 'property', and the distinctions between the different kinds of property contemplated by the Act). It is not possible here to examine the legislation in complete detail.[73] By way of illustration, however, consider the following issue, which demonstrates how and where the institutional approach might be interpretively useful. Because of conflictingly worded provisions, it was unclear whether property acquired during the marriage by virtue of separate property (which was exempt from equal distribution at the time of dissolution) would also be treated as separate, or as joint property, at the time of dissolution. The New Zealand Court of Appeal held in favour of the latter view. Woodhouse J noted that the purpose of the Act was to ensure 'the equal status of women in society'.[74] For this reason, it was explicitly noted that a departure from traditional property rules might be needed in order to secure the purposes of the Act. Thus:

> I emphasise the point against the background of s. 18 because in each of the eight areas some kind of assessment must be made; and it is not easy to add together the significance of unlike things (some tangible, some untangible), in order to estimate the total achievement of the one spouse, let alone compare it with a different achievement by the other. Furthermore, despite the injunction in s. 18(2) against preconceptions which would favour the value of monetary contributions, it is money which has the characteristic of being so easily measured for size that at a certain level weight alone might be allowed to submerge equally valuable or even superior but unquantifiable contributions of a non-monetary kind. The problem is accentuated by a tendency to attribute the whole of the money achievement to the husband or wife who seems to be directly responsible for it. Usually it is the husband. Yet it is the rare case where one spouse can properly claim sole credit for a monetary contribution

[70] See Property (Relationships) Act 1976, s 18; for an account of the Act's core principles, see P Tapp, 'The New Zealand Matrimonial Property Act 1976' (1981) 3 *OJLS* 421; for a summary of critiques, see B Atkin, 'Family Property Law Reform' (1995) 25 *Victoria University of Wellington Law Review* 77.

[71] AM Finlay 'Matrimonial Property – Comparable Sharing: An Explanation of the Matrimonial Property Bill 1975' [1975] II *Appendix to the Journals of the House of Representatives* E6.

[72] The New Zealand Law Commission, 'Review of the Property (Relationships) Act 1976' (n 68).

[73] See, eg PRH Webb, 'Achieving Inequality of Sharing under the Matrimonial Property Act of 1976: A Brief Survey', Auckland Law Faculty Seminar Paper Series, http://www.nzlii.org/nz/journals/NZLRFSP/1980/4.pdf; B Aitkin, 'What Kind of Property Is "Relationship Property"?' (2016) 47 *Victoria University of Wellington Law Review* 345. See also *Clayton v Clayton* [*Vaughan Road Property Trust*] [2016] NZSC 29.

[74] *Reid v Reid* [1979] 1 NZLR 572 (CA).

> which has been derived during the marriage from earnings or from some commercial enterprise. *Usually it is an accomplishment made possible by the support on the home front of the other spouse*; and whenever that is the position each should receive appropriate credit. (emphasis added)[75]

Thus the Court of Appeal held that, under the scheme of the Act, separate property was to be treated as a residual category, and any interpretive doubt had to be resolved in favour of joint property (and thereby equal division).[76]

As in the *Uber* case discussed in the previous chapter, the court did not explicitly contextualise what it was doing in terms of the institutional approach. However, much like in the *Uber* case, the institutional approach has explanatory power in helping understand the bases of the court's reasoning, and in deepening it, in the following two ways: first, as argued above, the 'cycle of vulnerability' that is baked into the institution of the domestic relationship commences before spouses formally enter the institution; and secondly, as we have seen, inequalities that are exacerbated during the course of the domestic relationship have a direct bearing on the difficulty of exit (which, in turn, results in a diminishing of 'voice' while in the relationship). The institutional approach, therefore, expands on the Court of Appeal's insight that the purpose of the law was to guarantee 'the equal status of women in society' by bringing an institutional lens to the question of what, precisely, constitutes 'equal status' in the context of patriarchal family structures and domestic relationships. Thus, it is the institutional approach that establishes the interpretive link between that abstract purpose – articulated by the term 'equal status' – and the specific finding that separate property is meant to be limited to a residual category.

It is important to reiterate, as indicated above, that this jurisprudential development has been broadly led by the courts, acting under the wide discretion provided by the New Zealand legislation. This provides an example for other jurisdictions where such development has not yet taken place, and where, therefore, the institutional approach can serve as an interpretive guide for the development of jurisprudence.

Consider, for example, the case of India (which also, for the purposes of this example, gives us an instance of our second constitutional context: where a written constitution with enforceable rights exists, but there is no direct horizontal right applicable to the case at hand). India's Domestic Violence Act already recognises that, in the case of domestic relationships, institutional differences in power require formal property rules to be overridden. Thus, section 19 of the Act allows judges to pass 'residence orders' that restrain the male spouse (or his family members) from evicting the female spouse from the shared household,

[75] ibid. See also *Allan v Allan* (1990) 7 FRNZ 102 (HC); *Martin v Martin* [2015] NZHC 1823. Another possible kind of judicial intervention consistent with the institutional approach would be to hold that the burden of proving separate property lies on the person who alleges it.

[76] *Reid v Reid* (n 74).

regardless of who has legal or equitable ownership over the shared household – and also prevents the male spouse from alienating the property while proceedings are pending.[77] However, despite significantly hemming in the male spouse's property rights, the Act stops short at according to the female spouse any legal right in the shared household. Consequently, if domestic violence proceedings end in separation, the protection accorded by the residence orders ends and common-law rules of maintenance – limited to the female spouse's 'reasonable needs' – become applicable. There is thus a gap between the Domestic Violence Act's recognition of institutional power imbalances (and its framing of property remedies, among others) and the absence of such recognition at the time of separation. In the absence of a statute equivalent to the Domestic Violence Act that governs the situation post-separation, the institutional approach (grounded within the Indian Constitution, which guarantees the rights to equal protection, life and livelihood, and forced labour) can serve as a source for female spouses to make post-separation claims upon male spouses. And, pending the enactment of a more detailed statutory framework, the evolution of the law can, indeed, be at the instance of the judiciary.

I will now consider the case of direct constitutional application. Previously in this chapter, I discussed the judgment of the Colombian Constitutional Court, which, in language very similar to the institutional approach, found a right to equal possession of the matrimonial property, based on uncounted domestic work. In that case, the Supreme Tribunal had refused to prevent the eviction of a widow from the matrimonial home that her husband had owned and had bequeathed to his sister.[78] The Supreme Tribunal noted that no quantification of the widow's contribution to the matrimonial home had been provided, and therefore she could not claim any interest in the property. While overturning this judgment, the Constitutional Court noted that it had the effect of 'invisiblising' domestic work,[79] which would only serve to deepen inequalities within social relations.[80] In language redolent of the institutional approach, the Court went on to observe that 'cultural, ideological, and *structural foundations*, and the logic of sexual subordination' (emphasis added), were constituted and sustained by the artificial distinction between 'productive' (and remunerated) and 'non-productive' (and non-remunerated) work, even though the latter was vital for the economy, for development and for the accumulation of capital.[81] On the basis of this analysis, the Court concluded that a refusal to factor in unpaid domestic work violated the Colombian Constitution's guarantee against

[77] Protection of Women from Domestic Violence Act 2005, s 19.

[78] This was thus a case of death, not divorce, but the underlying reasoning of the Constitutional Court is applicable to both situations.

[79] T-494/92 (n 57).

[80] ibid.

[81] ibid.

non-discrimination, and in this specific case created a right of possession in the matrimonial property and a protection against eviction without due process.[82]

The judgment of the Colombian Constitutional Court shows how institutional reasoning can be invoked by courts to apply constitutional rights *inter se* within a marriage or a domestic relationship, with respect to property claims. As indicated above, while the relationship in this case was ended by death, the Court's reasoning applies equally to separation. However, because of the narrow scope of the case before it, the Court was unable to go beyond finding a right of possession, and did not rule upon the larger claim before it: namely, that equal rights in the context of marriage required a stronger finding, that of a right to the *property*, and not only a right of *possession*.[83]

The last of my examples, however, does provide an illustration of the direct, horizontal application of constitutional rights in the manner discussed in this chapter: the case of Kenya.

Under old Kenyan family law, only financial contributions were taken into account in deciding the share of the parties upon separation.[84] Explicitly seeking to change this position,[85] the Kenyan Constitution of 2010 contained a directly applicable horizontal rights provision (Article 45(3)), borrowed from the UN Convention on the Elimination of all Discrimination against Women, which stated: 'Parties to a marriage are entitled to equal rights at the time of marriage, during the marriage and at the dissolution of the marriage.'[86]

In *Agnes Nanjala William v Jacob Petrus Nicholas Vandergoes*, the Court of Appeal held that Article 45 of the Kenyan Constitution could be applied directly – in the absence of an existing statutory framework – to require an even division of assets at the time of separation.[87] This is particularly relevant, as it involved the Court fashioning a remedy directly from a horizontal constitutional provision, broadly along the lines of what the institutional approach would require.

Subsequently, however, the Kenyan legislature passed the Matrimonial Property Act of 2013, which required judges to divide property in accordance with the 'relative contribution' of the spouses, where 'contribution' included non-monetary contributions, specifically listing domestic work, childcare and companionship. The constitutionality of the Act was challenged in *Federation of Women Lawyers v Attorney-General*, primarily on the basis that the difficulty in proving non-monetary contribution would, in effect, make it discriminatory

[82] ibid.

[83] ibid.

[84] *Peter Mburu Echaria v Priscilla Njeri Echaria*, Civil Appeal No 75 of 2001 (Court of Appeal of Kenya).

[85] *CMN v AWM*, Environment and Land Case 208 of 2012 (High Court of Kenya).

[86] Constitution of Kenya 2010, Art 45(3). Victoria Miyandazi notes that one of the reasons for Art 45 was to address 'harmful practices such as … unequal claims to matrimonial property upon divorce'. V Miyandazi, *Equality in Kenya's 2010 Constitution* (Hart Publishing, 2021) 42.

[87] Agnes Nanjala William *v* Jacob Petrus Nicholas Vandergoes, MSA CA Civil Appeal No 127 of 2011 (UR) (Court of Appeal of Kenya).

against women. The High Court of Kenya rejected this argument, however, on the grounds that the legislature had already taken into account, through its listing of non-monetary contribution, the gendered character of domestic work, and that it was equally essential to prevent non-contributing spouses from taking 'advantage' of marriage.[88]

But what was missing from the analysis of the High Court was the institutional insight that the disadvantage that the 50 per cent rule-of-thumb sought to mitigate was not dependent on the individual characteristics of the parties (and whether or not they 'contributed' to the marriage), but was, at least in part, structural in nature. An application of the institutional approach here may have led the High Court to understand that while the Matrimonial Property Act went some way to recognising and mitigating institutional inequalities within the marriage by explicitly listing domestic work, childcare and companionship as non-monetary contributions, it did not do enough to secure the constitutional guarantee of equal rights within the family. In other words, it would have led to a potentially different outcome.

Indeed, an interpretation of the Matrimonial Property Act that did not elevate an equal division to the status of an unalterable constitutional principle (as the *Agnes Nanjala Williams* case had done), but nonetheless maintained equality as a guiding principle that could be dislodged in exceptional circumstances, would have been well within the bounds of judicial remit. This, it may be noted, would also be consistent with the point made above, ie that the institutional approach provides a basic set of rights to mitigate imbalances in institutional power; however, legislatures and courts are always free to go beyond that when fashioning remedies.

The case of Kenya therefore illustrates the role that the institutional approach, and insights from that approach, can play when we consider institutional inequalities and rights violations within domestic relationships. First, Article 45(3) of the Kenyan Constitution provides us with an example of a horizontal constitutional right, as applied to domestic relationships, broadly in line with what the institutional approach would suggest. Secondly, the judgment of the Court of Appeal in *Agnes Nanjala Williams* is an illustration of how this horizontal right can be applied directly, in the absence of a legislative framework, in a manner that the institutional approach would broadly support and whose conclusions would be strengthened if it were to be invoked. And thirdly, the analysis in *Federation of Women Lawyers* shows how, when an (insufficient) statutory framework is enacted, the institutional approach could help judges in identifying where the inadequacy lies and how to mitigate it through interpretive techniques.

[88] *Federation of Women Lawyers v Attorney-General*, Petition No 164B of 2016 (High Court of Kenya).

V. CONCLUSION

The labour market and the family are two of the most consequential social institutions that structure contemporary life. Indeed, as this chapter has shown, in many ways, power structures in the labour market and in the family reinforce and complement each other. In the previous chapter, I examined the application of the institutional approach to the labour market by analysing how horizontal rights might work in the context of platform work. In this chapter, I ask whether the institutional approach might have a role to play in mitigating inequalities within the family, and specifically within domestic relationships.

Domestic relationships constitute 'institutions' within the meaning of the institutional approach (while also themselves being nested within the larger institution of the family). They are comprehensive, create a hierarchy of power between men and women, and impose structural barriers upon exit. This hierarchy of power enables the violation of rights, in particular through the extraction of unpaid domestic labour (which, even today, is performed predominantly by female spouses in many parts of the world). The rights at stake include the rights to non-discrimination and property, to life and livelihood, and against forced labour.

Inequalities of institutional power within the domestic relationship and the consequential violation of rights require multi-pronged solutions. These have included, for example, calls for wages for housework, for the state to fulfil its welfare obligations towards families and for a larger reconstruction of the world of work. Not all of these remedies are rights-based in nature, and the affective character of domestic relationships creates some challenges to transplanting the rights framework to this context. Nonetheless, I argue that the institutional approach may have an important role to play. One example of this is the distribution of property and claims to property at the time of separation. In many jurisdictions, there is a growing understanding that unpaid domestic work during the course of the domestic relationship must be taken into account at the time of separation. In some countries, this is now mandated by legislation, whereas in other countries, it has been developed incrementally by the judiciary. The institutional approach places this argument on constitutional footing and explains how it mitigates the violation of (constitutional horizontal) rights at issue, as well as helping to break the mutually reinforcing exit/voice inequalities within the domestic relationship.

Through illustrative examples from various jurisdictions, we can see the role that the institutional approach might play in the possible situations that were identified in chapter five: as an interpretive aid where there exists only a legislative framework (as in New Zealand); as modifying or altering an insufficient legislative framework by reference to constitutional rights, within the permissible bounds of adjudication (as in Kenya and India); and as a possible source of directly applicable horizontal rights under the constitution (as in Colombia and Kenya).

As in the previous chapter, the institutional approach works best when it is in conversation with existing law, as many of the issues involved are best addressed through legislation or judicial development, and not through direct constitutional rights enforcement. But it is a sign of the flexibility, and importance, of the institutional approach that it can play a supporting and interpretive role where law exists or a direct and leading role where it is absent – as well as a range of roles in between. The aim of this chapter has been to show that whether in the presence or absence of legislative frameworks, the institutional approach has an important part to play in articulating and addressing structural inequalities and rights violations within one of the most ubiquitous institutions of modern society.

In conclusion, it is important to reiterate that the institutional approach – which is an approach of bounded horizontality – operates within specific and limited contexts: identifying an institution where horizontality can place rights and obligations upon private parties located within that institution. The role of the institutional approach comes to the fore in conversation with legislation, in the absence of legislation (or judge-made law) or where legislation has gaps. The principles articulated by the institutional approach also indicate when the absence of a legal framework creates a constitutional issue and set boundary conditions for which potential solutions are acceptable and which are not. For example, in the context of this chapter, a legal regime governing separation that refused to take into account domestic labour at all would violate institutional horizontal rights, and would therefore be an unacceptable solution. Finally, as indicated at the beginning of this chapter, while the arguments here have focused on the domestic relationship, there exist a range of relationships within the family where the prerequisites of the institutional approach are fulfilled. The arguments advanced in this chapter, therefore, can be potentially extrapolated in a similar manner to other relationships within the family as well.

8

The Prospects of the Institutional Approach

I. INTRODUCTION

IN THIS BOOK, I have attempted to articulate a model of bounded horizontality that is both theoretically sound, and concretely applicable to adjudication. The need for such a model arises from the fact that while 'default verticality' – according to which constitutional rights are presumptively applicable between the individual and the state – has long been found to be unsatisfactory, attempts to depart from it have been equally so. This is because they have remained bound to one or more of its foundational assumptions. Furthermore, in the constitutions that have been studied in this book, which make provisions for direct horizontality, whether general or specific, constitutional courts have invoked them in a piecemeal, ad hoc fashion, without developing a principled approach to when horizontality should apply. A part of the reason for this is undoubtedly a fear that the floodgates might open if horizontal rights were applied indiscriminately, and the impact that would have on existing legislative frameworks, as well as on private law more generally.

* * * * *

For this reason, both theoretically and practically, it is important to articulate a model of bounded horizontality that specifies the scope and limitations upon the application of horizontal rights, the circumstances under which they may be invoked, the circumstances in which they are inapplicable, and the relationship between horizontal rights and private law. According to the institutional approach, horizontality applies within institutions (economic, social or cultural), where a private party's institutional location allows them to violate the rights of another. Institutions are characterised by their comprehensiveness and the difficulty of exit, while institutional power is characterised by its enduring and impersonal character, as well as by the fact that, in general, it is extremely difficult for a specific private party to overcome an institutional power difference or exit the institution. On the flip side, where any of these conditions are absent – ie where one private party alleges a violation of their rights by another but the relationship between the two is not mediated by an institution, or where there is no institutional difference in power – the constitution will not apply horizontally (ordinary law, of course, will continue to apply). To take a simple example, assault and battery will continue to be addressed through the laws of tort and crime, but not through a horizontally applicable constitutional right to life. Similarly, ordinary agreements will continue to be governed by the rules set out under contract law. Naturally, there are sub-domains of private law where this will not hold: domestic violence, for example, may require a sensitivity to the institutional context that takes it beyond the realm of tort and crime (see, for example, India's domestic violence legislation, which I discussed in the previous chapter). Similarly, labour law, as I discussed in chapter six, self-consciously departs from the law of contract and would benefit from an institutional analysis.

Following the structure of this book, this concluding chapter has two sections. In the first, backward-looking section, I will sum up the argument in part I, where the institutional approach was laid out in full (section II). In the second, forward-looking section, I will show how, in more recent constitutions (such as those of Kenya and South Africa), despite express provisions in the constitutional text, horizontal application remains 'a concept in search of content'.[1] Courts in both jurisdictions have avoided setting out a consistent, principled approach towards horizontality, thus demonstrating the present vacuum – and need – for a workable theory (such as the institutional approach). I will finish by examining a recent case from the Jamaican Court of Appeal (*Tomlinson*), which was delivered while this book was being written but which did address the question of horizontality head on. The case involved an unsuccessful attempt to apply the horizontal rights provision of the Jamaican Constitution (which, like South Africa's section 8, is framed in general terms) to a dispute between private parties. My analysis of this judgment will attempt to argue that an application of the institutional approach might have led to a different, intuitively more plausible outcome, thus demonstrating its practical utility to contemporary, comparative constitutional jurisprudence (section III). As the Jamaican Court of Appeal judgment as well as the recent jurisprudence of the Kenyan and South African judiciaries show, courts are presently grappling with conceptual issues around direct horizontality. For that reason, the analysis developed in this book will, it is hoped, be of relevance.

II. THE INSTITUTIONAL APPROACH: A SUMMARY

Modern constitutionalism is characterised by 'default verticality', according to which constitutional rights are presumptively applicable against the state. Horizontal application is a departure from this norm, and therefore exists

[1] YKB Sang, 'Horizontal Application of Constitutional Rights in Kenya' (2018) 26 *African Journal of International and Comparative Law* 1, 13.

only in a set of exceptional and narrowly defined circumstances. In the opening chapter, I argued that default verticality rests upon three interconnected conceptual assumptions: unitary sovereignty, abstract freedom and individual responsibility. Unitary sovereignty identifies the state as the sole locus of legitimate coercive power, and therefore accords special normative salience to the exercise of that power. Abstract freedom proposes a dematerialised conception of freedom, which is synonymous with constraining state coercion and ignores private individuals' material situation. Individual responsibility posits a private, 'horizontal' domain, where formally free individuals are equally responsible for shaping the terms of their relationships with each other.

These three assumptions are mutually reinforcing, and constitutive of the public/private divide (as it is popularly known). The concept of unitary sovereignty allows for the articulation of a 'private sphere' where the absence of state power can be treated as synonymous with freedom. Furthermore, the concept of individual responsibility is bound up with a vision of 'private individuals' within the 'private sphere' being formally equal, and therefore equally free when deciding whether and how to engage with each other. This, in turn, is enabled by the clean separation between the 'vertical' plane upon which the state (with its sovereign power) and the individual interact, and the 'horizontal' (ie formally equal) plane upon which private relationships are shaped.

Thus, as a result of these overlapping assumptions, the difference in power between the state and the individual (and the concomitant ability of the state to violate the individual's rights) is presumptively taken as an object of constitutional concern, and subjected to the framework of constitutional rights. On the other hand, private hierarchies (and the ability of private parties to violate each other's rights) are not, and are left to be dealt with by 'private law'. The content of private law, of course, remains subject to constitutional scrutiny, and in many jurisdictions can be subjected to judicial review for compliance with the constitution. This, in essence, is at the heart of default verticality.

Identifying the underlying assumptions of default verticality enables us to understand that even where courts have applied constitutional rights against private parties, the doctrinal bases remain tied to one or more of those very assumptions. This was considered in chapters two and three of this book. In chapter two, I looked at the 'state action doctrine', variants of which are applied by courts in multiple jurisdictions. Put simply, the 'state action doctrine' is a doctrine of functional equivalence that asks if the actions of a formally private entity can be 'attributed' to the state. Attribution is determined through a range of overlapping tests: the nature and extent of state control over the private party, the functions performed by the private party, the ability of the private party to infringe people's rights, and so on. The state action doctrine, as its name suggests, continues to centre the state as the primary object of analysis. A private party is subjected to constitutional rights if, in its structure or functioning, it bears a close enough resemblance to the state. While courts have disagreed over what constitutes sufficient resemblance, there has been agreement over the fact that a strong degree of resemblance has to be established.

The link between the state action doctrine and the concept of unitary sovereignty (one of the assumptions underlying default verticality) is particularly evident when we consider some of the indicators that courts have used to determine attribution: in particular, delegation and monopoly. Courts ask if a private party is performing a function that has been 'delegated' to it by the state, thus reinforcing a framework under which it is (delegable) state power that remains the subject of constitutional concern. Here, the key issue is that the power or function has been outsourced to a non-state body by the state. Courts also ask if the private party has a monopoly over the provision of a particular good or service (such as transportation services in an area, or electricity). The test of monopoly is particularly revealing, as it speaks directly to unitary sovereignty's conception of the concentration of power in one, identifiable entity (the state), and that it is that form of power that potentially merits the application of the rights framework. This conception, however, conflates monopoly and exit: it is possible that no single entity exercises a monopoly in a particular domain, while it is still impossible for individuals to exit that domain. Default verticality, in other words, operates with a personalised conception of power, as opposed to a depersonalised, structural or institutional conception.

Thus, upon unpacking the state action doctrine, we can see how it remains tied to the assumptions of default verticality, and therefore to its insufficiencies and limitations. There is, however, an important insight that the state action doctrine does provide in some of its iterations: by also asking whether a private party has the ability to impact an individual's rights, to that extent it places the rights bearer at the centre of the enquiry. It is equally clear, however, that not every circumstance in which a private party can violate the rights of another is a fit case for applying constitutional rights horizontally. There is, therefore, a need to develop a set of principles to determine which private relationships are appropriately subject to a horizontal rights framework.

If the state action doctrine remains primarily tied to the conception of unitary sovereignty, then the other prominent departure from verticality – indirect horizontality, the focus of chapter three of the book – often ends up being tied to abstract freedom and individual responsibility. Indirect horizontality uses the form of private law to apply constitutional rights between private parties, primarily by interpreting broadly worded private law provisions in conformity with constitutional rights. In this, however, indirect horizontality often suffers from the 'transplant problem' in its application. Even as it replaces the state with a private party as a duty bearer, indirect horizontality continues to see the two private parties as formally equal and equally free, and therefore focuses on how best to 'balance' their mutually enforceable rights and obligations. By going 'through' private law to apply constitutional rights, indirect horizontality frequently ignores the relational context that structures the relationships between private parties. Notably, it is possible to strengthen indirect horizontality to deal with the transplant problem; but other problems, such as a focus on unitary sovereignty and the state even when the rights violation is between two private parties, continue to exist.

Issues with both the state action doctrine and indirect horizontality raise the question of whether the resolution is simply direct horizontality, ie applying constitutional rights regardless of whether the duty bearer is the state or a private party. 'Unbounded direct horizontality', however, raises serious problems of overlap with existing regimes of private law and creates concerns around institutional competence as well as separation of powers, for both principled (ie democracy-based) and pragmatic reasons. In many circumstances, adjusting the rights and obligations between private parties is a task that is better left to legislatures through the law-making process, rather than courts through direct litigation.

It is therefore clear that any model of horizontality must be 'bounded' in nature, ie there must be a set of principles that determine which private relationships are subject to a horizontal rights framework and which are not. Furthermore, these principles must ensure that the three assumptions of default verticality – unitary sovereignty, abstract freedom and individual responsibility – do not constrain horizontality in the ways discussed above. The inadequacies of the state action doctrine and indirect horizontality suggest that there are two important aspects that a model of bounded horizontality ought to take into account: first, centring the rights bearer, and making the ability of a private party to impact the rights of another a relevant factor; and secondly, paying close attention to the relational context within which private parties engage with each other.

In recent years, scholars have articulated models of bounded direct horizontality along the lines indicated above. In chapter four, I considered two prominent contemporary models, advanced by Johan van der Walt and Jean Thomas. At the core of Van der Walt's critique of default verticality is how it treats private relationships in an atomised sense, ie simply as relationships between two formally equivalent private parties. Van der Walt argues, on the other hand, that certain private relationships can only be understood in the larger social context within which they are nested. For example, racially restrictive covenants do not only involve the property owner and the prospective buyer, but are located within the larger context of racial discrimination and private zoning, from which they cannot be separated. Van der Walt argues that in certain cases, this background context possesses the normative salience that justifies applying a horizontal rights framework to private relationships. He identifies the context as one involving 'social majorities and minorities'.

Van der Walt's model provides us with an important link between default verticality's assumptions of abstract freedom and individual responsibility on the one hand and the atomisation of private relationships on the other. He thus makes a convincing case for using social context as the basis to determine which private relationships ought to be subjected to a horizontal rights framework.

However, his solution – interactions between 'social majorities and minorities' – appears both underdetermined and insufficient.

A more persuasive account of what such a context might entail is provided by Jean Thomas. Thomas argues that what is morally salient in the relationship between the state and private parties is the existence of power on the one hand and dependency/vulnerability on the other. Private relationships that replicate this equation of power and dependency (here Thomas, like Van der Walt, takes issue with default verticality's assumption of private parties being formally equal and equally free to shape the terms of their relationships) are to be subjected to the horizontal rights framework.

Nonetheless, Thomas is aware that this is a necessary, but not sufficient, condition for the application of her model, as almost every private relationship will involve a power difference of some kind. In establishing a model of bounded horizontality, therefore, it must be the case that certain kinds of power relationships (which, in simpler terms, translates into the ability of one party to violate the rights of another, thus re-centring the perspective of the rights bearer) qualify, while others do not. However, in developing these further principled limits, Thomas appears to fall back into the assumptions of default verticality (especially unitary sovereignty) that bounded horizontally was meant to escape: a focus on monopoly control and a personalisation of power with respect to the duty bearer (by requiring, for example, that the duty bearer make an 'undertaking' that creates the relationship between themselves and the rights bearer).

The critique of Van der Walt and Thomas reveals that their models are complementary: Van der Walt's focus on social context (which, as a corollary, is predicated on a non-personalised, more structural account of power) and Thomas's stress on the rights bearer can, together, provide the foundations of a persuasive model of bounded direct horizontality. This model, which I call the institutional approach, is developed in chapter five of this book.

The institutional approach is a model of bounded horizontality. It argues for the application of horizontal rights to relationships between private parties where: first, both parties are located within the same institution; secondly, the parties' relative locations within the institution lead to a difference in power between them; and thirdly, this difference in power enables one party to violate the rights of the other. The institutional approach argues that in such a situation, horizontal rights may be invoked to mitigate this imbalance of power. Which rights are applicable, and to what extent, will depend upon the nature of the parties' relationship, the difference in power between them and the rights that one party is able to infringe or violate.

The institutional approach requires a working understanding of an 'institution'. While the concept of an institution has a long provenance in sociological literature, the institutional approach includes only a subset of the larger category of 'institutions', as commonly understood. 'Institutions' must be, first, comprehensive, ie they must exercise a significant influence upon an individual's life. Indicators of this might include, for instance, facilitating access to a range of basic goods, or requiring mandatory participation. Secondly, individual exit from an institution is extremely difficult in ordinary circumstances. Thus, while a particular school or hospital might not be an institution in this sense (although it might be in the broader, sociological sense), the labour market and the family do constitute institutions for the purposes of the institutional approach.

In chapter five, the workings of the institutional approach were illustrated through three judgments of the Supreme Court of India, interpreting the Indian Constitution's horizontal rights provisions. These provisions are specific and concrete: they proscribe discrimination in access to shops, the social practice of untouchability and forced labour. However, by interpreting them within an institutional framework, the Indian Supreme Court read into them wider prohibitions of social boycotts, menstruation-based practices of gender discrimination and the denial of minimum wages to workers by employers. The Court was able to do this by arguing that these specific provisions were nested within a range of institutional practices. What lent them their unique normative salience was how they were the most concrete manifestations of rights violations and inequalities within broader institutions: those of caste, of patriarchy and of the labour market. As an analysis of these judgments showed, an application of the institutional approach requires the Court to shift between levels of abstraction – from specific rights and obligations to institutional practices and to the institutions themselves. That notwithstanding, it is important to stress, as these cases show, that this is something well within the capacities and bounds of the adjudicatory process.

To be successful, the institutional approach must demonstrate two things: that it is not bound to the assumptions of default verticality, and that it does not suffer from the limitations of unbounded horizontality. With respect to the first, by making institutions the centre of its focus, the institutional approach displaces the assumption of unitary sovereignty. Its key contribution lies in how it depersonalises power and delinks it from the idea of monopoly. In this, it is enabled by taking the perspective of the rights bearer. Thus, while no individual private party may hold monopoly power, that power may exist within the institution itself – something that is revealed only if we focus upon the rights bearer and ask whether she has a feasible exit option from the institution. Furthermore, by making differences in power within institutions normatively salient, the institutional approach displaces the assumptions of abstract freedom and individual sovereignty: private parties' locations within institutions – often a function of their socioeconomic circumstances – are relevant to determining when and how the horizontal rights framework applies to their relationships.

The institutional approach has the added benefit of complementing existing regimes of private law instead of supplanting them. In situations where the institutional approach is applicable and private law is non-existent, there can be a straightforward direct application of horizontal rights to the private relationship at issue. However, where private law does exist, the institutional approach can play a supervisory role. To the extent that the private law regime does not adequately take into account institutional differences in power, the institutional approach can require reinterpretation or modification (in a manner similar to indirect horizontality). Another possibility is that a private party challenges legal obligations placed upon it by a private law regime on the grounds that its own rights are being violated. Here, the institutional approach comes in use to ensure that any 'balancing of rights' between the private parties factored in their institutional difference in power. For instance, a private property owner objecting to a law against racially restrictive covenanting on the grounds that it violates their property rights will fail in their claim once it becomes clear that the analysis does not require a balancing of equal rights – those of property and non-discrimination – between equal parties, but instead requires taking into account the constitutional commitment to eliminate institutional racism.

How the institutional approach might work in tandem with – and, when necessary, independent from – private law has been considered so far in part II of this book. Part II has considered the application of the institutional approach to two important domains: the labour market and the domestic relationship.

In chapter six, I examined the scope of the institutional approach in the context of the legal regulation of platform work. Platform work was chosen for the study for two reasons. First, it forms a part of the labour market, which constitutes an 'institution' for the purposes of the institutional approach. Secondly, the application of existing labour law frameworks to platform work is a subject of substantial contemporary controversy, and therefore provides an excellent case study for seeing how the institutional approach may work, both in the absence of legislation and complementary to it.

Applying the institutional approach to platform work allows us to see that the 'app' (which is under the proprietary control of the platform) constitutes the basis of the institutional power differential between platforms and workers. The 'app' is a gateway (through its algorithms) into accessing work, allows for price fixation and control over the manner of work, authorises control through surveillance, enables platforms to dismiss workers at any time and is the medium through which frequent changes in terms and conditions are communicated to workers on a take-it-or-leave-it basis. The institutional approach's power-centred approach is thus truer to the reality of platform work than 'traditional' labour law frameworks, where indicia such as ownership of equipment or ability to work for multiple employers are not easily transplanted to the flexible/precarious nature of digital platform work.

Furthermore, an application of the institutional approach allows us to derive a range of labour rights, enforceable by workers against employers, including rights to a minimum wage, to non-discrimination, to collective bargaining and against unfair dismissal. In many countries, these rights already exist in labour codes. The utility of the institutional approach is to ensure that platform workers fall within the scope of those codes, and to explain as well as provide further constitutional backing to judicial reasoning (such as in the UK) that has already begun to take the institutional power difference between the parties into account while considering these questions. Furthermore, in some cases, such as the scope of collective bargaining and algorithmic discrimination, the institutional approach provides reasons for courts to go beyond the existing limits of the law (this was discussed briefly, but a full exploration is beyond the scope of this book).

In the final substantive chapter of this book (chapter seven), I considered the case of domestic relationships. Nested within the larger institution of the family, domestic relationships also fulfil the criteria of 'institutions' for the purposes of the institutional approach, being both comprehensive and placing high costs upon exit. Domestic relationships are characterised by unpaid spousal domestic labour, which, according to global statistics, is overwhelmingly gendered and performed by women. Unpaid domestic labour is thus a ground for invoking constitutional rights horizontally, *inter se* between the spouses: it violates the rights to non-discrimination, to property, to livelihood and, arguably, against forced labour.

For the purposes of the chapter, I considered one specific remedy, that of presumptively equal property rights upon separation. This remedy flows directly from the fact that the gendered character of unpaid domestic work makes it likely that there will exist unequal property distribution between the parties in case of, and upon, separation. Presumptively equal property rights, by facilitating an exit from the domestic relationship, enable both a greater degree of rights protection within the relationship (as 'voice' and 'exit' are correlative) and protection upon separation. Thus, while the platform work chapter encourages the bringing of an institutional lens to contract, the domestic relationships chapter encourages the bringing of that lens to property.

Consideration of different jurisdictions illustrates how the institutional approach can be applied across a range of circumstances: as an interpretive aid in cases where legislation guarantees a form of equal property rights protection on separation but needs further judicial articulation to resolve disputes centring around, for example, what kind of property falls within the scope of equal division and what does not; as a guide to courts to enforce rights *inter se* when legislation does not yet exist; and finally, in situations such as in Kenya, where there exist specific horizontally applicable constitutional rights guaranteeing equality within marriages or domestic relationships and where existing legislation must be interpreted consistently with the country's constitution.

Chapters six and seven thus show that the institutional approach can carve out a principled and bounded domain for the operation of horizontal rights. Horizontality can complement or modify existing regimes of private law (without supplanting them), and also serve as a source of rights enforcement and remedies where private law does not exist or where there are gaps in the legal framework. In particular, the institutional approach can serve an important role in judicial adjudication. This is particularly important at a time when private power remains as consequential as ever, but courts continue to be in search of a principled approach towards direct horizontality.

III. CONTEMPORARY PROSPECTS

A. South Africa and Kenya: A Concept in Search of Content

In chapter five of this book, I discussed the judgment of the South African Constitutional Court in *Du Plessis v De Klerk*, where the Court declined to apply constitutional rights horizontally in the absence of a specific enabling provision in the interim South African Constitution. Numerous judges in *Du Plessis* gestured towards the institutional approach as a reason why a constitution might need to have a horizontal rights provision. Mahomed DP, for example, referred to the 'privatisation of apartheid', Ackermann J singled out the 'freedom of contract' as a historical device used to entrench and perpetuate existing (private) power structures and Madala J (in dissent) drew upon South African history to argue that the Constitution was intended to address oppressive practices and structural injustice and inequality 'at all levels'.[2]

The final version of the South African Constitution added a specific enabling provision – section 8(2) – for the implementation of horizontal rights, which was challenged by various parties in the *Certification Judgment* and upheld by the Constitutional Court without significant comment.[3] Section 8(2) stipulates that the Bill of Rights will be applicable to natural and juristic persons 'if, and to the extent that, it is applicable, taking into account the nature of the right and the nature of any duty imposed by the right'.[4] This, then, is an example of interpretive bounded horizontality: the qualifications expressed by the phrase 'if, and to the extent that, it is applicable' suggests that the Bill of Rights is not to be automatically applied to all private relations, but only to some. Furthermore, apart from nominal guidance (the nature of the right and the duty it imposes), section 8(2) leaves it up to the judiciary to evolve a theory, or set of principles, for horizontal rights application.[5]

The observations of the Constitutional Court in *Du Plessis* suggest that, taking into account South African context and history, the institutional approach is a plausible candidate for a theory of section 8(2). This has been affirmed by scholars, who note that 'many of the abuses of the apartheid system and much of the exploitation that marked apartheid society occurred on a horizontal level',[6] and that 'the current distribution of wealth and the *resulting power dynamics* within the private market is a product of the *socio-political* as well as legal *structures* of

[2] See ch 5 of this book.

[3] *Certification of the Constitution of the Republic of South Africa* 1996 (10) BCLR 1253 (CC).

[4] Constitution of South Africa 1996, s 8(2).

[5] H Cheadle and D Davis, 'The Application of the 1996 Constitution in the Private Sphere' (1997) 13 *South African Journal on Human Rights* 44, 57–58.

[6] PJ Sutherland, 'Ensuring Contractual Fairness in Consumer Contracts after *Barkhuizen v Napier* 2007 5 SA 323 CC – Part I' (2008) 19 *Stellenbosch Law Review* 390, 396.

the apartheid regime' (emphasis added).[7] The clearest gesture towards the institutional approach comes from Professor Sandra Liebenberg, who, in the context of applying socioeconomic rights to private law, notes that 'the commitment of the constitution to transform existing inequitable *power relations* and *patterns* of poverty supports an expansive interpretation of the provisions in the constitution governing horizontal application' (emphasis added).[8]

Thus far, however, in the few cases where section 8(2) has been invoked, the Constitutional Court of South Africa has avoided articulating a principled approach to horizontality.[9] In *Khumalo v Holomisa* – which was a case of indirect horizontality, as it involved the question of whether the common law of defamation was constitutionally compliant – the Constitutional Court noted that:

> given the intensity of the right in question coupled with the potential invasion of that right which could be occasioned by persons other than the state or organs of state, it is clear that the right to freedom of expression is of direct horizontal application in this case as contemplated by section 8(2) of the Constitution.[10]

The first part of this formulation ('intensity of the right') does little more than rephrase section 8(2) ('nature of the right'). The second part ('potential invasion') goes a little further by centring the rights bearer (which is also something that the institutional approach insists upon). However, as was seen in chapter two, it falls some way short of articulating a plausible theory for bounded horizontal rights application.

The *Holomisa* formulation has nevertheless become established wisdom over the years. In *Juma Musjid*, which involved a challenge to a decision by a private trust to evict what was a public school (on its premises), the Constitutional Court held that:

> the purpose of section 8(2) of the Constitution is not to *obstruct private autonomy* or to impose on a private party the duties of the state in protecting the Bill of Rights. It is rather to require private parties not to *interfere with or diminish* the enjoyment of a right. (emphasis added)[11]

The Court then went on to cite *Holomisa*. It should be noted, however, that much like the formulation in *Holomisa* itself, the formulation in *Juma Musjid* does not lay down any principle. The first part ('obstruct private autonomy')

[7] D Bhana, 'The Horizontal Application of the Bill of Rights: A Reconciliation of Sections 8 and 39 of the Constitution' (2013) 29 *South African Journal on Human Rights* 351, 353.

[8] S Liebenberg, 'The Application of Socio-Economic Rights to Private Law' [2008] *Journal of South African Law* 464, 467.

[9] For an overview, see I Currie and J de Waal, *The Bill of Rights Handbook*, 6th edn (JUTA Press, 2013) 45–50.

[10] *Khumalo v Holomisa* 2002 (8) BCLR 771 (CC).

[11] *Governing Body of the Juma Musjid Primary School v Essay NO* 2011 (8) BCLR 761 (CC).

is not entirely correct, as any constitutional obligation or duty imposed upon a private party must, by its very nature, 'obstruct' private autonomy at least to some extent (as recognised in the *Certification Judgment* itself). The second part ('duties of the state') is self-evidently true, but does not take us much further in understanding when those duties are to be enforced against private parties. The third part ('interfere with or diminish the enjoyment of a right') is at best incomplete without further articulation of what interference or diminishment entails. Furthermore, as a blanket statement that positive obligations could never apply to private parties, it is evidently too broad, and this position was subsequently negated by the Constitutional Court itself in *Daniels v Scribante*.[12]

In *Juma Musjid*, the Constitutional Court held that once the school was functioning on the premises of the private party, it had a negative obligation not to interfere with the learners' right to basic education – which, in this case, entailed not evicting the school without following principles of due process. While one may agree or disagree with the outcome, it is clear that the Court – as in *Holomisa* – preferred to limit itself to abstract statements about the applicability of section 8(2) instead of developing a concrete account of its scope and limits.

In *Daniels v Scribante*, the question before the Constitutional Court was whether an occupier of farmland, under a *sui generis* statutory regime, was entitled to make improvements to her dwelling over the objections of the owner. *Daniels v Scribante* came to the Court in the context of a long history, through the apartheid years, of systemic racial discrimination that denied security of tenure to the Black majority. In considering the applicability of horizontal rights, the Constitutional Court added a few more sub-clauses to the *Holomisa* and *Juma Musjid* formulations. It noted:

> Whether private persons will be bound depends on a number of factors. What is paramount includes: what is the nature of the right; what is the history behind the right; what does the right seek to achieve; how best can that be achieved; what is the 'potential of invasion of that right by persons other than the state or organs of state'; and, would letting private persons off the net not negate the essential content of the right?[13]

Once again, however, no further explanation was forthcoming. The Court did draw a distinction, for the purposes of horizontal obligations, between the state, which is supposed to act for the good of society as a whole and is therefore funded by public money, and private parties, who are not subject to any equivalent duty. While that observation is correct, as it goes, it is also not very helpful. With respect to its formulation of the test under section 8(2), the Constitutional Court issued no further guidance on what kind of history (behind a right), or

[12] *Daniels v Scribante* 2017 (8) BCLR 949 (CC).
[13] ibid [39].

what it sought to achieve, would be relevant to the issue of horizontal application. In other words, the formulations in *Khumalo*, *Juma Musjid* and *Daniels* all serve as precursors to a principled account of section 8(2). They stipulate what the Court must take into account in determining the question of horizontality, but do not explain how those factors must be taken into account or what their precise relationship is with horizontality (questions that the institutional approach has answers to).[14]

In his concurring opinion in *Daniels*, Froneman J gestured towards the institutional approach, in a manner similar to the opinions in *Du Plessis*. He noted that 'the absolutisation of ownership and property' would confirm and perpetuate 'the existing inequalities in personal, social, economic and political freedom'.[15] This was particularly important because, as noted above, the case involved a Black woman living on a farmstead without any formal right to the land, and a clash between the owner's property rights and the rights of the tenant to make improvements to her home so that she could live with dignity. Froneman J made the important point that existing property distribution, which had its origins in the apartheid regime and continued to be upheld by property law, was itself a potential source of the violation of rights.[16] This is particularly close to the institutional approach – without using its vocabulary – as, arguably, property distribution qualifies as an institution for our purposes.

More recently, in *AB v Pridwin Preparatory School*, the Constitutional Court considered the relationship between a private school and a learner whose parents had been asked to remove him from the school. Notwithstanding the existence of a contract between the private school and the learner's parents, the Court elected to apply the Constitution directly, albeit without detailed reasoning about the scope and limitations of horizontality under the Constitution.[17] Importantly, however, the Constitutional Court noted the growing 'power and significance of the independent school sector',[18] which therefore required Pridwin to give due consideration to the best interests of the child, as required by section 28 of the South African Constitution.[19] In the present case, that translated to adhering to principles of due process and natural justice before cancelling the parental contract with the learner's parents.[20]

[14] For a discussion and a bibliography on this point, see Bhana, 'The Horizontal Application of the Bill of Rights' (n 7) 365, fnn 75–78.

[15] *Daniels v Scribante* (n 12) [136].

[16] ibid [137].

[17] For a critique of the judgment, including the questionable use of direct horizontality when what was in issue was the validity of a contractual term, see M Finn, 'Befriending the Bogeyman: Direct Horizontal Analysis in *AB v Pridwin*' (2020) 137 *South African Law Journal* 591. For further analysis, see J Brickhill and M Bishop, 'Constitutional Law' (2020) 1 *Yearbook of South African Law* 227; Brickhill and Bishop also point out the inconsistency between *Pridwin* and *Beadica*, a judgment decided on the same day, where the court elected to apply indirect horizontality in examining another disputed contract.

[18] *AB v Pridwin Preparatory School* 2020 (9) BCLR 1029 (CC).

[19] ibid [149].

[20] ibid [204].

Finally, since *Pridwin*, the South African Constitutional Court has had two occasions to consider the scope of direct horizontality, in cases involving private bequests. In *King v De Jager*, a private will discriminated against female descendants and was challenged.[21] One question before the Court was whether the impugned clause could be subjected to direct horizontality. A majority of the Court applied the Constitution directly, and held the discriminatory clause to be unlawful, but provided no reasoning for why they had done so. In her separate opinion, Victor AJ, after recapitulating the *Daniels* dictum, also noted that direct horizontality would apply, inter alia, where 'not reaching into the private sphere could "perpetuate inequality and disadvantage"'.[22] Now, while this formulation gestures towards the institutional approach and could have been the starting point for a generative conversation about the institutional approach, private property regimes and testation, Victor AJ did not elaborate upon it further. She (correctly) found that there was no need to resort to the Constitution, as legislation – specifically, the Equality Act – already covered the field.[23] This is as it should be: as I have argued throughout this book, where legislation holds the field, the institutional approach seeks not to supplant it, but to inform its interpretation.

Interestingly, Victor AJ's testing of the will on the touchstone of the Equality Act bore traces of the institutional approach: she noted the contribution of the principle of freedom of testation to 'entrenching systemic disadvantage'[24] and 'iniquitous gender-based hierarchies',[25] especially in the 'private sphere'.[26] Indeed, it was this analysis that prompted Victor AJ to hold that the discrimination at issue constituted a '*system* of preventing women from inheriting family property' (emphasis added), as required by the Equality Act – even though the specific challenge was to a single clause in a single will. We therefore have a classic example of an individual act having specific salience because of the institutional, or systemic, relational context within which it is embedded. Thus, it is clear that Victor AJ's judgment marks an important advance in the direction of the institutional approach; however, as it did not command a majority and did not pertain specifically to theorising direct horizontality under the Constitution, it remains an incremental advance.

Furthermore, in *Wilkinson v Crawford*, which was at the same time as *King v De Jager*, the Constitutional Court had another opportunity to discuss the application of horizontal rights to private bequests, but declined to do so.[27] Considering a trust that arguably excluded adopted children from inheritance, a

[21] *King v De Jager* [2021] ZACC 4. I am grateful to Meghan Finn for bringing these judgments to my attention.

[22] ibid [178].

[23] ibid [179].

[24] ibid [208].

[25] ibid [216].

[26] ibid [219].

[27] *Wilkinson v Crawford* [2021] ZACC 8.

closely divided Court ultimately decided the case on public policy and statutory interpretation grounds, and did not therefore address the issue of horizontality.

Thus, an overview of the (few) judgments on section 8(2) reveals the following points. First, in various judgments, South African judges have indicated that the purpose of horizontality is to tackle private, institutional power, which is to be understood in the historical context of South Africa; secondly, the Constitutional Court has not, however, developed a theory, or an account, of the private relationships to which section 8(2) should apply, or how it should be applied[28] (although Victor AJ's concurrence in *King* gestures towards such a theory); and thirdly, a repeated concern appears to be the problem of opening the floodgates, or the numerous issues that will arise if private parties are indiscriminately subjected to obligations normally imposed upon the state (especially as the South African Constitution contains a range of socioeconomic rights).

It is here that the institutional approach, as developed in this book, can prove particularly helpful. Not only is it already implicit in the interpretive direct horizontality approach that the text of section 8(2) requires, and in the observations alluded to above, but it also (as I have attempted to show) addresses concerns around separation of powers and the transformation of all private law into applied constitutional law. It remains to be seen, however, whether the Constitutional Court will take its observations in cases like *Du Plessis*, *Pridwin* and *King* and develop them into a principled interpretive account of section 8(2) that centres the role of institutions and institutional differences of power in applying constitutional rights horizontally.

The experience of Kenyan courts in grappling with direct horizontality under the 2010 Constitution reveals a similar trajectory and a set of similar issues. Under Kenya's old Constitution, which did not have a horizontality provision, the position of law was that constitutional rights could not be applied against non-state parties.[29] The Kenyan Constitution of 2010 makes a conscious and specific departure from this position. Recall that, other than the specific horizontality contemplated by section 45 (which I discussed in chapter seven), Article 20(1) of the 2010 Constitution stipulates that the Bill of Rights applies to all law, and binds all state organs and persons. While at first blush this might appear to endorse unbounded direct horizontality, as Brian Sang YK argues, Article 20(2), which guarantees to every person the enjoyment of fundamental rights 'to the greatest extent consistent with the nature of the right',[30] prescribes an 'internal limitation' upon horizontal application.[31] In any event, it is evident that the scheme of Article 20 vests significant power and discretion in the

[28] Finn therefore calls the jurisprudence on s 8(2) 'casuistic'. Finn, 'Befriending the Bogeyman' (n 17).

[29] *Kenya Bus Service Ltd v Attorney General* [2005] KLR 788 (High Court).

[30] Constitution of Kenya, Art 20(2).

[31] Sang, 'Horizontal Application of Constitutional Rights in Kenya' (n 1) 7.

judiciary to determine the scope and limits of horizontality under the Kenyan Constitution.[32]

A study of the judgments applying Article 20 of the 2010 Constitution 'demonstrates an absence of conceptual clarity regarding when, how, and to what extent constitutional rights apply in private disputes',[33] including a normative account of the same. In one of the earliest cases under the 2010 Constitution, *Mwangi Stephen Mureithi v Hon'ble Daniel Toroitch Arap Moi*, the High Court of Kenya[34] noted two things: first, that the rationale of Article 20 was that 'private individuals and bodies … wield great power over the individual citizenry',[35] and that 'it will not matter who the duty holder is, rather, what matters is who should enjoy the rights as enshrined in the Constitution'.[36] However, the Court also held that claims for the application of horizontal rights would have to be examined on a case-by-case basis, because 'horizontal application does not and should not cut across the board'.[37] The Court thus made a beginning both by centring the rights bearer and noting that an analysis of power was integral to horizontal application, while also acknowledging that any account of horizontality would have to be bounded in character (ie only certain kinds of power would attract horizontal rights scrutiny). At the same time, the Court demonstrated the continuing pull of default verticality by noting that horizontality was not the rule but the exception, even though the text of Article 20(2) itself (unlike its South African counterpart) does not indicate that horizontality is meant to be subordinate to verticality.[38]

Therefore, while the High Court in *Mureithi* gestured towards some elements of the institutional approach, it did not parse out those elements in greater detail. Subsequent cases, like their South African counterparts, have also failed to build on this proto-formulation of the institutional approach. Consider the High Court's jurisprudence. The Court has pointed out, for instance, that 'the nature and extent of a particular right may be limited in scope to apply to the state and not a private individual';[39] that 'not every ill in society should attract a constitutional sanction … such sanctions should be reserved for appropriate and really serious occasions'[40] (in a defamation case); and 'the Constitution cannot

[32] See C Murray, 'Kenya's 2010 Constitution' (2013) 61 *Neue Folge Band Jarbuch des öffentlichen Rechts* 747, 761.

[33] ibid.

[34] The High Court of Kenya is a constitutional court. Appeals from the High Court's decisions are carried to the Court of Appeal and ultimately to the Supreme Court of Kenya.

[35] *Mwangi Stephen Mureithi v Hon'ble Danile Toroitch Arap Moi*, Petition No 625 of 2009, 17 (High Court of Kenya).

[36] ibid 18.

[37] ibid 17.

[38] ibid 18.

[39] *Law Society of Kenya v Betty Sungura Nyabuto*, Petition 21 of 2010, [18] (High Court).

[40] *Uhuru Muigai Kenyatta v Nairobi Star Publications Ltd*, Petition No 187 of 2012, [16] (High Court).

be used as a substitute where there are other remedies available in law'.[41] This last bit of reasoning has also served as a general basis for when horizontal rights might apply: that is, when, in the opinion of the Court, private law does not provide an adequate remedy for the constitutional rights violation.[42]

It should be obvious, however, that looking to the existence of a remedy in order to determine the application of constitutional rights horizontally risks putting the cart before the horse. Questions about the threshold application of horizontal rights, as well as their scope and limitations (and any balancing between private parties' rights), must be resolved before the question of what remedies exist in private law. This is also because – as pointed out in chapter three, during the discussion of Ireland's constitutional tort doctrine – a seeming gap in private law might well be the result of a conscious legislative choice not to impose obligations upon a private party in a particular context.[43] In any event, therefore, the threshold question of when horizontal rights ought to apply, independent of the landscape of private law, cannot be avoided.

A good example of this is the judgment in *Rose Wangui Mambo v Limuru Country Club*.[44] This case involved a challenge to a change in the by-laws of a private golf club that excluded women from holding executive positions. After recapitulating the legal position (as summarised above), the High Court reiterated that horizontal application 'is not an open cheque and whether and to what extent the Court will exercise jurisdiction will be informed by the circumstances of each individual case'.[45] With respect to the case at hand, the Court gestured towards the historical exclusion of women from economic, social, cultural and political spheres as a result of 'discriminatory *practices* … laws, policies and regulations … presenting itself as a manifestation of historically unequal *power relations* between men and women in Kenyan society' (emphasis added).[46] On that basis, the Court ruled that the Constitution's anti-discrimination provisions (under Article 27) would apply to both the public and the private domains.[47] Private clubs, therefore, 'are bound by the Constitution in the same way as any other legal person'.[48]

As in *Mureithi*, in *Rose Wangui Mambo* there is an intuitive articulation of the underlying basis for applying constitutional rights horizontally, without a

[41] *Jemimah Wambui Ikere v Standard Group Ltd*, Petition No 466 of 2012, [18] (High Court); see also *Stephen Saitoti Kapaiku v Cocacola Sabco Nairobi Bottlers Ltd*, Petition No 338 of 2012 (a case involving impurities in a Coca Cola bottle) (High Court).

[42] See, eg *Duncan Muriuki Kaguuru v Baobab Beach Resort and Spa Ltd*, Petition No 223 of 2012 (High Court); *Isaac Ngugi v The Nairobi Hospital*, Petition No 407 of 2012 (High Court).

[43] See ch 3 of this book.

[44] *Rose Wangui Mambo v Limuru Country Club*, Constitutional Petition No 160 of 2013 (High Court). For a discussion, see Victoria Miyandazi, *Equality in Kenya's 2010 Constitution* (Hart Publishing, 2021) 33.

[45] ibid [72].

[46] ibid [89].

[47] ibid [90].

[48] ibid [113].

full normative explication of the principles that are meant to guide the courts. The High Court elected to stick to the 'case by case' formulation that originated with *Mureithi*. In the present case, this also meant that the Court did not deal in any great detail with the issue of how to balance the club's countervailing rights (an issue that, as evidenced in chapter three, particularly needs something like the institutional approach). It noted only that while clubs were ordinarily permitted to discriminate with respect to their *membership*, the facts in this case did not involve any questions of membership: women could be members of the golf club, but they were prohibited from holding *executive positions* (ie positions with decision-making power). It is, however, unclear why the principle of private autonomy should apply with any lesser force to the framing of internal club rules than it does to the question of membership. Indeed, when we think of bodies such as clubs, it is important to remember that membership is often a sign of social status and that, historically, discriminatory membership criteria have been used to reinforce and entrench existing structures of power on racial, gender and class lines. Thus, if anything, there is greater reason for courts to override private club rules on membership than on the question of internal club hierarchies. Thus, as in the case of restrictive covenants, the institutional approach provides powerful reasons why formally 'private' clubs should, in certain circumstances, be subjected to constitutional obligations of non-discrimination. The institutional approach takes seriously the entrenching/reinforcing role that clubs have played, as discussed above.

An overview of the jurisprudence around direct horizontality under the Kenyan Constitutions reveals, therefore, that, like in South Africa, there exists an undercurrent of the institutional approach that informs judicial decisions on occasion, but that courts remain hesitant to articulate a normative account of horizontality that could be applied with principled consistency across cases. Needless to say, however, without a normative account, the application of horizontality will remain partial at best, and opens up courts to allegations of selective and inconsistent enforcement.[49] Thus, in both South Africa and Kenya, bounded horizontality is explicitly provided for in the Constitution, is litigated before the courts and is the subject of a growing body of contemporary case law, but remains in search of its normative foundations. The burden of this book has been to provide one plausible candidate to fill in that normative gap: the institutional approach.

B. Tomlinson's Case and the Potential of the Institutional Approach

In October 2020, the Jamaican Court of Appeal handed down its judgment in *Maurice Tomlinson v TVJ and Ors*.[50] The facts of the case were as follows.

[49] Sang, 'Horizontal Application of Constitutional Rights in Kenya' (n 1).

[50] *Maurice Tomlinson v TVJ and Ors* [2020] JMCA Civ 52 (Court of Appeal of Jamaica).

Mr Tomlinson, a gay man, wanted two of the most prominent Jamaican television stations (TVJ and CVM) to air a public service announcement/advertisement[51] calling for equal rights for Jamaica's LGBT community. TVJ declined to respond and CVM declined his request. Mr Tomlinson then approached the court, arguing that his rights to the freedom of speech and to the dissemination of information, guaranteed by sections 13(3)(c) and (d) of the Jamaican Charter of Fundamental Rights and Freedoms, had been infringed. In order to affix constitutional obligations upon commercial – and therefore private – television stations, Mr Tomlinson further relied upon section 13(5) of the Charter, which, following the South African Constitution, states that 'a provision of this chapter binds natural or juristic persons if, and to the extent that, it is applicable, taking account of the nature of the right and the nature of any duty imposed by the right'.[52] In essence, therefore, Mr Tomlinson's claim was that, via section 13(5), the (traditionally) vertical right of the freedom of speech and expression should be applied horizontally between him and the television stations that had refused to air his advertisement.

The first set of proceedings took place in the highest first-instance court of Jamaica, the Supreme Court[53] (Full Court), which found against Mr Tomlinson. Before the Full Court, Mr Tomlinson argued that the issue required a 'balancing' between the editorial and journalistic freedom enjoyed by TVJ and CVM on the one hand, and his right to access broadcast media and the public's right to be informed on matters of public interest on the other. 'In light of the dominance of the media',[54] he argued, the issue ought to be resolved by imposing 'an obligation on broadcasters to broadcast what reasonable private citizens desire to disseminate'.[55] Meanwhile, TVJ and CVM argued that the law 'did not create a right to use a person's private property to disseminate one's message',[56] and that the principles of the freedom of contract empowered them to 'decline or accept any advertisement or part thereof'.[57]

The judges of the Full Court framed the issue as one requiring a balance between the rights of the private parties under the Charter's horizontal rights clause. A declaration in favour of Mr Tomlinson would have 'prejudiced the rights and freedoms' of TVJ and CVM, and therefore could not have been within the contemplation of the drafters of the Jamaican Charter.[58] One of the judges, Sykes J, noted in addition that the wording of section 13(5) appeared

[51] The exact character was a subject matter of the controversy.

[52] Jamaican Charter of Fundamental Rights and Freedoms (Constitutional Amendment) Act 2011, s 13(5).

[53] The hierarchy of courts in Jamaica allows for appeals from the Supreme Court to be carried to the Court of Appeal and, subsequently, in the majority of cases, to the Privy Council.

[54] *Tomlinson v TVJ* (n 50) [37].

[55] ibid.

[56] ibid [38].

[57] ibid [40].

[58] ibid [54].

to indicate that 'a Charter right may not apply to a private citizen at all or if it does then it may not apply to the same extent as it would to the state'.[59] He also engaged in a 'transplant analysis', noting that if the government was not obligated to provide a forum to everyone who wished to speak, then it was difficult to argue that private citizens were subjected to more stringent obligations.[60]

Mr Tomlinson carried the case to the Court of Appeal. Before the Court of Appeal, he argued that the Full Court, when deciding on the application of horizontal rights, had failed to consider situations where 'private bodies that are akin to the state in both power and influence can use their position to restrict the rights and freedoms of individual members of the society', and that in this specific case the 'unequal power relations' between Mr Tomlinson and the television channels had not been examined.[61] Indeed, in this context, 'the influence, power and position of the respondents were such that they had the ability to unduly interfere with the free speech of a wide cross-section of the Jamaican population'.[62] This was because

> distribution or dissemination of ideas or opinions … would not be possible without access to the media … for an individual, therefore, to effectively access these avenues for expression and to disseminate information, the person who controls the access must be required to not deny access *arbitrarily, discriminatorily or unreasonably*. (emphasis added)[63]

Relying extensively upon South African precedent, the Court of Appeal began by noting that, unlike the vertical application of rights, horizontality under the Charter was conditional. In other words, it required the Court to first determine whether a particular Charter right was applicable horizontally, and if so, given the circumstances, to what extent.[64] In such a situation, the Court held that the test of proportionality, which is ordinarily applicable in the vertical domain, would have to be modified to apply to rights *inter se* between private parties. The Court borrowed the test from Lord Steyn's House of Lord's opinion in *Re (S): A Child*,[65] and held that 'the rights of each party are qualified according to the weight of the rights in a particular context'.[66] Thus, in the present case, the Court of Appeal then framed the issue as follows:

> Whether given the equal nature of the rights as between the parties, the respondents in not airing the advertisement, in effect, limited or restricted Mr Tomlinson's rights? In other words, whether there was, in fact and in law, an attempt by the respondents to control the message or the meaning Mr Tomlinson wished to have conveyed?[67]

[59] ibid [57].
[60] ibid [59].
[61] ibid [68].
[62] ibid [77].
[63] ibid [113].
[64] ibid [102].
[65] *Re S (A Child)* [2005] 1 AC 593.
[66] *Tomlinson v TVJ* (n 50) [211].
[67] ibid [138].

Having framed the question thus, the Court of Appeal answered it in the negative. The reason for this was that 'the respondents also have the same rights as Mr Tomlinson – the right to freedom of expression as well as the right to disseminate information, opinions and ideas. These rights are equal in content and in nature.'[68] Consequently, according to the Court of Appeal,

> one must query why Mr Tomlinson should be permitted to force the respondents, *who have no government association*, to permit him to use their television stations to carry his message to the public, or to encourage members of the public to listen to his ideas. (emphasis added)[69]

Furthermore, in the present case, the TV stations had opted not to air the public service announcement on the basis that they perceived its content might be viewed as a breach of law or lead to a breach of peace. The Court of Appeal held that this did not constitute arbitrary discrimination or an abuse of commercial institutional strength.

A close reading of the judgment in *Tomlinson* highlights almost all the issues that I have discussed in this book. Mr Tomlinson began by framing his argument in straightforward state action terms, seeking to equate big private TV stations with the state (see chapter two). As I have shown, however, this approach is very constrained in character. In due course, Mr Tomlinson's own arguments took a more nuanced and subtle form, focusing, among other things, on the TV stations' ability to impact his rights (see chapter two); the relational context, ie the impossibility of getting your voice heard in modern society without access to the infrastructure of speech, which is controlled by private parties (see chapter three); and the difference in power between the parties because of the TV stations' 'commercial institutional strength' (see chapter five). Thus, although Mr Tomlinson did not articulate the institutional approach in all the detail that has been elaborated in this book, elements of it featured prominently in his arguments.

The Court's judgment, on the other hand, was a textbook example of the 'transplant method', which has been critiqued earlier (see chapter three). On no less than seven occasions through the course of the judgment, the Court noted that the question involved the interaction between the 'equal rights' of Mr Tomlinson and the TV stations. Thus, even while applying the Jamaican Charter's horizontal rights provisions, the Court of Appeal continued to be bound to the assumptions of default verticality: in particular, individual responsibility and abstract freedom. It treated Mr Tomlinson and the TV stations as formally equal parties, equally free in shaping the terms of their relationship with each other. Once the Court had framed the issue thus, the conclusion was foregone: on a balancing between the 'equal rights' of Mr Tomlinson to free

[68] ibid [142], [169], [172], [179], [214].
[69] ibid [158].

speech (on the one hand) and the TV stations' to freedom of contract and editorial freedom – ie freedom of speech as well – on the other, it was the latter that would prevail. Tellingly, the Court relied extensively on judgments from jurisdictions that *did not* have horizontal rights provisions to substantiate its conclusion that Mr Tomlinson could not 'require' a private TV channel to make a certain, specific use of its property, ie carrying a particular message.

In short, therefore, the Court of Appeal's analysis was based on the following assumptions, all of which have been critiqued in this book: (i) that vertical rights remain the 'default' mode of constitutional rights application, with horizontal application serving as a limited exception; (ii) when one private party invokes the Constitution's horizontal rights provisions against another, the appropriate interpretive framework requires the Court to ask, first, whether the putative duty bearer has any 'governmental association'; (iii) if the answer to (ii) is no, then the Court ought to treat the two parties as formally equal, and balance their respective rights accordingly; and (iv) the balancing process entails weighing up the relative intensity of the rights against each other, and involves a modified application of the proportionality standard, the goal of which is to ensure that neither party's rights are nullified; it does not, however, require the Court to take into account the relational context within which the parties themselves operate, or their relative power vis-à-vis each other.

How might the institutional approach have differed in its examination and adjudication of this case? To begin with, recall that the institutional approach places the rights bearer at the centre of its analysis. Thus, the institutional approach would have taken seriously the contention that by denying Mr Tomlinson airtime, the TV stations had a non-trivial impact upon his rights. This seems to be straightforwardly true: in modern society, the ability to communicate one's thoughts, views or beliefs to an audience is often, if not always, conditioned by one's access to the instruments of mass media.

The institutional approach would have then asked: what gives these TV stations the ability to impact Mr Tomlinson's rights? The answer is, clearly, their control, through property rights, over the 'infrastructure of expression'.[70] In the Court of Appeal, this was a point in favour of the TV stations: ie the Court framed the issue as requiring a private entity to use their private property, against their will, for a particular purpose. For the institutional approach, however, proprietary control over the means of communication is the locus of the difference in power between the rights bearer and the duty bearer.

The third – and in this case, perhaps the most difficult – question that the institutional approach would need to ask is about the institution itself: while we have established that there is a difference in power between Mr Tomlinson and the TV stations that enables the latter to infringe the rights of the former, does there exist an institution, in the sense that this book has discussed? Here, I would

[70] JM Balkin, 'The First Amendment in a Second Guilded Age' (2018) 66 *Buffalo Law Review* 979.

give a tentative and exploratory answer: the institution is that of mass media.[71] Mass media is comprehensive, in the sense that its existence, in contemporary society, is ubiquitous and pervasive. The role of mass media in the process of 'socialisation', in shaping 'values and rules of behaviour'[72] and in 'defining the "appropriate" cultural boundaries around such factors as gender, race, and class'[73] (particularly relevant in the *Tomlinson* case) is also well documented. This makes effective 'exit' impossible, even for those who make individual decisions not to consume the said mass media.[74] Lastly, despite the more recent rise of social media, it is important to note that in several jurisdictions, social media usage remains relatively limited, and there is no (as yet) perceptible decline in the institutional influence of mass media.[75] In other words, it is probably not yet the case that social media serves as an effective substitute for mass media, at least as far as questions of socialisation go.

At first blush, therefore, the requirements of the institutional approach are fulfilled in the *Tomlinson* case: the existence of an institution (the mass media) and the ability of institutionally powerful actors (ie large private television stations, in the context of a political economy where the infrastructure of communication is largely privatised) to violate the rights of other individuals. The power of the television stations, of course, would be juxtaposed against the relative power of the speaker: Mr Tomlinson, being a private citizen, represents a particularly stark example of institutional difference in power. Needless to say, the enquiry is contextual in another way as well: it would depend on the (continuing) dominant position of mass media in a particular jurisdiction, and the fact that in that jurisdiction the ownership of mass media (to a non-trivial extent) is in private hands. If, in the context of Jamaica, those (empirically verifiable) conditions were fulfilled, Mr Tomlinson would have a strong horizontal rights claim against the two TV stations.

As a brief aside, interestingly, this is not the first time that a judicial body has made such an argument: in *De Geillustreerde Pers NV v The Netherlands*, the European Human Rights Commission indicated that the state's failure to 'protect against excessive press concentrations'[76] might implicate the freedom of expression rights under Article 10 of the European Convention on Human Rights. However, as the case itself did not involve a challenge to excessive media concentration, the Commission did not take this line of thought further.

[71] See, eg A Silverblatt, 'Media as Social Institution' (2004) 48(1) *American Behavioral Scientist* 35.
[72] ibid 39.
[73] M Kirk, *Gender and Information Technology* (IGI Global, 2009) 85.
[74] N Chomsky and ES Herman, *Manufacturing Consent: The Political Economy of Mass Media* (Pantheon Books, 1988).
[75] Specific to Jamaica, the most recent figures show social media is used by just over 50% of the population, 20 percentage points less than television access. See, eg Datareportal, 'Digital Jamaica: 2021', https://datareportal.com/reports/digital-2021-jamaica.
[76] *De Geillustreerde Pers NV v The Netherlands* App no 5178/71, Commission (Plenary) Report (31) (ECHR) [88].

Back to the *Tomlinson* case: it is important to note that the above argument would not, of course, be dispositive of the issue. As discussed in chapter five, the institutional approach does not argue that the rights of the institutionally more powerful party are to be discounted entirely. Rather, in cases where there is a clash, the balancing exercise requires factoring institutional power into the analysis (which the Court of Appeal refused to do). Thus, the institutional approach would not require a court to find that private TV broadcasters are always obligated to air advertisements or PSAs that are sent to them;[77] or that, all things considered, that the TV stations in the present case were obligated to air Mr Tomlinson's advertisement/PSA. A court might still find, even on applying the institutional approach, that the TV stations' rights outweigh those of Mr Tomlinson.

As indicated above, however, the TV stations' institutional power, and the violation of Mr Tomlinson's rights, would provide strong reasons for a finding in his favour. In particular, the institutional approach would find particularly persuasive the following arguments articulated by Mr Tomlinson: that 'the *unpopular but important* views promoted by Mr Tomlinson's advertisement are given fair consideration to secure expression in the media with the largest impact' (emphasis added);[78] and that, in view of private broadcasters' commitment to maximising profit, 'it would be naive to expect the majority of broadcasters to produce the variety and controversial material necessary to reflect *a full spectrum of viewpoints*' (emphasis added).[79] Indeed, the rights at issue are directly linked to the role that the institution of mass media plays as a social institution: insofar as it reflects dominant cultural values, the shutting out of Mr Tomlinson's message – which sought to use the infrastructure of communication to challenge those dominant values – would attract the private TV channels' horizontal obligations to an even greater extent. In the vertical context, two of the justifications underlying a strong free speech right are the role of free speech in sustaining democracy and the equal right of every person to use communication to shape their moral and cultural environment. It is easy to see how, in the specific case of Mr Tomlinson and the nature of his message, the institutional approach would find good reasons, all things considered, to apply the right horizontally against the private TV stations.

Furthermore, and as a related point, consider the situation if it was found that the TV stations had refused to air Mr Tomlinson's advertisement/PSA because of its unpopular content (ie advocating for the tolerance of same-sex relationships), and specifically because it was deemed to go against majoritarian views regarding matters of personal identity and decisional autonomy. In that

[77] Indeed, Mr Tomlinson himself framed the argument as one of arbitrary or discriminatory denial, and not of denial simpliciter.

[78] *Tomlinson v TVJ* (n 50) [192].

[79] ibid.

case, Mr Tomlinson's claim would rest upon both the right to free speech and the right to non-discrimination, and would, under the institutional approach, be likely to prevail. Indeed, the logic is somewhat similar to the logic of the restrictive covenant cases: just like the issue in those cases was not the specific denial of *a* house to *a* person but institutional discrimination creating, in essence, a system of private zoning, the issue in the *Tomlinson* case is, essentially, institutional exclusion of a certain set of anti-majoritarian viewpoints, enabled by private TV stations' control over the infrastructure of expression. It also, as pointed out by Mr Tomlinson, involves a conflict between the profit imperative and the necessity of reflecting 'a full spectrum of viewpoints'.

The Tomlinson case, which is one of the most recent instances where a Constitutional Court has been asked to apply horizontal rights directly, is thus a fascinating case study with which to conclude this book. The case itself is a 'hard case', where it is prima facie difficult to pinpoint why two private TV stations should be obligated to air Mr Tomlinson's advertisement/PSA; or, in other words, why Mr Tomlinson's free speech rights should prevail over the freedom of contract and the TV stations' rights to property and editorial judgment. The Court of Appeal's analysis suffers from the reflexive adherence to the principles of default verticality, which, as I have tried to argue, continue to constrain the development and evolution of a principled and independent approach towards bounded horizontality. The institutional approach, on the other hand, provides us with a grammar through which we can articulate our intuitions regarding the power differences between large TV stations and individuals seeking a platform to be able to communicate minority or unpopular views, in the context of a contemporary reality where communication without the mass media, and its control over the infrastructure of expression, remains chimerical. In particular, it helps us to move past the absence of governmental association, and the absence of an identifiable monopoly, by focusing on the rights bearer, and their institutionally mediated relationship with the putative private duty bearers.

As with the *Tomlinson* case, the institutional approach would provide a helpful framework for thinking through a number of contemporary controversies involving freedom of speech and formally private parties. A full analysis is beyond the scope of this book, but it is possible to flag some of the issues for future study. For example, when social media companies with wide reach (which makes them equivalent to mass media in the digital sphere) decide to ban individuals (including prominent politicians) from their platforms, the analysis would not be concluded by simply stating that a private company has an absolute right to enforce its terms and conditions as it sees fit. Rather, in cases where the scale and reach of the company grants it the institutional power that I have discussed in this book, it would amount to a prima facie infringement of the horizontally applicable right to free speech. Two responses might follow. First, it could be argued that for certain people, who wield considerable institutional power in their own right, ready access to alternate forms of communication already exists. Thus, there is no institutional difference in power that justifies applying the rights framework. However, even if this were not the case, the infringement could be justified by the platform by showing that the individual in question had, for instance, engaged in hate speech.

Similarly, we can consider a case like Lee v Ashers Baking Company[80] through the lens of the institutional approach. In *Lee v Ashers*, a private baking company (Ashers) refused the request of an individual (Lee) to bake a cake with a message promoting same-sex marriage. The baking company claimed that the message would violate their religious beliefs. The Supreme Court of the United Kingdom found in favour of Ashers, and overturned lower court rulings in favour of Lee. The primary reasons for the Supreme Court's holding were, first, that Lee had not been discriminated against 'on the ground of' his sexual orientation, as the baking company's objection was to the specific message that it had been asked to print on the cake, regardless of Lee's sexuality; and secondly, that the baking company could not be compelled to express a particular political belief.

The institutional approach, on the other hand, would consider this approach towards discrimination to be much too narrow. For the institutional approach, the issue would be less about the bakers' intention behind refusing to write 'support gay marriage' on a cake and more about (as in *Tomlinson*) a contextual enquiry into the use of private institutional power to reinforce existing institutional discrimination, as in restrictive covenanting cases. The institutional approach would ask, in particular, whether in Northern Ireland there was an institutional history of treating LGBTQ+ people as second-class citizens. It would ask whether and how denial of service was both constitutive and reflective of that discrimination (here again, the similarities with restrictive covenanting and, indeed, the Indian Supreme Court's judgment in the temple entry case are striking). It would ask whether that institutional discrimination still existed to an extent where there was a reasonable likelihood that Ashers's behaviour would be more the norm than the exception, and thus contribute to entrenching stigma against Lee, regardless of whether he was able to find an alternative. As Sandra Fredman puts the point, in cases of this kind, what is 'relevant is the extent to which such behaviour reinforces *existing dominant structures* and demands conformity to a dominant norm' (emphasis added).[81]

This is not to say, of course, that the final ruling would be necessarily different. The balancing of rights would still need to be undertaken. However, the institutional approach would bring a vital additional element to the judicial analysis (for example, Fredman argues that a court would consider the issues described above as part of the proportionality test when it balances competing rights[82]). This, I suggest, would help to place the relationship between the two

[80] *Lee v Ashers Baking Company* [2018] UKSC 49.

[81] S Fredman, 'Tolerating the Intolerant: Religious Freedom, Complicity, and the Right to Equality' (2020) 9 *Oxford Journal of Law and Religion* 305, 313; see also the discussion at 315–16; *Hall v Bull* [2013] UKSC 73.

[82] Fredman, 'Tolerating the Intolerant' (n 81) 314.

private parties, and the alleged rights violation, within their broader, institutional context.

IV. CONCLUSION

The institutional approach is characterised by the following features: centring the rights bearer, focusing on relational context and being sensitive to how power is exercised impersonally, through institutions. In the first part of this book, I argued that these features make it theoretically persuasive, as a model for the application of horizontal constitutional rights. In the second part, I argued that the institutional approach can do substantive work as part of the adjudicatory process, both in the absence of and complementary to existing regimes of private law. In this final chapter, bringing together parts I and II, I have attempted to show that as more and more constitutions begin to subscribe to bounded horizontality – whether through general provisions, as in South Africa and Jamaica, or specific provisions, as in India and Kenya – the need for a principled theoretical model to adjudicate horizontal rights claims will be felt more and more.

The institutional approach offers itself up as the beginning of a solution.

Bibliography

BOOKS

Ambedkar, BR, *The Untouchables: Who Were They and Why They Became Untouchables?*, http://drbacmahad.org/Speeches/the-untouchables-who-were-they-and-why-they-became.pdf.

Ambedkar, BR, *What Congress and Gandhi Have Done to the Untouchables* (Samyak Prakashan, 1945).

Anderson, E, *Private Government: How Employers Rule Our Lives (and Why We Don't Talk about It)* (Princeton University Press, 2017).

Atiyah, PS, *The Rise and Fall of the Freedom of Contract* (Oxford University Press, 1985).

Benhabib, S, *Situating the Self: Gender, Community, and Postmodernism in Contemporary Ethics* (Polity Press, 1992).

Banaji, J, *Theory as History: Essays on Modes of Production and Exploitation* (Brill, 2010).

Bhatia, G, *The Transformative Constitution* (HarperCollins India, 2019).

Brake, E, *After Marriage: Rethinking Marital Relationships* (Oxford University Press, 2016).

Chomsky, N and Herman, ES, *Manufacturing Consent: The Political Economy of Mass Media* (Pantheon Books, 1988).

Clapham, A, *Human Rights in the Private Sphere* (Oxford University Press, 1996).

Cohen, GA, *History, Labour, and Freedom: Themes from Marx* (Oxford University Press, 1989).

Currie, I and de Waal, J, *The Bill of Rights Handbook*, 6th edn (JUTA Press, 2013).

Davies, ACL, *Perspectives on Labour Law* (Cambridge University Press, 2004).

Davies, P and Freedland, M, *Kahn Freund's Labour and the Law*, 3rd edn (Stevens & Sons, 1983).

de Almeida Ribeiro, G, *The Decline of Private Law: A Philosophical History of Liberal Legalism* (Hart Publishing, 2019).

Dirks, N, *Castes of Mind: Colonialism and the Making of Modern India* (Princeton University Press, 2001).

Dukes, R, *Labour Constitution: The Enduring Idea of Labour Law* (Oxford University Press, 2014).

Elshtain, J, *Power Trips and Other Journeys* (University of Wisconsin Press, 1990).

Federici, S, *Revolution at Point Zero: Housework, Reproduction, and the Feminist Struggle* (PM Press, 2012).

Federici, S, *Caliban and the Witch: Women, The Body and Primitive Accumulation* (Autonomedia, 2004).

Folbre, N, *Who Pays for the Kids? Gender and the Structure of Constraint* (Routledge, 1994).

Foucault, M, *Power/Knowledge* (C Gordon ed, Pantheon, 1980).

Foucault, M, *The Will to Knowledge: The History of Sexuality I* (Penguin, 1976).

Frantziou, E, *The Horizontal Effects of the Charter of Fundamental Rights of the European Union* (Oxford University Press, 2019).

Fredman, S, *Human Rights Transformed: Positive Rights and Positive Duties* (Oxford University Press, 2008).

Fredman, S, *Women and the Law* (Oxford University Press, 1998).

Gordley, J, *The Philosophical Origins of the Modern Contract Doctrine* (Oxford University Press, 1993).

Griffin, J, *On Human Rights* (Oxford University Press, 2008).

Grimm, D, *Constitutionalism: Past, Present, and Future* (Oxford University Press, 2016).

Heinrich, M, *An Introduction to the three Volumes of Karl Marx's Capital* (Monthly Review Press, 2012).

Hobbes, T, *Leviathan* (first published 1651, Penguin Books, 1968).
Hochschild, A, *The Second Shift: Working Parents and the Revolution at Home* (Viking, 1989).
Isaac, JC, *Power and Marxist Theory: A Realist View* (Cornell University Press, 1987).
Kaviraj, S, *The Imaginary Institution of India* (Permanent Black, 2010).
Kaviraj, S, *Trajectories of the Indian State: Politics and Ideas* (Permanent Black, 2010).
Kirk, M, *Gender and Information Technology* (IGI Global, 2009).
Lerner, G, *The Creation of Patriarchy* (Oxford University Press, 1986).
Loughlin, M, *The Foundations of Public Law* (Oxford University Press, 2010).
Lovett, F, *General Theory of Domination and Justice* (Oxford University Press, 2010).
MacCormick, N, *Questioning Sovereignty: Law, State, and Nation in the European Commonwealth* (Oxford University Press, 1999).
Macpherson, CB, *The Political Theory of Possessive Individualism* (Clarendon Press, 1962).
Mau, S, *Mute Compulsion: A Marxist Theory of the Economic Power of Capital* (Verso, 2023).
Maine, H, *Ancient Law* (first published 1861, Cambridge University Press, 2013).
Mak, C, *Fundamental Rights in European Contract Law* (Wolters Kluwer, 2008).
Marks, S, *A False Tree of Liberty: Human Rights in Radical Thought* (Oxford University Press, 2019).
Marx, K, *Capital*, vol I (Penguin, 1990).
Marx, K, *Grundrisse* (Martin Nicolaus trans, Penguin Books, 1973).
Marx, K, *The German Ideology* (Progress Publishers, 1968).
Mathews, J, *Expanding Rights' Reach: Constitutions, Private Law, and Judicial Power* (Oxford University Press, 2018).
McMahon, BME and Binchy, W, *Irish Law of Torts*, 2nd edn (Butterworth (Ireland), 1990).
Mies, M, *Patriarchy and Accumulation on a World Scale* (Zed Books, 1986).
Miyandazi, V, *Equality in Kenya's, 2010 Constitution* (Hart Publishing, 2021).
Nedelsky, J, *Private Property and the Limits of American Constitutionalism* (University of Chicago Press, 1990).
Okin, SM, *Justice, Gender, and the Family* (Basic Books, 1989).
Pashukanis, E, *The General Theory of Law and Marxism* (Routledge, 2001).
Pateman, C, *The Sexual Contract* (Polity Press, 1988).
Pettit, P, *Republicanism: A Theory of Freedom and Government* (Oxford University Press, 1997).
Polanyi, K, *Economy and Society: Selected Writings* (Polity Press, 2018).
Polanyi, K, *The Great Transformation: The Political and Economic Origins of Our Time*, 2nd edn (Beacon Press, 2001).
Postone, M, *Time, Labor, and Social Domination* (Cambridge University Press, 1993).
Prassl, J, *Humans as a Service* (Oxford University Press, 2018).
Rahman, KS, *Democracy against Domination* (Oxford University Press, 2016).
Rawls, J, *A Theory of Justice* (Belknap Press, 1971).
Roberts, WC, *Marx's Inferno: The Political Theory of Capital* (Princeton University Press, 2016).
Rosenblatt, A, *Uberland: How Algorithms Are Rewriting the Rules of Work* (UC Press, 2018).
Saito, K, *Capital, Nature, and the Unfinished Critique of Political Economy: Karl Marx's Ecosocialism* (Monthly Review Press, 2017).
Sartre, J-P, *A Critique of Dialectical Reason*, vol 1 (A Sheridan-Smith trans, New Left Books, 1976).
Sciulli, D, *Theory of Societal Constitutionalism* (Cambridge University Press, 1992).
Seidman, L and Tushnet, M, *Remnants of Belief: Contemporary Constitutional Issues* (Oxford University Press, 1996).
Shoikhedbrod, I, *Revisiting Marx's Critique of Liberalism: Rethinking Justice, Legality and Rights* (Palgrave Macmillan, 2019).
Singha, R, *A Despotism of Law* (Oxford University Press, 1998).
Skinner, Q, *The Foundations of Modern Political Thought, vol 2: The Age of Reformation* (Cambridge University Press, 1978).
Slee, T, *What's Yours Is Mine: Against the Sharing Economy* (OR Books, 2015).

Sunstein, C, *The Partial Constitution* (Harvard University Press, 1998).
Taylor, R, *Exit Left: Markets and Morality in Republican Thought* (Oxford University Press, 2017).
Thomas, J, *Public Rights, Private Relations* (Oxford University Press, 2015).
Toupin, L, *Wages for Housework: A History of an International Feminist Movement, 1972–77* (Pluto Press, 2018).
Tribe, L, *American Constitutional Law*, 2nd edn (Foundation Press, 1988).
Van der Linden, M, *Workers of the World: Essays Toward a Global Labor History* (Brill, 2011).
Van der Walt, J, *The Horizontal Effect Revolution and the Question of Sovereignty* (De Gruyter, 2014).
Webber, G, Yowell, P, Ekins, R, Kopcke, M, Miller, BW and Urbina, FJ, *Legislated Rights* (Cambridge University Press, 2018).
Whyte, J, *The Morals of the Market: Human Rights and the Rise of Neoliberalism* (Verso, 2019).
Wittgenstein, L, *Philosophical Investigations* (MacMillan, 1953).
Wood, EM, *Democracy against Capitalism: Renewing Historical Materialism* (Cambridge University Press, 1995).
Young, IM, *Responsibility for Justice* (Oxford University Press, 2013).
Young, IM, *Justice and the Politics of Difference* (Princeton University Press, 1990).
Zelliott, E, *Ambedkar's World* (Navayana, 2012).

ARTICLES

Adams, RJ, 'From Statutory Right to Human Right: The Evolution and Current Status of Collective Bargaining' (2008) 12 *Just Labour* 48.
Adams, RJ, 'The Revolutionary Potential of *Dunmore*' (2003) 10 *Canadian Labour and Employment Law Journal* 117.
Aitkin, B, 'What Kind of Property Is "Relationship Property"?' (2016) 47 *Victoria University of Wellington Law Review* 345.
Aitkin, B, 'Family Property Law Reform' (1995) 25 *Victoria University of Wellington Law Review* 77.
Alexander, L, 'The Public/Private Distinction and Constitutional Limits on Private Power' (1993) 10 *Constitutional Commentary* 361.
Alstott, AL, 'Neoliberalism in US Family Law: Negative Liberty and Laissez-Faire Markets in the Minimal State' (2014) 77 *Law and Contemporary Problems* 25.
Altman, A, 'Discrimination', *The Stanford Encyclopedia of Philosophy*, https://plato.stanford.edu/entries/discrimination/.
Aloisi, A, 'Demystifying Flexibility, Exposing the Algorithmic Boss: A Note on the First Italian Case Classifying a (Food-Delivery) Platform Worker as an Employee' [2021] *Comparative Labor Law & Policy Journal* Dispatch No 35 – Italy 1.
Arruzza, C, 'Remarks on Gender' (*Viewpoint Magazine*, 2 September 2014) https://viewpointmag.com/2014/09/02/remarks-on-gender/.
Arthurs, H, 'Labor Law as the Law of Economic Subordination and Resistance: A Thought Experiment' (2013) 34 *Comparative Labor Law & Policy Journal* 585.
Arthurs, H, 'The Constitutionalisation of Employment Relations: Multiple Models, Pernicious Problems' (2010) 19 *Social & Legal Studies* 403.
Balkin, JM, 'The First Amendment in a Second Guilded Age' (2018) 66 *Buffalo Law Review* 979.
Banks, K, 'The Role and Promise of International Law in Canada's New Labour Law Constitutionalism' (2012) 16 *Canadian Labour Law and Employment Journal* 233.
Barak-Erez, D, 'Civil Rights in the Privatized State: A Comparative View' (1999) 28 *Anglo-American Law Review* 503.
Barlow, A, 'Configuration(s) of Unpaid Caregiving within Current Legal Discourse in and around the Family' (2007) 58 *Northern Ireland Law Quarterly* 251.

Berle Jr, AA, 'Constitutional Limitations on Corporate Activity – Protection of Personal Rights from Invasion through Economic Power' (1952) 100 *University of Pennsylvania Law Review*.

BeVier, L and Harrison, J, 'The State Action Principle and Its Critics' (2010) 96 *Virginia Law Review* 1767.

Bhana, D, 'The Horizontal Application of the Bill of Rights: A Reconciliation of Sections 8 and 39 of the Constitution' (2013) 29 *South African Journal on Human Rights* 351.

Binchey, W, '*Meskell*, the Constitution and Tort Law' (2011) 33 *Dublin University Law Journal* 339.

Black Jr, CL, 'The Supreme Court, 1966 Term – Foreword: "State Action", Equal Protection, and California's Proposition 14' (1967) 81 *Harvard Law Review* 71.

Bogg, A, 'Taken for a Ride: Workers in the Gig Economy' (2019) 135 *Law Quarterly Review* 135.

Bogg, A, 'Republican Non-Domination and Labour Law: New Normativity or a Trojan Horse?' (2017) 33 *International Journal of Comparative Labour Law & Industrial Relations* 391.

Brake, E, 'Marriage and Domestic Partnership', *The Stanford Encyclopedia of Philosophy*, https://plato.stanford.edu/entries/marriage/.

Breen, K, 'Non-Domination, Workplace Republicanism, and the Justification of Worker Voice and Control' (2017) 33 *International Journal of Comparative Labour Law & Industrial Relations* 419.

Brest, P, 'State Action and Liberal Theory: A Casenote on *Flagg Brothers v Brooks* (1982) 130 *University of Pennsylvania Law Review* 1296.

Brickhill, J and Bishop, M, 'Constitutional Law' (2020) 1 *Yearbook of South African Law* 227.

Butler, AS, 'Constitutional Rights in Private Litigation: A Critique and Comparative Analysis' (1993) 22 *Anglo-American Law Review* 1.

Card, C, 'Against Marriage and Motherhood' (1996) 11(3) *Hypatia* 1.

Cetty, C, 'Talking about Private Government: A Review of the Economic Claims Made to Rebut Anderson's Analysis' (2022) 3(1) *Journal of Law and Political Economy* 28.

Chatterjee, P, 'Nationalism, Internationalism, and Cosmopolitanism: Some Observations from Modern Indian History' (2016) 36 *Comparative Studies of South Asia, Africa and the Middle East* 320.

Cheadle, H and Davis, D, 'The Application of the 1996 Constitution in the Private Sphere' (1997) 13 *South African Journal on Human Rights* 44.

Chemerinsky, E, 'Rethinking State Action' (1985) 80 *Northwestern University Law Review* 503.

Cherednychenko, OH, 'Fundamental Rights and Private Law: A Relationship of Subordination or Complementarity?' (2007) 3(2) *Utrecht Law Review* 1.

Cohen, GA, 'The Structure of Proletarian Unfreedom' (1983) 12 *Philosophy and Public Affairs* 3.

Cohen, M, 'The Basis of Contract' (1933) 46 *Harvard Law Review* 553.

Collins, H, 'Independent Contractors and the Challenge of Vertical Disintegration to Employment Protection Laws' (1990) 10 *OJLS* 353.

Collins, H, 'Market Power, Bureaucratic Power, and the Contract of Employment' (1986) 15 *Industrial Law Journal* 1.

Compa, LA, 'Labor's New Opening to International Human Rights Standards' (2008) 11(1) *WorkingUSA: The Journal of Labor and Society* 99.

Craig, P, 'The Legal Effect of Directives: Policy, Rules and Exceptions' (2009) 34 *EL Rev* 349.

Dagan, H and Dorfman, A, 'Interpersonal Human Rights' (2018) 51 *Cornell International Law Journal* 361.

Davidov, G, 'The Three Axes of Employment Relationships: A Characterization of Workers in Need of Protection' (2002) 52 *University of Toronto Law Journal* 357.

Davies, ACL, 'Wages and Working Time in the "Gig Economy"' (2020) 31 *King's Law Journal* 250.

de Mol, M, 'The Novel Approach of the CJEU on the Horizontal Direct Effect of the EU Principle of Non-Discrimination: (Unbridled) Expansion of EU Law?' (2011) 18 *Maastricht Journal of European and Comparative Law* 109.

de Stefano, V, 'The Rise of the "Just-in-Time Workforce": On-Demand Work, Crowdwork, and Labor Protection in the Gig Economy' (2016) 37 *Comparative Labor Law & Policy Journal* 471.

Deakin, S, 'Decoding Employment Status' (2020) 31 *King's Law Journal* 180.

Deakin, S and Wilkinson, F, 'Rights v Efficiency? The Economic Case for Transnational Labour Standards' (1994) 23 *Industrial Law Journal* 289.
Doherty, M and Franca, V, 'Solving the "Gig-Saw"? Collective Rights and Platform Work' (2020) 49 *Industrial Law Journal* 352.
Drzemczewski, A, 'The European Human Rights Convention and Relations between Private Parties' (1979) 26 *Netherlands International Law Review* 163.
Elliott, JE, 'Social and Institutional Dimensions of Marx's Theory of Capitalism' (1979) 37 *Review of Social Economy* 261.
Elliott, JE, 'The *Grundrisse* as Social Theory: Link between Young Marx and Mature Marx' (1978) 59 *Social Science Quarterly* 239.
Engle, E, 'Third Party Effect of Fundamental Rights (Drittwirkung)' (2009) 5 *Hanseativ Law Review* 16.
Ewing, KD, 'Democratic Socialism and Labour Law' (1995) 24 *Industrial Law Journal* 103.
Finlay, AM, 'Matrimonial Property – Comparable Sharing: An Explanation of the Matrimonial Property Bill 1975' (1975) II *Appendix to the Journal of the House of Representatives* E6.
Finn, M, 'Befriending the Bogeyman: Direct Horizontal Analysis in *AB v Pridwin*' (2020) 137 *South African Law Journal* 591.
Finn, M, 'Organs of State: An Anatomy' (2015) 31 *South African Journal on Human Rights* 631.
Forbath, WE, 'Constitutional Rights: A History, Critique, and Reconstruction' (2001) 69 *Fordham Law Review* 1821.
Frantziou, E, 'Case C-176/12 Association de Médiation Sociale: Some Reflections on the Horizontal Effect of the Charter and the Reach of Fundamental Employment Rights in the European Union' (2014) 10 *European Constitutional Law Review* 332.
Fraser, N, 'Beyond the Master/Subject Model: Reflections on Carole Pateman's Sexual Contract' (1993) 37 *Social Text* 173.
Fredman, S and Du Toit, D, 'Tolerating the Intolerant: Religious Freedom, Complicity, and the Right to Equality' (2020) 9 *Oxford Journal of Law and Religion* 305.
Fredman, S and Du Toit, D, 'One Small Step Towards Decent Work: *Uber v Aslam* in the Court of Appeal' (2019) 48 *Industrial Law Journal* 260.
Fredman, S and Du Toit, D, 'Substantive Equality Revisited' (2016) 14 *International Journal of Constitutional Law* 712.
Fredman, S and Du Toit, D, 'Breaking the Mold: Equality as a Proactive Duty' (2012) 60 *American Journal of Comparative Law* 265.
Fredman, S and Du Toit, D, 'Engendering Socio-Economic Rights' (2009) 25 *South African Journal on Human Rights* 410.
Fudge, J, 'The New Discourse of Labor Rights: From Social to Fundamental Rights' (2007) 29 *Comparative Labor Law & Policy Journal* 29.
Gardbaum, S, 'The "Horizontal Effect" of Constitutional Rights' (2003) 102 *Michigan Law Review* 387.
Gardbaum, S, 'Where the (State) Action Is' (2006) 4 *International Journal of Constitutional Law* 760.
Gerstenberg, O, 'Private Law and the New European Settlement' (2004) 10 *European Law Journal* 766.
Gibson, D, 'Distinguishing the Governors from the Governed: The Meaning of Government under Section 32(1) of the Charter' (1983) 13 *Manitoba Law Journal* 505.
Gibson, D, 'The Charter of Rights and Private Litigation' (1982–83) 12 *Manitoba Law Journal* 213.
Gourevitch, A, 'Labor Republicanism akjhhj nd the Transformation of Work' (2013) 41 *Political Theory* 591.
Grellette, M, 'Review: *Jean Thomas*, Public Rights, Private Relations' (2016) 79 *MLR* 924.
Hale, R, 'Force and the State: A Comparison of "Political" and "Economic" Compulsion' (1935) 35 *Columbia Law Review* 149.
Henkin, L, '*Shelley v Kraemer:* Notes for a Revised Opinion' (1962) 110 *University of Pennsylvania Law Review* 473.

Hershkoff, H, 'The Private Life of Public Rights: State Constitutions and the Common Law' (2013) 88 *New York University Law Review* 1.

Horwitz, MJ, 'The History of the Public/Private Distinction' (1982) 130 *University of Pennsylvania Law Review* 1423.

Horwitz, MJ, 'The Historical Foundations of Modern Contract Law' (1974) 87 *Harvard Law Review* 917.

Hoskyns, C and Rai, SM, 'Recasting the Global Political Economy: Counting Women's Unpaid Work' (2007) 12 *New Political Economy* 297.

Hsieh, N, 'Rawlsian Justice and Workplace Republicanism' (2005) 31 *Social Theory and Practice* 115.

Hunter, R, 'Critical Legal Studies and Marx's Critique: A Reappraisal' (2021) 31 *Yale Journal of Law and the Humanities* 389.

Jager, S, Noy, S and Schoefer, B, 'Codetermination and Power in the Workplace' (2022) 3(1) *Journal of Law and Political Economy* 198.

Jowell, J, 'Is Equality a Constitutional Principle?' (1994) 47(2) *Current Legal Problems* 1.

Kay, RS, 'The State Action Doctrine, the Public–Private Distinction, and the Independence of Constitutional Law' (1993) 10 *Constitutional Commentary* 329.

Kennedy, D, 'The Role of Law in Economic Thought: Essays on the Fetishism of Commodities' (1985) 34 *American University Law Review* 939.

Kerr, T and Cooney, T, 'Constitutional Aspects of Irish Tort Law' (1981) 3 *Dublin University Law Journal* 1.

Klare, K, 'The Public/Private Distinction in Labor Law' [1982] *University of Pennsylvania Law Review* 1358.

Klare, K, 'Judicial Deradicalization of the Wagner Act and the Origins of Modern Legal Consciousness 1937–1941' [1977–78] *Minnesota Law Review* 265.

Kleingeld, P, 'Just Love? Marriage and the Question of Justice' (1998) 24 *Social Theory and Practice* 261.

Konstantinidis, P, 'The Horizontal Effect of Fundamental Rights in the Jurisprudence of the Supreme Court of Cyprus' (2018) 30(1) *The Cyprus Review* 145.

Kotiswaran, P, 'The Laws of Social Reproduction: A Lesson in Appropriation' (2013) 64 *Northern Ireland Law Quarterly* 317.

Kotiswaran, P, 'An Ode to Altruism: How Indian Courts Value Unpaid Work' (2021) 56(36) *Economic and Political Weekly* 45.

Kruse, SR, 'Beyond Non-Domination: Agency, Inequality and the Meaning of Freedom' (2013) 39 *Philosophy and Social Criticism* 187.

Kumm, M, 'Who Is Afraid of the Total Constitution? Constitutional Rights as Principles and the Constitutionalization of Private Law' (2006) 7 *German Law Journal* 341.

Kumm, M, 'Constitutional Rights as Principles: On the Structure and Domain of Constitutional Justice' (2003) 2 *International Journal of Constitutional Law* 574.

Lang, JT, 'Private Law Aspects of the Irish Constitution' (1971) 6 *Irish Jurist* 237.

Langille, BA and Davidov, G, 'Beyond Employees and Independent Contractors: A View from Canada' (1999) 21(7) *Comparative Labor Law & Policy Journal* 7.

Langille, BA, 'Why Are Canadian Judges Drafting Labour Codes – and Constitutionalising the Wagner Act Model?' (2010) 15 *Canadian Labour and Employment Law Journal* 101.

Langille, BA, 'The Freedom of Association Mess: How We Got into It and How We Can Get Out of It' (2009) 54 *McGill Law Journal* 177.

Langille, BA, 'Core Labour Rights – the True Story (Reply to Alston) (2005) 16 *European Journal of International Law* 409.

Layder, D, 'Power, Structure, and Agency' (1985) 15 *Journal for the Theory of Social Behaviour* 131.

Leczykiewicz, D, 'Horizontal Application of the Charter of Fundamental Rights' (2013) 4 *EL Rev* 479.

Lessard, H, 'The Idea of the 'Private': A Discussion of State Action Doctrine and Separate Sphere Ideology' (1956) 10 *Dalhousie Law Journal* 107.

Lewan, KM, 'The Significance of Constitutional Rights for Private Law: Theory and Practice in West Germany' (1968) 17 *ICLQ* 571.

Lewis, TP, 'Book Review: Larry Alexander & Paul Horton, *Whom Does the Constitution Command?*' (1991) 8 *Constitutional Commentary* 486.
Lianos, I, Countouris, N and De Stefano, V, 'Rethinking the Competition Law/Labour Law Interaction: Promoting a Fairer Labour Market' (2019) 10 *European Labour Law Journal* 291.
Liebenberg, S, 'The Application of Socio-economic Rights to Private Law' [2008] *Journal of South African Law* 464.
Lovett, F, 'Republicanism', *The Stanford Encyclopedia of Philosophy*, https://plato.stanford.edu/entries/republicanism.
Mantouvalou, V, 'Welfare to Work, Structural Injustice and Human Rights' (2020) 83 *MLR* 929.
Marx, K, 'On the Jewish Question' (1844) www.marxists.org/archive/marx/works/1844/jewish-question/.
McAffee, TB, 'Restoring the Lost World of Classical Legal Thought: The Presumption in Favor of Liberty over Law and the Court over the Constitution' (2006–07) 75 *University of Cincinnati Law Review* 1499.
Mensch, B, 'Freedom of Contract as Ideology' (1981) 33 *Stanford Law Review* 753.
Michel, L, 'The Goliath in the Room: How the False Assumption of Equal Worker–Employer Power Undercuts Workplace Protections' (2022) 3(1) *Journal of Law and Political Economy* 4.
Michelman, F, 'W(h)ither the Constitution?' (2000) 21 *Cardozo Law Review* 1063.
Miller, S, 'Social Institutions', *The Stanford Encyclopedia of Philosophy*, https://plato.stanford.edu/entries/social-institutions/.
Munro, K, '"Social Reproduction Theory", Social Reproduction, and Household Production' (2019) 83 *Science and Society* 451.
Murphy, CC, 'Using the EU Charter of Fundamental Rights Against Private Parties after Association De Médiation Sociale' (2014) *European Human Rights Law Review* 170.
Murray, C, 'Kenya's 2010 Constitution' (2013) 61 *Neue Folge Band Jarbuch des öffentlichen Rechts* 747, 761.
Naidu, S and Carr, M, 'If You Don't Like Your Job, Can You Always Quit? Pervasive Monopsony Power and Freedom in the Labor Market' (2022) 3(1) *Journal of Law and Political Economy* 131.
Naidu, SC, 'Domestic Labour and Female Labou Force Participation: Adding a Piece to the Puzzle' (2016) LI(44/45) *Economic and Political Weekly* 101.
Nerken, I, 'A New Deal for Fourteenth Amendment Rights: Challenging the Doctrinal Bases of the Civil Rights Cases and State Action Theory' (1977) 12 *Harvard Civil Rights-Civil Liberties Law Review* 297.
Oeter, S, 'Fundamental Rights and Their Impact on Private Law – Doctrine and Practice under the German Constitution' (1994) 12 *Tel Aviv University Student Law Review* 7.
Okin, SM, 'Women and the Making of the Sentimental Family' (1981) 11 *Philosophy and Public Affairs* 65.
Olsen, F, 'The Myth of State Intervention in the Family' (1985) *Journal of Law Reform* 835.
Parekh, S, 'Getting to the Root of Gender Inequality: Structural Injustice and Political Responsibility' (2011) 26 *Hypatia* 672.
Parkman, AM, 'Bargaining over Housework: The Frustrating Situation of Secondary Wage Earners' (2004) 63 *American Journal of Economics and Sociology* 765.
Peller, G and Tushnet, M, 'State Action and a New Birth of Freedom' (2004) 92 *Georgia Law Journal* 779.
Pietrogiovanni, V, 'Between *Sein* and *Sollen* of Labour Law: Civil (and Constitutional) Law Perspectives on Platform Workers' (2020) 31 *King's Law Journal* 313.
Pincus, FL, 'Discrimination Comes in Many Forms: Individual, Institutional, and Structural' (1996) 40 *American Behavioural Scientist* 186.
Prassl, J and Risak, M, '*Uber, TaskRabbit, and Co:* Platforms as Employers? Rethinking the Legal Analysis of Crowdwork' (2015–16) 37 *Comparative Labor Law & Policy Journal* 619.
Quinn, KL, 'Mommy Dearest: The Focus of the Family in Legal Feminism' (2002) 37 *Harvard Civil Rights-Civil Liberties Law Review* 447.
Quint, RE, 'Free Speech and Private Law in German Constitutional Theory' (1989) 48 *Maryland Law Review* 247.

Reeves, AR, 'Book Review: Jean Thomas, *Public Rights, Private Relations*' (2016) 35 *Law and Philosophy* 529.

Rivera-Perez, W, 'What's the Constitution Got to Do with It? Expanding the Scope of Constitutional Rights into the Private Sphere' (2012) 1 *Creighton International and Comparative Law Journal* 189.

Robin, C and Gourevitch, A, 'Freedom Now' (2020) 52 *University of Chicago Law Journal* 384.

Rogers, B, 'Employment Rights in the Platform Economy: Getting Back to Basics' (2016) 10 *Harvard Law & Policy Review* 479.

Sang, YKB, 'Horizontal Application of Constitutional Rights in Kenya' (2018) 26 *African Journal of International and Comparative Law* 1.

Sarkar, T, 'Something Like Rights? Faith, Law and Widow Immolation Debates in Colonial Bengal' (2012) 49 *Indian Economic and Social History Review* 295.

Sarkar, T, 'A Prehistory of Rights: The Age of Consent Debate in Colonial Bengal' (2000) 26 *Feminist Studies* 601.

Satz, D, 'Feminist Perspectives on Reproduction and the Family', *The Stanford Encyclopedia of Philosophy*, https://plato.stanford.edu/entries/feminism-family/.

Sedley, S, 'No Ordinary Law' (2008) 30(11) *London Review of Books*, www.lrb.co.uk/the-paper/v30/n11/stephen-sedley/no-ordinary-law.

Seidman, L, 'The State Action Paradox' (1993) 10 *Constitutional Commentary* 379.

Signes, AT, 'Notes on the Spanish Supreme Court Ruling that Considered Riders to Be Employees' [2020] *Comparative Labor Law & Policy Journal* Dispatch No 30 – Spain 1.

Silbaugh, K, 'Turning Labor into Love: Housework and the Law' (1996) 91 *Northwestern University Law Review* 1.

Silverblatt, A, 'Media as Social Institution' (2004) 48(1) *American Behavioral Scientist* 35.

Sprigman, C and Osborne, M, 'Du Plessis Is *Not* Dead: South Africa's 1996 Constitution and the Application of the Bill of Rights to Private Disputes' (1999) 15 *South African Journal on Human Rights* 25.

Sunstein, C and Thaler, R, 'Privatizing Marriage' (2008) 91 *The Monist* 377.

Supiot, A, 'A Labour Code for the 21st Century' (27 May 2018) *Green European Journal*, www.greeneuropeanjournal.eu/a-labour-code-for-the-21st-century/.

Supiot, A, 'The Public–Private Relation in the Context of Today's Refeudalisation' (2013) 11 *International Journal of Constitutional Law* 129.

Sutherland, PJ, 'Ensuring Contractual Fairness in Consumer Contracts after *Barkhuizen v Napier* 2007 5 SA 323 CC – Part I' (2008) 19 *Stellenbosch Law Review* 390.

Tapp, P, 'The New Zealand Matrimonial Property Act 1976' (1981) 1 *OJLS* 421.

Teitel, R, 'Transitional Jurisprudence: The Role of Law in Political Transformation' (1997) 106 *Yale Law Journal* 2009.

Tushnet, M, 'A Review of Jean Thomas, *Public Rights, Private Relations*' (2016) 7 *Jurisprudence* 355.

Unseld, C, 'Horizontal Application', *The Max Planck Encyclopedia of Comparative Constitutional Law*, https://oxcon.ouplaw.com/view/10.1093/law-mpeccol/law-mpeccol-e308?prd=MPECCOL.

Van Aswegen, A, 'The Implications of a Bill of Rights for the Law of Contract and Delict' (1995) 11 *South African Journal on Human Rights* 50.

Van der Walt, J, 'Progressive Indirect Horizontal Application of the Bill of Rights: Towards a Co-operative Relation between Common-Law and Constitutional Jurisprudence' (2001) 17 *South African Journal on Human Rights* 341.

Van der Wyver, JD, 'The Private Sphere in Constitutional Litigation' (1994) 57 *Tydskrif vir Hedendaagse Romeins-Hollands Reg* 378.

Von Prondzynski, FFVR, 'Protection of Constitutional Rights: Comparisons between Ireland and Germany' (1980) 2 *Dublin University Law Journal* 14.

Waldron, J, 'When Justice Replaces Affection: The Need for Rights' (1988) 11 *Harvard Journal of Law and Public Policy* 625.

Whyte, G, 'Industrial Relations and the Irish Constitution' (1981) 16 *Irish Jurist* 35.
Wolff, J, 'Marx and Exploitation' (1999) 3 *Journal of Ethics* 105.
Wood, A et al, 'Good Gig, Bad Gig: Autonomy and Algorithmic Control in the Gig Economy' [2018] *Work, Employment and Society* 1.
Wood, EM, 'From Opportunity to Imperative: The History of the Market' [1994] *The Monthly Review* 14.
Woolman, S and Davis, D, 'The Last Laugh: *Du Plessis v De Klerk*, Classical Liberalism, Creole Liberalism and the Application of Fundamental Rights under the Interim and the Final Constitutions' (1996) 12 *South African Journal on Human Rights* 361.
Zakson, LS, 'Worker Participation: Industrial Democracy and Managerial Prerogative in the Federal Republic of Germany, Sweden, and the United States' (1984) 8(1) *Hastings International and Comparative Law Review* 93.
Zatz, ND, 'The Minimum Wage as a Civil Rights Protection: An Alternative to Antipoverty Arguments?' (2009) 2009 *University of Chicago Law Forum* 1.
Zipperer, B, 'Turnover, Prices, and Reallocation: Why Minimum Wages Raise the Incomes of Low-Wage Workers' (2022) 3(1) *Journal of Law and Political Economy* 160.
Zwolinski, M, 'Structural Exploitation' (2012) 29(1) *Social Philosophy & Policy* 154.

ARTICLES IN EDITED COLLECTIONS

Akrivopoulou, C, 'Greece: Taking Private Law Seriously in the Application of Constitutional Rights' in D Oliver and J Fedtke (eds), *Human Rights and the Private Sphere: A Comparative Study* (Routledge, 2007).
Ambedkar, BR, 'Memorandum and Draft Articles on the Rights of States and Minorities, 24 March 1947' in B Shiva Rao (ed), *The Framing of India's Constitution: Select Documents*, vol II (Universal Law Publishing, 1968) 84.
Bak McKenna, M, 'Feminist Materialism and the Laws of Social Reproduction' in P O'Connell and U Ozsu (eds), *The Research Handbook on Law and Marxism* (Edward Elgar, 2021) 283.
Barak, A, 'Constitutional Human Rights and Private Law' in D Friedmann and D Barak-Erez (eds), *Human Rights and Private Law* (Hart Publishing, 2001).
Benson, P, 'Equality of Opportunity and Private Law' in D Friedmann and D Barak-Erez (eds), *Human Rights and Private Law* (Hart Publishing, 2001).
Bhattacharya, T, 'Introduction: Mapping Social Reproduction Theory' in T Bhattacharya (ed), *Social Reproduction Theory: Remapping Class, Recentering Oppression* ((Pluto Press, 2017).
Bogg, A, 'Economic Coordination as Freedom of Association' in S McCrystal, E McGaughey and S Paul (eds), *Labour in Competition Law* (Cambridge University Press, 2021).
Bogg, A and Estlund, C, 'Freedom of Association and the Right to Contest: Getting Back to the Basics' in A Bogg and T Novitz (eds), *Voices at Work* (Oxford University Press, 2014).
Collins, H, 'Is the Contract of Employment Illiberal?' in H Collins, G Lester and V Mantouvalou (eds), *Philosophical Foundations of Labour Law* (Oxford University Press, 2018).
Collins, H, 'Theories of Rights as Justifications for Labour Law' in G Davidov and B Langille (eds), *The Idea of Labour Law* (Oxford University Press, 2011).
Collins, H, Lester, G and Mantouvalou, V, 'Introduction' in H Collins, G Lester and V Mantouvalou (eds), *Philosophical Foundations of Labour Law* (Oxford University Press, 2018).
Davies, P and Freedland, M, 'Changing Perspectives on the Employment Relationship in British Labour Law' in C Barnard, S Deakin and GS Morris (eds), *The Future of Labour Law: Liber Amicorum Sir Bob Hepple QC* (Hart Publishing, 2004).
De Almeida Ribeiro, G, 'The Effects of Fundamental Rights in Private Disputes' in H Collins (ed), *European Contract Law and the Charter of Fundamental Rights*, vol 2 (Intersentia, 2017) 219.

Dimick, M, 'Pashukanis' Commodity-Form Theory of Law' in P O'Connell and U Ozsu (eds), *The Research Handbook on Law and Marxism* (Edward Elgar, 2021).

Dowdle, MW and Wilkinson, MA, 'Introduction' in MW Dowdle and MA Wilkinson (eds), *Constitutionalism beyond Liberalism* (Cambridge University Press, 2017).

Ellgar, R, 'The European Convention of Human Rights and Fundamental Freedoms and German Private Law' in D Friedmann and D Barak-Erez (eds), *Human Rights and Private Law* (Hart Publishing, 2001).

Fraser, N, 'Crisis of Care? On the Social-Reproductive Contradictions of Contemporary Capitalism' in T Bhattacharya (ed), *Social Reproduction Theory: Remapping Class, Recentering Oppression* (Pluto Press, 2017) 21.

Forde, M, 'Who Can Remedy Human Rights Abuses? The "State Action" Question' in KD Ewing et al (eds), *Human Rights and Labour Law: Essays for Paul Higgins* (Mansell Publishing, 1994).

Gilabert, P, 'Dignity at Work' in H Collins, G Lester and V Mantouvalou (eds), *Philosophical Foundations of Labour Law* (Oxford University Press, 2018).

Heldrich, A and Rehm, GM, 'Importing Constitutional Values through Blanket Clauses' in D Friedmann and D Barak-Erez (eds), *Human Rights and Private Law* (Hart Publishing, 2001).

Hepple, B, 'Four Approaches to the Modernisation of Individual Employment Rights' in R Blanpain and M Weiss (eds), *Changing Industrial Relations and Modernisation of Labour Law: Liber Amicorum in Honour of Professor Marco Biagi* (Kluwer Law International, 2003).

Hershkoff, H, 'Privatising Public Rights: Common Law and State Action in the United States' in T Kahana and A Scolnicov (eds), *Boundaries of State, Boundaries of Rights: Human Rights, Private Actors, and Positive Obligations* (Cambridge University Press, 2016).

Lucy, W, 'Private and Public: Some Banalities about a Platitude' in C Mac Amhlaigh, C Michelon and N Walker (eds), *After Public Law* (Oxford University Press, 2013).

Mantouvalou, V, 'Legal Construction of Structures of Exploitation' in H Collins, G Lester and V Mantouvalou (eds), *Philosophical Foundations of Labour Law* (Oxford University Press, 2018).

Markesinis, B and Enchelmaier, E, 'The Applicability of Human Rights as between Individuals under German Constitutional Law' in B Markesinis (ed), *Protecting Privacy* (Oxford University Press, 1999).

McLoughlin, D and Hurzeler, T, 'Marx on the Factory Act: Law, Exploitation and Class Struggle' in P O'Connell and U Ozsu (eds), *The Research Handbook on Law and Marxism* (Edward Elgar, 2021).

Michelman, F, 'Constitutions and the Public/Private Divide' in M Rosenfeld and A Sajo (eds), *The Oxford Handbook of Comparative Constitutional Law* (Oxford University Press, 2012).

Miller, PB, 'Principles of Public Fiduciary Administration' in T Kahana and A Scolnicov (eds), *Boundaries of State, Boundaries of Rights* (Cambridge University Press, 2016).

O'Cinneide, C, 'Ireland: Irish Constitutional law and Direct Horizontal Effect – A Successful Experiment?' in D Oliver and J Fedtke (eds), *Human Rights and the Private Sphere: A Comparative Study* (Routledge, 2007).

Oliver, D, 'Introduction' in D Oliver and J Fedtke (eds), *Human Rights and the Private Sphere: A Comparative Study* (Routledge, 2007).

Regan, MC, 'Between Justice and Commitment' in J Cohen and D Chasman (eds), *Just Marriage* (Oxford University Press, 2004).

Rodriguez Liboreiro, A, 'Spain: A Jurisdiction Recognising the Direct Horizontal Application of Human Rights' in D Oliver and J Fedtke (eds), *Human Rights and the Private Sphere: A Comparative Study* (Routledge, 2007).

Saunders, C, 'Constitutional Rights and the Common Law' in A Sajo and R Uitz (eds), *The Constitution in Private Relations* (Eleven International Publishing, 2005).

Schein, R, 'From Free Time to Idle Time: Time, Work-Discipline, and the Gig Economy' in P O'Connell and U Ozsu (eds), *The Research Handbook on Law and Marxism* (Edward Elgar, 2021) 400.

Sen, A, 'Gender and Cooperative Conflict' in I Tinker (ed), *Persistent Inequalities: Women and World Development* (Oxford University Press, 1991).

Shanley, ML, 'Just Marriage' in J Cohen and D Chasman (eds), *Just Marriage* (Oxford University Press, 2004).

Smits, JM, 'Private Law and Fundamental Rights: A Sceptical View' in T Barkhuysen and S Lindenbergh (eds), *Constitutionalisation of Private Law* (Martinus Nijhoff, 2006).

Teubner, G, 'Societal Constitutionalism beyond the Nation State' in P Dobner and M Loughlin (eds), *The Twilight of Constitutionalism* (Oxford University Press, 2010).

Thomas, J, 'Our Rights, but Whose Duties? Re-conceptualizing Rights in the Era of Globalization' in T Kahana and A Scolnicov (eds), *Boundaries of State, Boundaries of Rights: Human Rights, Private Actors, and Positive Obligations* (Cambridge University Press, 2016) 1.

Van der Walt, J, 'Rethinking the Fundamental Structures of the State with Reference to the Horizontal Application of Fundamental Rights' in M Sachs, H Siekmann, H-J Blanke, J Dietlein, M Nierhaus and G Puttner (eds), *Der grundrechtsgeprägte Verfassungsstaat. Festschrift für Klaus Stern zum 80* (Geburtstag Duncker & Humblot, 2012).

White, A, 'Marxism, Labour and Employment Law and the Limits of Legal Reform in Class Society' in P O'Connell and U Ozsu (eds), *The Research Handbook on Law and Marxism* (Edward Elgar, 2021).

Whittington, K, 'Constitutionalism' in R Scott and S Kosslyn (eds), *Emerging Trends in the Social and Behavioral Sciences* (John Wiley, 2015).

WORKING PAPERS

Collins, H, 'Utility and Rights in Common Law Reasoning: Rebalancing Private Law through Constitutionalization' (2007) LSE Law, Society and Economy Working Papers 6/2007, www.lse.ac.uk/law/working-paper-series/2007-08/WPS06-2007Collins.pdf.

Herr, H, Kazandziska, M and Mahnkopf-Praprotnik, S, 'The Theoretical Debate about minimum wages' (International Labour Organisation) Global Labour University Working Paper No 6, www.econstor.eu/bitstream/10419/96384/1/glu-wp_no-6.pdf.

Tomasetti, J, 'Rebalancing Worker Rights and Property Rights in Digitalised Work', https://papers.ssrn.com/sol3/papers.cfm?abstract_id=3345808.

Webb, PRH, 'Achieving Inequality of Sharing under the Matrimonial Property Act of 1976: A Brief Survey', Auckland Law Faculty Seminar Paper Series, www.nzlii.org/nz/journals/NZLRFSP/1980/4.pdf.

NEWSPAPER ARTICLES

Bhat, K, 'Wages for Housework?', *The Hindu* (Chennai, 21 February 2021).

Chandrasekharan, A, 'Wages for Housework', *The Indian Express* (New Delhi, 20 January 2021).

Sunil, A, 'Wages of Housework', *The Hindu* (Chennai, 31 January 2021).

REPORTS

Datareportal, *Digital Jamaica: 2021*, https://datareportal.com/reports/digital-2021-jamaica.

International Labour Organisation, *Care Work and Care Jobs for the Future of Decent Work*, www.ilo.org/wcmsp5/groups/public/---dgreports/---dcomm/---publ/documents/publication/wcms_633135.pdf.

New Zealand Law Commission, *Review of the Property (Relationships) Act, 1976*, www.lawcom.govt.nz/sites/default/files/projectAvailableFormats/NZLC%20-%20PRA%20Review%20Project%20-%20Final%20Report%20R143_0.pdf.

UN Women, 'Promoting Women's Economic Empowerment: Reorganizing and Investing in the Care Economy' (May 2018), www.unwomen.org/-/media/headquarters/attachments/sections/library/publications/2018/issue-paper-recognizing-and-investing-in-the-care-economy-en.pdf?la=en&v=2004.

UN Women, 'Redistributing Unpaid Care and Sustaining Quality Care Services: A Prerequisite for Gender Equality' (2016) Policy Brief No 5, www.unwomen.org/-/media/headquarters/attachments/sections/library/publications/2016/un-women-policy-brief-05-redistributing-unpaid-care-en.pdf?la=en&v=2644.

UNHCR, 'A Practitioner's Toolkit on Women's Access to Justice Programming: Marriage, Family and Property Rights', www.unodc.org/pdf/criminal_justice/WA2J_Consolidated.pdf.

UNRISD, 'Research and Policy Brief 9: Why Care Matters for Social Development', www.unrisd.org/80256B3C005BCCF9/(httpAuxPages)/25697FE238192066C12576D4004CFE50/%24file/RPB9e.pdf.

MISCELLANEOUS

Anandhi, S, 'Middle Class Women in Colonial Tamil Nadu, 1920–1947: Gender Relation and the Problem of Consciousness' (PhD thesis, Jawaharlal Nehru University, 1992) https://shodhganga.inflibnet.ac.in/handle/10603/14993.

The Oxford English Dictionary (Oxford University Press, 2020) www.oed.com/.

Index

abstract freedom/autonomy, 15–18
balancing competing concerns (indirect horizontality) and, 58–59, 60
constraint of state's power as supposed *ipso facto* promotion of, 16, 28–29, 202
erosion by civil rights legislation imposing obligations on private parties, 16–17
as 'freedom from' vs 'freedom to' concept/ abstract dematerialisation, 16–18, 29
individual responsibility compared, 18–19
historical development, 18
institutionalism's approach to: *see* 'constituted freedom' (institutional approach)
jurisprudence
Civil Rights Cases, 17
Cruickshank, 17–18
Du Plessis, 18
Jackson, 4
Lugar, 16
McKinney, 16
PUDR, 115–20
state action doctrine and, 16
see also state action doctrine
vertical approach, as supporting pillar of, 15–16, 202
see also default vertical approach, core concepts/underlying assumptions
views of
Atiyah, 18
Dowdle and Wilkinson, 16
Gardbaum, 16
Grimm, 16, 17, 18, 23, 126
Henkin, 16
Hershkoff, 16
Hobbes, 17
Lewis, 16
Pashukanis, 18
Peller and Tushnet, 17
Polyani, 18
Sciulli, 126
Seidman, 16
Sunstein, 17–18
van der Walt, 73–74, 127
Whittington, 16
algorithms: *see* **'app'**
'app'
algorithmic transparency
EU guarantees, 162
institutional approach to, 165, 171
as basis of difference in power between platforms and workers, 138–39, 153–55
collective bargaining, applicability to, 165
definition/role, 138–39, 153–55, 157–58, 161, 207
jurisprudence
ICTU (ECSR), 155
Palermo Tribunal decision of November 2020, 155
Spanish Supreme Court decision of 25 September 2020, 154
Uber app, 153–55
use as violation of rights
algorithmic bias and discrimination, 162
collective bargaining, 165
determination of status of drivers as 'Limb B' workers, 143, 167, 168–69
discriminatory effect, burden of proof, 162
right against unfair labour practices, 162
right to a fair trial, 161
views of
Aloisi, 155
Bogg, 155
Pietrogiovanni, 153, 154
Prassl and Risak, 153–54
Rogers, 154
Rosenblatt, 153, 154, 162
Schein, 154–55, 162
Signes, 154
Slee, 154
Tomasetti, 154
'application': *see* **'app'**
attribution: *see* **state action doctrine**

balancing competing concerns (direct horizontality), 62–63, 102–03
  Tomlinson, 217–24
balancing competing concerns (indirect horizontality), 57–61
  as an intuition, 58–59, 61–62
  comparison with
    abstract freedom/autonomy (second assumption), 58–59, 60
    individual responsibility (third assumption), 58
    third-party effect, 57
  criticisms of
    an 'open-ended and unwieldy process', 57
    domination of balancing requirement, 58
  equal treatment vs freedom of contract rights, 56–57, 58–60
  institutionalist approach compared, 128–29
  jurisprudence
    Lee v Ashers, 225–26
    Shelley v Kraemer, 56–57
  social and economic background, resistance to consideration of, 58
  transplant problem, 57–58
    see also transplant problem (indirect horizontality),
  views of
    Barak, 58–59, 128–29
    Collins, 57
    Frantziou (ECJ jurisprudence), 59 n55
    Gerstenberg, 57
    Kumm, 57
    Leisner, 57
    Lewan, 57
    Oeter, 57
    Sprigman and Osborne, 58
    Thomas, 58, 59
    Van der Walt, 58
    Von Prondzynski, 58
  see also equality
balancing competing concerns (institutional approach), 207
bills of rights
  centrality of the relationship between the individual and the state, 4, 14, 31
  jurisprudence
    Barsky (Douglas J (dissenting)), 4
    Du Plessis, 4
  private parties, applicability to, 35, 70
  public/private divide, particular applicability to, 4
  sovereignty and, 14, 24, 31
  views of
    Grimm, 4
  see also default vertical approach
'bounded direct horizontality', overview
  approach (direct application of specific constitutional rights), 50
    applicability of default verticality in case of unspecified rights, 50
  constitutional provision for
    Kenya, 214–17
      see also Kenya
    South Africa, 209
      see also South Africa
  enforcement of rights, requirements, 187
  principled framework, direct horizontality's need for, 45, 46, 47, 64–69, 71, 84–85, 128, 191, 200, 201–02, 204, 205, 208, 210–14
  scholarly models (Van der Walt/Thomas), overview, 71–72, 204–05
    as basis for the institutional approach, 72, 86–87, 205
    models compared, 78–79, 84–85, 86–87
  state action approach/indirect horizontality, lessons from, 47
'bounded direct horizontality' (Thomas model), 83, 85, 86–87
  as basis for institutional approach, 205
  concerns, 205
    need to avoid subjecting all private law disputes to constitutional review, 130
    principled limits in the private domain, 45, 69, 77, 79, 128, 205
    transplant problem, 77–79
  default verticality, rejection
    existence of power structures other than states similarly capable of violating rights, 76
    as historically contingent phenomenon, 76
  key features
    dependency relationship, 76–78, 79–82, 95, 129
    extrapolation of normatively significant features of state/individual relationship, 76–77, 79, 85, 122–23
    focus on questions of power and vulnerability, 42, 44–45, 72, 86, 128, 205
    monopoly over core goods, 72, 77, 79–82, 124

monopoly/no exit relationship, 81, 124
retention of structure of established public law rights, 72, 83
rights bearer as priority, 76
sufficiency of link between private rights holder and duty bearer to establish responsibility, 76–82, 95, 129, 205
transplant problem, 58, 76, 77–82
voluntary undertaking by the more powerful party, 77–78, 79
purpose of horizontal rights programme, 76
strengths and weaknesses, 79–82, 205
'bounded direct horizontality' (van der Walt model)
as basis for institutional approach, 72
default vertical approach, rejection of underlying assumptions, 73–76
abstract freedom/individual responsibility, 73–74
presumed equality of private parties operating in the same plane, 73–74
sovereign monopoly as threat to liberty/ proposed replacement with 'différantial sovereignty', 75
key elements
limitation of institutional conflict to that between 'social majorities and minorities', 72, 75, 84, 204–05
location of horizontality in private transactions embodying 'institutional conflict', 75, 78–79, 83–84
principled framework, 69, 74–75, 76, 83
rejection of transplant of the rights framework to private 'hierarchies', 83
rejection of verticality's three assumptions, 75
need to avoid subjecting all private law disputes to constitutional review, 24, 130
purpose of horizontality
determination of normatively significant power relations/inequalities, importance, 72, 74
identification of institutional conflict in individual forms of action, 74–75
strengths and weaknesses, 82–84, 204–05
Teubner, 74
views considered
Shelley, 74–75
Tribe ('subjugation' thesis), 75
'bounded (institutional approach): *see* **institutional approach**
'bounded interpretive direct horizontality'
approach (generic terms left to judicial interpretation), 50, 209
'bounded direct horizontality distinguished, 50
South African Constitution 8(2) as, 209

Canada
collective bargaining, 144–45, 150–51, 165–66
Constitution as definition and limits of the state, 3–4, 15
indirect horizontality approach
balancing competing concerns, 57
ubiquity of the state, 49, 55
platform work, 142 n16
state action doctrine, 32 n3, 36, 39, 43–44
caste
caste hierarchy, 189
as institution
'comprehensive' status, 123
powerlessness of individual to counter, 123
cis-heteropatriarchy: *see* **patriarchy**
Civil Rights Cases **(US)**, 6–10
as constitutional challenge to the Civil Rights Act 1875, 6–7
default vertical approach, 5
Harlan J (dissenting)
summary, 8–9
institutional approach, 8–9
'institution' (S-G Phillips)
Harland J's endorsement of slavery/ involuntary servitude as race-based institution, 99
historical context and social backdrop indicating a 'social tendency', 98
majority's rejection of S-G's interpretation, 98–99
widely practiced custom vs scattered practice, 98–99
the issues/Court's decision to strike down the Act
clean separability of issues/order of determination, 7–8
rejection of applicability of Fourteenth Amendment (section 5 enforcement powers) to private conduct, 7–8
state action doctrine and, 9–10
strict limitation of Thirteenth Amendment discrimination amounting to renewal of slavery, 8

public/private divide and, 6, 7–9
see also discrimination; race/racism; racially restrictive covenants
collective bargaining
attempts to impede, 165–66
as constitutional/fundamental right
Canadian Charter of Rights and Freedoms, 145
constitutional tort claims, 67
EU Charter of Fundamental Rights (2000), 165
European Works Council Directive (2009), 165
freedom of association as basis, 139, 144–45, 163–64
invalidation of substantive interference or undue burden, 165–66
US Wagner Act, 145, 150–51, 163
difficulty of exit as justification for right, 150–51
as feature of collective *laissez-faire*, 143
immunities approach to protection of, 143
constitutional protection, role, 144
insufficiency, 144
institutional approach, 144, 158, 163–67
explanatory role, 167–69
extension of right, 138, 163–67, 171
jurisprudence
First National Maintenance Corp v NLRB, 164
Fraser, 165
Health Services & Support, 144–45, 150–51, 165
IWUGB v Deliveroo, 166–67
IWUGB v DWP, 138, 169
NLRB v Jones & Laughlin Steel Corp, 145
Sindicatul 'Pastorul Cel Bun', 166
Swedish Engine Drivers' Union, 165
means/methods, variety, 143, 164–65
participation in government deriving from associational rights, 163–64
'apps', applicability to, 165
codetermination, 164 n108
constitutionalisation of, 165
European Social Charter (Revised) (1995), 164 n108
institutional approach to, 164–65
workers' councils, 164 n108
platform work and, 165
redress of structural imbalance between employers and workers as goal, 145, 151, 163
scope
extension under the institutional approach, 163–67
wages/working hours, 164
see also participation in government deriving from associational rights *above*
trade union involvement, 164 n106
lack of 'institutional' status, 164 n106
views of
Banks, 165–66
Bogg, 164, 166
Compa, 164, 166
Davies, 164 n108
Ewing, 164
Fudge, 165–66
Hsieh, 164
Jager et al, 164
Klare, 164
Langille, 165 n109
Michel, 164
Rosenblatt, 165
Tomasetti, 164
collective *laissez-faire*
applicability to platform work, 143–44
collective bargaining as feature of, 143
description of, 143
equality of employers and workers as goal, 143
as immunities regime, 143
limitations of/alternative approaches, 144, 165–66
as response to changing capital–labour relationships, 141
role of trade unions, 143
effect of their decline, 143
UK labour law and, 143
views of
Collins et al, 144
Davies and Freedland, 143
Doherty and Franca, 144
Kahn-Freund, 143
Wood et al, 143
Colombia
horizontal approach, 32–33
property rights, 195–96, 198
'constituted freedom' (institutional approach), 126–27
definitions, 126

distinguishing features
coercion as act of individual vs act of institution, 126–27
irrelevance of context vs socioeconomic status/institutional location, 126
views of
Grimm, 126
Marx, 127
Mau, 126
Sciulli, 126
constitutional models, overview, 3
centrality of state, 4
Constitution as definition and limits of the state, 3–4
public/private divide: *see* public/private divide
constitutional scrutiny
failure of
definition, 51
indirect horizontality resulting from, 51–52
Irish constitutional tort cases and, 67–68
family relationships, traditional exclusion of, 173–74, 179–80
'going through the state' requirement and, 61–62
jurisprudence
Du Plessis (Mahomed DP), 102
PUDR, 117
striking down/modification of law and, 49, 64
ubiquity of the state approach and, 55
constitutionalisation of labour rights: *see* **labour and employment rights, constitutionalisation of**
Cyprus
constitutional scrutiny, failure of, 68

default vertical approach, 3–30
bills of rights, particular applicability to, 4
see also bills of rights
core concepts/underlying assumptions
overview, 4–5, 29–30, 201–05
alternative justifications/reservations regarding, 5–6, 23–25
constraint of state's power as *ipso facto* promotion of freedom and autonomy, 16, 28–29
dependence on a clean separation between 'state' and 'society', 10–11
interdependence/mutual reinforcement, 29–30
as justification for constraint of sovereign power/failure to protect against non-state violation of rights, 5–6
see also abstract freedom/autonomy; sovereignty (verticality); state action doctrine
as justification for counterintuitive nature of the vertical approach, 5–6
protection of private space from destruction by the state, 16
state monopoly of [lawful] force/binding conflict resolution, 10, 11, 12–13
see also abstract freedom/autonomy; individual responsibility; sovereignty
departures from/alternative approaches
classification of, 31–32
comparative approach to, 32–33
constitutionalisation of horizontal rights, 6, 52–54
see also horizontality; India; labour and employment rights, constitutionalisation of; state action doctrine
forces militating against, 25, 29
legislative intervention in the 'private sphere', 6
privatisation of public functions, pressure from, 33–34
departures from/alternative approaches, analysis
Akrivopoulou, 32
Black, 33
Gardbaum, 31–32
Mathews, 32, 33
Rivera-Perez, 31–32
Rodriguez Liboreiro, 32
Supiot, 34
Thomas, 31–32, 33, 34
jurisprudence
Civil Rights Cases (US): *see Civil Rights Cases* (US)
Du Plessis (Madala J (concurring/ dissenting)), 3
Jackson, 4
Kenya Bus Service, 3
McKinney, 3
normative foundation, need for, 5
origin
context-specific, 6, 25, 86
public/private divide, 4
see also public/private divide
US constitutional jurisprudence, 4–5, 32

views of
Chemerinsky, 4
Dowdle and Wilkinson, 4–5, 25
Gardbaum, 4
Gibson, 3–4
Grimm, 4, 6, 10, 86
Kay, 3
Michelman, 5, 10, 14
Peller and Tushnet, 5, 6
Seidman and Tushnet, 6

discrimination, protection from
balancing competing concerns (indirect horizontality), 56–57, 58–61, 128–29
EU/EC Treaty (on grounds of nationality), 65–66
gender-based discrimination in a marriage/domestic relationship, 187–88
gendered nature of the public divide, 181–89
Indian Constitution, 25, 27–28, 91, 105–14
IMA, 106–11, 149, 177, 188–89
Sabarimala Case, 110–14
see also India (institutional approach) (constitutional horizontal rights provisions)
institutional approach to, 188
court's focus, 132–33
recognition of direct and indirect discrimination claims, 132
'structural'/'institutional' discrimination as norm, 97, 127
motivation, relevance, 127
platform work
Uber's obligation to comply with US non-discrimination laws, 161–62
use of 'app' as, 162
state action doctrine and, 35–36, 56
see also state action doctrine
US
Civil Rights Act/*Civil Rights Cases*, 6–10, 19–21, 97–101
see also Civil Rights Cases (US)
Shelley, 56–57, 75
see also caste; 'equality' of parties operating within the same plane; patriarchy; race/racism; racially restrictive covenants; unpaid domestic labour

domestic relationship
Note: to avoid unnecessary repetition most 'domestic relationship' entries have been consolidated under 'marriage'.
definition (in present context), 174–75
embedding in the institution of the patriarchal family, 176
as institution
comprehensive nature, 176, 185, 198, 208
constituting the 'basic structure of society, 185
hierarchies of power, 175, 176, 198
nesting within the social institution of the family, 174–75, 176, 185, 187, 198, 208
scope for violation of party's rights/examples
equality, 177
forced labour, 177
non-discrimination, 177
rights to property, 177
unpaid labour, 177
see also family, as social institution; marriage, applicability of the institutional approach/issues; patriarchy; unpaid domestic labour

'equality' of parties operating within the same plane
dematerialisation/separation of law from socio-economic bases, 17, 18–19, 21, 73–74
a flawed assumption, 28–29, 46, 58, 60–61, 63, 91–92
imbalance of institutional power between the parties, 91–92
systematic and structured violation of right, 108–10
'horizontal' as indicator of 'flattening'/'equ ality', 18–19, 127
individuals as abstract wills and, 17, 18–19
institutionalism's approach to, 91–92, 127–29, 132–33
jurisprudence
Drummond Wren, 59
Du Plessis, 101–02
Wilson, 60
relational context, importance, 59–60, 70, 77–79, 123–25, 128–29
transplant problem and, 58, 63, 69, 74
views of
Atiya, 18
Benson, 60
Kumm, 60
Sunstein, 17
Thomas, 58, 76–79, 123
Tribe, 127–28
van der Walt, 21, 73–74, 78–79, 127–28

see also abstract freedom/autonomy; balancing competing concerns; individual responsibility (verticality)

family
hierarchies, 173, 174–75
as social institution, 174–75, 176, 185, 187, 198, 208
pervasiveness, 174
variety of relationships qualifying as, 173
see also domestic relationship; patriarchy

feminist perspectives/constraints on women, 173–99
colonial India, 27
patriarchal institutions and structures, 96
views of
Arruzza, 173
Mau, 173
Satz, 174
see also India (institutional approach) (constitutional horizontal rights provisions), jurisprudence (Constitution 17 and 'untouchability') (*Sabarimala Case*)

forced labour
unpaid domestic labour as, 177, 188–89, 190, 208

freedom: *see* **abstract freedom/autonomy; 'constituted freedom' (institutional approach)**

functional equivalence: *see* **state action doctrine**

gender
gendered hierarchies, 91, 114, 176, 189, 198, 213
as institution, 91, 110, 111, 112, 113
public/private divide and, 181–89

Germany
indirect horizontality/third-party effect (*mittelbare Drittwirkung*), 32, 49, 51, 52–55, 62 n70, 130
Lüth, 52–54
institutional approach/*Handelsverter*, 103–04, 120, 131–32
presumed equality of private parties operating in the same plane, 58 n51

Grimm, D
abstract freedom/autonomy, 16, 17, 18, 23, 126
default vertical approach, 4, 6, 10, 86
institutional approach, 124–25
public/private divide, 4, 6
sovereignty, 10–11, 14
vertical approach, 4, 6, 10

hierarchies
institutional/structural power hierarchies
caste hierarchy, 189
domestic relationships, 175, 187, 198
family hierarchies, 173–74
gendered hierarchies, 91, 114, 176, 189, 198, 213
impossibility of escape from, 88
interrelationship with existence of an institution, 90, 121
as natural outcomes of virtuous diligence and natural talent (Van der Walt), 21
permanence/endurance, 88, 128, 187
racism/racially restrictive covenants and, 94–95, 189
subjugation theory (Tribe) and, 128
workplace hierarchies, 147–48, 159
private hierarchies
applicability of private law, 202
applicability of the rights framework, 74, 81–82, 83, 85
horizontality and, 74
vs public, 21, 82–83
stigmatised hierarchies (IMA (Chandrachud J)), 111, 113

horizontality (overview), 46–47
as archetypal model of departure from verticality, 46
definition (Unwin), 48
as exception requiring strict interpretation (*Civil Rights Cases*), 8
as flattening concept/treatment of parties as equals, 18–19, 78
see also 'equality' of parties operating within the same plane
indirect and direct horizontality, distinguishability, 46, 47, 48–51
counter-arguments, 61–63
a matter of form?, 61–62
purpose of: *see* 'bounded direct horizontality' (van der Walt model)
see also 'bounded direct horizontality'; 'bounded interpretive direct horizontality'; horizontality (direct); horizontality (indirect); institutional approach; positive obligations theory

horizontality (direct)
concerns
overlap with existing private law regimes/ persistence of the transplant problem, 46, 64
separation of powers issues, 64
unworkability, 3
examples
Indian Constitution: *see* India (institutional approach) (constitutional horizontal rights provisions)
Irish constitutional tort doctrine, 32, 62, 67–68, 216
Kenyan Constitution s 20, 49–50, 63
South African Constitution 8(2), 29, 41–42, 49, 145
Thirteenth Amendment (slavery and involuntary servitude), 49
positive aspects, 63–64
abolition of distinction between state and non-state parties, 46
'direct' subjection of private conduct to the constitution, 47, 49, 63–64
principled framework, need for, 45, 46, 47, 64–69, 71, 84–85, 128, 191, 200, 201–02, 204, 205, 208, 210–14
see also 'bounded interpretive direct horizontality'
horizontality (indirect) (critique)
concerns
individual responsibility and abstract freedom, 57–61
infringement of separation of powers, 47, 68, 130, 204, 214
vagueness, 47
see also balancing competing concerns (indirect horizontality); transplant problem (indirect horizontality)
positive features, 62–63
displacement of state/avoidance of the sovereignty requirement, 62–63
views of
Gerstenberg, 57
Kumm, 57
Leisner, 57
Lewan, 57
Oeter, 57
Oliver, 57
Webber, 63
horizontality (indirect), forms and limits, 51–57
bases for
'inadequate constraints'/'a failure of constitutional scrutiny' (Thomas), 51, 55, 62, 64
features
application of rights to the private domain, 46
non-constitutional law mediation between the Constitution and the individual dispute, 48
state's pervasive presence/inevitable implication in 'private' transactions, 46, 55
jurisprudence
Khumalo v Holomisa, 48 n3
New York Times v Sullivan, 48–49
RWDSU v Dolphin Delivery Ltd, 49
positive obligations as source of indirect horizontal effect/overlap with, 51
see also positive obligations theory
third-party effect/ubiquity of the state, conceptual differences, 51–52
see also horizontality (indirect) (third-party effect); horizontality (indirect) (ubiquity of the state)
views of
Gardbaum, 49, 51
Thomas, 51
weak vs strong indirect horizontality, 49
horizontality (indirect) (third-party effect)
absolute constitutional sovereignty concept, 54
constitution as 'objective order of values' pervading the private legal realm, 51
global reach, 52, 54
'going through the state' requirement, 51–52
as interpretive technique leaving private law rules unaffected, 53, 54
jurisprudence
Burghschaft case, 53
Lüth, 52–54
positive obligations distinguished, 54
post-war German constitutional doctrine (*mittelbare Drittwirkung*) as origin, 51, 52, 130
views of
Barak, 54
Benson, 55
Cohen, M, 53
Drzemczewski, 52
Ellgar, 54

Engel, 54
Gerstenberg, 54
Heldrich and Rehm, 54
Kumm, 54
Mak, 53
Mathews, 52
Quint, 52
Smits, 53
Van Aswegen, 52
Van der Walt, 52 n52

horizontality (indirect) (ubiquity of the state), 55–57
adoption in Canada, 49, 55
constitutional scrutiny and, 55
description/examples, 55–56
'going through the state' requirement, 51–52, 61–62
state as public/private divide and continuing presence in the private legal realm, 51, 55
jurisprudence
Du Plessis (Ackerman J), 62–63
Du Plessis (Mahomed DP), 55–56
Shelley, 56–57
US legal realist scholarship as origin, 51, 55–56
views of
Alexander, 55
Benson, 55
Cohen, 55
De Almeida Ribeiro, 56
Gibson, 55
Hale, 56
Henkin, 55–56
Klare, 55
Kumm, 61–62
Mathews, 55
Thomas, 61
Woolman and Davis, 55

India: *see* **India (Constitution) (fundamental rights) by article; India (Constitution/bill of rights) (public/private divide); India (institutional approach) (constitutional horizontal rights provisions)**

India (Constitution) (fundamental rights) by article
12 ('State'), 25
14 (equal protection of laws), 25
15(2) (non-discrimination), 25, 91, 105
direct horizontal applicability, 105
examples, 26
IMA, 106–11, 149, 177, 188–89
legislative history, 27–28, 107–09
15(2)(a) (grounds/discrimination), 25
17 (untouchability), 26, 91, 105
direct horizontal applicability, 105, 111
examples, 26, 108–09
legislative history, 111, 112
PUDR, 114–20
Sabarimala Case, 110–14
21 (life and personal liberty), 25, 114
23(1) (forced labour), 91, 105
direct horizontal applicability, 105
examples, 26
legislative history, 118–19
minimum wage as corollary, 114–20, 133, 139, 149, 160–61
PUDR, 115–20
24 (child labour), 26
historical evolution, 26–29

India (Constitution/bill of rights) (public/private divide), 25–29
bill of rights' departures from the default verticality model, 25–27
as attempt to remedy community-sanctioned 'legacies of injustice', 26–28
examples of injustice, 26–28
specificity/absence of reference to the state, 26, 105
women's rights, 27
default verticality features, 25
layered sovereignty/non-interference with personal laws of self-regulating communities', 26–28
sources (US, Ireland, Japan), 25, 26
state action/applicability of bill of rights to private body, 35–36
views of
Ambedkar, 27, 28–29
Chatterjee, 26
Dirks, 26
Kaviraj, 26–27
Sarkar, 27
Singha, 26
Teitel, 26
Zelliott, 27–28

India (institutional approach) (constitutional horizontal rights provisions)
evidence of institutional approach (general)
focus on social practices, 105–06

references to social institutions, 105
specificity of provisions, 26, 105
jurisprudence (Constitution 15(2) and shops) (*IMA*), 106–10
summary of the case, 106–09
applicability to 'all service providers', 107–08
applicability to economic transactions, 107–08
enforceability by private parties, 107
injustices covered by, 108–09
legislative history, 107–09
'shop' as generic term (Ambedkar), 107–08
jurisprudence (Constitution 15(2) and shops) (*IMA*), evidence of institutional approach
dependence of individual's economic and social power on relative position in institution of caste, 109
diagrammatic representation, 114
enforcement of social boycotts, 110
identification of caste as 'institution', 109
remedy (constitutional provision applied horizontally), 110
jurisprudence (Constitution 17 and 'untouchability') (*Sabarimala Case*), 110–14
Chandrachud J (concurring), 110–14
legislative history, 111, 112
summary of the case, 110–11
Supreme Court's decision/review, 110–11
'untouchability' as generic term covering other cases of social exclusion, 111–14
jurisprudence (Constitution 17 and 'untouchability') (*Sabarimala Case*), evidence of institutional approach
diagrammatic representation, 114
identification of 'patriarchy' as institution, 112–14
identification of practices, patterns of behaviour, and social norms (legislative history), 113
jurisprudence (Constitution 23 and 'forced labour') (*PUDR*)
constitutionalisation of institutionally grounded relationship, 116–20
criticisms of Court's decision, 117–19
'other similar forms of forced labour', wide applicability, 115–16
summary of the case, 115–17
jurisprudence (Constitution 23 and 'forced labour') (*PUDR*), evidence of institutional approach
Court's articulation of an institutionally grounded understanding of freedom, 117
diagrammatic representation, 119
labour market as 'institution', 118, 119–20
significance of institutional location of the parties, 116
mechanics of the institutional approach, 120–22
property rights, absence of a direct applicable horizontal right/ Domestic Violence Act, scope, 194–95
social institutions
diversity of, 105
forced labour (*begar*) (*Vasudevan*), 105
untouchability, 105
see also India (Constitution) (fundamental rights) by article
individual responsibility (institutional approach), 127–29
balancing competing concerns, 128–29
departure from default verticality approach/ determination of horizontality
equality of responsibility, 202
existence of social coercion as test, 127
rejection of formal equality, 127–28
relative institutional location as the salient factor, 127
remedies, limitations on, 129
views of
Fredman, 129
Van der Walt, 127–28
see also individual responsibility (verticality)
individual responsibility (verticality), 18–23
'abstraction' (separation of law from socio-economic environment), 18–23
European comparisons, 22–23
freedom/autonomy compared, 18–19, 21
high-water mark of US freedom on contract supremacy, 20–21
replacement of rights holder/duty bearer relationship with contractual relationship, 19–20
as core concept/supporting pillar of vertical approach, 5, 19–21
see also default vertical approach, core concepts/underlying assumptions

freedom of contract principle, 18–23
evolution of contract law, 22–23
insulation of the private sphere from rights, 23
presumption of the equality of parties, 58, 60
'will' theory/rejection of material differences between parties, 22–23
impairment vs invasion/denial vs obstacles, 13, 20
jurisprudence
Civil Rights Cases, 19–20
Coppage, 20–21
Dartmouth College v Woodward, 19
Fletcher v Peck, 19
Rives, 20
sovereignty and, 6
views of
Attiyah, 17, 18, 23
De Almeida Ribeiro, 21, 23
Gordley, 23
Grimm, 23
Horwitz, 22–23
Kennedy, 23
McPherson, 23
Maine, 21
Marx, 22
Nerken ('atomisation' of private relationships), 19–20, 22, 98–99, 127
Olsen, 23
Pashukanis, 22
Van der Linden, 22
Van der Walt, 18–19, 21, 73–74
see also individual responsibility (institutional approach)

institutional approach: *see* **'constituted freedom' (institutional approach); individual responsibility (institutional approach); 'institution', examples; 'institution', key features; institutional approach, general; institutional approach, judicial leanings towards; institutional approach, philosophical foundations; institutional approach, private law relationship; sovereignty (institutionalism's approach to)**

'institution', examples of qualifying/ non-qualifying groups
caste, 27–28, 88, 91, 108–10, 111–13, 114, 123, 126, 206
domestic relationship, 174–75, 176–77, 178–80, 185–89, 191–92, 194, 198, 208
family, 174–75, 176, 185, 187, 197, 198, 208
gender, 91, 110, 111, 112, 113
involuntary servitude, 97–99
labour market, 90, 91, 119–20, 138, 140, 149–52, 157–58, 168–69, 171–72, 198, 206, 207
marriage: *see* marriage, applicability of the institutional approach/issues
status as social institution
mass media, 221–24
patriarchy, 91, 96, 113, 114, 123, 174–75, 176, 178–79, 194, 206
race/racism, 88, 97–105, 123
school/hospital (exclusion), 88, 206

'institution', key features (for purposes of a horizontal rights framework)
coherence and unity, 87
determination of power by relative locations within the institution, 87, 95, 104, 109, 119, 120, 123, 147, 148, 151, 179, 205
difficulty of exit/absence of a right, 81, 88, 98, 123, 124, 125, 138, 147, 150–51, 152, 176–78, 187, 190–92, 194, 200, 206, 208
dominance of the structural/'institutional' power, 88, 176, 185–86
institutionally assigned roles, functions and powers, 87
institutionally mediated difference in power, 88, 138
low threshold/establishment as a first step, value of, 89–90, 120–22
monopoly, 81, 124–25, 152
norms (created by prolonged convergence of behaviour by multiple actors), 87
pervasive influence over individual's everyday life, 98, 123, 138, 149–51, 176, 185, 205–06
powerlessness of individual to counter, 123
a set of 'social relations which have an ongoing, organised and relatively enduring quality to them' (Layder), 87, 200
structure
differantial sovereignty (Van der Walt), 75, 126
individuals as key players, 87–88, 129

limitation to interactions between social majorities and minorities (van der Walt), 72, 75, 79, 84, 85, 126, 127, 203, 204–05
nesting of/within institutions, 72, 174–75, 176, 185, 187, 198, 204, 208
views of
Grimm, 86, 124–25
Harlan J (slavery as institution), 8–9
Isaac, 88
Layder, 87, 88
Miller, 87
Postone, 87
Van der Walt, 72
Wittgenstein, 75, 89, 126

institutional approach, general
introduction/summary, 90–92, 201–08
application to
domestic relationships: *see* marriage, applicability of the institutional approach/issues
platform work: *see* 'app'; platform work
'comprehensive' institution
definition/requirements, 123, 138, 149, 176, 185, 205–06, 222
examples, 123, 138, 149, 176, 185–87, 198, 200, 205–06
continued centrality of the state, 120
'institutional approach' (replacement of the concept of interpersonal domination with an institutional one), 186, 189
objections to the concept/rejoinders
vagueness, 88
width, 88, 89–90
principled framework, need for, 45, 46, 47, 64–69, 71, 84–85, 128, 191, 200, 201–02, 204, 205, 208, 210–14
rule of law/legal stability issues, 89
AMS v Union locale des syndicats CGT (AG Villalon), 89, 156
Langille and Davidov, 89
sources for construction of
state action/indirect horizontality, 47
Van der Walt/Thomas models of bounded direct horizontality, 72, 86–87, 205
tentative leanings towards (South Africa/Kenya/Jamaica), 41–42, 209–25

institutional approach, judicial leanings towards, 97–104
AB v Pridwin, 212
Blinkfuer, 104
Certification Judgment, 209, 211
Civil Rights Cases, 98–99
see also *Civil Rights Cases*, 'institution'
Daniels, 211–12, 213
Du Plessis, 101–03, 130–31, 209–10
Duncan Muriuki Kaguuru, 216
Griggs v Duke Power, 100–101
Handelsvertreter, 103–04
Holomisa, 210–11
IMA, 106–11
see also India (institutional approach) (constitutional horizontal rights provisions), jurisprudence (Constitution 15(2) and shops) (*IMA*)
Inclusive Communities Project, 100, 132
Jemimah Wambui Ikere, 215–16
Jones v Alfred H Mayer, 100
Juma Musjid, 210–11
Kenya Bus Service, 214–15
Khumalo v Holomisa, 210
King (Victor AJ), 213, 214
Law Society of Kenya v Betty Sungura Nyabuto, 215
Lee v Ashers, 225–26
Mureithi, 215
Reitman v Mulkey, 99
Rose Wangui Mambo, 216–17
Shelley, 99
Stephen Saitoti Kapaiku, 216 n41
Tomlinson, 217–26
Uhuru Muigai Kenyatta, 215
Wilkinson v Crawford, 213–14

institutional approach, philosophical foundations, 92–97
issues considered
class-based vs intra class relationships, 93 n18
contractual exchange of labour power as social coercion, 93
'domination'/'oppression', definitions, 94
exploitative practices, 96–97
feminist legal tradition, 96
formal vs substantive relationship, 93
individual acts of oppression vs structural constraints, 92–93, 95–96
institutional power derived from capital, 93
non-dyadic relationships, 93–94
right to work, 96
social power, importance of, 92
structural injustice, factors contributing to, 94–97

views of
Altman, 97
Cohen, GA, 93, 124
Elliott, 92–93
Foucault, 96 n34
Fredman, 95, 129
Heinrich, 92
Kruse, 95–96
Mantouvalou, 96–97
Marks, 93 n16
Marx, 92–93
Mau, 92, 93–94
Parekh, 95
Pincus, 97
Roberts, 93
Shoikhedbrod, 92, 93
Wolff, 93
Wood, 92
Young, 94–95
Zwolinski, 97

institutional approach, private law relationship
overview
as bounded horizontality approach, 133–34, 187, 200, 205
complementary role, 90, 92, 130–33, 192, 199, 206–07
summary, 133
existence of both an applicable constitutional right and an existing legislative or common law regime, 92
analytical primacy of statutory scheme, 63, 130–31, 139
examples, 131
inadequacy of the legislative framework, 197, 198
existence of a constitution without applicable direct horizontal right, 135, 194–95, 196, 197
existence only of a legislative framework, 192–95, 199
New Zealand (Property (Relationships) Act (1976/2001)), 135–36, 192–95
institutional approach
explanatory role, 167, 168, 194
interpretive support, 131, 132, 133, 140, 141, 158, 159, 167, 180, 191–94, 197, 206–07, 208, 209–10, 213–14, 221
jurisprudence
Du Plessis, 131 n164
IMA, 133
Inclusive Communities Project, 132
PUDR, 133
legislative vacuum, 92, 133, 192
parties' challenge to private law regime as curtailment of their rights, 92, 132–33
views of
Cherednychenko, 130
Kumm, 130 n161
Langille, 138–39, 140
van der Walt, 130
Webber and Yowel, 130–31

intuitions
articulation of, 224
balance between competing rights, 58–59, 61–62
relationship between parties vs state's successful balancing of the interests, 61–62
bills of rights as primarily constraints on the state, 3
grounding the intuition, 59
normatively significant features of state–individual relationship as key, 123
state legislation as appropriate response to rights infringement, 45
views of
Barak, 45, 58–59
Barak-Erez, 45
Thomas, 45

Ireland
abortion cases, 68
constitutional tort doctrine
as direct horizontality, 32
lack of conceptual clarity, 67
principled framework, absence, 67
constitutional tort doctrine, jurisprudence
Byrne, 67
Educational Company v Fitzpatrick (No 2), 67
Grogan, 68
Hanrahan v Merck Sharp, 68
Hosford, 68
Meskell, 67
Open Door Counselling, 68
W v Ireland, 68
constitutional tort doctrine, views of
Butler, 67
Forde, 67, 68
McMahon and Binchy, 68
O'Cinneide, 67, 68

Temple Lang, 67
Von Prondzynki, 67
Whyte, 67

Jamaica (*Tomlinson*)
balancing competing concerns (direct horizontality), 217–24
failure to develop a principled framework, 217, 224
institutional approach alternative, 221–24

Kenya
Constitution as definition and limits of the state, 3–4
direct horizontal approach (Constitutional provisions by section)
20 (application of the Bill of Rights), 29 n123, 49–50, 63, 214–16
27 (non-discrimination), 216–17
45 (family), 196–97
institutional approach, leanings towards, jurisprudence, 197, 214–17
Ikere, 214–15
Kaguuru, 215
Kapaiku, 214–15
Kenya Bus Service (Sang YK), 214–15
Kenyatta, 214
Mureithi, 215–17
Ngugi, 215
Nyabuto, 214
Rose Wangui Mambo, 215–16
institutional approach, leanings towards, views of
Miyandazi, 216 n44
Murray, 215
Sang, 217
principled framework, courts' hesitation to adopt, 217
property rights upon separation (Constitution 45(3) (equality of parties to a marriage))
CMN v AWM, 196
as directly applicable horizontal right, 196–97
Echaria, 196
William, 196, 197
property rights upon separation (Matrimonial Property Act 2013)
Federation of Women Lawyers, 196–97
relative contribution of the spouses test, 196–97

labour and employment rights, constitutionalisation of, 144–49
applicability of institutional approach, 149–52, 170–72
see also labour market as institution; labour market regulation, applicability of the institutional approach
definition, 144
as fundamental/human rights, 144
as peremptory/constitutional rights, 144
international examples of constitutional provision
EC Treaty, 65–66
EU Charter of Fundamental Rights (2000), 146
ILO Declaration on Fundamental Principles and Rights at Work (1998), 146
UDHR (1948) and, 146
jurisprudence
Health Services & Support, 144–45, 150–51, 165
Murray v Minister of Defence, 145
NLRB v Jones & Laughlin Steel Corp, 145
PUDR, 115–20, 149
SANDU v Minister of Defence, 145
Vertreter, 120
justification for constitutional approach/ purpose
protection against politicised legislation, 144
protection of right to collective bargaining, 144–45
protection of workers from asymmetric power/remedies, 148–49
as remedy for imbalances of power in the workplace, 144, 145
national examples of constitutional provision, 144–45
structural power, significance, 147–49
see also hierarchies, institutional/ structural power hierarchies
theories
Irish constitutional tort doctrine, 32, 64 n78, 67–68, 216
see also Ireland, constitutional tort doctrine
republican theories, 146–48, 150
see also republican theories
vertical approach, dominance, 146

views of
Adams, 145, 146
Ambedkar, 118–19
Anderson, 119
Breen, 148
Collins, 142 n16, 144
Collins et al, 144, 148
Doherty and Franca, 142, 144
Fudge, 145
Gilabert, 148, 150, 151
Kahn-Freund, 143
Mau., 148
Michel, 148 n48
see also republican theories (labour market)
see also platform work

labour market 'freedom'
constitutionalisation of institutionally grounded relationship, 116–20
contractual exchange of labour power
as social coercion/exploitation, 93, 115–16
formal (contractual) vs substantive (relative institutional locations) relationship, 93, 116
institution-based exploitation, 96–97
views of
Banaji, 116 n123
Herr, Kazandziska and Mahnkopf-Praprotnik, 117 n124
Mantouvalou, 96–97
Marks, 92–93
Sartre, 117 n123
Young, 96
Zipperer, 117 n124
Zwolinski, 97
wage-fixation, effect, 117–18
women and, 96
see also India (institutional approach) (constitutional horizontal rights provisions), jurisprudence (Constitution 23 and 'forced labour') (*PUDR*)

labour market as institution
qualifying features
asymmetry of relationship at point of entry and during, 139, 151–52, 159
comprehensive nature, 138, 149, 151
difficulty of exit, 125, 138, 147, 150–51, 152
pervasive influence over individual's everyday life, 138, 149–51
power determined by relative locations within the institution, 151–52
right to work for multiple employers, 152
views of
Anderson, 151
Cetty, 151
Cohen, 150–51
Collins, 150, 151
Gilabert, 150, 151
Heinrich, 151
Hunter, 150
Klare, 149–50
Marx, 149
Mau, 149
Naidu and Carr, 150
van der Linden, 149, 151
Wood, 150

labour market regulation, applicability of the institutional approach, 149–52, 170–72
advantages
applicability beyond labour law, 171
practicality, 171
responsiveness to realities, 171
as complementary approach to existing accounts, 170
contributions
avoidance of the employment/contractor binary, 171
as brake on legislative attempts to roll back basic rights, 170–71
facilitation of relations between statutory labour law regimes and constitutional rights, 170
justification for algorithmic transparency, 171
see also 'app'
promotion of increased worker participation in management, 171
see also collective bargaining
qualifying criteria
existence of a difference in power flowing from parties' institutional location, 151–52
'inequality of power' justification for labour law, 149, 170
labour market as 'institution': *see* labour market as institution

marriage, applicability of the institutional approach/issues, 185–89
definitions/qualification as

domestic relationship, interchangeability of terms, 175
non-heterosexual relationships, importance of, 180
institutional approach (replacement of the concept of interpersonal domination with an institutional one), 146, 168, 186, 189
institutional inequality of power
as 'a set of impersonal structural mechanisms', 186
as contribution to difficulty of exit, 176–77, 187
exacerbation by legal framework/marital property rules, 176–77
examples of impact on women, 185–86
marriage contract as a set of 'master/subject' relations, 186
as permanent feature inherent in the institution, 186, 187
persistence of gender inequality, 192–93
scope for violation of a party's rights, 177
jurisprudence
Columbian Constitutional Court, 188
Olga Tellis, 188
PUDR, 188–89
rights at issue
enforcement requirements, dependence on compliance with, 187
livelihood/right to life, 188, 190
non-discrimination on grounds of gender, 187–88
property/factors contributing to breach, 188
protection against forced labour, 188–89
status as social institution, 176
comprehensiveness, 187
difficulty of exit, 176–78, 180, 187, 190–91, 198, 208
dominant and pervasive influence on individual, 176, 185
gender-based structure, 185–86
non-applicability of justice requirement/response to, 151, 173–75, 176, 179–80, 181–86, 187, 198, 208
ongoing impact of norms and expectations, 185, 186, 189
views of
Barlow, 180
Brake, 186, 187
Fraser, 182, 186, 187, 190–91
Kleingeld, 182, 185–86
Kotiswaran, 180, 189
Naidu, 189
Okin, 173, 181, 185, 186, 187
Pateman, 181, 182, 186
Quinn, 180
Rawls, 185
Regan, 185
Satz, 189
Sen, 187
Shanley, 189
Waldron, 187
see also domestic relationship; unpaid domestic labour
marriage contracts
institutional constraints on, 191–92
structural inequality of, 186, 192
views of
Fraser/Pateman, 186
Sunstein and Thaler, 191–92
mass media as institution, 221–24
difficulty of exit, 222
Michelman, F
Fourteenth (due process clause), 9
default vertical approach, 5, 10, 14
public/private divide, 10, 41
sovereignty, 10, 12–13, 14, 15, 18
state action doctrine, 9–10, 33
minimum wage, right to
constitutionalisation of, 120, 131
court's declaratory judgment confirming constitutional right, 139, 149
as a corollary of the right to protection against forced labour, 115–20, 160
as evidence of unequal institutional power structure, 117, 160–61
institutional approach to, 160–61, 207
jurisprudence
PUDR, 115–20, 133, 139, 149, 160–61
legislative vacuum, 133, 139, 156, 158
platform workers and, 131
as remedy/mitigation of inequality of power, 117, 119, 120, 129, 133
views of
Collins et al, 160
Davies, 160
Prassl, 160
monopoly as feature of institution, 81
default verticality/Thomas's approach distinguished, 124–25
difficulty of exit, relationship with, 81, 124, 147, 152
monopoly vs monopolist, 125, 147
see also state monopoly of coercive powers

nationality, discrimination on grounds of, 65–66
New Zealand (Property (Relationships) Act (1976/2001))
establishment of a presumption of equal sharing of property at time of separation, 170, 192–94, 198
displacement of presumption, 192–93
gendered division of labour, as attempt to address/persistence of, 192–93
institutional approach (interpretive support), 135–36, 193–94
interpretive disputes, 193–94
jurisprudence, 192
Alan v Alan, 194
B v B, 192
Clayton v Clayton, 193
Martin v Martin, 192, 194
P v P, 192
Reid v Reid, 194
Williams v Williams, 192
non-discrimination: *see* **discrimination; race/ racism; racially restrictive covenants**

patriarchy
definition, 174
as institution
'comprehensive' status, 123
powerlessness of individual to counter, 123
normative primacy, 174–75
platform work
'app': *see* 'app'
collective *laissez-faire*, 143–44
see also collective *laissez-faire*
definition, 131, 137
range of possibilities, 155
examples
Deliveroo, 142, 166–67
Uber, 104 n74, 137–38, 142–43, 153–55, 167–69, 194
institutional approach
advantages, 157–58
purpose (determination of workers' rights), 156–57
jurisprudence
AMS v Union locale des syndicats CGT (AG Villalon), 156, 158
Cotter v Lyft, 142
David Heller v Uber Technologies, 104
Douglas O'Connor v Uber Technologies, 142
Dynamex, 142
Inake v Deliveroo, 142
IWUGB v Deliveroo, 166–67
IWUGB v DWP, 138, 169
Lawson v Grubhub, 142
M Kaseris v Rasier Pacific, 142
Pallage v Rasier, 142
Uber v Aslam, 137–38, 142
Uber v Bensalem, 142
Vega v Postmates, 142
views of
Boggs, 152
Davidos, 157
Davies, 140 n11, 141, 142, 155, 156
Davies and Freedland, 143
de Stefano, 141
Deakin, 157
Deakin and Wilkinson, 140 n11
Dukes, 143
Fredman and Du Toit, 137, 142
Hepple, 140 n11
Jowell, 140 n11
Klare, 141
Langille, 139–40
Langille and Davidov, 89, 142 n16
Mau, 137
Prassl, 137, 143
Prassl and Risak, 141
Rosenblatt, 137
Schein, 137, 142
Supiot, 157–58
Wood et al, 143
Zatz, 140 n11
workforce
characteristics, 137
uncertain status, 131, 137
see also labour and employment rights, constitutionalisation of; platform workers' rights, application according to the institutional approach; platform workers' rights, traditional entitlement/legal framework
platform workers' rights, application according to the institutional approach, 139–40, 158–72
applicable law
constitutional charter, disadvantages, 139
constitutional context, importance, 158–59
constitutional and labour code rights, parallel existence, 139, 158

applicable rights at point of entry to and during the relationship, 139, 151–52, 159
applicable rights (collective rights), 139, 159–60
collective bargaining, 139
applicable rights (individual)
minimum wage, 139
see also minimum wage, right to
non-discrimination, 139
safe working conditions, 139
see also safe working conditions, right to
courts' role
declaratory judgments in case of legislative gaps, 139, 156, 158
incremental extension of legislative rights, 138, 158
interpretive support, 131, 132, 133, 140, 141, 158, 159, 167
'judicially-created labour code', rejection, 139
jurisprudence
AMS v Union locale des syndicats CGT (AG Villalon), 158
legislative gaps, 158
purpose (aid to determination of workers' rights), 156–57
sources
legislation as primary source, 139
traditional approach to rebalancing of power differentials, 140
utility of institutional approach, 140
views of
Langille, 139–40, 158

platform workers' rights, traditional entitlement/legal framework
courts' focus on substantial content of parties' relationship, 152
courts' 'indicators' for determining status of worker
existence of a substitution clause, 166–67
freedom to work for more than one employer (flawed monopoly approach), 138, 151, 152
provision of equipment, 138, 153
see also "app'
similarity of indicators across jurisdictions, 152
variety/range of possibilities, 138–39, 155
traditional legal framework, difficulties with, 131–36, 157–58
ambiguity, 131
employer/contractor binary as basis, 140–41, 152, 155
legislative gaps, 89, 131, 133, 136, 138, 140, 141, 158
uncertain status of parties/categorisation of 'worker', 155–57

positive obligations theory
continued centrality of the state, 45
definition (omission or inaction as violation/obligation to act positively), 45, 50–51
determination of rights violations, 'going through the state' requirement, 45 n70
Fourteenth Amendment and, 9–10
imposition of positive obligations on private parties, 211
Lüth, 54
overlap with/source of indirect horizontality, 51
'privatisation' of the family/abdication of welfare obligations, 178–80
state action distinguished, 33
views of
Fredman, 9–10, 50
Gardbaum, 51
Michelman, 9

principled framework (bounded horizontal/ institutional approach): *see* **'bounded direct horizontality', overview**

public/private divide
bills of rights, particular applicability to, 4
constitutional dichotomy between deprivation of rights by the state/ deprivation by private conduct as basis of divide, 4
core assumptions (abstract freedom/unitary sovereignty/individual sovereignty), 202
freedom/autonomy and, 16–18
deprivatisation of society's ruling power/privatisation of society, 9–10, 18
erosion by civil rights legislation imposing obligations on private parties, 16–17
see also abstract freedom/autonomy
gendered nature, 181–89

jurisprudence
Civil Rights Cases, 6, 7–9
Du Plessis, 55–56, 62–63
Jackson, 82
Shelley, 56–57
justice requirement, applicability, 151, 173–75, 176, 179–80, 181–86, 187, 198, 208
vertical approach, 4, 6, 28–29
views of
Ambedkar, 28–29
Dowdle and Wilkinson, 6
Grimm, 4
Horwitz, 6
Michelman, 10, 41
see also unpaid domestic labour (context/historical review), public/private divide

race/racism
as institution
'comprehensive' status, 123
difficulty of exit, 81, 98, 123, 124
powerlessness of individual to counter, 123
racially restrictive covenants as evidence of, 94–95, 99, 121, 123, 124, 204
see also discrimination
racially restrictive covenants
constitutional obligations to equalize the relationship between the parties/eliminate institutional racism, 129, 209, 217
as evidence of racism as institution, 80, 123, 124, 204
jurisprudence
Griggs v Duke Power, 100–101
Inclusive Communities Project, 100, 132
Jones v *Mayer*, 100
Reitman, 99
Shelley, 56–57, 74–75, 80, 99, 127–28
as part of the larger social context, 204, 223–24
as part of a pattern of discriminatory conduct constitutive of the institution of racism, 99
as reflection of relative locations of power within the social institution of race/race, 80, 94–95
as reinforcement of existing institutional discrimination, 80, 225
remedies, 132–33
views of
Tribe (subjugation theory), 74–75, 80, 127–28
Van der Walt, 74–75
see also discrimination
republican theories (labour market), 146–48, 150
chief concerns
dominant relationships, 146
location of arbitrary sources of power, 146–48
viability of exit option, 147
exemplars, 146
genealogy of the term, 146
views of
Bogg, 147
Breen, 147
Gourevitch, 147–48
Lovett, 146, 147
Marx, 147
Pettit, 146
Taylor, 147
Whyte, 146
restrictive covenants: *see* **racially restrictive covenants**

safe working conditions, right to, 139, 155
institutional approach to, 169
IWUGB v DWP, 138, 169
jurisprudence, 169
platform work and, 162–63
slavery: *see* ***Civil Rights Cases*** **(US); US Constitution/bill of rights**
social reproduction
definition, 173
family as central social institution, 173
see also family
views of
Arruzza, 173
Bhattacharya, 173
Hoskyns and Rai, 173
Mau, 173
Wood, 150
South Africa
Constitution as definition and limits of the state, 3–4
default vertical approach (Constitution 8(1)), 29, 39
direct horizontal approach (Constitution 8(2)), 29, 41–42, 49, 145, 209–14
as 'bounded interpretive direct horizontality', 209

negotiating history, 101, 102–03, 209
principled framework, need for, 65, 102, 210–14
summary of jurisprudence, 214
direct horizontal approach (Constitution 8(2)), jurisprudence
AB v Pridwin, 212
Certification Judgment, 209, 210–11
Daniels, 211–12, 213
Daniels (Froneman J concurring), 212
Du Plessis, 101–03, 209–10
Du Plessis (Madala dissenting), 102, 209
Du Plessis (Mahomed DP concurring), 55–56, 102, 209
Juma Musjid, 210
Khumalo v Holomisa, 210
King (Victor AJ), 213, 214
Wilkinson v Crawford, 213–14
direct horizontal approach (Constitution 8(2)), views of
Bhana, 212
Brickhill and Bishop, 212
Currie and de Waal, 210
Finn, 212
indirect horizontal approach
balancing competing concerns, 58
Du Plessis (Mahomed DP), 55–56
third-party effect, 48 n3, 52, 54
ubiquity of the state, 55–56
institutional approach, tentative leanings towards, 41–42, 209–14
Bhana, 209–10
Cheadle and Davis, 209
Liebenberg, 210
Sutherland, 209
labour rights, constitutional protection of (Constitution 23), 145
complementarity to existing labour legislation/subsidiarity, 145
race issues/apartheid
Du Plessis, 101–03
state action/applicability of bill of rights to private persons, 32
AAA Investments, 35, 39–40
Allpay, 40, 42
Calibre Clinical Consultants, 34–35, 43–44
evasion of responsibilities considerations, 39
functional equivalence, 39–40, 43–44
Khumalo v Holomisa, 41–42
monopoly test, 39–40
private body as 'organ of state' (Constitution 239), 35, 39–40
private body's ability to affect rights as determining factor, 41–42
sovereignty: *see* **default vertical approach; default vertical approach, core concepts/underlying assumptions; sovereignty (overview); sovereignty (institutionalism's approach to); sovereignty (verticality)**
sovereignty (overview)
definition (concentration of power in the state), 10–11
horizontality and, 54, 62–63
'layered sovereignty' (India), 26–28
state monopoly of coercive powers and, 10–11, 12–14, 29, 34, 44
state/sovereignty link, inextricability, 12
views of
Loughlin, 13, 14
sovereignty (institutionalism's approach to), 122–26
default verticality's approach to distinguished, 123–26
rejection of verticality's unitary concept, 92
focus on
normatively significant features of state–individual relationship, 123–26
parties' relative locations within an institution, 123
sovereignty (verticality)
as a centralised and unitary concept, 10–11, 27, 31, 34, 37, 69, 80, 84, 122–26, 202
as basis for limiting rights claims to the individual–state relationship, 78, 122, 125
deprivatisation of society's ruling power/ privatisation of society, 9–10, 18
monopolistic powers, 34, 80, 125
constraint of state's powers
role of sovereignty in determining state's normatively salient attributes, 10–15, 122
vs the exercise of unconstrained non-state powers, 14–15
jurisprudence
Flagg Bros, 11–14
Flagg Bros (Marshall J dissenting), 37
Flagg Bros (Stevens J dissenting), 11

normative salience
historical origins, 14
uniqueness, 14
views of
Grimm, 10–11, 14
Kay, 13
Michelman, 10, 12–13, 14, 15, 18
Thomas, J, 13, 14
state action doctrine
overview, 31, 33–34
as archetypal model of departure from verticality, 46
definition, 5
lack of a principled framework, 33, 44–45, 47
normative political theory vs conceptual basis, 10
attribution of acts of non-state body to the state, 31, 35–36
delegation/monopoly alternatives, 33–34
effacement vs close nexus, 35–36
functional test: *see* functional equivalence *below*
imposition of obligations on the state distinguished, 33
attribution of acts of non-state body to the state, jurisprudence
AAA Investments, 35, 39–40
Burton, 35–36
Calibre Clinical Consultants, 35
Jackson, 35
Jackson (Douglas J (dissenting)), 36
Moose Lodge v Irvis, 35–36
Pollack, 35
Pradeep Kumar Biswas Case, 35
elements of
applicability of bill of rights to non-state actors, 12
denial of rights vs obstacles to, 13, 20
focus on the state/entrenchment of sovereignty, 34, 36, 40, 46–47, 203
functional equivalence: *see below*
impairment of a constitutional right vs invasion, 13, 20
'natural monopolies'/outcomes of unregulated markets, exclusion, 17–18, 40
normative difference between sovereign and non-sovereign powers, 13–14
performance of core sovereign acts by non-state actors, dependence on state authorisation, 11–12
functional equivalence, 36–40, 202–03
tests for, 34–35
functional equivalence (delegation), 38–39
evasion of responsibilities considerations, 38, 39, 51
functional equivalence (delegation), jurisprudence
AAA Investments, 39
Blum v Yaretsky, 37, 43
Civil Rights Cases, 9–10
Cruikshank, 9
Evans v Newton, 38
Flagg Bros, 11–14
Hudgens, 38
Jackson, 17–18, 35, 43
Jackson (Douglas J (dissenting)), 41
Jackson (Marshall J (dissenting)), 40
Logan Valley, 38–39
Marsh, 38–39
Reitman v Mulkey (Douglas J (concurring)), 43
Rives, 9
functional equivalence (monopoly status)
South Africa, 39–40
US, 40
functional equivalence (monopoly status), jurisprudence
AAA Investments, 39–40
Allpay, 40, 42
Hudgen, 40
Jackson, 40
Kohn, 40
McKinney, 44
Marsh, 40
functional equivalence (traditional functions), 37
Clapham on, 37
historical vacuum, 37
functional equivalence (traditional functions), jurisprudence
Calibre Clinical Consulting, 43–44
Flagg Bros, 37
Jackson, 37
Kohn, 37
San Francisco Arts and Athletics v USOC, 37
individual freedom and, 16
see also abstract freedom/autonomy
private body's ability to affect rights as determining factor, 41–42, 203
Barak-Erez on, 42, 45
Khumalo v Holomisa, 41–42

Marsh, 41
Thomas on, 42, 45
privatisation of public functions, effect, 33–34
'inadequate constraint' hypothesis, 28–29, 34–35, 51
views of
Barak-Erez, 33, 42, 43
Berle, 33
Black, 33
Brest, 33
Finn, 39
Hershkoff, 34
Michelman, 9–10, 33
Sedley, 33
Wyver, 43
state monopoly of coercive powers
as justification for
constraint of state's powers/default verticality, 10–11
as mark of 'sovereignty', 10–11, 12–14, 29, 34, 44
'différantial sovereignty', 75, 126
transplant process and, 80–81
monopoly as component of functional equivalence, 39–40, 44
monopoly as 'flawed' concept, 80–81, 138–39
monopoly over law-making powers, 29, 122
as uniquely significant threat to core individual interests, 34, 41, 43–44, 122
'subjugation' thesis (Tribe), 74–75, 80, 127–28

third-party effect: *see* **horizontality (indirect) (third-party effect)**
Thomas, J
horizontality (bounded): *see* 'bounded direct horizontality' (Thomas model)
horizontality (direct), 64, 69
horizontality (indirect), 51, 58, 59, 61, 62
institutional approach, 205
sovereignty, 13, 14, 122–24, 126
state action, 32, 33, 43
public character of private actors, 34
transplant problem, 58, 76
'vulnerable valuable interests diagnosis', 42, 44–45, 86, 128, 205
trade unions: *see* **labour and employment rights, constitutionalisation of**
transplant problem (indirect horizontality), 47, 57–61, 63
presumptions
equal applicability of rights framework in private and public contexts, 58
equality of non-state/private parties, 58
Tomlinson, 220–21
unilateral enforceability of rights against state vs mutual rights and obligations of private parties, 58
views of
Collins, 57
Thomas, 58, 76, 77–82

Uber, 104 n74, 137–38, 142–43, 153–55, 167–69, 194
see also platform work
UK
collective bargaining, 166–70
collective *laissez-faire* in, 143
Lee v Ashers, 225–26
unpaid domestic labour, overview
features of
as facet of social reproduction, 173
inclusion of goods and services, 173
feminist views on, 175
institutional approach
effectiveness, 180
justification, 179–80
modalities, 208
as reinforcement of
exit difficulties, 190–91
pre-existing differences in institutional power, 190
as violation of rights to
livelihood, 190, 208
non-discrimination, 177, 190, 208
property, 177, 190, 208
protection from forced labour, 177, 188–89, 190, 208
see also unpaid domestic labour (context/historical review); unpaid domestic labour, remedy (equal property rights upon separation)
unpaid domestic labour (context/historical review), 181–85
increasing acknowledgment of direct and indirect contribution to the economy, 176
public/private divide
as basis for non-remuneration of domestic work, 182

exceptions to the unwaged and gendered character of domestic work, 183
gendered nature/as on-going phenomenon, 181–89
Hibbs, 184
justice requirement, non-applicability to civil society institutions, 151, 173–75, 176, 179–80, 181–86, 187, 198, 208
production vs reproduction, 181
state vs non-state, 181
traditional view of domestic work
female as unwaged private support of male public wage-earner, 182–83
housework/care work as 'nurture', 175–76, 182
as part of the wife's job not eligible for remuneration, 175–76, 182
UN/ILO publications
'Care Work and Care Jobs for the Future of Decent Work' (ILO), 184
'Promoting Women's Economic Empowerment: Reorganizing and Investing in the Care Economy' (UN Women, May 2018), 176
'Redistributing Unpaid Care and Sustaining Quality Care Services' (UN Women, 2016), 176
'Why Care Matters for Social Development' (UNRISD), 184
views of
Anandhi, 183
Benhabib, 181
Chandrasekharan, 183
Federici, 181, 183
Folbre, 184
Fraser, 182
Fredman, 96, 182
Hochschild, 184
Hoskyns and Rai, 184
Hughes, 181
Kleingeld, 182
Kotiswaran, 179 n15
Lucy, 181
McKenna, 183, 190
Mies, 183
Okin, 181
Olsen, 183
Parkman, 190
Pateman, 181, 182
Satz, 175, 181
Silbaugh, 190
unpaid domestic labour, remedy (equal property rights upon separation), 190–97, 208
advantages, 208
applicability
domestic relationships departing from the traditional norm, 191
exclusion (for present purposes) of on-going relationships/remedies other than property rights, 175, 190
marriage contracts: *see* marriage contracts
application, examples
Colombia, 195–96
India, 194–95
New Zealand, 192–94
see also New Zealand
UK, 195
application, methods
direct horizontal application of constitutional rights, 195–96, 198
existence of a constitution without applicable direct horizontal right, 194–95, 196, 197
interpretation of existing legislative frameworks, 192
limitation to a legislative framework, 192–94, 198
statute/judge-made law, 179, 192
compatibility with state's positive obligations towards domestic relationships, 179, 180
institutional approach
benefits (facilitation of relationship with private law), 192
purpose/criticisms, 191
justification, 208
as recognition of unpaid domestic work as equal contribution to the domestic relationship as remunerated outside work, 190
relevant factors
distinguishing 'relationship property' and 'separate property', 192
length of relationship, 191
marital home, 191
views of
'A Practitioner's Toolkit on Women's Access to Justice Programming' (UNHCR), 191
Shanley, 179 n15, 184, 191

US
  abstract freedom, 18
  collective bargaining (Wagner Act), 145, 163
  default vertical approach, origin in, 4–6, 32
  horizontal approach (ubiquity of the state), 55–56
  institutional approach, leanings towards, 97–101
  labour rights/collective bargaining (Wagner Act), 145
  Reconstruction era, 6, 17
  state action doctrine, 5, 35–36, 39, 42–44
  see also US Constitution/bill of rights
US Constitution/bill of rights
  Thirteenth Amendment (proscription of slavery and involuntary servitude), 7, 49
    applicability to acts of private parties, 97–98, 100
    applicability to racial discrimination not amounting to slavery, 7
    as direct horizontality, 49
    Indian Constitution compared, 26
    'involuntary servitude' as institution, 98–99
  Fourteenth Amendment (due process clause)
    applicability to federal regulation of private conduct, 7
    limitation to exclusively sovereign acts, 11–12
    Michelman on, 9
    positive obligations theory and, 9–10
  constitutional jurisprudence as dominant default verticality influence, 4–5, 32
  extending common law rights to state action/making the domain of rights gapless, 15
    see also individual responsibility
  key concepts, 5
  views of
    Chemerinsky, 15
    McAffee, 5
  see also Civil Rights Cases (US)

Van der Walt, J: *see* **'bounded direct horizontality' (van der Walt model)**
vertical approach: *see* **default vertical approach**

women: *see* **domestic relationship; family; feminist perspectives/ constraints on women; India (institutional approach) (constitutional horizontal rights provisions); India (institutional approach) (constitutional horizontal rights provisions), jurisprudence (Constitution 17 and 'untouchability') (*Sabarimala Case*); marriage, applicability of the institutional approach/issues; unpaid domestic labour**

Milton Keynes UK
Ingram Content Group UK Ltd.
UKHW010623070224
437347UK00004B/83

9 781509 967612